Sir William Davenant's

Gondibert

Sir William Davenant's
Gondibert

EDITED BY

DAVID F. GLADISH

OXFORD

AT THE CLARENDON PRESS

1971

Oxford University Press, Ely House, London W. 1

GLASGOW NEW YORK TORONTO MELBOURNE WELLINGTON
CAPE TOWN SALISBURY IBADAN NAIROBI DAR ES SALAAM LUSAKA ADDIS ABABA
BOMBAY CALCUTTA MADRAS KARACHI LAHORE DACCA
KUALA LUMPUR SINGAPORE HONG KONG TOKYO

PRINTED IN GREAT BRITAIN

TO S. G.

CONTENTS

INTRODUCTION

I. THE POEM

'Fame', says Sir William Davenant, 'is like a river . . . narrowest where 'tis bred and broadest afar off.' Davenant's river, it must be admitted, has run through rather sandy soil. He wrote *Gondibert: An Heroick Poem* with the most solemn intentions, but he begot it, to use his own figure, 'in an unseasonable time' (*Postscript*, p. 250 below). His long *Preface* to *Gondibert* came out in 1650, but without the poem. The first three of Davenant's five books of *Gondibert* came out in 1651. The other two books were never written at all. By 1653 there had been time for the humorists to get the flavour of *Gondibert*, so there appeared a delightful collection of impudencies called *Certain Verses Written by Several of the Author's Friends; to Be Reprinted with the Second Edition of Gondibert* (Appendix B). The 'author's friends'—John Denham can be identified as one of them —mainly twit the author's pretensions. They also mock his style and his language and recommend a most unliterary use for the pages of *Gondibert*. In other words, the 'author's friends' inaugurated a tradition which is faithfully carried on today by most graduate students in literature and by many scholars.

To attempt to combine all the highest forms of literature in one poem (for that is what Davenant's *Preface* promises) is to undertake a great deal, and the fact that he dropped it half-finished argues the impracticability of the whole plan. But parts of the whole, particularly Davenant's metaphysical wit and his wry observations about human nature, have always recommended the poem to a little circle. A pleasant little volume of verse could be put together out of excerpts from *Gondibert*, even though the story is hardly gripping.

The realistic Davenant preaches the 'new philosophy' of Bacon and the Deism of Hobbes; thus his epistemology is closer to our own than to, say, Spenser's or Milton's. In *Gondibert* Davenant speaks to us from the threshold of our own era, from the time when the idea of the 'Golden Age' became, so to speak, a promise for the future rather than a regrettable loss of the past. And critically speaking, he helps bring into English literature the formalities of French

neo-classicism; his *Preface* is an analytical and prescriptive statement
of rules for the construction of a heroic poem. Moreover, *Gondibert*
contains specimens of many favourite seventeenth-century poetic
forms—the love lyric, the prospect poem, the 'character', the literary
curse, the ode, the description of a painting.

In brief, *Gondibert* is a poetic museum of seventeenth-century
literature and theory, written with an anti-scholastic slant by the
semi-official poet-laureate.

The 'Heroick Poem'

The tag 'Heroick Poem' which Davenant attaches to *Gondibert*
is a misnomer if one takes the term *heroic* in any classic sense.
Gondibert is much more in the style of the Restoration 'heroic play'
than in that of the classical epic. The love interest in *Gondibert* is
handled in the manner of the romance. Love (rather than honour,
dignity, or ambition) is the primary motivation, for Gondibert is
reluctant to fight, he falls in love with an insignificant country girl,
and he staunchly tries to refuse fame, renown, and power. He is a
competent warrior and a competent leader and much admired as
such, but his real preoccupation is his love for Birtha. He has much
of Ariosto's Orlando about him in this respect. Certain details of the
plot seem closely associated with Kynaston's *Leoline and Sydanis*,
which itself comes out of the tradition of the romance, and the five-
'act' structure of Davenant's plot seems imitative of Kynaston's
poem, and of other models like d'Urfé's *Astrée*, and Thomas May's
The Reign of King Henry the Second. The poem clearly grows out of
the tradition of the romance rather than reaches back to the classical
epic for its rationale.[1]

As to subject matter, the real substance of *Gondibert* is the popular
notions of seventeenth-century England, set to verse—notions
which one finds everywhere in the works of Davenant's contem-
poraries: in *Eikon Basilike*, in Dryden's *State of Innocence*, in Bacon's
New Atlantis, not to say in Burton, Browne, and the metaphysical
poets. He says in his *Preface* that he is 'obliged to men of any science
as well mechanicall as liberall', and indeed the poem bristles with
what Jonson and Dryden called 'terms of art'. Many of the poetic
figures are based on alchemy and many on philosophy. Seamanship
is well represented, since Davenant was so good a sailor as to be

---

[1] Cornell March Dowlin, *Sir William D'avenant's* Gondibert, *its Preface, and Hobbes'*
Answer (Philadelphia, 1934), pp. 21 ff.

called a 'great pirott' by one enemy,[1] and so are many other 'sciences' from medicine to bird-catching. Davenant, in his *Preface*, likens his story to the river system of Lombardy, a figure which Hobbes enthusiastically seizes on in his *Answer*, and if the ideas in *Gondibert* are also a river, the headwaters from which they first trickle are Pliny, Browne, Harvey, Gerard, Bacon, Hobbes, and such 'philosophers'. Davenant is concerned with camp and court, science and 'schools', the Church and the State. Love and honour are his declared theme, but the former is romantically idealized, and the latter is a kind of enlightened self-interest. He calls ambition a 'lifting of the feet in the rough ways of honor'.

Instead of dealing with his subject in the context of the Immortals and immortality, as the epic must do, Davenant presumes to scan only mankind and the material environment. The age of reason had begun, and the classical epic's theme of interdependence between the world of men and the world of gods has no place in a poem which is concerned with 'men's business and their Bosoms' (cf. *Preface*, line 679 and note). In omitting the supernatural as an operative, causative, and reciprocating agent, Davenant presents a realistic, or at least a Deistic, world, at the sacrifice of the profundity which true epics normally gain from themes of immortality, whether of the race, of the Olymp, or of Heaven.

To enrich the mixture further, the poem is a dramatic poem, too. Davenant's dramatic method, as Alfred Harbage points out, causes him to expend considerable effort just to keep the secret of the outcome, even from canto to canto.[2] The result is a series of calculated surprises rather than the majestic historical panorama we might expect in a 'heroick poem'. *Gondibert*, like a play, is really only the account of one crucial event. The action of the first two and a half books seems to take place in a matter of days, or weeks at the most. Preceding events are not supplied by flashback, and the future is not prophesied. Probably the outcome, whatever it was to have been if the poem had been completed, is no more than a month away when the story breaks off half-finished, for the plot hinges partly on the marriage of the minor characters Orna and Hurgonil, which marriage, by Lombard custom, is to take place a month after their betrothal.

---

[1] Alfred Harbage, *Sir William Davenant: Poet Venturer* (University of Pennsylvania, 1935), pp. 94–5.
[2] Harbage, p. 183.

The neo-classical *Gondibert* punctiliously displays certain appointments of the classical heroic poem—a hunt, a duel of champions, a descent into the Elysium of Astragon's academe, murals like those in Dido's temple, a classical funeral celebration, and many verbal echoes,[1] but these trappings are only the surface. Generally speaking, the real poem is a hybrid—a texture of romance and drama with recognizable features of the epic and the lyric woven in. But in its effort to deal in some measure with domestic and material realities *Gondibert* rather anticipates more modern forms of narrative and drama.

Substance and Sources

Gondibert is just as eclectic in its contents as in its genre.

Some of the names in Paulus Diaconus' *De Gestis Regum Langobardorum* do resemble those in *Gondibert* (Ariburtus is the eighteenth king, Gundebertus is the twentieth, another Aribertus is the twenty-seventh, and there are a Rodalinda and an Vbertus), but Paulus offers no satisfactory source for the plot of the story.

Apart from the names which come out of Lombard history, two of the events in the poem belong to the eighth century, in a manner of speaking. At least so Davenant would have us believe. One of these events is interpolated into the passage on Astragon's studies in astronomy:

> Nine hasty Centuries are now fulfill'd
> Since Opticks first were known to *Astragon*;
> By whom the Moderns are become so skill'd,
> They dream of seeing to the Maker's Throne.
>
> (II. v. 17)

The 'nine hasty centuries' are evidently supposed to date Astragon about A.D. 750.

The other allusion hinges on a seventeenth-century legend about the discovery of the compass. Davenant must have felt that it was worth going out of his way to celebrate the mariner's compass, because when Ulfin conducts a tour of Astragon's college, it is on the very day when Astragon is rejoicing over the discovery of the 'loadstone'. The House of Praise rings with thanksgiving. Then Davenant adds a curious note (slightly violating his conviction that heroic poems should not contain supernatural trappings),

---

[1] For extensive parallels see Georg Gronauer's *Sir William D'avenants 'Gondibert'* (Munich, 1911), pp. 63–8 and the notes to the present edition.

And this, in sleepy Vision, he was bid
To register in Characters unknown;
Which Heav'n will have from Navigators hid,
Till *Saturn*'s walk be twenty circuits grown.

(II. vi. 30)

Saturn's period is about twenty-nine and a half years, so the know-
ledge of the mariner's compass was to be hidden for about 590 years
after Astragon's discovery. In the seventeenth century there was a
legend that the compass was invented in 1302.[1] A little arithmetic
again makes Davenant's date for Astragon fall in the first half of the
eighth century.

Why Davenant took these pains to verify his medieval setting is
an unanswered question. He may, of course, have done it in obed-
ience to some source we have not discovered. More likely, I think,
he was merely following a time-honoured convention of the romance
and endowing myth with a semblance of reality.

Davenant makes his ostensible source an ancient Lombard record
by an unidentified author, but this source seems to be, in the words
of Dowlin, 'a pleasant fiction',[2] because most of the poem's substance
belongs to Davenant's own seventeenth century.

The fact seems to be that under the mask of historicity the poem
is a prodigious collection of literary, philosophical, and historical
bits and pieces. Outstanding in the *mélange*, and among the most
intriguing aspects of the poem, are many allusions, apparently, to
contemporary history. *Gondibert* plays about the fringes of the *roman
à clef*. For example, Davenant ends the first canto of the poem with
the stanza

And fatally (as even if souls were made
Of warring Elements as Bodies are)
Our Reason our Religion does invade,
Till from the schools to Camps it carry warre.

(I. i. 80)

The poem was started in 1648 or 1649, when a Royalist had special
cause to be bitter about the religious war.

Henrietta Maria, long a patroness of Davenant, admired the
Astrée of Honoré d'Urfé,[3] and, inspired by that novel, had earlier
commissioned Davenant to write the *Temple of Love* (1635). He

---

[1] *Encyclopedia Britannica*, 14th edn., vi. 176b.   [2] Dowlin, p. 112.
[3] Harbage, pp. 55–6.

would consequently have been familiar with the genre. And there are connections between *Gondibert* and the mid-seventeenth-century scene which seem too close to be merely casual. When the poem was begun, Charles I, Charles the Martyr, had just been beheaded, or was about to be. In Charles's works there appears a favourite commonplace about him, in the phrase 'Providence seeming to consecrate Him to Suffering from the Womb, and to accustome Him to the exchange of the strictures of Greatness for the clouds of Tears'.[1] Compare Davenant's words about King Aribert:

> But yet the early King (from Childhood bred
> To dangers, toyles, and courser wants of warre) . . .
> $\hfill$ (II. ii. 2)

Eikon Basilike 27, 'To the Prince of Wales', affords another parallel of the same sort. The letter is a parting 'advice' to his son, in which Charles says, 'I had rather you should be *Charles le Bon*, then *le Grand*, good, then great . . .'. Compare the passage in *Gondibert* where Ulfin advises his departing son, Ulfinor,

> Be good! and then in pitty soon be great!
> For vertuous men should toile to compass power,
> Least when the Bad possess Dominion's Seat,
> We vainly weep for those whom they devowr.
> $\hfill$ (III. vi. 4)

Further, Charles's most insistent adjuration to his son is to be forgiving, and Davenant makes clemency one of Gondibert's and Aribert's chief virtues. Ulfin, too, emphasizes clemency in his advice to Ulfinor:

> To kill, shows Fear dares not more fears endure!
> When wrong'd, destroy not with thy Foes thy fame;
> The Valiant by forgiving mischief, cure;
> And it is Heav'n's great conquest to reclame!
> $\hfill$ (III. vi. 16)

Gondibert may well be a kind of veiled allegorical discussion of current vital issues. Charles Cotton the younger, it will be noticed, found his father among the heroes in the poem (see Appendix C), and he makes the imprisoned Davenant a light shining out of a dark lantern.

---

[1] *Basilika*, p. 1. Emblems here and in *Eikon Basilike* show palm trees weighted and inscribed, *Crescit sub pondere virtus*, a legend which would fit King Aribert as Davenant describes him.

One is on fascinating but shaky ground in trying to construct a 'key' to the characters in *Gondibert*, but the princess Rhodalind suggests Henrietta Maria, Gondibert the younger Buckingham or Charles II, and the crafty counsellor Hermegild Sir Edward Nicholas, Secretary of State to both Charleses. Astragon the scientist seems patterned after Bacon or William Gilbert (cf. II. v, *Arg.* n.), but as a physician he may also owe something to Gideon Delaune and Thomas Cademan, both old medical friends of Davenant.[1] Oswald, like Oliver Cromwell, is a famous general of horse, commanding an old veteran army (Fairfax's?), whose general had been Gondibert's father, while he lived.

Davenant devotes the second canto of his poem to the account of a hunt in which the ancient and mighty stag very clearly takes on symbolic proportions.[2] He seems the figure of nobility, and Davenant persistently impresses us with the injustice of his being pestered by lesser creatures, hounded to exhaustion, and, finally, slaughtered mercilessly and triumphantly, deserted by his subjects. His fate certainly suggests that of Charles I.

A better historian than I might make more (or perhaps less) of these seeming allusions, but I would suggest that they are likely to be more serious than polite. Davenant repeatedly insists, in his *Preface*, that the poet, by means of his moral examples, can promote righteousness better than divines or statesmen; he virtually, like Shelley, makes the poet an 'unacknowledged legislator'. Davenant took this obligation to heart, for the earlier poem 'Madagascar' was an attempt to coax Prince Rupert into invading the island of that name.[3] Rupert and others appear in the poem under romantic sobriquets by which they were known at court, and it may also be that Gondibert's noble (and ignoble) deeds were designed to coax Charles into rescuing England from the Commonwealth. The poem *Gondibert*, then, seems to have its principal motivation, if not actual sources, in contemporary figures and events.

There is one portion of the poem of which a literary source can be certainly identified, and that is the plot to defame Gondibert's sister, Orna. It is apparently a reworking of Don John's plot against Hero in Shakespeare's *Much Ado*. It emerges as follows.

---

[1] Arthur H. Nethercot, *Sir William D'avenant: Poet Laureate and Playwright-Manager* (Chicago, 1938), pp. 94 and 288.
[2] See I. ii, *Arg.* n., and I. ii. 32 ff. n.
[3] Harbage, p. 64. See also *Preface*, 388-9 and notes.

After the alliance is established among Hermegild, Gartha, and Hubert (II. iv. 15–30), we learn that Hurgonil and Orna are to marry in a month (III. i. 34). The poet predicts unhappiness for them before the wedding (III. i. 44–5). Next, Hermegild broaches his plan to prevent the union of Gondibert's family with that of Hurgonil (III. i. 46–52), and, presenting Gartha a chest containing a complete outfit of man's clothing (III. i. 53–7), persuades her that disguise is common in court, and urges secrecy (III. i. 58–71). We next see Hermegild and Gartha when the whole court appears at Astragon's palace (III. iii. 53–64). He is urging her to be patient and to have confidence in his plan. Here the poem proper breaks off.

But in the *Seventh and Last Canto* (which was not printed until after the poem had been abandoned and the author was dead) the plot against Orna is continued. Hurgonil, singing 'Reveillees' at Orna's window (23–4), thinks he sees a youth briefly appear behind the glass (25–8). He is not jealous, but he takes it as some strategy of Orna's to test his faith in her (35–43). Then we learn that the 'youth' was Gartha (44–50) and hear about her management of the ruse (73–4). When the conspirators part at the end of the canto, Gartha 'hastes to Court to hasten Orna's shame' (104). The sequel, of course, is lacking.

Prayer, Penitence, and Praise

As to its moral intention, *Gondibert* may be considered a philosophical poem somewhat related to Sir John Davies's *Nosce Teipsum*, which, incidentally, seems to have provided Davenant his stanza of four iambic pentameter lines rhyming *abab*—the so-called 'heroic stanza'. In *Gondibert* the most concentratedly philosophical passage consists of cantos v and vi in Book II. These cantos happen also to contain some of Davenant's best poetry and most inspired comments about the contemporary scene. They are a long digression, in which the Court of Astragon is described and his pursuits commented upon. Canto v is essentially an account of a 'little academe', its organization, its apparatus, and its library. Canto vi is an account of three temples, dedicated to Prayer, Penitence, and Praise. In a general sense, this part of the poem, as Harbage notes,[1] derives from Bacon's *New Atlantis*.

Astragon, the proprietor of this conservatory, deserves some

---

[1] Harbage, p. 186, with footnote. There are also parallels with *Advancement of Learning* and with Cowley's *Davideis*. But cf. II. v, *Arg.* n, below.

attention, because he seems to be Davenant's tribute to science and to Deism. Astragon's studies represent a return to nature for truth, while scientific investigation replaces the intuitive knowledge of Adam and the scholastic learning of the Middle Ages as an instrument. Astragon is the Baconian philosopher, seeking truth in a new way, the 'schools' having corrupted, hidden, and confused the greater part of revelation. In Astragon's library, stocked with all sorts of ancient and modern literature, one of the specially noted exhibits is 'The Souls chief Book', of which Davenant approves if it is used discreetly and by the right people; but

> About this sacred little Book did stand
> Unwieldy Volumes, and in number great;
> And long it was since any Readers hand
> Had reach'd them from their unfrequented Seat.
>
> For a deep Dust (which Time does softly shed,
> Where only Time does come) their Covers beare;
> On which, grave Spyders, streets of Webbs had spred;
> Subtle, and slight, as the grave Writers were.
>
> In these, Heav'ns holy fire does vainly burn;
> Not warms, nor lights, but is in Sparkles spent;
> Where froward Authors, with disputes, have torn
> The Garment seamlesse as the Firmament.
>
> (II. v. 48–50)

The whole fifth canto of Book II is a definition, so to speak, of the 'new philosophy'. It starts with a description of the endeavours of Astragon and his students:

> Here Art by such a diligence is serv'd,
> As does th'unwearied Planets imitate;
> Whose motion (life of Nature) has preserv'd
> The world, which God vouchsaf'd but to create.
>
> (II. v. 7)

They are 'as busy as intentive Emmets' at their furnaces and in the fields. They investigate the sea, the earth, and the heavens. All forms of animal life are studied in Nature's Office, where also records are kept. In Nature's Nursery the vegetable kingdom is ransacked for knowledge, and in the Cabinet of Death, or the Monument of Bodies, are preserved all sorts of archaeological relics—even (so Davenant would tell us) the bodies of Adam and Eve. The library, where all the world's important books are kept, from Egyptian scrolls to modern commentaries, is called the 'Monument of Vanish'd Mindes'.

For Astragon, and presumably for Davenant, the chief characteristics of learning are universality, objectivity, and observation—not words. This is not to deny that specious words are part of man's proper study; Astragon had long since read (and shut) the 'old Polemicks' (II. v. 51), and the 'Monk's audacious stealths' lie open for all to read (II. v. 52, and note).

Not all Davenant's philosophical remarks and admonishments, however, are found in the two cantos about Astragon's college. *Gondibert* is full of digressions and observations designed to edify the reader. One prominent strain, amounting to a theme in the poem, is a resigned but puzzled and sometimes amused—almost Swiftian—sense of the bestiality in man's bloodthirstiness. First it is the Stag Hunt in Book I:

> Tirranique Man! thy subjects Enemy!
> And more through wantonesse than need or hate;
> From whom the winged to their Coverts flie;
> And to their Dennes even those that lay in waite.
>
> (I. ii. 38)

And a little later,

> But now the Monarch Murderer comes in,
> Destructive Man! whom Nature would not arme,
> As when in madness mischief is foreseen
> We leave it weaponless for fear of harme.
>
> (I. ii. 52)

And Oswald's retainers are the quintessence of human perversity:

> To all but to themselves they cruel were,
> And to themselves chiefly by mischief Friends.
>
> (I. ii. 74)

When the bodies of Arnold and Hugo are brought to Verona for a proper burial, the priest refuses, saying, among other things,

> These by their bloody marks in Combat di'de;
> Through anger, the disease of Beasts untam'd;
> Whose wrath is hunger, but in Men 'tis pride,
> Yet theirs is cruelty, ours courage nam'd.
>
> (II. i. 44)

Nevertheless, Davenant is far from timid about warfare, however much he may regret its necessity. His rather Machiavellian attitude is that, since the worst people are the most ambitious, order must be maintained by violent means. Practically every passage about man's bloodthirstiness can be matched with a passage about the necessity of slaughter in a good cause.[1]

On a close reading, *Gondibert* turns out to be a rather rich statement of a poet's personal philosophy. It is not certain, but Davenant may have been converted to Catholicism about 1646.[2] Judging by certain passages in *Gondibert*, however, he seems sensitive about the kind of clerical abuses which had led to the Reformation. In Book II, where the priest refuses burial for the heroes killed in war, Davenant's other characters become the voice of the Reformation, citing abuses of the priesthood—particularly the heavy taxation it exacts and the lack of genuine Christianity in its habits of secrecy —and pointing out that the Church depends upon warriors in temporal matters as much as these depend on the Church in spiritual (II. i. 50 ff.).

The sixth canto of Book II is full of moral and spiritual dicta. The stanzas on Prayer, Praise, and Penitence, quoted in the *Preface*, would argue for Davenant's belief in the essentials of religious observance which we associate with the Deists, as well as for his reservations about the efficacy of mere formalities.

Two later poems, 'To my Friend Mr. Ogilby Upon the Fables of Aesop Paraphras'd in Verse' and 'The Death of Astragon' (which is apparently a fragment of *Gondibert* composed after the main work was printed), leave the poet's faith just as much a mystery as *Gondibert* does. The first few stanzas of 'To my Friend Mr. Ogilby' are a clever, Deistic statement. Davenant frets that the 'Schools' removed religion from 'God's clear book of Nature' and obscured it so that only they could know the truth. Then he praises the translator of Aesop for restoring that simple truth. The 'Death of Astragon' is really two poems, 'The Philosophers Disquisition to the Dying Christian' and 'The Christians Reply'. The 'Disquisition' again amounts to a statement of Deistic principles, and we might take it as Davenant's *credo*, except that the 'Christians Reply', very brief, and in a still small voice reminiscent of the one at the end of Herbert's 'The Collar', powerfully affirms a rather more orthodox belief.

---

[1] See *Gondibert*, I. i. 2; I. iii. 34–40; II. i. 73–4; II. viii. 26 ff.
[2] Harbage, pp. 104–6.

Davenant straddles Deism and orthodoxy. So do Dryden and Pope, of course. This is one of the respects in which our poet anticipates the spirit of the Englightenment.

The Plot

The first *Act* is the generall preparative, by rendring the Cheefest characters of persons and ending with something that looks like an obscure promise of designe. The second begins with an introducement of new persons, so finishes all the characters, and ends with some little performance of that designe which was promis'd at the parting of the first Act. The Third makes a visible correspondence in the Underwalks (or lesser intrigues) of persons; and ends with an ample turne of the maine designe, and expectation of a new. The fourth (ever having occasion to be the longest) gives a notorious turn to all the Underwalks, and a counter-turne to that maine designe which changed in the Third. The Fifth begins with an intire diversion of the mayne, and dependant Plotts; then makes the generall correspondence of the persons more discernable, and ends with an easy untying of those particular knots, which makes a contexture of the whole; leaving such satisfaction of probabilities with the Spectator, as may persuade him that neither Fortune in the fate of the persons, nor the Writer in the Representment, have been unnaturall or exorbitant. (*Preface*, ll. 506–23)

The student of drama and the reader of Professor T. W. Baldwin's *Shakespeare's Five-Act Structure* will recognize this play 'recipe' as deriving from the Elizabethan combination of Horace and Donatus.[1] The pattern, described so prominently in the *Preface*, applies remarkably well to *Gondibert*, so that, among other things, we have in *Gondibert* an illustrative example of the author's compositional theory.

Specifically, the pattern applies to the poem as follows. All the characters in the poem, except Dalga (who seems to be an afterthought), are introduced in the first two books, and so are the settings. The 'obscure promise of designe' at the end of Book I is the chance which takes Gondibert to the court of Astragon, where he is to meet Birtha. In the last two cantos of Book II, Gondibert and Birtha fall in love, and thus we have 'some little performance of that designe which was promised at the parting of the first Act'. In the opening of Book III, Hurgonil woos Orna, and Tybalt Laura, providing 'a visible correspondence in the Underwalks (or lesser

---

[1] Richard H. Perkinson, 'The Epic in Five Acts', *SP* xliii (1946), 465–81. Perkinson discusses the various antecedents of *Gondibert* as a heroic poem in five 'acts'.

intrigues) of persons'. The 'ample turne of the maine designe', which should come at the end of Act (or Book) III, is apparently the King's insistence on Gondibert's presence at court. The 'expectation of a new' is somewhat puzzling. In the next-to-last canto, Birtha is planning to follow Gondibert in disguise, but if this is the 'expectation', then canto vi must be some kind of addendum, for in it the mystery of Dalga is raised. Until a source (or the missing two books) is found, the puzzle must remain.

The events develop in a fairly standard type of the boy-meets-girl formula,[1] and this is one reason why the story seems a romance, rather than a heroic poem in the classical sense of the term. Gondibert's romantic interest, however, promises to ruin his brilliant prospects as a political and military leader, and so the poem presents a perplexed conflict between *love* and *honour*, thus anticipating the formula of the Restoration 'heroic play'.

The development of opposing forces and conflicting resolutions in the poem can be summarized quite briefly. If it obeyed the classical tradition of the epic, there would be a conflict between ambitious factions. Curiously, the conflict between Aribert and Gondibert is the reverse of ambitious: instead of burning for power, both are resolved to give away the throne! Gondibert secretly wishes to marry Birtha and is frustrated by King Aribert, who would like to bow out and give him Princess Rhodalind and the throne. The king's plans are, at the same time, the target of a counterplot by Hubert, Hermegild, and Gartha, who are brewing a treacherous scheme to get rid of Gondibert and seize the kingdom. They do not realize, of course, that Gondibert has never bothered to envisage himself as king and really prefers a secluded country life.

No doubt, in the final outcome, Gondibert was to reform his ambition, but thus far he is a hero with a kind of inverted *hubris*. The humane but unfortunate clemency which in Book I is pre-figured in his failure to dispose of Hubert grows into the pathetic lack of ambition with which he abandons himself to Birtha and the quiet life of Astragon's little academe. But by the end of Book II Gondibert's love for Birtha is the focus of all the forces operating in the poem, even though, ironically, few of the agents for these forces are aware of his love for her. The most crucial point in the plot is reached in stanza 53, canto viii, of Book II. Everyone's hope rests on Gondibert at this point, either in his promotion or (for

[1] See *Preface*, ll. 457-67 and note, concerning Davenant's interest in young love.

Hubert's faction) in his elimination. Goltho and the rest of Gondibert's retainers (and perhaps a disappointed reader) might well fume when the hero demurs, saying,

> Bid all our Worthys to unarm, and rest!

After this, either love or honour will almost surely lose the day—we at least hope not by default. At this crucial moment *Gondibert* is quite an unheroic poem with a 'non-hero'.

At the end of Book III, however, the situation is more satisfactorily explosive. Gondibert is about to wed Rhodalind. Birtha is about to follow them to Verona. Hermegild and Gartha are treacherously about to undermine the marriage of Hurgonil and Orna, and thus to divide Gondibert from his trusted lieutenant. Gartha entertains an intense hatred of Rhodalind and Gondibert, both of whom seem to her responsible for her brother's death. Aribert's kingdom is newly united and perhaps fragile, and he is getting old. Goltho and Ulfinor both love Gondibert's Birtha. Hubert and Borgio seem to be plotting to burn Verona down (canto vii, st. 19).

We can expect a counterturn in the Gondibert–Birtha–Rhodalind plot in Book IV, and a 'notorious turn to all the Underwalks'. One cannot help putting two and two together, be conjecture worth what it may; thus, if Gondibert's security and his marriage to Rhodalind were undermined by means of the sabotaging of Hurgonil's marriage to Gondibert's sister (which seems to be Hermegild's plan), then both the conditions proper to the fourth 'act' would be satisfied. This process of undermining is begun in the *Seventh and Last Canto*, which we can reasonably assume, therefore, is organically part of the hypothetical fourth Book, even though its title attaches it to the third.

Book V would presumably have presented an 'entire diversion' in the Gondibert–Birtha–Rhodalind plot, and also in the sub-plots involving Hermegild, Hubert, and Gartha; Hurgonil and Orna; and Ulfinor, Goltho, and Birtha. There ought also to be another battle to balance the one in Book I. Who can say what was to take place, exactly? One appropriate tragicomic denouement might allow for Gondibert to marry Birtha *and* get the throne. Perhaps Hermegild is only pretending to be a traitor and is to betray his new allies. Perhaps Gondibert will turn out to be a long-lost son of Aribert or Astragon and will be able thus to love both women, one as a sister. Goltho and Ulfinor would be eagerly waiting, if it were Birtha who remained unclaimed. What *Gondibert* is (rather than what it might have been if finished) concerns us more practically. It is, first of all, an anthology of seventeenth-century commonplaces, often put very wittily and often quite lyrically. It is also, I suspect, a veiled commentary on some of the spectacular events and personages of Davenant's lifetime. Moreover, it is a unique effort to apply the structural principles of drama to the plotting of a romantic story. It rings down the curtain on the Renaissance, too, for literary history has followed Davenant, though it has celebrated Milton, and the realism of Davenant adumbrates a much more prominent strain in our present culture than does the theism of his predecessors.

[The following two pages (xxiv and xxv) are specimens taken from the first edition of *Gondibert* (quarto, 1651), showing examples of Davenant's manuscript corrections in the printed text. Corrections appear in stanza 79 on page xxiv (page 100 of the quarto) and in stanzas 11 and 12 on page xxv (page 294 of the quarto). These are only three of the fifty-four such corrections discussed on pages xxxiv ff. below.]

'78

And now the weary world's great Med'cin, Sleep
  This learned Hoft difpenc'd to ev'ry Gueft;
Which fhuts thofe wounds where injur'd Lovers weep,
  And flies Oppreffors to relieve th' Oppreft.

79.

It loves the Cotage, and from Court abftaines,
  It ftills the Sea-man though the Storm be high;
closeft Frees the griev'd Captive in his ~~clofet~~ Chaines,
  Stops wants lowd Mouth, & blinds the treach'rous
                            (Spie!

80.

Kinde Sleep, Night's welcome Officer, does ceafe
  All whom this Houfe containes till day return;
And me, Grief's Chronicler, does gently eafe,
  Who have behind fo great a task to mourn.

The End of the Firft Book.

8.

A Crown foon taught, by whom Pow'r firft was given;
 When Victors (of Dominion cautious made
By hearing of that old revolt in Heaven)
 Kept Pow'r too high for Subjects to invade,

9.

A Crown, which ends by Armies their debate,
 Who queftion height of Pow'r; who by the Law
(Till plain obedience they make intricate)
 Would not the People, but their Rulers aw.

10.

To Pow'r adoption makes thy title good;
 Preferring worth, as birth gives Princes place;
And Vertue's claim exceeds the right of blood,
 As Souls extraction does the Bodies Race.

11.

Yet for thy Bloods long walk through Princes veins,
 Thou maift with any *Lombard* meafure time;
Though he his hidden houfe in *Illium* feigns ; *would*
 And not ftep fhort, when *Hubert*'s felf *could* climbe.

12.

And *Hubert* is of higheft Victors ~~bred~~; *Bred*;
 Whofe worth I fhall for diftant Empire chufe;
If he will learn, that you by Fate precede,
 And what he never had, he cannot lofe.

His

II. THE TEXT

'*50a*   *The Preface to Gondibert.* Mattieu Gvillemot. Paris, 1650. 8vo. Copies used are those at Harvard and Bibliothèque Nationale. Copy-text for *The Preface to Gondibert* and Hobbes's *Answer to the Preface.*

'*50b*   *A Discourse upon Gondibert.* Mattieu Gvillemot. Paris [London?], 1650. 12mo.

'*51a*   *Gondibert: An Heroick Poem.* Thomas Newcomb for John Holden. London, 1651 [1650?]. 4to. 13 copies used (see alphabetical list below). Copy-text for *Gondibert.*

'*51b*   *Gondibert: An Heroick Poem.* Printed for John Holden. London, 1651. 8vo.

'*73*   *The Works of Sir William D'avenant Knight.* Henry Herringman. London, 1673. Folio.

Arg.   The Argument prefixed to canto, etc.

BM   George Thomason's copy of '*51a*. British Museum No. E782. (The date on the title-page of this copy has been changed by pen to 1650.)

Bodl   Copy of '*51a* inscribed by Davenant to John Selden. Bodleian shelf-mark 4to D. 8. Art. Seld.

Chap   Copy of '*51a* at Chapin Library, Williams College.

cor   Corrected forme.

Folg   Copy of '*51a* at Folger Library.

Hn¹   Copy of '*51a* at Huntington Library, No. 29n57.

Hn²   Copy of '*51a* at Huntington Library, No. 142324.

IU   Copy of '*51a* at Indiana University. Title-page inscribed, 'Elisa Cotes given me by my Uncle E. Cotes 1722'.

MS   Manuscript correction in printed text.

Nethercot   Copy of '*51a* owned by Professor Arthur H. Nethercot with signature of Charles Boynton.

P   Copy of '*51a* at Princeton, Ex3706.7.34.

Pen   Copy of '*51a* at the University of Pennsylvania.

u   Uncorrected forme.

UI¹   Copy 1 of '*51a* at the University of Illinois. Trimmed.

UI²   Copy 2 of '*51a* at the University of Illinois. Untrimmed.

WC   Copy of '*51a* at Wellesley College.

Y   Copy of '*51a* at Yale, Ih.D272.651.

NOTE ON LINE NUMBERS AND CITATIONS

The lines in the *Preface* are numbered consecutively throughout. The *Answer to the Preface* is numbered separately. In references to the poem *Gondibert*, upper-case roman numerals refer to books, lower-case Roman to cantos, and arabic to stanzas. In the 'Seventh Canto' all references are to stanzas.

EDITORIAL PRACTICES AND POLICIES

It has been my principal endeavour to present a critical edition of Sir William Davenant's *Gondibert*, based on a collation of the seventeenth-century editions of the poem. For the sake of completeness I have included texts of three other works: *The Author's Preface*, Hobbes's *Answer to the Preface*, and *The Seventh Canto of the Third Book of 'Gondibert'*. The *Preface* and *Answer* together form a statement of the principles according to which the poem was written. The *Seventh Canto* advances the plot from the point where the poem itself breaks off. Two other poems which are apparently fragments of *Gondibert*, namely 'The Philosopher's Disquisition' and 'The Christian's Reply', will be found among the minor poems (ed. A. M. Gibbs).

Inasmuch as '*51a*, the copy-text for *Gondibert*, shows evidence of extensive correction by both the author and his printer, (cf. pp. xxxiv f. below), I have followed its punctuation and orthography rather slavishly, with the following exceptions: long *ſ* is rendered as *s*; *u* and *v*, and *i* and *j*, are distinguished according to modern practice; possessive '*s* is italicized when it is the suffix of an italicized noun; proper nouns are italicized, even in the few cases where the copy-text fails to do so.

In the textual notes,] signifies 'the reading of the copy-text and all other witnesses not specified as reading otherwise' (McKerrow's *Prolegomena*, pp. 73–4). But where manuscript corrections, cancels, and corrected formes are involved, all the witnesses are listed for the sake of clarity.

There are five seventeenth-century editions of the *Preface* and *Answer*: '*50a*, '*50b*, '*51a*, '*51b*, and '*73*. '*50a* is the first edition; '*50b* is practically a line-for-line reprint of '*50a*; '*51a* is a reprint of '*50a* with revisions and corrections; '*51b* is a reprint of '*51a*; and '*73* is a reprint of '*51a* with revisions and corrections. There are, therefore, three substantive editions of the *Preface*: '*50a*, '*51a*, and '*73*. There is one substantive edition of the *Answer*, '*50a*.

There are three seventeenth-century editions of *Gondibert*: '*51a*, '*51b*, and '*73*. '*51a* is the first edition, '*51b* is a reprint of '*51a*, and '*73* is a reprint of '*51a* with revisions and corrections. Therefore, there are two substantive editions of *Gondibert*.

There is one seventeenth-century edition of 'The Seventh Canto', which was printed separately in 1685.

The copy-text for each work in the present edition is the first edition of that work. The general editorial policy has been to follow the punctuation and spelling of the earliest edition and to adopt the substantive and semi-substantive readings of the last substantive edition, where there are variants which are not apparently printer's errors. The same policy has governed the treatment of cancels and in-process changes in '*51a*; that is, the punctuation and spelling of the *cancellandum* and of the uncorrected forme have been followed, but the substantive readings of the *cancellans* and of the corrected forme have been adopted, in each case. The following table is a discussion of the relatively few passages in which this policy could not be followed.

Preface line 208 hath] had '*73*. This is apparently a printer's error in '*73*, since *had* is inconsistent with the tense of the passage.

Line 594 workes] work '*51a–b*.

Line 1056 is] though '*73*. '*73* is rejected here because, although some revision was evidently intended, it is not certain what. Perhaps '*73* was to have read *though a restraint . . . liberty, hath the same. . . .*

Line 1451 as] then '*73*. Here, again, some improvement may have been intended, but it is not clear what; *then* makes no sense.

Answer line 371 going] '*51a–b*, '*73*: go '*50a–b*. Here the sense demands the correction, even though it was probably not made by Hobbes.

Gondibert I. iii. 62 which] have '*73*. *have* is nonsense. Whatever revision was intended is not clear.

I. iii. 75 doom] dooms '*73*. *NED* lists no *dooms* to fit this context.

II. iii. 58 sing] sign '*73*. *Sign* is scarcely possible. Apparently the letters were transposed by the compositor.

II. iv. 61 there] their '*73*. Perhaps the compositor was misled by *their*, appearing later in the line.

II. v. 63 Life like] Like life '*73*. The sense demands the earlier reading. (The same is true of the next three passages)

II. viii. 12 who to] to who '73.

II. viii. 24 Were] Where '51b, '73. (This variant suggests that there may be another state of '51a (u), which was used as copy-text for both '51b and '73.)

II. viii. 60 met] meet '73.

III. vi. 40 That he to] That to '73. The later reading makes an awkward trochaic line.

The *MS* corrections in '50a and '51a have all been adopted, regardless of whether they are changes in punctuation or changes in wording.

THE TEXT OF THE 'PREFACE' AND 'ANSWER'

There are three modern texts of the *Preface* and Hobbes's *Answer*, in *The Works of the British Poets*, R. Anderson, ed., London, iv (1795), 765–874; *The Works of the English Poets*, A. Chalmers, ed., London, vi (1810), 374–435; and *Critical Essays of the Seventeenth Century*, J. E. Spingarn, ed., Oxford (1908), vol. ii. The first two of these are reprints from '73. The third is based on '73 and corrected by '51a; therefore none of these texts uses the first edition, '50a.

The copy-text for the *Preface to 'Gondibert'* and Hobbes's *Answer* is '50a, the first edition. Films of the two known copies were collated, one from Harvard and one from the Bibliothèque Nationale. A brief description follows.

Title: THE PREFACE | TO | GONDIBERT, | AN HEROICK POEM | WRITTEN BY | SIR WILLIAM D'AVENANT: | WITH AN ANSWER TO THE | PREFACE BY Mr HOBBES. | [Ornament: Staff twined with snakes between two cornucopias] | À PARIS, | Chez MATTHIEV GVILLEMOT, ruë Sainct | Iacques au coin de la ruë de la Parcheminerie, | à l'Enseigne de la Bibliotheque. | M.DC.L.

Format and collation: 8vo. π A–K⁸ L².

Errors: Sig. C3 is signed Aiij; Sig. D2 is signed Cij.

Pagination: 1–164.

Error: p. 153 is numbered 15.

'50a contains the following *MS* corrections in an unidentified hand. With the one exception listed below, these *MS* corrections appear in both copies.

Preface line 315 should *MS*: hould
Line 415 warmth *MS*: warmt'h
Line 796 fortune *MS*: fotune
Line 1380 think-not *MS*: think
Line 1389 our *MS*: their

Answer lines 361–2 weak- | nesse of body, *MS*: weak- | nesse, of body (uncorrected in the BN copy).

'50b is the second edition of the *Preface* and *Answer*. A brief description follows.

Title: A | DISCOURSE | UPON | *GONDIBERT*. | An Heroick *POEM* | Written by | Sʳ *WILLIAM D'AVENANT* | With an Answer to it by | Mʳ HOBBS. | - | [three fleurs de lis] | - | *A PARIS*, | Chez MATTHIEV GVILLEMOT, | ruë Sainct Jaques au Coin de la ruë de la | Parcheminerie, à l'Enseigne de la | Bibliotheque, M. DC. L.

Format and collation: 12mo. A–F¹² G⁵.
Errors: A4, D5, G4, G5 are unsigned.

Pagination: 2–145.
That *'50a* is an earlier edition than *'50b* may be inferred from a comparison of the two editions. In *'50a*, the text begins on sig. A1; the commendatory poems of Waller and Cowley appear at the end of the volume, on sig. L–L2ᵛ. In *'50b*, the title-page is [A], and the commendatory poems occupy sigs. A2–A3ᵛ.
That *'50b* was set up from *'50a* is apparent from the following readings.

Preface lines 133–4 Poet (. . . Invention)] Poet, . . . Invention, *'51a–b*, *'73*
Lines 287–8 palpably *'51a–b*, *'73*: palpably, and with horror *'50a–b*
Line 415 warmth *'50a MS*, *'51a–b*, *'73*: warmt'h *'50a–b*
Line 1578 make way for *'51a–b*, *'73*: perfect *'50a–b*

Answer line 54 Poesy] Prose *'51a–b*, *'73*
Line 160 findeth] findes *'51a cor*, *'73*: finding *'51a u*, *'51b*
Line 176 observation] observations *'51a–b*, *'73*
Line 320 persons] person *'51a–b*, *'73*
Line 323 possibly] possible *'51a–b*, *'73*

'50b may have been printed in England—not Paris, as the title-page says. The best indication of this is that the conventions of

spelling followed in '*50b* are closer to those appearing in the *Preface* and *Answer* as printed in '*51b*, the second edition of *Gondibert* (London), than to those of '*50a*, the bona-fide Paris edition of the *Preface* and *Answer*.

The text appearing in '*51a* was apparently set up from '*50a*, as the following readings show. (For a description of '*51a*, see below, p. xxxviii.)

Preface line 711 Seaven years '*50b*, '*73*: Seaven '*50a*, '*51a–b*
Line 965 Int'rests '*50b*, '*51b*: Intr'ests '*50a*, '*51a*, '*73*
Line 1475 finds '*51b*, '*73*: find's '*50a–b*, '*51a*
Answer line 56 with '*50b*, '*51b*: which '*50a*, '*51a*, '*73*
Line 88 syllables '*50b*, '*51b*, '*73*: syllabes '*50a*, '*51a*
Line 246 *Battaile*, '*73*: Battayle. '*50a–b*, '*51a–b*
Line 337 Judgement, '*51b*: Judgement. '*50a*, '*51a*, '*73*: Judgement: '*50b*

'*51b* contains the fourth edition of the *Preface* and *Answer*. It is the second edition of *Gondibert*. A brief description follows.

Title: GONDIBERT: | AN HEROICK | POEM; | WRITTEN BY | Sir WILLIAM D'AVENANT. | [ornament: hands with mortars and pestles on either side of fountain; banner above with motto: DVM PREMOR ATTOLOR] | *LONDON*, | Printed for *John Holden*, and are | to be sold at his Shop at the sign of the An- | chor in the *New-Exchange*, 1651.

Format and collation: 8vo. A–V⁸.

Pagination: 1–64; four unnumbered pp.; 1–243; six unnumbered pp.; unnumbered errata sheet.

'*51b* was set up from '*51a*. This has been established by Cornell March Dowlin,[1] in a demonstration based on misnumbered stanzas and misplaced marks of punctuation in the text of the poem. Dowlin does not discuss the text of the *Preface*. One would naturally assume that here, too, '*51b* was set up from '*51a*, and support for this assumption appears in the following readings.

Preface line 143 Empires '*51a–b*, '*73*: Empire '*50a–b*
Lines 387–8 palpably discerne '*51a–b*, '*73*: palpably, and with horrour . . . '*50a–b*
Line 477–8 Drunkennesse '*51a–b*, '*73*: Drunkenesse '*50a–b*

---

[1] Cornell March Dowlin, 'The First Edition of *Gondibert*: Quarto or Octavo?', *Library*, Ser. 4, xx (1939–40), 167–79.

Line 556 does '*50a*: doth '*51a–b*, '*73*: do's '*50b*
Line 700 Guest '*51a–b*, '*73*: Guests '*50a–b*
Line 1311 dissuaded '*51a–b*, '*73*: dissuades '*50a–b*
Line 1578 would make way for '*51a–b*, '*73*: would perfect '*50a–b*
Answer line 54 Prose '*51a–b*, '*73*: Poesy '*50a–b*
Line 160 finding '*51a u*, '*51b*: findeth '*50a–b*: findes '*51a cor*, *73*'
Line 176 observations '*51a–b*, '*73*: observation '*50a–b*
Line 320 person '*51a–b*, '*73*: persons '*50a–b*
Line 323 possible '*51a–b*, '*73*: possibly '*50a–b*
Line 371 going '*51a–b*, '*73*: go '*50a–b*

'*73* contains the fifth edition of the *Preface* and *Answer* and the third edition of *Gondibert*. It is THE | WORKS | OF | Sʳ William D'avenant Kᵗ | Consisting of | *Those which were formerly Printed*, | AND | *Those which he design'd for the Press*: | NOW PUBLISHED | Out of the AUTHORS | Originall Copies. | - | [design] | - | *LONDON*: | Printed by *T. N.* for *Henry Herringman*, at the Sign of the | *Blew Anchor* in the Lower Walk of the *New* | *Exchange*. 1673. *Folio*. The 'Authors Original Copies' had apparently been corrected by him, for '*73* contains a number of substantive changes, and yet it was set up from '*51a*, as an examination of the table just above will show. That it was not set up from '*51b* is shown by the variant readings of line 160 of Hobbes' *Answer*, where '*73* follows '*51a cor* and '*51b* follows '*51a u*. The characteristics of spelling and punctuation in '*51a* and '*73* are very similar.

One other thing should be said about the authority of '*73*. While it follows its copy-text, '*51a*, very closely in most places, there is evidence that it may have been corrected by reference to other editions of the *Preface* and *Answer*. The following collation may suggest this inference, although it will be noticed that every one of these changes could have been made by an alert compositor, including the one substantive change (*Preface*, l. 711).

Preface line 711 Seaven] Seaven years '*50*, '*73*

Answer line 88 syllabes] syllables '*50b*, '*51b*, '*73*
Lines 111–12 lustification '*51a*: Iustification '*50a*: Justification '*50b*, '*51b*: justification '*73*

THE TEXT OF 'GONDIBERT'

The copy-text for *Gondibert* is '*51a*, the first edition of the poem. (There is no known manuscript of the poem.) A description follows.

Title: GONDIBERT: | AN HEROICK | POEM, | WRITTEN BY| Sr *WILLIAM D'AVENANT*. | [ornament: two hands with mortars and pestles, one on either side of a fountain; a banner above with the legend DVM PREMOR ATTOLLOR] | LON-DON, | Printed by *Tho. Newcomb* for *John Holden*, and are to | be sold at his Shop at the sign of the Anchor in the | NEVV-EX-CHANGE, 1651. [In the Thomason copy, *1651* is struck out by pen and *Jan: 1650* is inserted.]

Format and collation: 4to. A–3K^4 (–3K4 = N2).

N2 and N4 are cancels in some copies. 2G3 is signed G 3 in some copies. 2O3 is unsigned. 3H3 is signed Ggg3. 3K4 is the cancellans N2 in *Hn²*.

Pagination: 1–88, four unnumbered pp., 1–344, six unnumbered pp. Misnumbered pp.: 82 misnumbered 84 in some copies, 68 misnumbered 98, 242–243 misnumbered 234–235 in some copies, 246–247 misnumbered 238–239 in some copies.

'*51a* is the earliest available form of the poem, and there is evidence that it was set up from a manuscript while the author was still revising and adjusting his text. The stanzas quoted in the *Preface* (ll. 959–74) are numbered 89–92, but they appear in the text of the poem as stanzas 84–87 (of Book II, canto vi). The authority of '*51a* is further established by the fact that all copies examined contain a large number of pen-and-ink corrections (see p. xxxiv below) which are in Davenant's hand, judging by the specimen in Gregg's *Literary Autographs*. Moreover, '*51a* is full of stop-press corrections, and some copies contain two cancels (see pp. xxxvi–xxxviii).

The second edition of *Gondibert*, '*51b* (described p. xxxi. above), is a reprint of '*51a*, as may be seen from the following table. References are to the *verse* in each case.

I. i. 9 lasting '*51a cor*, '*51b Errata*, '*73*: lusty '*51a u*, '*51b*
I. i. 28 Time '*51a cor*, '*51b Errata*: Trine '*51a u*, '*51b*, '*73*
I. v. 76 Threds '*73*: Thirds '*51a–b*: Thrids '*51b Errata*
II. iv. 7 grow '*51a MS*: grew '*51a–b*, '*73*
II. vii. 89 *Florist* '*51a cor*, '*73*: Florist '*51a u*, '*51b*
II. viii. 8 Needles '*51a cor*, '*51b Errata*, '*73*: Beedles '*51a u*, '*51b*
II. viii. 24 feed '*51a cor*: fed '*51a u*, '*51b*, '*73*
III. i. 34 Moon '*51a MS*, '*51b Errata*: Morn '*51a–b*, '*73*
III. v. 41 the weaker '*51a MS*: weak '*51a–b*, '*73*: our weaker '*51b Errata*

Moreover, on the basis of certain misnumbered stanzas, Dowlin has already established that '51b derives from '51a (see p. xxxi above).

'51b offers no improvements on '51a, and some passages are considerably worse. Some copies contain an errata sheet which makes certain important corrections, but which, again, adds nothing to what is found in the various states of '51a. '51b contributes little, substantively, to the present edition, though all its substantive variants are noted.

'73 also derives from '51a but contains 202 substantive variants. It has been assumed that these are Davenant's corrections (except where they are obviously printer's errors), and they have been accepted in the present text, due note being made.

The following table lists printer's errors (other than those in the table just above) in '51a which are carried over into '73. These errors prove that '73 was set up from '51a.

I. i. 47 Rhodalind '51b: Rodalind '51a, '73
I. v. 14 provoke: '51a MS, '51b: provoke '51a, '73
III. iv. 51 fals-hood Ed: falsh-hood '51a MS, '73: falshood '51b: falsh hood '51a
III. v. 37 err'd, '51b: err'd. '51a, '73

In addition, '51a often has to displace a word at the end of a long line, setting it above or below, within a parenthesis, (. '73 confuses these with marks of parenthesis in the following lines: I. ii. 35. 4, I. iii. 7. 2; and II. iv. 61. 4.

Manuscript Corrections in '51a

The manuscript corrections, apparently in Davenant's hand (see p. xxxiii above), in '51a, total fifty-four—at least in the copies examined. All but a few of these corrections appear in every copy of '51a, and they appear to have been made in the printing-house when the sheets were still unfolded. Dowlin observes that the corrections in the Millington copy, at the Library of the University of Pennsylvania, are made in black printer's ink, although this is not the case with other copies.[1] There is more cogent evidence in the fact that the corrections in Sheet 3D are all on the inner forme, but

---

[1] Dowlin, p. 169. In the two copies at the University of Illinois, in the Nethercot copy, and in the copy at Indiana University these corrections are in faded brown ink, and I have examined all other copies only on film.

on two separate pages, 3D1ᵛ and 3D3ᵛ, and none of these correct-ions appears in *UI*², which of course contains the other corrections. This circumstance would hardly have occurred if the corrector had been paging through a bound volume. The *MS* readings are accepted in the present text.

Many of the *MS* corrections are marks of punctuation inserted or deleted; although they cannot be definitely ascribed to Davenant, they are in the same ink as the other corrections, and they have been accepted, duly noted.

The *MS* corrections in '*51a* are as follows, the first reading being the correction in each case. They appear in every copy examined, except as noted.

Preface line 51 Censurers: Censures
Line 451 unprofitable: profitable
Line 529 *Proem*: *Poem*
Line 703 posting: boasting
Line 713 implys: inplys
Line 898 weare: ware
Line 904 of *Lay-men*; and the newest: of the *Lay-men*; and newest.
Line 1428 in contriving: in the contriving (Uncorrected in Nether-cot's copy)
(Remaining references are to *Gondibert*)

I. i. Arg., 1 ARIBERT'S: ARIBERTS
      5 forth,: forth
I. i. 1. 1 Lombards,: Lombards
      2 long,: long
I. i. 19 eye: ey
I. i. 43 sung: song
I. i. 57 Armies are,: Armies; are
I. ii. 77 ne'r: neer
I. v. 1 wept: weep'd
I. v. 14 provoke:: provoke
I. v. 25 in-large: in large
I. vi. 79 clossest: closet
II. i. 35 Priests: Priest
II. iii. 3 her: his
II. iv. 7 grow: grew (some copies uncorrected)
II. v. 46 Tomes: tombs
II. vi. 7 neither: never (some copies uncorrected)

p. 194 *catchword* By: This

II. vi. 76 comment: commet

II. vii. 53 excesse,: success

II. vii. 58 false: fase

II. vii. 81, 4 Whom: When

II. vii. 81, 4 winde: winde, (some copies uncorrected)

II. viii. 53 place: place (*UI*[1] only)
peace: place (*UI*[2], *Hn*[2], *Nethercot* only)
make: may

II. viii. 67 whom: home (*Bodl* only)
harm'd: arm'd

II. viii. 78 worth,: worth

III. i. 2 her: their

III. i. 29 where: wuere (some copies uncorrected)

III. i. 30 kinde: kinde,
forward: foward

III. i. 34 Moon: Morn (*Bodl* and *Nethercot* only)

III. i. 73 Traytors: Tyrants

III. iii. 36 Grates: Gates

III. iii. 41 *Nethercot* copy has an illegible correction of strait, which
looks like stryait

III. iv. 11 would: could

III. iv. 12 Breed;: bred;

III. iv. 28 Votaries: Victories (Uncorrected: *UI*[2])

III. iv. 51 falsh-hood: falsh hood (Uncorrected: *UI*[2])

III. iv. 51 sleep.: sleep (Uncorrected: *UI*[2])

III. v. 41 the weaker: weak (*Chap* only)

III. vi. 2 path: ph, at

III. vi. 32 As if he fain: As if fain (some copies uncorrected)

III. vi. 78 back: black (*Folg*, *Hn*[2] only)

Cancels in '51a

There are two cancels in '*51a*, sig. N2 and sig. N4. It has been
observed that 'D'avenant, by means of numerous cancellations and
inserts, is attempting to revise his text, although the corrections are
so varied and irregularly bound-in that an ideal copy would need
to be a composite'.[1] No two copies of '*51a* come near to being identi-

---

[1] Fredson Bowers, *Principles of Bibliographical Description* (Princeton University,
1949), p. 71. Professor Bowers speaks further of 'insertions . . . possibly placed only in
unbound copies and the bound copies . . . partially corrected by hand' (ibid., p. 72).

cal, but 'numerous cancellations' is misleading. '*51a* does contain an unusually large number of in-process changes (at least twenty-two formes have been corrected), but none of the copies I have examined shows evidence of more than two cancellations.

The two leaves which have been corrected by cancellation have not been corrected in *MS* in any of the copies containing the cancellandum. Both cancels are in the first gathering of the poem, but the corrections made by the cancellation of these leaves are neither more numerous nor more important than those made elsewhere merely by *MS*. Some of the in-process changes, however, have been duplicated by *MS* in the uncorrected states of some formes. The various types of corrections in '*51a*, then, must have been made as follows. Stop-press corrections were made by the press-corrector as errors were discovered during the imposition of the text. At some time before 3K had been completely run off, the errors on N2 and N4 were discovered, and two cancels were printed, one of them (N2) on the otherwise blank 3K4. But it soon became evident that there were many more errors of the same sort—too many to be corrected by cancellation, and so Davenant did the best he could with pen and ink. Finally, the 8vo second edition was brought out (in the same year), incorporating most of the corrections in '*51a*. It may have been brought out principally in an attempt to correct the text of the bungled quarto, for as late as 1653 some of Davenant's contemporaries did not realize that there had already been a second edition of *Gondibert*.[2]

Cancels

Sig. N2
Cancellans in: *UI²*, *Chap*, *Hn¹*, *Hn²* (on 3K4), *Y*, *P*, *Nethercot*
Cancellandum in: *UI¹*, *BM*, *Folg*, *Hn²*, *Bodl*, *Pen*, *WC*, *IU*
Sig. N2ʳ
I. i. 9. 1 lasting] lusty
        2 Bed;] bed,
        3 Sex] sex

But the *MS* corrections in '*51a* were apparently made even before the sheets were folded, as has been shown above, and not after some volumes were bound. The fact that they are in the same hand in all copies suggests that they were all made at once, very likely sheet by sheet.

  [2] The satirical volume *Certain Verses* was published in 1653 as though to accompany the 'Second Edition of *Gondibert*', if one should come out. More recent readers have also taken the 8vo for the first edition; see Dowlin's 'The First Edition of *Gondibert*'.

I. i. 11. 1 Sphear,] Sphear
      3 appear,] appear
Sig. N2^v
I. i. 12. 4 beauty] beauty
I. i. 15. 4 sicknes] sickness
Sig. N4
Cancellans in: *UI*², *Hn*¹⁻², *Chap, Y, P, Nethercot*
Cancellandum in: *UI*¹, *BM, Folg, Bodl, Pen, WC, IU*
Sig. N4^r
I. i. 27. 3 War's] Warr's
      4 far] farr
I. i. 28. 1 Time . . . Judge] *Trine* . . . Judg
      2 yeilds] yields
      3 less . . . misteries] lesse . . . mysteries
      4 peaceful] peacefull
I. i. 31. 3 Fate] fate
Sig. N4^v
I. i. 32. 3 bus'ness] bus'nesse
I. i. 33. 3 Ambition's] Ambitions
I. i. 34. 1 steddy] stedy
      3 goodness] goodnesse
I. i. 35. 1 war] warr
      4 toile] toyl
I. i. 36. 2 war] warr
      3 war] warr

Press-Variants in '51a

The following table of press-variants in '51a is based on a complete collation of five copies: *UI*¹⁻², *BM, Folg,* and *Hn*¹. The other nine copies which appear in the table have been examined only in respect to the variants found in the examination of the first five.[1]

[Note: The variants are apparently mere failures to print in the following cases:

Sheet Q inner forme
    ,,   2B   ,,   ,,
    ,,   2E   ,,   ,,
    ,,   2F   ,,   ,,   (a)
    ,,   2G outer ,,   (b)

---

[1] I am indebted to Professor Fredson Bowers, *The Dramatic Works of Thomas Dekker.* Cambridge, 1935, for the general scheme of this table.

Sheet 2T outer forme
   ,,   2Z   ,,   ,,
   ,,   3C   ,,   ,,]

Sheet L (inner forme)
Corrected: *UI²*, *P*, *Chap*, *Bodl*, *Pen*, *WC*, *IU*
Uncorrected: *UI¹*, *BM*, *Folg*, *Hn¹⁻²*, *Y*, *Nethercot*
Sig. Lᵛ
Answer, l. 160 findes] finding

Sheet Q (inner forme)
Corrected: *UI²*, *BM*, *Hn¹*, *Y*, *Pen*, *P*, *WC*, *Chap*, *IU*, *Nethercot*
  (impression, but without ink)
Uncorrected: *UI¹*, *Folg*, *Hn²*, *Bodl*
Sig. Q3ᵛ
I. ii. 61. 4 from] fron

Sheet Y (inner forme)
Corrected: *UI²*, *BM*, *Folg*, *Hn¹*, *Chap*, *Bodl*, *Y*, *P*, *WC*, *IU*,
  Nethercot
Uncorrected: *UI¹*, *Hn²*
Sig. Yᵛ
I. v. 40. 4 stay:] stay.
I. v. 41. 4 inrag'd!] inrag'd
Sig. Y3ᵛ
I. v. 61. 3 flesh;] flesh:

Sheet 2B (inner forme)
Sig. 2Bᵛ
I. vi. 71. 1 But] -t *Hn¹*
        3 And] d *Hn¹*
Catchword Who] Whₒ *UI¹*
Sig. 2B3ᵛ
II. i. 2. 2 Beames] Be mes *BM*

Sheet 2E (inner forme)
Corrected: *UI¹*, *Folg*, *Hn¹⁻²*, *Chap*, *Bodl*, *Pen*, *P*, *WC*, *IU*, *Nethercot*
Uncorrected: *UI²*, *BM*, *Y*
Sig. 2E4
Catchword This] Thi
Sheet 2F (inner forme)[a]
Corrected: *UI¹*, *Folg*, *Chap*, *Hn²*, *WC*, *Bodl*, *Y*, *Pen*, *P*, *IU*, *Nethercot*
Uncorrected: *UI²*, *BM*, *Hn¹*

Sig. 2F3^v

II. ii. 78. 4 who devoures] who█devoures

Sheet 2F (inner forme)^b
Corrected: *UI*[1], *Folg, Chap, Hn*[2], *WC, IU, Nethercot*
Uncorrected: *UI*[2], *BM, Hn*[1], *Bodl, Y, Pen, P*
Sig. 2F^v

II. ii. 58. 2 Oracles . . . taught,] Oracles, . . . taught
Sig. 2F2

II. ii. 66. 1 Liver] liver
Sig. 2F3^v

II. ii. 81. 3 Slaves] Slaves,

Sheet 2G (outer forme)^a
Corrected: *UI*[1], *Folg, Hn*[2], *Nethercot*
Uncorrected: *UI*[2], *BM, Hn*[1], *Chap, Bodl, Y, Pen, P, WC, IU*
Sig. 2G

II. iii. Arg., 1 HUBERT] HΩBERT

Sheet 2G (outer forme)^b
Corrected: *UI*[1–2], *Folg, Hn*[2], *Y, Nethercot*
Uncorrected: *BM, Hn*[1], *Chap, Bodl, Pen, P, WC, IU*
Sig. 2G3
Signature Gg3] G 3

Sheet 2H (outer forme)
Corrected: *UI*[2], *Hn*[1–2], *WC, IU*
Uncorrected: *UI*[1], *BM, Folg, Chap, Bodl, Y, Pen, P, Nethercot*
Sig. 2H3
Signature line (prais'd. Hh3 Like: Hh3 (prais'd.

Sheet 2L (outer forme)^a
Corrected: *UI*[1], *Chap, Hn*[2]
Uncorrected: *UI*[2], *BM, Folg, Hn*[1], *Bodl, Y, Pen, P, WC, IU*
Sig. 2L2^v

II. v. 33. 1 wall] Wall
II. v. 34. 2 controul] controul;
II. v. 37. 1 There] Where

Sheet 2L (outer forme)^b
Corrected: *UI*[1], *Folg, Chap, Hn*[2], *Nethercot*
Uncorrected: UI[2], *BM, Hn*[1], *Bodl, Y, Pen, P, WC, IU*
Sig. 2L4^v

II. v. 54. 3 lie,] lie;

II. v. 56. 2 display'd,] display'd;
      3 Princes] Princes,

Sheet 2Q (outer forme)
Corrected: *UI¹, BM, Folg, HN¹⁻², Bodl, Y, Pen, P, Nethercot*
Uncorrected: *UI², Chap, WC, IU*
Sig. 2Q
II. vii. 53. 3 treat . . . want . . . success,] treat, . . . want, . . . success;
II. vii. 56. 3 wounds] wounds,
II. vii. 57. 2 from] fr m
Sig. 2Q2ᵛ
II. vii. 68. 1 bow:] bow;
II. vii. 69. 3 way] way,
Sig. 2Q3
II. vii. 73. 1 onward] outward
II. vii. 77. 4 midst] midst,
Sig. 2Q4ᵛ
II. vii. 88. 3 proceed,] proceed;
II. vii. 89. 2 *Florist*] Florist

Sheet 2R (inner forme)
Corrected: *UI², BM, Folg, Hn¹, Bodl, Pen, Nethercot*
Uncorrected: *UI¹, Hn², Y, P, WC, IU*
Sig. 2Rᵛ
II. viii. 4. 1 soon] soon,
II. viii. 5. 3 Maids] Maids,
      4 carry'd] carry'd,
II. viii. 7. 3 Love] Love,
Sig. 2R2
II. viii. 8. 3 Needles] Beedles
II. viii. 10. 2 Spie?] Spie;
II. viii. 12. 2 Saints] Saints,
Sig. 2R3ᵛ
II. viii. 24. 2 Toyles;] Toyles,
      3 feed] fed
Catchword Though] Thoug
Sig. 2R4
II. viii. 30. 1 Sick] stck

Sheet 2S (outer forme)ᵃ
Corrected: *BM, Folg, Hn¹, Chap, Bodl, Y, Pen, P, WC, IU*
Uncorrected: *UI¹⁻², Hn², Nethercot*

Sig. 2S
II. viii. 39. 4 seem,] seem
Sig. 2S2ᵛ
II. viii. 53. 4 peace] place
Sheet 2S (outer forme)ᵇ
Corrected: *UI²*, *BM*, *Folg*, *Hn¹*, *Chap*, *Bodl*, *Y*, *Pen*, *P*, *WC*, *IU*,
    Nethercot
Uncorrected: *UI¹*, *Hn²*
Sig. 2S
II. viii. 42. 2 Romans] Romvns
            3 boast] hoast
Sheet 2T (outer forme)
Sig. 2T
II. viii. 81. 4 desert.] desert *UI¹*, *Hn¹*, *Pen*, *P*
Sheet 2U (inner forme)
Corrected: *UI²*, *Chap*, *P*, *WC*, *IU*
Uncorrected: *UI¹*, *BM*, *Hn ¹⁻²*, *Bodl*, *Y*, *Pen*, *Folg*, *Nethercot*
Sig. 2Uᵛ
Page number 242] 234
III. i. 22. 1 Eies,] Eies
            4 Eies] Eys
Sig. 2U2
Page number 243] 235
III. i. 29. 4 where] wuere
III. i. 30. 4 bloomy] blooming
Sig. 2U3ᵛ
Page number 246] 238
III. i. 45. 4 cruell] cruest
Sig. 2U4
Page number 247] 239
III. i. 48. 1 grows,] grows.
Sheet 2Z (inner forme)
Corrected: *UI²*, *Folg*, *Hn²*, *Y*, *WC*
Uncorrected: *UI¹*, *BM*, *Hn¹*, *Chap*, *Bodl*, *Pen*, *P*, *IU*, *Nethercot*
Sig. 2Zᵛ
III. ii. 53. 1 moves;] moves,
Sig. 2Z2
III. ii. 58. 1 chide,] chide
III. ii. 60. 4 then, . . . froward,] then . . . froward

III. ii. 61. 3 garish] garnish
Sig. 2Z3ᵛ
III. ii. 74. 3 vow,] vow
III. ii. 75. 2 me] we
            3 wait;] wait,
Sig. 2Z4
III. ii. 80. 4 a█] an (*except Hn² reads* a)

Sheet 2Z (outer forme)
Sig. 2Z3
III. ii. 71. 2 threatning Beams;] threatnin   Beam *BM*

Sheet 3A (inner forme)
Corrected: *UI², BM, Folg, Hn¹, Bodl, Y, Pen, IU, Nethercot*
Uncorrected: *UI¹, Chap, Hn², P, WC*
Sig. 3Aᵛ
III. ii. 97. 3 truth;] truth,
Sig. 3A2
III. ii. 98. 2 mourn:] mourn;
            3 Breast!] Breast,
            4 return!] return.
III. ii. 99. 3 Chiefs,] Chiefs
Sig. 3A3ᵛ
III. iii. 1. 4 de-|vowr:] de-|vowr.
III. iii. 2. 4 cease:] cease,
Sig. 3A4
III. iii. 3. 4 die:] die.
III. iii. 4. 3 Light;] Light,

Sheet 3B (outer forme)
Corrected: *UI², Folg, Bodl*
Uncorrected: *UI¹, BM, Hn¹⁻², Chap, Y, Pen, P, WC, IU, Nethercot*
Sig. 3B
III. iii. 17. 1 live,] live!
            2 Powers!] Powers;
            4 fall] full

Sheet 3C (outer forme)
Sig. 3C4ᵛ
III. iv. 19. 4 con-|ceal.] con|ceal *UI¹*

Sheet 3F (outer forme)

Corrected: *BM*, *Y*, *Pen*, *WC*, *IU*
Uncorrected: *UI*¹⁻², *Folg*, *Hn*¹⁻², *Chap*, *Bodl*, *P*, *Nethercot*
Sig. 3F4ᵛ
III. v. 39. 3 Seed] seed
Sheet 3G (inner forme)
Corrected: *UI*², *Y*
Uncorrected: *UI*¹, *BM*, *Folg*, *Hn*¹⁻², *Chap*, *Bodl*, *Pen*, *P*, *WC*,
   IU, *Nethercot*
Sig. 3Gᵛ
III. v. 52. 1 Lord] Lord,
Sig. 3G2
III. v. 54. 3 haste,] haste?
III. v. 55. 4 scape?] scape!
III. v. 56. 1 those but] but those
III. v. 57. 4 feare?] feare.
Sig. 3G3ᵛ
III. v. 72. 1 She] she

Sheet 3H (inner forme)
Corrected: *UI*¹⁻², *Chap*, *Hn*², *Y*, *P*
Uncorrected: *BM*, *Folg*, *Hn*¹, *Bodl*, *Pen*, *WC*, *IU*, *Nethercot*
Sig. 3Hᵛ
III. vi. 9. 4 *Greeks*] *Greeks*,
Sig. 3H2
III. vi. 13. 1 Valor,] Valor!
          2 Cowardise,)] Cowardise!)
III. vi. 14. 1 Fear,] Fear!
III. vi. 15. 3 war] war,
III. vi. 17. 2 bold] bold,
          3 his] this
Sig. 3H3ᵛ
III. vi. 28. 2 ere] e're
III. vi. 29. 4 fame] fame,
III. vi. 32. 3 if he fain] if fain
Sig. 3H4
III. vi. 34. 4 dispos'd.] dispos'd

THE TEXT OF 'THE SEVENTH CANTO'

'The Seventh Canto' was first printed in 1685 as THE |
SEVENTH | And Last | CANTO | OF THE | THIRD BOOK |

OF | GONDIBERT, | Never yet Printed. | - | By Sir *William D'avenant*. | - | *LONDON,* | Printed for *William Miller* and *Joseph Watts* at the | *Gilded Acorn* in St. *Paul*'s Church-Yard, over] against the little North Door, 1685. 8vo.

In 1940 Professor James G. McManaway printed a modern text of the fragment (*MLQ* i. 1 (1940)) based on a comparison of two extant copies of the 1685 edition, one at the Folger Library, and one at the Wellesley Library. The present text is based on a collation of the two copies of 1685 and checked against McManaway's text.

I am deeply indebted to Professor G. B. Evans for his help in the original preparation of this edition. The University of Illinois Library was most generous in purchasing books, and Franklin College has given me considerable aid in travelling. Of the many colleagues who have contributed to this work in a variety of ways I owe particular thanks to Professor Eva Benton and Professor A. M. Gibbs. The Clarendon Press deserves my very humble gratitude for their patience and meticulous care in the printing of this book.

GONDIBERT

THE AUTHOR'S
PREFACE TO HIS
MUCH HONOR'D FRIEND,
M. Hobbes

SIR, Since you have done me the honour to allow this Poem a
daylie examination as it was writing, I will presume now it hath
attain'd more length, to give you a longer trouble; that you may
yeild me as great advantages by censuring the method, as by judging
the Numbers, and the matter. And because you shall passe through 5
this new Building with more ease to your disquisition, I will acquaint
you, what care I tooke of my materialls, ere I began to worke.

But first give me leave (remembring with what difficulty the world
can shew any Heroick Poem, that in a perfect glasse of Nature gives
us a familiar and easy view of our selves) to take notice of those 10
quarrells, which the Living have with the Dead: and I will (accord-
ing as all times have apply'd their reverence) begin with *Homer*, who
though he seemes to me standing upon the Poets famous hill, like the
eminent Sea-marke, by which they have in former ages steer'd; and
though he ought not to be remov'd from that eminence, least 15
Posterity should presumptuously mistake their course; yet some
(sharply observing how his successors have proceeded no farther
than a perfection of imitating him) say, that as Sea-markes are
cheefly usefull to Coasters, and serve not those who have the ambi-
tion of Discoverers, that love to sayle in untry'd Seas; so he hath 20
rather prov'd a Guide for those, whose satisfy'd witt will not venture
beyond the track of others, then to them, who affect a new and
remote way of thinking; who esteem it a deficiency and meanesse of
minde, to stay and depend upon the authority of example.

Some there are, that object that even in the likelyhoods of Story 25
(and Story, where ever it seemes most likely, growes most pleasant)
he doth too frequently intermixe such Fables, as are objects lifted
above the Eyes of Nature; and as he often interrogates his Muse,
not as his rationall Spirit but as a *Familiar*, separated from his body,
so her replyes bring him where he spends time in immortall con- 30
versation; whilst supernaturally he doth often advance his men

to the quality of Gods, and depose his Gods to the condition of men.

His Successor to fame, (and consequently to censure) is *Virgill*;
35 whose toyles nor vertue cannot free him from the peevishnesse (or rather curiosity) of divers Readers. He is upbrayed by some (who perhaps are affected Antiquaries, and make priority of time the measure of excellence) for gayning his renowne by imitation of *Homer*: Whilst others (no lesse bold with that ancient Guide) say,
40 he hath so often led him into Heaven, and Hell, till by conversation with Gods and Ghosts, he sometimes deprives us of those naturall probabilities in Story, which are instructive to humane life: And others affirme (if it be not irreverence to record their opinion) that even in witte, he seemes deficient by many omissions; as if he had
45 design'd a pennance of gravity to himselfe and to posterity: And by their observing that continu'd gravity, me thinks they looke upon him, as on a Musitian composing of Anthemes; whose excellence consists more in the solemnesse, then in the fancy; and upon the body of his Worke as on the body of a Giant, whose force hath more
50 of strength, then quicknesse, and of patience, then activity.

But these bold Censurers are in danger of so many Enemies, as I shall wisely shrinke from them; and only observe, that if any Disciples of unimitable *Virgill* can prove so formall, as to esteeme witte (as if it were levity) an imputation to the Heroique Muse (by
55 which malevolent word, Witt, they would disgrace her extraordinarie heights) yet if those grave Judges will be held wise, they must endure the fate of Wise men; who always have but few of their societie; for many more then consist of their number (perhaps not having the sullennesse to be of it) are taken with those bold flights,
60 and thinke tis with the Muse (whose noble Quarry is men) as with the Eagle, who when he soares high stoopes more prosperously, and is most certaine of his prey. And surely Poets (whose businesse should represent the Worlds true image often to our view) are not lesse prudent than Painters, who when they draw Landschaps enter-
65 taine not the Eye wholy with even Prospect, and a continu'd Flatte; but (for variety) terminate the sight with lofty Hills, whose obscure heads are sometimes in the Clowdes.

Lucan who chose to write the greatest actions that ever were allow'd to be true (which for feare of contemporary witnesses,
70 oblig'd him to a very close attendance upon Fame) did not observe

51 Censurers *'50a–b*, *'51a MS*, *'51b*, *'73*: Censures *'51a*

that such an enterprize rather beseem'd an Historian then a Poet: for wise Poets think it more worthy to seeke out truth in the passions, then to record the truth of actions; and practise to describe Mankinde just as wee are persuaded or guided by instinct, not particular persons, as they are lifted, or levell'd by the force of Fate, it being nobler to contemplate the generall History of Nature, then a selected Diary of Fortune: And Painters are no more then Historians, when they draw eminent persons (though they tearme that drawing to the life) but when by assembling divers figures in a larger volume, they draw passions (though they terme it but Story) then they increase in dignity and become Poets.

I have been thus hard to call him to account for the choyce of his Argument, not meerly as it was Story, but because the actions he recorded were so eminent, and so neere his time, that he could not assist Truth, with such ornaments as Poets, for usefull pleasure, have allow'd her; least the feign'd complexion might render the true suspected. And now I will leave to others the presumption of measuring his Hyperboles, by whose space and height they malitiously take the dimension of witt; and so mistake him in his boyling Youth (which had merveilous forces) as wee disrellish excellent Wine when fuming in the Lee.

Statius (with whome wee may conclude the old Heroicks) is as accomptable to some for his obligations to *Virgill*, as *Virgill* is to others for what he owes to *Homer*; and more closely then *Virgill* waits on *Homer*, doth *Statius* attend *Virgill*, and follows him there also where Nature never comes, even into Heaven, and Hell: and therefore he cannot escape such as approve the wisdome of the best Dramaticks; who in representation of examples, beleeve they prevaile most on our manners when they lay the Scene at home in their owne Country, so much they avoid those remote regions of Heaven and Hell: as if the People (whom they make civill by an easy communication with reason (and familiar reason is that which is call'd the civility of the Stage) were become more discreet than to have their eyes persuaded by the descending of Gods in gay Clowds, and more manly than to be frighted with the rising of Ghosts in Smoake.

Tasso (who reviv'd the Heroick flame after it was many ages quench'd) is held both in time and merit, the first of the Modernes; an honour by which he gaines not much; because the number he excells must needs be few, which affords but one fit to succeed him;

82 hard '73: hardy '50a–'51b.

110 for I will yeild to their opinion, who permit not *Ariosto*, no nor *Du Bartas* in this eminent ranck of the Heroicks; rather than to make way by their admission for *Dante*, *Marino*, and others. *Tasso's* honnour too is cheefly allow'd him, where he most endevors to make *Virgill* his Patterne: And againe, when we consider from whom
115 *Virgill's* spirit is deriv'd, wee may observe how rarely humane excellence is found; for Heroick Poesy (which, if exact in it selfe, yeelds not to any other humane worke) flow'd but in few, and even those streames descended but from one Grecian Spring: And tis with Originall Poems as with the Originall Peeces of Painters, whose
120 Coppies abate the excessive price of the first Hand.

But *Tasso* though he came late into the world must have his share in that Criticall warre which never ceases amongst the Learned; and he seemes most unfortunate, because his errors which are deriv'd from the Ancients, when examin'd, grow in a great degree
125 excusable in them, and by being his, admit no pardon. Such as are his Councell assembled in Heaven, his Witches Expeditions through the Aire, and enchanted Woods inhabited with Ghosts. For though the elder Poets (which were then the sacred Priests) fed the world with supernaturall Tales, and so compounded the Religion,
130 of Pleasure and Mysterie (two Ingredients which never fail'd to worke upon the People) whilst for the eternity of their Chiefs (more refin'd by education) they surely intended no such vaine provision. Yet a Christian Poet (whose Religion little needs the aydes of invention) hath lesse occasion to imitate such Fables, as meanly
135 illustrate a probable Heaven, by the fashion, and dignity of Courts; and make a resemblance of Hell, out of the Dreames of frighted Women; by which they continue and increase the melancholy mistakes of the People.

Spencer may stand here as the last of this short File of Heroick
140 Poets; Men, whose intellectualls were of so great a making, (though some have thought them lyable to those few censures wee have mention'd) as perhaps they will in worthy memory outlast, even Makers of Lawes, and Founders of Empires, and all but such as must therefore live equally with them, because they have recorded
145 their names[; and consequently with their owne hands led them to the Temple of Fame]. And since wee have dar'd to remember those

132 provision. *Ed*: provision) *'50a–b*, *'51a*: provision.) *'51b*, *'73*.   143 Empires *'51a–b*, *'73*: Empire *'50a–b*   145–6 names . . . Fame. And] names. And *'73*

exceptions which the Curious have against them, it will not be expected I should forget what is objected against *Spencer*; whose obsolete language wee are constrain'd to mention, though it be grown the most vulgar accusation that is lay'd to his charge.   150
Language (which is the only Creature of Man's creation) hath like a Plant, seasons of flourishing, and decay; like Plants is remov'd from one soile to an other, and by being so transplanted, doth often gather vigour and increase. But as it is false husbandry to graft old branches upon young stocks: so wee may wonder that our Language   155
(not long before his time created out of a confusion of others, and then beginning to flourish like a new plant) should (as helps to its increase) receive from his hand, new grafts of old wither'd words. But this vulgar exception, shall only have the vulgar excuse; which is, that the unlucky choice of his *Stanza* hath by repetition of Rime   160
brought him to the necessity of many exploded words.

If wee proceed from his Language to his Argument, wee must observe with others, that his noble and most artfull hands deservd to be employ'd upon matter of a more naturall, and therefore of a more usefull kinde. His allegoricall Story (by many held defective in   165
the connexion) resembling (me thinks) a continuance of extra-ordinary Dreames; such as excellent Poets, and Painters, by being overstudious may have in the beginning of Feavers: And those morall visions are just of so much use to humane application, as painted History, when with the cousenage of lights it is represented   170
in Scenes, by which wee are much lesse inform'd then by actions on the Stage.

Thus, Sir, I have (perhaps) taken paines to make you think me malitious, in observing how farre the Curious have look'd into the errors of others; Errors which the naturall humor of imitation hath   175
made so like in all (even from *Homer* to *Spencer*) as the accusations against the first, appear but little more then repetition in every processe against the rest: and comparing the resemblance of error in persons of one generation, to that which is in those of an other age; wee may finde it exceeds not any where, notoriously, the   180
ordinary proportion. Such limits to the progresse of every thing (even of worthiness as well as defect) doth Imitation give: for whilst wee imitate others, wee can no more excell them, then he that sailes by others Mapps can make a new discovery: and to Imitation, Nature (which is the only visible power, and operation of God) perhaps doth   185
needfully encline us, to keepe us from excesses. For though every

man be capable of worthinesse and unworthinesse (as they are
defin'd by Opinion) yet no man is built strong enough to beare the
extremities of either, without unloading himselfe upon others
190 shoulders, even to the wearinesse of many. If courage be worthinesse,
yet where it is overgrowne into extreames, it becomes as wilde
and hurtfull as ambition; and so what was reverenc'd for protection
growes to be abhor'd for oppression: If *Learning* (which is not
Knowledge, but a continu'd Sayling by fantastick and uncertaine
195 windes towards it) be worthynesse, yet it hath bounds in all Philo-
sophers; and Nature that measur'd those bounds, seemes not so
partiall, as to allow it in any one a much larger extent then in an
other; as if in our fleshy building, she consider'd the furniture and
the roome, alike, and together; for as the compasse of Diadems
200 commonly fits the whole succession of those kings that weare them;
so throughout the whole World, a very few inches may distinguish
the circumference of the heads of their Subjects: Nor need wee
repine that Nature hath not some Favorites, to whom she doth
dispense this Treasure, Knowledge, with a prodigious Liberalitie.
205 For as there is no one that can be said vastly to exceed all mankinde;
so divers that have in learning transcended all in some one province,
have corrupted many with that great quantity of false gold; and the
authority of their stronger Science hath often serv'd to distract, or
pervert their weaker disciples.
210   And as the qualities which are term'd good, are bounded, so are
the bad; and likewise limited, as well as gotten by imitation; for
amongst those that are extraordinary, either by birth or brayne (for
with the usuall pride of Poets, I passe by common crowds, as
negligently as Princes move from throngs that are not their owne
215 Subjects) wee cannot finde any one so egregious (admitting cruelty
and avarice for the chiefest evills; and errors in goverment or
doctrine, to be the greatest errors) but that divers of former or
succeeding times may enter the scales with them, and make the
Ballance even; though the passion of Historians would impose the
220 contrary on our belief; who in dispraise of evill Princes are often as
unjust and excessive as the common People: for there was never any
Monarch so cruell but he had living subjects, nor so avaritious but
that his subjects were richer then himself; nor ever any disease in
goverment so extreamly infectious as to make universall Anarchy,
225 or any error in Doctrine so strong by the Maintayner, but that Truth

208 hath] had '73

(though it wrastled with her often, and in many places) hath at some season, and on some grownd, made her advantages and successe apparent: Therefore wee may conclude, that Nature, for the safety of mankinde, hath as well (by dulling and stopping our progresse with the constant humor of imitation) given limits to courage 230 and to learning, to wickednes and to erour, as it hath ordain'd the shelves before the shore, to restraine the rage and excesses of the Sea.

But I feele (Sir) that I am falling into the dangerous Fitte of a hott Writer; for in stead of performing the promise which begins 235 this Preface, and doth oblige me (after I had given you the judgment of some upon others) to present my selfe to your censure, I am wandring after new thoughts: but I shall aske your pardon, and returne to my undertaking.

My Argument I resolv'd should consist of Christian persons; for 240 since Religion doth generally beget, and governe manners, I thought the example of their actions would prevaile most upon our owne, by being deriv'd from the same doctrine and authority; as the particular Sects educated by Philosophers were diligent and pliant to the dictates and fashions of such as deriv'd them selves from the same 245 Master; but lazy and froward to those who convers'd in other Schooles: Yet all these Sects pretended to the same beauty, *Vertue*; though each did court her more fondly, when she was dress'd at their owne homes, by the hands of their acquaintance: And so Subjects bred under the lawes of a Prince (though Lawes differ 250 not much in Morality, or priviledge throughout the civill World; being every where made for direction of Life, more then for sentences of Death) will rather dye neer that Prince, defending those they have been taught, then live by taking new from an other.

These were partly the reasons why I chose a Story of such Persons 255 as profess'd Christian Religion; but I ought to have been most enclin'd to it, because the Principles of our Religion conduce more to explicable vertue, to plaine demonstrative justice, and even to Honor (if Vertue the Mother of Honor be voluntary, and active in the darke, so as she need not lawes to compell her, nor looke for 260 witnesses to proclaime her) then any other Religion that e're assembl'd men to Divine Worship. For that of the *Jewes* doth still consist in a sullen separation of them selves from the rest of humane flesh, which is a fantasticall pride of their owne cleanesse, and an

247 pretended '50b–'73: pretented '50a

265 uncivill disdaine of the imagin'd contagiousnes of others; and at this
day, their cantonizing in Tribes, and shynesse of allyance with
neighbours, deservs not the terme of mutuall love, but rather seemes
a bestiall melancholy of hearding in their owne Walks. That of the
Ethnicks, like this of *Mahomet*, consisted in the vaine pride of
270 Empire, and never enjoyn'd a Jewish separation, but drew all Nations
together; yet not as their companyons of the same species, but as
slaves to a Yoke: Their sanctity was Honor, and their Honor only
an impudent courage, or dexterity in destroying. But Christian
Religion hath the innocence of Village neighbourhood, and did
275 anciently in its politicks rather promote the interest of Mankinde
then of States; and rather of all States then of one; for particular
endeavors only in behalfe of our owne homes, are signes of a narrow
morall education, not of the vast kindnesse of Christian Religion,
which likewise ordain'd as well an universall communion of bosoms,
280 as a community of Wealth. Such is Christian Religion in the pre-
cepts, and was once so in the practise. But I resolv'd my Poem should
represent those of a former age, perceiving tis with the servants of
Christ, as with other servants under temporall power, who with all
cleanenesse, and even with officious diligence performe their duty
285 in their Masters sight; but still as he grow's longer absent, become
more slothfull, uncleane, and false. And this, who ere compares the
present with the Primitive times, may too palpably [, and with
horrour] discerne.

When I consider'd the actions which I ment to describe, (those
290 inferring the persons) I was againe persuaded rather to chuse those
of a former age, then the present; and in a Century so farre remov'd,
as might preserve me from their improper examinations who know
not the requisites of a Poem, nor how much pleasure they lose (and
even the pleasures of Heroick Poesy are not unprofitable) who take
295 away the liberty of a Poet, and fetter his feet in the shackles of an
Historian: For why should a Poet doubt in Story to mend the
intrigues of Fortune by more delightfull conveyances of probable
fictions, because austere Historians have enter'd into bond to truth?
an obligation which were in Poets, as foolish and unnecessary as is
300 the bondage of false Martyrs, who lye in chaines for a mistaken
opinion: But by this I would imply, that Truth narrative, and past,
is the Idoll of Historians, (who worship a dead thing) and truth

---

operative, and by effects continually alive, is the Mistresse of Poets, who hath not her existence in matter, but in reason.

I was likewise more willing to derive my theame from elder times, as thinking it no little marke of skilfulnesse to comply with the common Infirmity; for men (even of the best education) discover their eyes to be weake, when they looke upon the glory of Vertue (which is great actions) and rather endure it at distance then neer; being more apt to beleeve, and love the renowne of Predecessors, then of Contemporaries, whose deeds excelling theirs in their owne sight, seeme to upbraid them, and are not reverenc'd as examples of Vertue, but envy'd as the favours of Fortune: But to make great actions credible is the principall Art of Poets; who though they avouch the utility of Fictions, should not (by altering and subliming Story) make use of their Priviledge to the detriment of the Reader: whose incredulity (when things are not represented in proportion) doth much allay the rellish of his pitty, hope, joy, and other Passions: For wee may descend to compare the deceptions in Poesy to those of them that professe dexterity of Hand, which resembles Conjuring, and to such wee come not with the intention of *Lawyers* to examine the evidence of facts, but are content (if wee like the carriage of their feign'd motion) to pay for being well deceiv'd.

As in the choice of time, so of place, I have comply'd with the weaknes of the generality of men; who think the best objects of their owne country so little to the size of those abroad, as if they were shew'd them by the wrong end of a Prospective: for Man (continuing the appetites of his first Childhood, till he arrive at his second, which is more froward) must be quieted with something that he thinks excellent, which he may call his owne; but when he sees the like in other places (not staying to compare them) wrangles at all he has. This leads us to observe the craftines of the *Comicks*, who are only willing when they describe humor (and humor is the Drunckenesse of a Nation which no sleep can cure) to lay the Scene in their owne country; as knowing wee are (like the Sonne of *Noah*) so little distasted to behold each others shame, that wee delight to see even that of a Father: yet when they would set forth greatnesse and excellent vertue (which is the Theame of *Tragedy*) publiquely to the people; they wisely (to avoid the quarrells of neighbourly envy) remove the Scene from home. And by their example I travail'd too; and *Italie* (which was once the Stage of the World) I have

305
310
315
320
325
330
335
340

315 should '50a MS–'73: hould '50a

made the Theater, where I shew in either Sex, some patternes of human life, that are (perhaps) fit to be follow'd.

Having told you why I tooke the actions that should be my
345 Argument, from men of our owne Religion, and given you reasons for the choyce of the time and place design'd for those actions; I must next acquaint you with the Schooles where they were bred; not meaning the Schooles where they tooke their Religion, but Morality; for I know Religion is universally rather inherited then
350 taught: and the most effectuall Schooles of Morality, are Courts and Camps: Yet towards the first, the people are unquiet through envy; and towards the other through feare; and always jealous of both for Injustice, which is the naturall scandall cast upon authority, and great force. They looke upon the outward glory or blaze of Courts,
355 as Wilde beasts in darke nights stare on their Hunters Torches; but though the expences of Courts (whereby they shine) is that consuming glory in which the people think their liberty is wasted (for wealth is their liberty and lov'd by them even to jealousy (being themselves a courser sort of Princes, apter to take then to pay) yet
360 Courts (I meane all abstracts of the Multitude; either by King, or Assemblyes) are not the Schooles where men are bred to oppression, but the Temples where some times Oppressors take Sanctuary; a safety which our reason must allow them. For the ancient laws of Sanctuary (deriv'd from God) provided chiefly for actions that pro-
365 ceeded from necessity; and who can imagine lesse then a necessity of oppressing the people, since they are never willing either to buy their peace or to pay for Warre?

Nor are Camps the Schooles of wicked Destroyers, more then the *Inns of Court* (being the Nursery of Judges) are the Schooles of
370 Murderers; for as Judges are avengers of private men against private Robbers, so are Armys the avengers of the publique against publique Invaders (either civill or forraigne) and Invaders are Robbers, though more in countenance then those of the high-way, because of their number. Nor is there other difference between
375 Armys, when they move towards Sieges, or battaile, and Judges moving in their Circuit (during the danger of extraordinary Malefactors) with the guards of the County; but that the latter is a lesse Army, and of lesse discipline. If any man can yet doubt of the necessary use of Armys, let him study that which was anciently
380 call'd a Monster, the Multitude (for Wolves are commonly harm-

363 laws '50b–'73: law's '50a

lesse when they are met alone, but very uncivill in Heards) and he
will not finde that all his kindred by *Adam* are so tame, and gentle,
as those Lovers that were bred in *Arcadia*: or to reforme his opinion,
let him aske why (during the utmost age of History) Cittys have
been at the charge of defensive Walls and why Fortification hath   385
been practis'd so long, till it is growne an Art?

I may now beleeve I have usefully taken from Courts and Camps,
the patterns of such as will be fit to be imitated by the most neces-
sary Men; and the most necessary men are those who become
principall by prerogative of blood (which is seldom unassisted with   390
education) or by greatnes of minde, which in exact definition is
Vertue. The common Crowd (of whom wee are hopelesse) wee
desert; being rather to be corrected by lawes (where precept is
accompany'd with punishment) then to be taught by Poesy; for few
have arriv'd at the skill of *Orpheus*, or at his good fortune, whom wee   395
may suppose to have met with extraordinary Grecian Beasts, when
so successfully he reclaim'd them with his Harpe. Nor is it needfull
that Heroique Poesy should be levell'd to the reach of Common men;
for if the examples it presents prevaile upon their Chiefs, the delight
of Imitation (which wee hope wee have prov'd to be as effectuall to   400
good as to evill) will rectify by the rules, which those Chiefs estab-
lish of their owne lives, the lives of all that behold them; for the
example of life, doth as much surpasse the force of precept, as Life
doth exceed Death.

In the choyce of these Objects (which are as Sea-markes to direct   405
the dangerous voyage of life) I thought fitt to follow the rule of
Coasting Mapps, where the Shelv's and Rocks are describ'd as well
as the safe Channell; the care being equall how to avoyd, as to
proceed: and the Characters of men (whose passions are to be
eschew'd) I have deriv'd from the distempers of Love, or Ambition: 410
for Love and Ambition are too often the raging Feavers of great
mindes. Yet Ambition (if the vulgar accepcion of the Word were
corrected) would signifie no more then an extraordinary lifting of
the feet in the rough ways of Honor, over the impediments of
Fortune; and hath a warmth (till it be chaf'd into a Feaver)   415
which is necessary for every vertuous breast: for good men are
guilty of too little appetite to greatnesse, and it either proceeds from
that they call contentednesse (but contentednesse when examin'd
doth meane something of Lasynesse as well as moderation) or from

415 warmth '*50a MS*, '*51a–b*, '*73*: warmt'h '*50a–b*

420 some melancholy precept of the Cloyster; where they would make
life (for which the world was only made) more unpleasant then
Death; as if Nature, the Vicegerent of God (who in providing
delightfull varietyes, which vertuous greatnesse can best possesse,
or assure peaceably to others, implicitly commanded the use of
425 them) should in the necessaries of life (life being her chiefe businesse)
though in her whole reigne she never committed one error, need the
councell of Fryars; whose solitude makes them no more fitt for such
direction, then Prisoners long fetter'd are for a race.

In saying this, I only awaken such retir'd men, as evaporate their
430 strength of minde by close and long thinking; and would every
where separate the soule from the body, ere wee are dead, by
persuading us (though they were both created and have been long
companions together) that the preferment of the one must meerly
consist in deserting the other; teaching us to court the Grave, as if
435 during the whole lease of life wee were like Moles to live under
grownd; or as if long and well dying, were the certaine means to live
in Heaven: Yet Reason (which though the most profitable Talent
God hath given us, some Divines would have Philosophers to bury
in the Napkin, and not put it to use) persuads us, that the painfull
440 activenesse of Vertue (for Faith on which some wholly depend,
seems but a contemplative boast till the effects of it grow exemplary
by action) will more probably acquire everlasting dignities. And
surely if these severe Masters (who though obscure in Cells, take it
ill if their very opinions rule not all abroad) did give good men leave
445 to be industrious in getting a Share of governing the world, the
Multitudes (which are but Tenants to a few Monarchs) would
endure that subjection which God hath decreed them, with better
order, and more ease; for the world is only ill govern'd because the
wicked take more paines to get authority, then the vertuous; for the
450 vertuous are often preach'd into retirement; which is to the publique
as unprofitable as their sleep; and the erroneousnesse of such lazy
rest let Philosophers judge; since Nature (of whose body man
thinks himself the cheefest member) hath not any where, at any
time, been respited from action (in her, cal'd motion) by which she
455 universally preserves and makes Life. Thus much of Ambition
which should have succeeded something I was saying of Love.

Love in the Interpretation of the Envious, is softnesse; in the

425 businesse '50b, '51a: business '51b, '73: busniesse '50a   451 unprofitable
'50a–b, '51a MS, '51b, '73: profitable '51a

Wicked, good men suspect it for Lust; and in the good, some spirituall men have given it the name of Charity: And these are but termes to this which seemes a more consider'd Definition; that indefinite Love is Lust; and Lust when it is determin'd to one, is Love; This Definition too but intrudes it selfe on what I was about to say, which is, [(and spoken with sobernesse though like a *Layman*)] that Love is the most acceptable imposition of Nature, the cause and preservation of Life, and the very healthfulnesse, of the minde, as well as of the body; but Lust (our raging Feaver) is more dangerous in Citties, then the Calenture in Ships.

Now (Sir) I againe aske you pardon, for I have againe digress'd; my immediate businesse being to tell you; that the distempers of Love and Ambition are the only characters I design'd to expose as objects of terrour: and [my purpose was also to assure you,] that I never meant to prostitute Wickednesse in the Images of low and contemptible people, as if I expected the meanest of the multitude for my Readers (since only the Rabble is seen at common executions) nor intended to raise iniquity to that height of horrour, till it seemed the fury of something worse then a beast. In order to the first I beleeve the *Spartans* (who to deterre their children from Drunkenesse accustom'd their Slaves to vomit before them) did by such fulsome examples rather teach them to disdaine the Slaves, then to loath Wine, for men seldome take notice of the vice in abject persons, especially where necessity constraines it. And in observation of the second, I have thought, that those horrid spectacles (when the latter race of *Gladiators* made up the excesses of Roman feasts) did more induce the Guests to detest the cruelty of mankinde, then increase their courage by beholding such an impudent scorne of Life.

I have now given you the accompt of such provisions as I made for this new Building; and you may next please (having examin'd the substance) to take a view of the forme; and observe if I have methodically and with discretion dispos'd of the materialls, which with some curiosity I had collected. I cannot discerne by any help from reading, or learned men, (who have been to me the best and briefest Indexes of Books) that any Nation hath in represment of great actions (either by *Heroicks* or *Dramaticks*) digested Story into so pleasant and instructive a method as the English by their *Drama*:

460
465
470
475
480
485
490
495

and by that regular species (though narratively and not in Dialogue) I have drawn the body of an Heroick Poem: In which I did not only observe the Symmetry (proportioning five bookes to five *Acts*, and *Canto's* to *Scenes* (the Scenes, having their number ever govern'd by occasion) but all the *shadowings, happy strokes, secret graces*, and even the *drapery* (which together make the second beauty) I have (I hope) exactly follow'd: and those compositions of second beauty, I observe in the *Drama* to be the underwalks, interweaving, or correspondence of lesser designe in *Scenes*, not the great motion of the maine plot, and coherence of the *Acts*.

The first *Act* is the generall preparative, by rendring the cheefest characters of persons, and ending with something that lookes like an obscure promise of designe. The second begins with an introducement of new persons, so finishes all the characters, and ends with some little performance of that designe which was promis'd at the parting of the first *Act*. The Third makes a visible correspondence in the Underwalks (or lesser intrigues) of persons; and ends with an ample turne of the maine designe, and expectation of a new. The fourth (ever having occasion to be the longest) gives a notorious turne to all the Underwalks, and a conterturne to that maine designe which chang'd in the Third. The Fifth begins with an intire diversion of the mayne, and dependant Plotts; then makes the generall correspondence of the persons more discernable, and ends with an easy untying of those particular knots, which made a contexture of the whole; leaving such satisfaction of probabilities with the Spectator, as may persuade him that neither Fortune in the fate of the Persons, nor the Writer in the Representment, have been unnaturall or exorbitant. To these Meanders of the English Stage I have cut out the Walkes of my Poem; which in this description may seeme intricate and tedious; but will I hope (when men take paines to visit what they have heard describ'd) appear to them as pleasant as a sommer passage on a crooked River, where going about, and turning back, is as delightfull as the delays of parting Lovers.

In placing the Argument (as a *Proem*) before every *Canto*, I have not wholly follow'd the example of the Moderns; but averted it from that purpose to which I found it frequently us'd: for it hath been intended by others, as the contents of the Chapter, or as a Bill of Fare at a Venetian Feast; which is not brought before the meate

501 beauty)] beautys '73   517 Plotts] Plott '73   529 *Proem* '50a-b, '51a
MS, '51b, '73: *Poem* '51a

to rayse an expectation, but to satisfy the longing curiosity of the Guests. And that which I have call'd my Argument, is only meant as 535 an assistance to the Readers memory, by contayning breef hints, such, as if all the Arguments were successively read, would make him easily remember the mutuall dependancies of the generall designe; yet each rather mentions every person acting, then their actions: But he is very unskilfull that by Narratives before an 540 Historicall Poem, prevents expectation; for so he comes to have as little successe over the Reader (whom the Writer should surprize, and as it were keep prisoner for a time) as he hath on his Enemy's, who commanding a party out to take them (and commonly Readers are justly Enemyes to Writers) imparts openly the designe ere he 545 begins the action: Or he may be said to be as unluckily officious as he that leads a wooing to a Mistresse, one that already hath newly enjoy'd her.

I shall say a little, why I have chosen my interwoven *Stanza* of foure, though I am not oblig'd to excuse the choyce; for numbers in 550 Verse must, like distinct kindes of Musick, be expos'd to the un-certaine and different taste of severall Eares. Yet I may declare that I beleev'd it would be more pleasant to the Reader, in a Worke of Length, to give this respite or pause, between every *Stanza* (having endevor'd that each should containe a period) then to run him out of 555 breath with continu'd *Couplets*. Nor does alternate Rime by any lowlinesse of cadence make the sound lesse Heroick, but rather adapt it to a plaine and stately composing of Musick; and the brevity of the *Stanza* renders it lesse subtle to the Composer, and more easy to the Singer; which in *stilo recitativo*, when the Story is long, is 560 cheefly requisite. And this was indeed (if I shall not betray vanity in my Confession) the reason that prevail'd most towards my choyce of this *Stanza*, and my division of the maine worke into *Cantos*, every *Canto* including a sufficient accomplishment of some worthy designe or action; for I had so much heat (which you, Sir, may call 565 pride, [since pride may be allow'd in *Pegasus*, if it be a praise to other Horses)] as to presume they might (like the Works of *Homer* ere they were joyn'd together and made a Volume by the Athenian King) be sung at Village-feasts; though not to Monarchs after Victory, nor to Armys before battaile. For so (as an inspiration of 570 glory into the one, and of valour into the other) did *Homer's* Spirit, long after his body's rest, wander in musick about *Greece*.

556 does] do's '*50b*: doth '*51a–b*, '*73*   565–7 call pride . . . as] call pride as '*73*

Thus you have the Modell of what I have already built, or shall hereafter joine to the same frame. If I be accus'd of Innovation, or
575 to have transgress'd against the method of the Ancients; I shall think my selfe secure in beleeving, that a Poet who hath wrought with his owne Instruments at a new designe, is no more answerable for disobedience to Predecessors, then *Law-makers* are lyable to those old Lawes which themselves have repeal'd.

580 Having describ'd the outward frame, the large roomes within, the lesser conveyances, and now the furniture; it were orderly to let you examine the matter of which that furniture is made: But though every Owner who hath the Vanity to shew his ornaments, or Hangings, must endure the curiosity, and censure of him that
585 beholds them; yet I shall not give you the trouble of inquiring what is, but tell you of what I design'd their substance; which is, *Witte*: And *Witte* is the laborious, and the lucky resultances of thought, having towards its excellence (as wee say of the strokes of Painting) as well a happinesse, as care. [It is a Webb consisting of the subtlest
590 threds, and like that of the *Spider* is considerately woven out of our selves; for a *Spider* may be said to consider, not only respecting his solemnesse, and tacite posture (like a grave Scowte in ambush for his Enemy) but because all things done, are either from consideration, or chance; and the workes of chance are accomplishments of an
595 instant, having commonly a dissimilitude; but hers are the works of time, and have their contextures alike.]

Witte is not only the luck and labour, but also the dexterity of thought; rounding the world, like the Sun, with unimaginable motion; and bringing swiftly home to the memory universall
600 survays. It is the Soules *Powder*, which when supprest (as forbidden from flying upward) blowes up the restraint; and loseth all force in a farther ascension towards Heaven [(the region of God)] and yet by nature is much lesse able to make any inquisition downward towards Hell, [the Cell of the Devill;] But breaks through all about it
605 (as farr as the utmost it can reach) removes, uncovers, makes way for Light, where darknesse was inclos'd, till great bodyes are more examinable by being scatter'd into parcells; and till all that finde its strength (but most of mankinde are strangers to *Witt*, as *Indians* are to *Powder*) worship it for the effects, as deriv'd from the Deity. It is

---

583 ornaments] ornament '51b   589–96 It is . . . alike.] *not in* '73
594 workes] work '51a–b   602 Heaven . . . and] Heaven, and '73   604 Hell
. . . But] Hell, but '73

in Divines Humility, Exemplarinesse, and Moderation; In States- 610
men Gravity, Vigilance, Benigne Complaisancy, Secrecy, Patience,
and Dispatch. In Leaders of Armys Valor, Painfulnesse, Temper-
ance, Bounty, Dexterity in Punishing, and rewarding, and a sacred
Certitude of promise. It is in Poets a full comprehension of all
recited in all these; and an ability to bring those comprehensions 615
into action, when they shall so farre forget the true measure of
what is of greatest consequence to humanity, (which are things
righteous, pleasant and usefull) as to think the delights of greatnesse
equall to that of Poesy; or the Cheifs of any Profession more neces-
sary to the World then excellent Poets. Lastly though *Wit* be not 620
the envy of ignorant Men, tis often of evill *Statesmen*, and of all such
imperfect great spirits, as have it in a lesse degree then Poets: for
though no man envys the excellence of that which in no proportion
he ever tasted (as men cannot be said to envy the condition of Angells)
yet wee may say the Devill envys the Supremacy of God, because 625
he was in some degree partaker of his glory.

That which is not, yet is accompted, *Wit*, I will but sleightly
remember; which seemes very incident to imperfect youth, and
sickly age; Yong men (as if they were not quite deliver'd from Child-
hood whose first exercise is Language) imagine it consists in the 630
Musick of words, and believe they are made wise by refining their
speech, above the vulgar Dialect: which is a mistake almost as
great, as that of the people, who think Orators, (which is a title that
crowns at riper years those that have practis'd the dexterity of
tongue) the ablest men; who are indeed so much more unapt for 635
governing, as they are more fit for Sedition: and it may be said of
them as of the Witches of *Norway*, who can sell a Storme for a
Doller, which for Ten Thousand they cannot allay. From the esteem
of speaking they proceed to the admiration of what are commonly
call'd *Conceits*, things that sound like the knacks or toyes of ordinary 640
Epigrammatists: and from thence, after more conversation and
variety of objects, grow up to some force of *Fancy*; Yet even then
like young Hawks they stray and fly farr off; using their liberty as if
they would ne're returne to the Lure; and often goe at check ere
they can make a stedy view, and know their game. 645

Old men, that have forgot their first Childhood and are returning
to their second, think it lyes in [*agnominations*, and in] a kinde of [an

alike] tinkling of words; or else in a grave telling of wonderfull things, or in comparing of times without a discover'd partiality; 650 which they performe so ill by favoring the past, that, as tis observ'd, if the bodys of men should grow lesse, though but an unmeasurable proportion in Seaven yeares; Yet reckoning from the *Flood*, they would not remaine in the Stature of Froggs; so if States and particular persons had impar'd in goverment, and increas'd in wickednesse, 655 proportionably to what Old men affirme they have done, from their owne infancy, to their age; all publique Policy had been long since Confusion, and the congregated world would not suffise now to people a Village.

The last thing they suppose to be *Witte*, is their bitter Moralls, 660 when they almost declare themselves Enemys to Youth, and Beauty; by which Severity they seem cruell as *Herod* when he surpris'd the sleeping Children of *Bethlem*: For Youth is so farre from wanting Enemys, that it is mortally its owne; so unpractis'd, that it is every where cosen'd more then a Stranger among *Jewes*; and hath an 665 Infirmity of sight more hurtfull then Blindnesse to Blinde men; for though it cannot chuse the way it scorns to be led. And Beauty, though many call themselves her Frends, hath few but such as are false to her: Though the World sets her in a Throne, yet all about her (even her gravest Councellers) are Traytors, though not in 670 conspiracy, yet in their distinct designes; and to make her certaine not only of distresse but ruine, she is ever pursu'd by her most cruell enemy, the greate Destroyer, *Time*. But I will proceed no farther upon Old men, nor in recording mistakes; least finding so many more, then there be Verities, wee might beleeve wee walke in 675 as great obscurity as the Egyptians when Darknesse was their Plague. Nor will I presume to call the matter of which the Ornaments or Substantiall parts of this Poem are compos'd, *Witte*; but only tell you my endevour was, in bringing Truth (too often absent) home to mens bosoms, to lead her through unfrequented and new 680 ways, and from the most remote Shades; by representing Nature, though not in an affected, yet in an unusuall dresse.

Tis now fitt, after I have given you so long a survay of the Building, to render you some accompt of the Builder, that you may know by what time, pains, and assistance I have already proceeded, 685 or may hereafter finish my worke: and in this I shall take occasion to accuse, and condemne, as papers unworthy of light, all those hasty digestions of thought which were publish'd in my Youth; a sentence

not pronounc'd out of melancholy rigour, but from a cheerfull
obedience to the just authority of experience: For that grave
mistresse of the World, *Experience* (in whose profitable Schoole 690
those before the Flood stay'd long, but wee like wanton children
come thither late, yet too soone are call'd out of it, and fetch'd home
by Death) hath taught me, that the engendrings of unripe age
become abortive, and deform'd; and that after obtayning more yeares,
those must needs prophecy with ill successe, who make use of their 695
Visions in Wine; That when the ancient Poets were vallew'd as
Prophets, they were long and painfull in watching the correspon-
dence of Causes, ere they presum'd to foretell effects: and that tis a
high presumption to entertaine a Nation (who are a Poets standing
Guest, and require Monarchicall respect) with hasty provisions 700
[; as if a Poet might imitate the familiar dispatch of Faulkoners,
mount his *Pegasus*, unhood his *Muse*, and with a few flights boast he
hath provided a feast for a Prince]. Such posting [upon *Pegasus*] I
have long since forborne; and during my Journey in this Worke
have mov'd with a slow pace; that I might make my survays as one 705
that travaild not to bring home the names, but the proportion, and
nature of things: and in this I am made wise by two great examples;
for the friends of *Virgill* acnowledge he was many yeares in doing
honor to *Æneas* (still contracting at night into a closer force the
abundance of his morning strengths) and *Statius* rather seems to 710
boast, then blush, when he confesses he was twice Seaven years in
renowning the warre between *Argos* and *Thebes*.

Next to the usefullnesse of Time (which here implys ripe Age) I
beleev'd paines most requisite to this undertaking: for though
painfulnesse in Poets (according to the usuall negligence of our 715
Nation in examining, and their diligence to censure) seems always
to discover a want of naturall force, and is traduc'd, as if Poesy
concern'd the world no more then Dancing; whose only grace is the
quicknesse and facility of motion; and whose perfection is not of
such publique consequence, that any man can merit much by at- 720
taining it with long labour; yet let them consider, and they will
finde (nor can I stay long ere I convince them in the important use
of Poesy) the naturall force of a Poet more apparent, by but

700 Guest '51a–b, '73: Guests '50a–b   700–3 provisions . . . Such posting
upon *Pegasus* I '50a–b, '51a MS, '51b: . . . such boasting . . . '51a: provisions. Such
posting I '73   706 not to] not '51b   711 Seaven years in '50b, '73: Seaven in
'50a, '51a–b: six in '51b errata   713 implys '50a–b, '51a MS,' 51b, '73: inplys '51a

confessing that great forces aske great labour in managing; then by
725 an arrogant braving the world, when he enters the field with his
undisciplin'd first thoughts: For a wise Poet, like a wise Generall,
will not shew his strengths till they are in exact government and
order; which are not the postures of chance, but proceed from
Vigilance and labour.

730   Yet to such painfull Poets some upbraid the want of extemporary
fury, or rather *inspiration*; a dangerous word; which many have of
late successfully us'd; and *inspiration* is a spirituall Fitt, deriv'd
from the ancient Ethnick Poets, who then, as they were Priests,
were Statesmen too, and probably lov'd dominion; and as their well
735 dissembling of inspiration begot them reverence then, equall to that
which was payd to Lawes; so these who now professe the same fury,
may perhaps by such authentick example pretend authority over
the people; It being not unreasonable to imagine, they rather imitate
the *Greeke* Poets then the *Hebrew* Prophets, since the later were
740 inspir'd for the use of others; and these, like the former, prophecy
for themselves. But though the ancient Poets are excus'd, as know-
ing the weake constitution of those Deities from whom they tooke
their Priesthood; and the frequent necessity of dissembling for the
ease of goverment; yet these (who also from the cheef to the meanest
745 are Statesmen and Priests, but have not the luck to be Poets)
should not assume such saucy familiarity with a true God.

From the time and labour requir'd to my Poem, let me proceed
to my Assistants; by which I shall not so much attest my owne
weaknesse, as discover the difficulties and greatnesse of such a worke.
750 For when *Salomon* made use of his Neighbours towards his building,
he lost no reputation, nor by demanding those aides was thought a
lesser Prince; but rather publish'd his Wisdome, in rightly under-
standing the vast extent of his enterprise: who likewise with as much
glory made use of Fellers of wood, and Hewers of Stone, as of
755 learned Architects: Nor have I refrayn'd to be oblig'd to men of any
science, as well mechanicall, as liberall: Nor when Memory (from
that various and plentifull stock, with which all observers are
furnish'd, that have had diversity of life) presented me by chance
with any figure, did I lay it aside as uselesse, because at that instant
760 I was not skilfull to manage it artfully; but I have stayd and recorded
such objects, till by consulting with right Masters I have dispos'd of
them without mistake; It being no more shame to get Learning at

743 Priesthood '51a: Priesthoo'd 50a

that very time, and from the same Text; when, and by which, wee
instruct others; then for a forward Scoute, discovering the Enemy,
to save his owne life at a Passe, where he then teaches his Party to   765
escape.

In remembring mine owne helps, I have consider'd those which
others in the same necessity have taken; and finde that Writers
(contrary to my inclination) are apter to be beholding to Bookes,
then to Men; not only as the first are more in their possession (being   770
more constant Companions then dearest frends) but because they
commonly make such use of treasure found in Bookes, as of other
treasure belonging to the Dead, and hidden under ground; for they
dispose of both with great secrecy, defacing the shape, or images of
the one, as much as of the other; through feare of having the Origin-   775
all of their stealth, or aboundance discover'd. And the next cause
why Writers are more in Libraries, then in company, is, that Bookes
are easily open'd, and learned men are usually shut up, by a froward
or envious humor of retention; or els unfold themselves, so as wee
may read more of their weaknesse, and vanity, then Wisdome;   780
imitating the Holiday-custome in great Cittys, where the shops of
Chaundry, and slight wares, are familiarly open, but those of solid
and staple marchandise are proudly lockd up.

Nor indeed can it be expected that all great Doctors are of so
benigne a nature, as to take pains in gaining treasure (of which   785
Knowledge is the greatest) with intent to inrich others so easily, as if
they stood every where with their Pockets spred, and ready to be
pickt: Nor can wee read of any Father, who so farre and secretly
adopted his Sonne to a Booke of his owne writing, as that his Sonne
might be thought Author of that written Witte, as much as his   790
Father was Author of him: Nor of any Husband that to his darling
Wife would so farre surrender his Wisdome, as that in publique, he
could endure to let her use his Dictates, as if she would have others
think her wiser then himselfe. By this remembrance of that usuall
parsimony in owners of Wit, towards such as would make use of their   795
plenty, I lament the fortune of others, and may wish the Reader to
congratulate mine; For I have found Frends as ready as Bookes, to
regulate my conceptions, or make them more correct, easy, and
apparent. But though I am become so wise, by knowing my selfe,
as to beleeve the thoughts of divers transcend the best which I have   800
written; yet I have admitted from no man any change of my Designe,

796 fortune '50a MS, '50b, '51a–b, '73: fotune '50a

nor very seldome of my sence; For I resolv'd to have this Poem
subsist, and continue throughout, with the same complexion and
spirit; though it appeare but like a plaine Family, of a neighbourly
805 alliance, who marry into the same moderate quality and garbe, and
are fearfull of introducing strangers of greater ranke, least the
shining presence of such, might seem to upbraid, and put all about
them out of countenance.

And now, Sir, that the Reader may (whom Writers are faine to
810 court, draw in, and keep with artifice, so shy men grow of Bookes)
beleeve me worthy of him, I cannot forbeare to thank you in pub-
lique, for examining, correcting, and allowing this Poem in parcells
ere it arriv'd at the contexture: by which you have perform'd the
just degrees of proceeding with Poets; who during the gayety and
815 wantonnesse of the Muse, are but as children to Philosophers
(though of some Giant race) whose first thoughts (wilde, and
roaming farre off) must be brought home, watch'd, and interro-
gated, and after they are made more regular, be encourag'd and
prais'd for doing well, that they may delight in ayming at perfection.
820 By such a Method the Muse is taught to become Mistress of her
owne, and others strength: and who is he so learn'd (how proud so
ever with being cherish'd, in the bosome of Fame) that can hope,
(when through the severall ways of Science, he seeks Nature in her
hidden walks) to make his Journy short, unlesse he call you to be his
825 Guide? and who so guided can suspect his safety, even when he
travails through the Enemy's country? For such is the vast field of
Learning, where the Learned (though not numerous enough to be
an Army) lye as small Partys, malitiously in Ambush, to destroy all
new Men that looke into their Quarters. And from such, you, and
830 those you lead, are secure; because you move not by common
Mapps, but have painfully made your owne Prospect; and travaile
now like the Sun, not to informe your selfe, but enlighten the World.

And likewise, when by the strict survay and Goverment that hath
been had over this Poem, I shall think to governe the Reader (who
835 though he be noble, may perhaps judge of supreme power like a very
Commoner, and rather approve authority, when it is in many, then
in one) I must acquaint him, that you had not alone the trouble of
establishing, and destroying; but injoy'd your intervalls and ease by
Two Colleagues; Two that are worthy to follow you into the Closets
840 of Princes; if the knowledge of Men past, (of whom Bookes are the

820 Mistress '73: Master '50a–b, '51a–b

remayning mindes) or of the present (of whom Conversation is the usefull and lawfull Spy) may make up such greatnesse, as is fit for great Courts: or if the rayes that proceed from Poetry, be not a little too strong for the sight of moderne Princes; who now are too seldome taught in their youth, like Eaglets to fortify their eyes by often soaring neere the Sun. And though this be here but my testimony, it is too late for any of you to disclaime it; for since you have made it valid by giving yours of GONDIBERT under your hands, you must be content to be us'd by me, as Princes are by their prefer'd Subjects; who in the very act of taking honor returne it to the Giver; as benefits receav'd by the Creature manifest the power, and redound to the glory of the Creator.

I am now, Sir, (to your great comfort, that have been thus ill, and long diverted) arriv'd at my last consideration, which is to satisfy those who may inquire why I have taken so much paines to become an Author? or why any man stays so long sweating at [the fire of] Invention, [to dresse the food of the Minde,] when [most] Readers have so imperfect Stomacks, as they either devoure Bookes with over hasty Digestion, or grow to loath them from a Surfet. And why I more especially made my taske an Heroick Poem? I shall involve the two first Questions in one; as submitting to be concern'd amongst the generality of Writers; whose Enemys being many, and now mine, wee must joyne forces to oppose them.

Men are cheefly provok'd to the toyle of compiling Bookes, by love of Fame, and often by officiousnesse of Conscience, but seldome with expectation of Riches: for those that spend time in writing to instruct others, may finde leasure to informe themselves, how meane the provisions are which busy and studious mindes can make for their owne sedentary bodys: And Learned men (to whom the rest of the world are but Infants) have the same foolish affection in nourishing others mindes, as Pellicans in feeding their young; which is, at the expence of the very subsistance of Life. Tis then apparent they proceed by the instigation of Fame, or Conscience; and I beleeve many are persuaded by the first (of which I am One) and some are commanded by the second. Nor is the desire of Fame so vaine as divers have rigidly imagin'd; Fame being (when belonging

845

850

855

860

865

870

875

843 from . . . be '73: from the Poetick Planet, be '50a–b, '51a–b   844 Princes
'73: Monarchs '50a–b, '51a–b   856–8 at . . . Readers Ed: . . . when Readers
'50a–b, '51a–b: at invention when most Readers '73

to the Living) that which is more gravely call'd, a steddy and necessary reputation; and without it, hereditary Power, or acquir'd
880 greatnesse can never quietly governe the World. Tis of the Dead a musicall glory, in which God, the author of excellent goodnesse, vouchsafes to take a continuall share; For the remember'd vertues of great men are cheefly such of his workes (mention'd by King *David*) as perpetually praise him: and the good fame of the Dead prevails
885 by example much more then the reputation of the Living, because the later is always suspected by our Envy, but the other is cheerfully allow'd, and religiously admir'd: for Admiration (whose Eyes are ever weake) stands still, and at gaze upon great things acted farre off; but when they are neere, walks slightly away as from familiar
890 objects. Fame is to our Sonnes a solid Inheritance, and not unusefull to remote Posterity; and to our Reason, tis the first, though but a little taste of Eternity.

Those that write by the command of Conscience (thinking themselves able to instruct others, and consequently oblig'd to it) grow
895 commonly the most voluminous; because the pressures of Conscience are so incessant, that she is never satisfy'd with doing enough: for such as be newly made the captives of God (many appearing so to themselves, when they first begin to weare the Fetters of Conscience) are like common Slaves, when newly taken; who terrify'd
900 with a fancy of the severity of absolute Masters, abuse their diligence out of feare, and doe ill, rather then appeare idle. And this may be the cause why Libraries are more then double lin'd with Spirituall Bookes, or Tracts of Morality; the latter being the Spirituall Counsels of *Lay-men*; and the newest of such great volumes (being
905 usually but transcriptions or translations) differ so much from the Ancients, as later days from those of old, which difference is no more then an alteration of names by removing the *Ethnicks* to make way for the *Saints*. These are the effects of their labours, who are provok'd to become Authors, meerly out of Conscience; and
910 Conscience wee may againe averre to be often so unskilfull and timerous, that it seldome gives a wise and steddy accompt of God; but growes jealous of him as of an Adversary, and is after melancholy visions like a fearfull Scout, after he hath ill survayd the Enemy, who then makes incongruous, long, and terrible Tales.
915 Having confess'd that the desire of Fame made me a Writer; I

---

898 weare *'50a*, *'51a* MS, *'51b*, *'73*: ware *'51a*: wear *'50b*   904 of ... newest
'50a-b, *'51a* MS, *'51b*, *'73*: of the Lay-men and newest *'51a*

must declare, why in my riper age I chose to gaine it more especially
by an Heroicall Poem; and the Heroick being by most allow'd to be
the most beautifull of Poems, I shall not need to decide the quarrels
of Poets about the Degrees of Excellence in Poesy: but tis not amisse
ere I avow the usefulnesse of the science in generall (which was the   920
cause of my undertaking) to remember the value it had from the
greatest and most worthy spirits in all Ages: for I will not abstaine
(though it may give me the reputation but of common reading) to
mention, that *Pisistratus*, (though a Tyrant) liv'd with the praise,
and dy'd with the blessing of all *Greece*, for gathering the scatter'd   925
limbs of *Homer's* Workes into a Body; and that Great *Alexander* by
publiquely conversing with it attain'd the universall opinion of wit;
the fame of such inward forces conducing as much to his Conquests,
as his Armys abroad: That the *Athenian* Prisoners were thought
worthy of life and liberty for singing the Tragedies of *Euripides*:   930
That *Thebes* was sav'd from destruction by the Victors reverence to
the memory of *Pindar*: That the elder *Scipio* (who govern'd all the
civill world) lay continually in the bosome of *Ennius*: That the great
Numantin and *Lælius* (no lesse renownd) were openly proud when
the Romans beleev'd they assisted *Terence* in his Comedies: That   935
Augustus (to whom the mysteries of universall Empire were more
familiar then domestique Dominion to Moderne Kings) made
Virgill the partner of his joyes, and would have divided his business
with *Horace*: and that *Lucan* was the feare, and envy of *Nero*. If wee
approach neerer our owne times, wee may adde the triumphall   940
Entry which the Papacy gave to *Petrarch*; and now much *Tasso* is
still the glory and delight of *Italy*.

   But as in this hasty Muster of Poets and listing their confederates,
I shall by omitting many, deprive them of that pay which is due
from Fame; so I may now by the opinion of some Divines (whom   945
notwithstanding I will reverence in all their distinct habits and
fashions of the minde) be held partiall, and too bold, by adding to
the first number (though I range them upon holy grownd, and
aside) *Moses*, *David*, and *Salomon*, for their Songs, Psalmes, and
Anthemes; the Second being the acknowledg'd Favorite of God;   950
whom he had gain'd by excellent Praises in sacred Poesy. And I
feare (since Poesy is the clearest light by which they finde the soule
who seeke it) that Poets have in their fluent kindnesse diverted
from the right use, and spent too much of that spirituall talent in
the honor of mortall Princes: for divine Praise (when in the high   955

perfection, as in Poets, and only in them) is so much the uttermost and whole of Religious worship, that all other parts of Devotion serve but to make it up.

89. Praise, *is Devotion fit for mighty Mindes;*
The *diffr'ing World's agreeing Sacrifice;*
Where Heaven divided Fayths united findes:
But Pray'r *in various discord upward flyes.*

Gondi-
bert
lib. 2.
Canto.
6.

90. For Pray'r *the Ocean is, where diversly*
Men Steere their course, each to a sev'rall Coast;
Where all our Intr'ests so discordant be,
That halfe begg windes by which the rest are lost.

91. By Penitence *when Wee our selves forsake,*
Tis but in wise designe on piteous Heaven;
In Praise *Wee nobly give what God may take,*
And are without a Beggars blush forgiven.

92. *Its utmost force, like* Powder's, *is unknowne;*
And though weake Kings excesse of Praise *may feare,*
Yet when tis here, like Powder *dang'rous growne,*
Heaven's Vault receaves what would the Pallace teare.

After this contemplation, how acceptable the voyce of Poesy hath been to God, wee may (by descending from Heaven to Earth) consider how usefull it is to Men; and among Men, Divines are the cheef, because ordain'd to temper the rage of human power by spirituall menaces, as by suddaine and strange threatnings, madnesse is frighted into Reason; and they are sent hither as Liegers from God, to conserve in stedfast motion the slippery joints of Goverment; and to persuade an amity in divided Nations: therefore to Divines I first addresse my selfe; and presume to ask them, why, ever since their dominion was first allow'd, at the great change of Religions, (though ours more then any inculcates obedience, as an easy Medicine to coole the impatient and raging world into a quiet rest) mankinde hath been more unruly then before? it being visible that Empire decreas'd with the encrease of Christianity; and that one weake Prince did anciently suffise to governe many strong Nations: but now one little Province is too hard for their owne wise King: and a small Republique hath Seventy yeares maintain'd their revolt to the disquiet of many Monarchs. Or if Divines reply, wee

959–74 *These stanzas are 84–7 in every text of the poem.*

cannot expect the good effects of their office, because their spirituall
Dominion is not allow'd as absolute, then it may be ask'd them more
severely, why tis not allow'd? for where ever there hath been great 995
degrees of power (which have been often, and long in the Church)
it discovers (though worldly vicissitude be objected as an excuse)
that the Mannagers of such power, since they endeavor'd not to
enlarge it, beleev'd the increase unrighteous; or were in acting, or
contriving that endeavour, either negligent or weake: For Power 1000
like the hasty Vine, climbes up apace to the Supporter; but if not
skilfully attended and dress'd, instead of spreading, and bearing
fruit, grows high, and naked; and then (like empty title) being
soone uselesse to others, becomes neglected, and unable to support
it selfe. 1005
   But if Divines have fail'd in governing Princes (that is, of being
intirely beleev'd by them) yet they might have obliquely rul'd
them, in ruling the People; by whom of late, Princes have been
govern'd; and they might probably rule the People, because the
heads of the Church (where ever Christianity is preach'd) are 1010
Tetrarchs of Time; of which they command the fourth Division;
for to no lesse the Sabbaths, and Days of Saints amount; and during
those days of spirituall triumph, Pulpits are Thrones; and the
people oblig'd to open their Eares, and let in the ordinances and
commands of Preachers; who likewise are not without some little 1015
Regency throughout the rest of the Yeare; for then they may
converse with the Laity, from whom they have commonly such
respect (and respect soone opens the doore to persuasion) as shew's
their Congregations not deaf in those holy seasons, when Speaking
predominates. 1020
   But notwithstanding these advantages, the Pulpit hath little
prevail'd; for the world is in all Regions revers'd, or shaken by
disobedience; an Engine with which the great Angells (for such
were the Devills, and had faculties much more sublim'd then Men)
beleev'd they could disorder Heaven. And tis not want of capacity 1025
in the lower Auditory that makes Doctrine so unsuccesfull; for the
People are not simple, since the Gentry (even of strongest education)
lack sufficient defense against them, and are hourely surpris'd in
(their common Ambushes) their Shops: For on sacred Days they
walke gravely and sadly from Temples, as if they had newly bury'd 1030

996 have '73: hath '50a–b, '51a–b   1007 have obliquely '73: obliquely have
'50a–b, '51a–b

their sinfull Fathers; at night sleep as if they never needed forgive-
nesse; and rise with the next Sun, to ly in waite for the Noble, and
the Studious. And though these quiet Cousners are amongst the
People, esteem'd their steddy Men; yet they honor the Courage,
1035 and more active parts of such disobedient Spirits, as disdayning thus
tamely to deceave, attempt bravely to robb the State; and the State
they beleeve (though the Helme were held by Apostles) would
always consist of such Arch-robbers, as who ever stripps them, but
waves the tedious satisfaction which the Lasy expect from Lawes,
1040 and comes a shorter way to his owne.

Thus unapt for obedience (in the condition of Beasts whose
appetite is Liberty, and their Liberty a license of Lust) the People
have often been, since a long, and notorious power hath continu'd
with Divines; whom though with reverence we accuse for mistaken
1045 lenity; yet are wee not so cruell to expect they should behave
themselves to Sinners like fierce *Phineas*, or preach with their
Swords drawne, to kill all they cannot perswade: But our meaning
is to shew how much their Christian meeknesse hath deceav'd them
in taming this wilde Monster the People; and a little to rebuke
1050 them for neglecting the assistance of Poets; and for upbraiding the
Ethnicks, because the Poets mannag'd their Religion; as if Religion
could walk more prosperously abroad, then when Morality (res-
pectfully, and bareheaded as her Usher) prepares the way: it being
no lesse true that during the Dominion of Poesy, a willing and
1055 peacefull obedience to Superiors becalm'd the World; then that
obedience like the Marriage yoke, is a restraint more needful and
advantagious then liberty; and hath the same reward of pleasant
quietnesse, which it anciently had, when *Adam*, till his disobedience,
injoy'd Paradise. Such are the effects of sacred Poesy, which
1060 charm's the People, with harmonious precepts; and whose aide
Divines should not disdaine, since their Lord, (the Saviour of the
World) vouchsaf'd to deliver his Doctrine in Parabolicall Fictions.

Those that be of next importance are Leaders of Armys; and such
I measure not by the suffrages of the People, who give them respect
1065 as Indians worship the evill Spirit, rather for feare of harme, then
for affection; but esteem them as the painfull Protectors, and en-
largers of Empire; by whom it actively moves; and such active
motion of Empire is as necessary as the motion of the Sea; where all
things would putrifie, and infect one an other, if the Element were

1056 is] thaugh '73   1062 vauchsaf'd 50b, '51a–b, '73: vouchaf'd '50a

quiet; so is it with mens mindes on shore, when that Element of 1070
greatnesse and honor, *Empire*, stands still; of which the largenesse
is likewise as needfull, as the vastnesse of the Sea; For God ordain'd
not huge Empire as proportionable to the Bodies, but to the Mindes
of Men; and the Mindes of Men are more monstrous, and require
more space for agitation and the hunting of others, then the Bodies 1075
of Whales: But he that beleevs men such moderate Sheep as that
many are peacefully contain'd in a narrow Folde, may be better
inform'd in *America*; where little Kings never injoy a harmlesse
neighborhood, unlesse protected defensively amongst them selves,
by an Emperour that hath wide possessions, and priority over them 1080
(as in some few places) but when restraind in narrow dominion,
where no body commands and hinders their nature, they quarrell
like Cocks in a Pitt; and the Sun in a days travaile there, sees more
battailes (but not of consequence, because their Kings though many,
are little) then in *Europe* in a Yeare. 1085

To *Leaders of Armies*, as to very necessary Men (whose office
requires the uttermost aides of art, and Nature, and rescues the
sword of Justice, when tis wrested from supreme Power by Com-
motion) I now address myself; and must put them in minde (though
not upbraidingly) how much their Mighty Predecessors were 1090
anciently oblig'd to Poets; whose Songs (recording the praises of
Conduct and Valor) were esteem'd the cheefest rewards of Victory;
And since Nature hath made us prone to Imitation (by which wee
equall the best or the worst) how much those Images of Action
prevaile upon our mindes, which are delightfully drawne by Poets? 1095
For the greatest of the Grecian Captains have confess'd, that their
Counsells have been made wise, and their Courages warme by
Homer: and since Praise is a Pleasure which God hath invited, and
with which he often vouchsaf'd to be pleas'd when it was sent him
by his owne Poet; why is it not lawfull for vertuous men to be 1100
cherish'd, and magnify'd with hearing their vigilance, Valour, and
good fortune (the latter being more the immediate guift of Heaven,
because the effect of an unknowne cause) commended, and made
eternall in Poesy? But perhaps the art of praising Armies into great,
and instant action, by singing their former deeds (an Art with which 1105
the Ancients made *Empire* so large) is too subtle for moderne
Leaders; who as they cannot reach the heights of Poesy, must be

1089 I now address myself '73: I am now address'd '50a–b, '51a–b   1102 being
'50b, '51a–b, '73: bring '50a

content with a narrow space of Dominion: and narrow Dominion breeds evill, peevish, and vexatious mindes, and a nationall self-
1110 opinion, like simple Jewish arrogance; and the *Jewes* were extra-ordinary proud in a very little Country: For men in contracted goverments are but a kinde of Prisoners; and Prisoners by long restraint grow wicked, malitious to all abroad, and foolish esteemers of themselves; as if they had wrong in not enjoying every thing
1115 which they can only see out of Windowes.

Our last application is to *Statesmen*, and Makers of *Lawes*; who may be reasonably reduc'd to one; since the second differ no more from the first, then Judges (the Copies of *Law-makers*) differ from their Originalls: for Judges, like all bold Interpreters, by often
1120 altering the Text, make it quite new; and *Statesmen* (who differ not from Law-makers in the act, but in the manner of doing) make new Lawes presumptuously without the consent of the People; but *Legislators* more civilly seeme to whistle to the Beast, and stroake him into the Yoke: and in the Yoke of State, the People (with too
1125 much pampering) grow soone unruly and draw awry; Yet *Statesmen* and *Judges* (whose businesse is governing, and the thing to be govern'd is the People) have amongst us (wee being more proud and mistaken then any other famous Nation) look'd gravely upon Poetry, and with a negligence that betrayd a Northerly Ignorance; as if they
1130 beleev'd they could performe their worke without it. But Poets (who with wise diligence study the People, and have in all ages, by an in-sensible influence govern'd their manners) may justly smile when they perceive that *Divines*, *Leaders of Armies*, *Statesmen*, and *Judges*, think *Religion*, the *Sword*, or (which is unwritten *Law*, and a secret
1135 confederacy of Cheefs) *Policy*, or *Law* (which is written, but seldome rightly read) can give, without the helpe of the *Muses*, a long and quiet satisfaction in goverment: For *Religion* is to the wicked and faithlesse (who are many) a jurisdiction against which they readily rebell: because it rules severely, yet promiseth no
1140 worldly recompense for obedience: obedience being by every human power invited with assurances of visible advantage. The Good (who are but few) need not the power of *Religion* to make them better, the power of *Religion* proceeding from her threatnings, which though meane Weapons, are fitly us'd, since she hath none but
1145 base Enemies. Wee may observe too, that all Vertuous men are so taken up with the rewards of Heaven, that they live as if out of the World; and no goverment receaves assistance from any man

meerly as he is good; but as that goodnesse is active in temporall things.

The *Sword* is in the hand of *Justice* no guard to Goverment, but then when *Justice* hath an Army for her owne defense; and Armies, if they were not pervertible by Faction, yet are to Commonwealths like kings Physitians to poore Patients; who buy the cure of their disorderd bodies at so high a rate, that they may be said to change their Sicknesse for Famine. *Policy* (I meane of the Living, not of the Dead; the one being the last rules or designes governing the Instant; the other those lawes that began Empire) is as mortall as *Statesmen* themselves; whose incessant labors make that Hectick feaver of the minde, which insensibly dispatches the Body: and when Wee trace *Statesmen* through all the Histories of Courts, wee finde their Inventions so unnecessary to those that succeed at the Helme, or so much envy'd as they scarce last in authority till the Inventors are buried: and change of Designes in *Statesmen* (their designes being the Weapons by which States are defended) growes as destructive to Goverment, as a continuall change of various Weapons is to Armies; which must receave with ruine any suddaine assault, when want of practise makes unactivenesse. Wee cannot urge that the ambition of Statesmen (who are obnoxious to the People) doth much disorder goverment; because the Peoples anger, by a perpetuall comming in of new Oppressors is so diverted in considering those whom their Eyes but lately left, as they have not time enough to rise for the Publique: and evill successors to power are in the troubled Streame of State like succeeding Tides in Rivers, where the Mudd of the former is hidden by the filth of the last.

Lawes, if very ancient, grow as doubtfull and difficult as Letters on bury'd Marble, which only Antiquaries read; but if not Old, they want that reverence which is therefore paid to the vertues of Ancestors, because their crimes come not to our remembrance; and yet Great Men must be long dead whose ills are forgotten. If *Lawes* be New they must be made either by very Angells, or by Men that have some vices; and those being seen make their Vertues suspected; for the People no more esteeme able men, whose defects they know, (though but errors incident to Humanity) then an Enemy values a Strong Army having experience of their Errors. And new Lawes are held but the projects of necessitous Power, new Nets spred to intangle Us; the Old being accompted too many, since most are beleev'd to be made for Forfeitures: and such letting of blood

1150

1155

1160

1165

1170

1175

1180

1185

(though intended by Law makers for our health) is to the People
always out of Season: for those that love life with too much Passion
1190 (and Mony is the life blood of the People) ever feare a Consumption.
But be Law makers as able as Nature or Experience (which is the
best Art) can make them; yet, though I will not yeild the Wicked to
be wiser then the Vertuous, I may say, offences are too hard for the
Lawes, as some Beasts are too wylie for their Hunters; and that Vice
1195 overgrowes Vertue, as much as Weeds grow faster then Medicin-
able Hearbs: or rather that Sinne, like the fruitfull Slime of *Nilus*,
doth increase into so many various shapes of Serpents (whose walks
and retreats are winding and unknowne) that even *Justice* (the
painfull pursuer of Mischief) is become weary, and amaz'd.
1200   After these Meditations, me thinks Goverment resembles a Ship,
where though *Divines, Leaders* of *Armys, Statesmen,* and *Judges*
are the trusted Pilots; yet it moves by the means of Windes, as un-
certaine as the breath of Opinion; and is laden with the People; a
Freight much loosser, and more dangerous then any other living
1205 stowage; being as troublesome in faire weather, as Horses in a
Storme. And how can these Pilots Stedily maintaine their Course to
the Land of Peace and Plenty, since they are often divided at the
Helme? For *Divines,* (when they consider great *Chiefs*) suppose
Armys to be sent from God for a temporary Plague, not for con-
1210 tinuall Jurisdiction; and that Gods extreame punishments (of
which Armys be the most violent) are ordaind to have no more
lastingnesse, then the extreames in Nature. They think, (when they
consider *Statesmen*) Policy hath nothing of the Dove, and being all
Serpent, is more dangerous, then the dangers it pretends to pre-
1215 vent: and that outwitting (by falshood and corruption) adverse
States, or the People (though the people be often the greater enemy
and more perilsome being neerest) is but giving reputation to
Sinne, and that to maintaine the Publique by Politique evills, is a
base prostitution of Religion, and the prostitution of Religion is that
1220 unpardonable whoredome which so much anger'd the Prophets.
They think *Law* nothing but the Bible forcibly usurp'd by covetous
Lawyers, and disguis'd in a Paraphrase more obscure then the
Text; and that tis only want of just reverence to Religion which
doth expose us to the charges and vexations of *Law.*
1225   The *Leaders* of *Armys,* accuse *Divines* for unwisely raising the
Warre of the World by opposite Doctrine, and for being more
indiscreet in thinking to appease it by persuasion; forgetting that

the dispatchfull ending of Warre is blows; and that the naturall
region for Disputes, when Nations are engag'd, (though by Religion)
is the Field of Battaile, not Schooles and Academies; which they 1230
beleeve (by their restlesse controversies) lesse civill then Camps; as
intestine Quarrell is held more barbarous then forraign Warr. They
think *Statesmen* to them (unlesse dignifyd with military office) but
mean Spys, that like *African Foxes* (who attend on *Lyons*, ranging
before and about, for their valiant prey) shrink back till the danger 1235
be subdu'd, and then with insatiate hunger come in for a Share:
Yet Sometimes with the Eye of Envy (which inlarges objects like a
multiplying-glasse) they behold these *Statesmen*, and think them
immense as *Whales*; the motion of whose vast bodys can in a
peacefull calme trouble the Ocean till it boyle; After a little hasty 1240
wonder, they consider them againe with disdaine of their low con-
straints at Court; where they must patiently endure the little
follies of such small Favorites as wait even neer the wisest Thrones;
so fantastically weake seem Monarchs in the sicknesse of Care (a
feaver in the head) when for the humerous pleasure of Diversity, 1245
they descend from Purple Beds, and seeke their ease upon the
grownd. These great *Leaders* say also that *Law* moves slowly, as
with fetter'd feet, and is too tedious in redresse of wrongs; whilste in
Armys *Justice* seems to ride poste, and overtakes Offenders ere the
contagion of crimes can infect others: and though in Courts and 1250
Cittys great men fence often with her, and with a forcive sleight but
by her sword; yet when she retires to *Camps*, she is in a posture
not only to punish the offences of particular Greatnesse, but of
injurious Nations.

Statesmen looke on *Divines* as men whose long solitude and 1255
Meditations on Heaven hath made them Strangers upon Earth:
and tis acquaintance with the World, and knowledge of Man that
makes abilities of Ruling: for though it may be said that a sufficient
beleef of Doctrine would beget obedience (which is the uttermost
designe of governing) yet since diversity of Doctrine doth distract 1260
all Auditors, and makes them doubtfully dispose their obedience
(even towards spirituall powers, on which many would have the
temporall depend) therefore *Statesmen* think themselves more fitt to
manage *Empire*, then *Divines*; whose usefulnesse consists in persua-
sion; and persuasion is the last medicine (being the most desperate) 1265
which *Statesmen* apply to the distemper of the People: for their

1231 (by '51a–b, '73: by '50a–b

distemper is madnesse, and Madnesse is best cur'd with terror and force. They think that *Leaders* of *Armys* are to great Empire, as great Rivers to the Continent; which make an easy accesse of such 1270 benefitts as the Metropolis (the seat of Power) would els at vast distances with difficulty reach: yet often like proud Rivers when they swell, they destroy more by once overflowing their borders at home, then they have in long time acquir'd from abroad: They are to little Empire like the Sea to low Islands; by nature a defense from 1275 Forreigners, but by accident, when they rage, a deluge to their owne land. And at all seasons *Statesmen* beleeve them more dangerous to goverment then themselves: for the popularity of *Statesmen* is not so frequent as that of *Generalls*; or if by rare sufficiency of Art it be gain'd; yet the force of Crowds in Cittys, compar'd to the validity 1280 of men of Armes, and discipline, would appeare like the great number of Sheep to a few Wolves, rather a cause of Comfort then of Terror. They think that cheef *Ministers of Law* by unskilfull integrity, or love of popularity (which shewes the Minde, as meanly borne as bred) so earnestly pursue the protection of the Peoples 1285 right, that they neglect the publique Interest; and though the Peoples right, and publique Interest be the same, yet usually by the People, the Ministers of Law meane Private men, and by the other the State; and so the State and the People are divided, as wee may say a man is divided within him selfe, when reason and passion [(and 1290 Passion is folly)] dispute about consequent actions; and if wee were calld to assist at such intestine warre, wee must side with Reason, according to our duty, by the Law of Nature; and Natures Law, though not written in Stone (as was the Law of Religion) hath taken deep impression in the Heart of Man, which is harder then 1295 marble of *Mount-Sinai*.

Cheef *Ministers* of *Law*, think *Divines* in goverment should like the *Penall Statutes*, be choicely, and but seldome us'd; for as those Statutes are rigorously inquisitive after veniall faults, (punishing our very manners and weake constitution, as well as insolent 1300 appetite) so Divines (that are made vehement with contemplating the dignity of the Offended, (which is God) more then the frailty of the Offender) governe as if men could be made Angells, ere they come to Heaven.

Great *Ministers* of *Law* think likewise that Leaders of Armys are

1276 land '73: shore '50a–b, '51a–b   1289–90 passion . . . dispute] passion
dispute '73   1300 appetite) *Ed*: appetite: '50a–'73

like ill Physitians, only fitt for desperate cures, whose boldnesse 1305
calls in the assistance of Fortune, during the feares and troubles of
Art; Yet the health they give to a distemperd State is not more
accidentall then the preservation of it is uncertaine; because they
often grow vaine with successe, and encourage a restor'd State to
such hazards, as shew like irregularity of life in other recover'd 1310
bodys; such as the cautious and ancient gravity of *Law* dissuaded:
For *Law* (whose temperate designe is safety) rather prevents by
constancy of Medicine (like a continu'd Dyet) diseases in the Body-
politick, then depends after a permitted Sicknesse upon the chance
of recovery. They think *Statesmen* strive to be as much Judges of 1315
Law, as them selves, being cheef Ministers of Law, are Judges of
the People; and that even good *Statesmen* pervert the Law more then
Evill Judges: For Law was anciently meant a Defensive Armor, and
the People tooke it as from the Magazin of Justice, to keep them
safe from each others violence; but *Statesmen* use it as offensive 1320
Armes, with which in forraging to get releef for Supreme Power,
they often wound the Publique.

Thus wee have first observ'd the Foure cheef aides of Gover-
ment, (*Religion*, *Armes*, *Policy*, and *Law*) defectivly apply'd, and
then wee have found them weake by an emulous warr amongst 1325
themselves: it follows next, wee should introduce to strengthen
those principall aides (still making the People our direct object)
some collaterall help; which I will safely presume to consist in
Poesy.

Wee have observ'd that the People since the latter time of 1330
Christian religion, are more unquiet then in former Ages; so dis-
obedient and fierce, as if they would shake off the ancient imputation
of being Beasts, by shewing their Masters they know their owne
strength: and wee shall not erre by supposing that this conjunction
of Fourefold Power hath faild in the effects of authority, by a mis- 1335
application; for it hath rather endeavord to prevaile upon their
bodys, then their mindes; forgetting that the martiall art of con-
straining is the best; which assaults the weaker part; and the weakest
part of the People is their mindes; for want of that which is the
Mindes only Strength, *Education*; but their Bodys are strong by 1340
continuall labour; for Labour is the Education of the Body. Yet
when I mention the misapplication of force, I should have said, they

1311 cautious '50a, '51a–b, '73: cautions '50b   1311 dissuaded '51a–b, '73:
dissuades '50a–b

have not only faild by that, but by a maine error; Because the sub-
ject on which they should worke is the Minde; and the Minde can
1345 never be constrain'd, though it may be gain'd by Persuasion: And
since Persuasion is the principall Instrument which can bring to
fashion the brittle and misshapen mettall of the Minde, none are so
fitt aides to this important worke as Poets: whose art is more then
any enabled with a voluntary, and cheerfull assistance of Nature;
1350 and whose operations are as resistlesse, secret, easy, and subtle, as
is the influence of Planetts.

I must not forget (least I be prevented by the Vigilance of the
Reader) that I have profes'd not to represent the beauty of vertue
in my Poem, with hope to persuade common men; and I have said
1355 that *Divines* have faild in discharging their share of Government,
by depending upon the effects of Persuasion; and that Statesmen in
managing the People rely not upon the persuasion of Divines, but
upon force. In my despaire of reducing the mindes of Common men,
I have not confest any weaknesse of Poesy in the generall Science;
1360 but rather infer'd the particular strength of the Heroick; which
hath a force that overmatches the infancy of such mindes as are not
enabled by degrees of Education; but there are lesser forces in
other kinds of Poesy, by which they may traine, and prepare their
understandings; and Princes, and Nobles being reform'd and made
1365 Angelicall by the Heroick, will be predomanant lights, which the
People cannot chuse but use for direction; as Glowormes take
in, and keep the Sunns beames till they shine, and make day to
themselves.

In saying that *Divines* have vainly hop'd to continue the peace of
1370 Goverment by persuasion, I have imply'd such persuasions as are
accompany'd with threatnings, and seconded by force; which are
the persuasions of Pulpits; where is presented to the Obstinate, Hell
after Death; and the civill Magistrate during Life constrains such
obedience as the Church doth ordaine. But the persuasions of
1375 Poesy in stead of menaces, are Harmonious and delightfull insinu-
ations, and never any constraint; unlesse the ravishment of Reason
may be call'd Force. And such Force, (contrary to that which
Divines, *Commanders*, *Statesmen* and *Lawyers* use) begets such
obedience as is never weary or griev'd.
1380   In declaring that *Statesmen* think-not the State wholly secure by

1361–2 are not enabled] are enabled '51*b*   1380 think-not '50*a MS*, '50*b*, '51*a–b*,
'73: think '50*a*

such manners as are bred from the persuasions of *Divines*, but more
willingly make Goverment rely upon military force, I have neither
concluded that Poets are unprofitable, nor that *Statesmen* think so;
for the wisdome of Poets, would first make the Images of Vertue so
amiable that her beholders should not be able to looke off (rather   1385
gently, and delightfully infusing, then inculcating Precepts) and
then when the minde is conquer'd, like a willing Bride, Force
should so behave it selfe, as noble Husbands use their power; that is,
by letting their Wives see the Dignity and prerogative of our Sex
(which is the Husbands harmlesse conquest of Peace) continually   1390
maintain'd to hinder Disobedience, rather then rigorously impose
Duty: But to such an easy goverment, neither the People (which
are subjects to Kings and States) nor Wives (which are subject to
Husbands) can peacefully yeild, unlesse they are first conquer'd by
Vertue; and the Conquests of Vertue be never easy, but where her   1395
forces are commanded by Poets.

It may be objected that the education of the Peoples mindes
(from whence Vertuous manners are deriv'd) by the severall kindes
of Poesy (of which the *Dramatick* hath been in all Ages very succes-
full) is opposite to the receav'd opinion, that the People ought to be   1400
continu'd in ignorance; a Maxime sounding like the little subtilty of
one that is a Statesman only by Birth or Beard, and merits not his
place by much thinking: For Ignorance is rude, censorious, jealous,
obstinate, and proud; these being exactly the ingredients of which
Disobedience is made; and Obedience proceeds from ample con-   1405
sideration, of which knowledge consists; and knowledge will soone
put into one Scale the weight of oppression, and in the other, the
heavy burden which Disobedience lays on us in the effects of civill
Warr: and then even Tyranny will seem much lighter, when the
hand of supreme Power bindes up our Load, and lays it artfully on   1410
us, then Disobedience (the Parent of Confusion) when wee all
load one an other; in which every one irregularly increases his
fellows burden, to lessen his owne.

Others may object that Poesy on our Stage, or the Heroick in
Musick (for so the latter was anciently us'd) is prejudiciall to a   1415
State; as begetting Levity, and giving the People too great a diver-
sion by pleasure and mirth. To these (if they be worthy of Satis-
faction) I reply; That whoever in Goverment endeavors to make the
People serious and grave, (which are attributes that may become the

1389 our *'50a MS*, *'50b*, *'51a–b*, *'73*: their *'50a*

1420 Peoples *Representatives*, but not the People) doth practice a new
way to enlarge the State, by making every Subject a *Statesman*: and
he that means to governe so mournfully (as it were, without any
Musick in his Dominion) must lay but light burdens on his Subjects;
or else he wants the ordinary wisdome of those, who to their Beasts
1425 that are much loaden whistle all the day to encourage their Travail:
For that supreme power which expects a firme obedience in those,
who are not us'd to rejoycing, but live sadly, as if they were still
preparing for the funerall of Peace, hath little skill in contriving the
lastingnesse of Goverment, which is the principall worke of Art;
1430 And lesse hath that Power consider'd Nature; as if such new auster-
ity did seem to tax, even her, for want of gravity, in bringing in the
Spring so merrily with a musicall variety of Birds; And such sullen
power doth forget that Battails (the most solemne and serious
businesse of Death) are begun with Trumpets and Fifes; and
1435 anciently were continu'd with more diversity of Musick. And that
the Grecian Lawes (Lawes being the gravest endeavour of human
Councells, for the ease of Life) were long before the Days of
Lycurgus (to make them more pleasant to memory) publishd in
Verse: And that the wise *Athenians* (dividing into Three parts the
1440 publique Revenew) expended one in Plays and Showes, to divert
the People from meeting to consult of their Rulers merit, and the
defects of Goverment: And that the *Romans* had not so long con-
tinu'd their Empire, but for the same diversions, at a vaster charge.
      Againe it may be objected, that the Precepts of Christian Religion
1445 are sufficient towards our regulation, by appointment of manners;
and towards the ease of Life, by imposing obedience; so that the
morall assistance of Poesy, is but vainly intruded. To this I may
answer, that as no man should suspect the sufficiency of Religion by
its insuccesfulnesse, so if the insuccesfulnesse be confess'd, wee
1450 shall as little disparage Religion, by bringing in more aides when tis
in action, as a Generall dishonors himselfe by endeavoring with
more of his owne Forces to make sure an attempt that hath a while
miscarry'd: For Poesy, which (like contracted *Essences* seemes the
utmost strength and activity of Nature) is as all good Arts, sub-
1455 servient to Religion; all marching under the same Banner, though of
lesse discipline and esteeme. And as Poesy is the best Expositor of
Nature (Nature being mysterious to such as use not to consider) so

Nature is the best Interpreter of God; and more cannot be said of Religion. And when the Judges of Religion (which are the Chiefs of the Church) neglect the help of Moralists in reforming the People 1460 (and Poets are of all Moralists the most usefull) they give a sentence against the Law of Nature: For Nature performes all things by correspondent aides and harmony. And tis injurious not to think Poets the most usefull Moralists; for as Poesy is adorned and sublim'd by Musick, which makes it more pleasant and acceptable; so 1465 morality is sweetned and made more amiable by Poesy. And the Austerity of some Divines may be the cause why Religion hath not more prevaild upon the manners of Men: for great Doctors should rather comply with things that please (as the wise Apostle did with Ceremonies) then lose a Proselyte. And even *Honor* (taught by 1470 morall Philosophers, but more delightfully infus'd by Poets) will appear (notwithstanding the sad severity of some latter Divines) no unsafe Guide towards Piety; for it is as wary and nice as *Conscience*, though more cheerfull and couragious. And however *Honor* be more pleasing to flesh and blood, because in this World it find's 1475 applause; yet tis not so mercenarie as Piety: for Piety (being of all her expectations inwardly assur'd) expects a reward in Heaven; to which all earthly payments compar'd, are but Shaddows, and Sand.

And it appeares that Poesy hath for its naturall prevailings over the Understandings of Men (sometimes making her conquests with 1480 easy plainesse, like native country Beauty) been very succesful in the most grave, and important occasions that the necessities of States or Mankinde have produc'd. For it may be said that *Demosthenes* sav'd the *Athenians* by the Fable or Parable of the Doggs and Wolves, in answer to King *Philip's* proposition; And that *Menenius* 1485 *Agrippa* sav'd the Senate, if not *Rome*, by that of the Belly and the Hands: and that even our Saviour was pleas'd (as the most prevalent way of Doctrine) wholy to use such kinde of Parables in his converting, or saving of Soules; it being written, *Without a Parable spake he not to them*. And had not the learned Apostle thought the 1490 wisdome of Poets worthy his remembrance, and instructive, not only to Heathens, but to Christians, he had not cited *Epimenides* to the *Cretans*, as well as *Aratus* to the *Athenians*.

I cannot also be ignorant that divers (whose consciencious Melancholy amazes and discourages others Devotion) will accuse Poets as 1495 the Admirers of Beauty; and Inventors, or Provokers of that which

1461 useful '51a, '73: usefull '51b: usefuful '50a

by way of aspersion they call *Love*. But such, in their first accusation seeme to looke carelesly and unthankfully upon the wonderfull works of God; or else through low education, or age, become in-
1500 competent Judges of what is the chief of his works upon Earth. And Poets, when they praise Beauty, are at least as lawfully thankfull to God, as when they praise Seas, Woods, Rivers, or any other parts that make up a prospect of the World. Nor can it be imagin'd but that Poets in praising them, praise wholy the Maker; and so in
1505 praising Beauty: For that Woman who beleev's she is prais'd when her Beauty is commended, may as well suppose that Poets think she created her selfe: And he that praises the inward Beauty of Women, which is their Vertue, doth more performe his duty then before: for our envious silence in not approving, and so encouraging what is
1510 good, is the cause that Vice is more in fashion and countenance then Vertue. But when Poets praise that which is not beauty, or the minde which is not vertuous, they erre through their mistake, or by flattery; and flattery is a crime so much more prosperous in others who are Companions to greatnesse, that it may be held in Poets
1515 rather Kindnesse then designe.

They who accuse Poets as Provokers of Love, are Enemys to Nature; and all affronts to Nature are offences to God, as insolencies to all subordinate Officers of the Crowne are rudenesses to the King. *Love* (in the most obnoxious interpretation) is Natur's Preparative
1520 to her greatest worke, which is the making of *Life*. And since the severest Divines of these latter times have not been asham'd publiquely to command and define the most secret duty, and enter-tainments of Love in the Married; why should not Poets civilly endevour to make a Frendship between the Guests before they
1525 meet, by teaching them to dignify each other with the utmost of estimation. And Mariage in Mankinde were as rude and unprepar'd as the hasty elections of other Creatures, but for acquaintance, and conversation before it: and that must be an acquaintance of Mindes, not of Bodys; and of the Minde, Poesy is the most naturall and
1530 delightfull Interpreter.

When neither Religion (which is our Art towards God) nor Nature (which is Gods first law to Man, though by Man least study'd) nor when Reason (which is Nature, and made Art by Experience) can by the Enemys of Poesy be sufficiently urg'd against
1535 it; then some (whose frowardnesse will not let them quitt an evill

1522 duty '73: dutys '50a–b, '51a–b

cause) plead written Authoritie. And though such authoritie be a Weapon, which even in the warr of Religion, distress'd Disputers take up, as their last shift; yet here wee would protest against it, but that wee finde it makes a false deffence, and leaves the Enemy more open. This authoritie (which is but single too) is from *Plato*; 1540 and him some have malitiously quoted; as if in his feign'd Commonwealth he had banish'd all Poets. But *Plato* says nothing against Poets in generall; and in his particular quarrell (which is to *Homer*, and *Hesiod*) only condemnes such errors as wee mention'd in the begining of this *Preface*, when wee look'd upon the Ancients. And 1545 those errors consist in their abasing Religion, by representing the Gods in evill proportion, and their *Heroes* with as unequal Characters; and so brought Vices into fashion, by intermixing them with the vertues of great Persons. Yet even during this divine anger of *Plato*, he concludes not against Poesy, but the Poems then most 1550 in request: for these be the words of his Law. *If any Man (having abilitie to imitate what he pleases) imitate in his Poems both good and evill, let him be reverenc'd, as a sacred, admirable, and pleasant Person; but be it likewise knowne, he must have no place in our Commonwealth.* And yet before his banishment he allows him, *the honor of a* 1555 *Diadem, and sweet Odours to annoint his Head*: and afterwards says, *Let us make use of more profitable, though more severe, and lesse pleasant Poets, who can imitate that which is for the honor and benefit of the Common-wealth.* But those who make use of this just indignation of *Plato* to the unjust scandall of Poesy, have the common 1560 craft of False-Witnesses, inlarging every circomstance, when it may hurt, and concealing all things that may deffend him they oppose. For they will not remember how much the Scholler of *Plato* (who like an absolute Monarch over Arts, hath almost silenc'd his Master throughout the Schooles of *Europe*) labours to make Poesy uni- 1565 versally current, by giving Lawes to the Science: Nor will they take notice, in what dignitie it continu'd whilst the *Greeks* kept their dominion, or Language; and how much the *Romans* cherish'd even the publique repetition of *Verses*: Nor will they vouchsafe to observe (though *Juvenall* takes care to record it) how gladly all 1570 *Rome* (during that exercise) ranne to the voice of *Statius*.

Thus having taken measure (though hastily) of the extent of those great Professions that in Goverment contribute to the necessities,

1537 which '51b, '73: that '50a–b: swich '51a   1570 takes '73: take '50a–b,
'51a–b

ease, and lawfull pleasures of Men; and finding Poesy as usefull
1575 now, as the Ancients found it towards perfection and happinesse;
I will, Sir, (unlesse with these Two Bookes you returne me a dis-
couragment) cheerfully proceed: and though a little time would
make way for the Third, and make it fitt for the Presse; I am resolv'd
rather to hazard the inconvenience which expectation breeds, (for
1580 divers with no ill satisfaction have had a taste of *Gondibert*) then
endure that violent envy which assaults all Writers whilst they live;
though their Papers be but fill'd with very negligent and ordinary
thoughts: and therfore I delay the publication of any part of the
Poem, till I can send it you from *America*; whither I now speedily
1585 prepare; having the folly to hope, that when I am in another World
(though not in the common sense of dying) I shall finde my Readers
(even the Poets of the present Age) as temperate, and benigne, as
wee are all to the Dead, whose remote excellence cannot hinder our
reputation. And now, Sir, to end with the Allegory which I have so
1590 long continu'd, I shall (after all my busy vanitie in shewing and
describing my new Building) with great quietnesse (being almost
as weary as your selfe) bring you to the Back dore, that you may
make no review but in my absence; and steale hastely from you,
as one who is asham'd of all the trouble you have receav'd from,
1595 (SIR) Your most humble, and most affectionate Servant WILL.
D'AVENANT.

From the Louvre in Paris
January 2. 1650.

1577-8 would make way for '*51a-b*, '*73*: would perfect '*50a-b*

THE ANSWER
OF
Mr. HOBBES
TO
SIR WILL. D'AVENANT'S
PREFACE
BEFORE GONDIBERT

SIR, If to commend your Poeme, I should onely say (in generall Termes) that in choyce of your Argument, the disposition of the partes, the maintenance of the Characters of your Persons, the dignity and vigour of your expression you have performed all the parts of various experience, ready memory, cleare judgment, swift 5 and well govern'd fancy, though it were enough for the truth, it were too little for the weight and credit of my testimony. For I lie open to two Exceptions, one of an incompetent, the other of a corrupted Witnesse. Incompetent, because I am not a Poet; and corrupted with the Honor done me by your Preface. The former obliges me to 10 say something (by the way) of the Nature and differences of Poesy.

As Philosophers have divided the Universe (their subject) into three Regions, *Caelestiall*, *Aëriall*, and *Terrestriall*; so the Poets, (whose worke it is by imitating humane life, in delightfull and measur'd lines, to avert men from vice, and encline them to vertuous 15 and honorable actions) have lodg'd themselves in the three Regions of mankind, *Court*, *Citty*, and *Country*, correspondent in some proportion, to those three Regions of the World. For there is in Princes, and men of conspicuous power (anciently called *Heroes*) a lustre and influence upon the rest of men, resembling that of the Heavens; and 20 an insincerenesse, inconstancy, and troublesome humor of those that dwell in populous Citties, like the mobility, blustring, and impurity of the Aire; and a plainesse, and (though dull) yet a nutritive faculty in rurall people, that endures a comparison with the Earth they labour. 25

From hence have proceeded three sorts of Poesy. *Heroique*, *Scommatique*, and *Pastorall*. Every one of these is distinguished againe in the manner of *Representation*, which sometimes is *Narrative*,

wherein the Poet himselfe relateth, and sometimes *Dramatique*,
30 as when the persons are every one adorned and brought upon the
Theater, to speake and act their owne parts. There is therefore
neither more nor lesse then six sorts of Poesy. For the Heroique
Poeme narrative (such as is yours) is called an *Epique Poeme*;
The Heroique Poeme Dramatique, is *Tragedy*. The Scommatique
35 Narrative, is *Satyre*, Dramatique is *Comedy*. The Pastorall narrative,
is called simply *Pastorall* (anciently *Bucolique*) the same Dramatique,
Pastorall comedy. The Figure therefore of an Epique Poeme, and of
a Tragedy, ought to be the same, for they differ no more but in that
they are pronounced by one, or many persons. Which I insert to
40 justify the figure of yours, consisting of five bookes divided into
Songs, or Cantoes, as five Acts divided into Scenes has ever bene
the approved figure of a Tragedy.

They that take for Poesy whatsoever is Writ in Verse, will thinke
this division imperfect, and call in Sonnets, Epigrammes, Eclogues,
45 and the like peeces (which are but Essayes, and parts of an entire
Poeme) and reckon *Empedocles*, and *Lucretius* (naturall Philosophers)
for Poets, and the morall precepts of *Phocylides*, *Theognis*, and the
Quatraines of *Pybrach*, and the History of *Lucan*, and others of that
kind amongst Poemes; bestowing on such Writers for honor, the
50 name of Poets, rather then of Historians, or Philosophers. But the
subject of a Poeme is the manners of men, not naturall causes;
manners presented, not dictated; and manners feyned (as the name
of Poesy importes) not found in men. They that give entrance to
Fictions writ in Prose, erre not so much, but they erre. For Poesy
55 requireth delightfulnesse, not onely of fiction, but of stile; in which
if Prose contend with Verse it is with disadvantage and (as it were)
on foot against the strength and winges of *Pegasus*.

For Verse amongst the *Greekes* was appropriated anciently to the
service of their Gods, and was the Holy stile; the stile of the Oracles;
60 the stile of the Lawes; and the stile of men that publiquely recom-
mended to their Gods, the vowes and thankes of the people; which
was done in their holy songes called Hymnes; and the Composers of
them were called Prophets and Priests before the name of Poet was
knowne. When afterwards the majesty of that stile was observed,
65 the Poets chose it as best becomming their high invention. And for
the Antiquity of Verse it is greater then the antiquity of Letters.

54 Poesy] Prose '*51a–b*, '*73*   56 contend with '*50b*, '*51b*: contend which '*50a*,
'*51a*, '*73*

For it is certaine, *Cadmus* was the first that (from *Phœnicia*, a country that neighboureth *Judæa*) brought the use of Letters into *Greece*. But the service of the Gods, and the lawes (which by measured Sounds were easily committed to the memory) had bene 70 long time in use, before the arrivall of *Cadmus* there.

There is besides the grace of stile, another cause why the antient Poets chose to write in measured language, which is this. Their Poemes were made at first with intention to have them sung, as well Epique, as Dramatique (which custome hath been long time layd 75 aside, but began to be revived in part, of late yeres in *Italy*) and could not be made commensurable to the Voyce or Instruments, in Prose; the wayes and motions whereof are so uncertayne and undistinguished, (like the way and motion of a Ship in the Sea) as not onely to discompose the best Composers, but also to disappoint 80 some times the most attentive Reader, and put him to hunt counter for the sense. It was therefore necessary for Poets in those times, to write in Verse.

The verse which the *Greekes*, and *Latines* (considering the nature of their owne languages) found by experience most grave, and for 85 an Epique Poeme most decent, was their *Hexameter*; a Verse limited, not onely in the length of the line, but also in the quantity of the syllables. In steed of which wee use the line of ten syllables, recompensing the neglect of their quantity, with the diligence of Rime. And this measure is so proper for an Heroique Poeme, as 90 without some losse of gravity and dignity, it was never changed. A longer is not farre from ill Prose, and a shorter, is a kind of whisking (you know) like the unlacing, rather then the singing of a Muse. In an Epigramme or a Sonnet, a man may vary his measures, and seeke glory from a needlesse difficulty, as he that contrived 95 verses into the formes of an Organ, a Hatchet, an Egge, an Altar, and a payre of Winges; but in so great and noble a worke as is an Epique Poeme, for a man to obstruct his owne way with unprofitable difficulties, is great imprudence. So likewise to chuse a needelesse and difficult correspondence of Rime, is but a difficult toy, and forces 100 a man some times for the stopping of a chinke to say some what he did never thinke; I cannot therefore but very much approve your *Stanza*, where in the syllables in every verse are ten, and the Rime Alternate.

105   For the choyse of your subject your have sufficiently justified
your selfe in your Preface. But because I have observed in *Virgil*,
that the Honor done to *Æneas* and his companions, has so bright a
reflexion upon *Augustus Cæsar*, and other great *Romanes* of that
time, as a man may suspect him not constantly possessed with the
110   noble spirit of those his *Heroes*, and beleeve you are not acquainted
with any great man of the Race of *Gondibert*, I adde to your Justifi-
cation of the purity of your purpose, in having no other motive of
your labour, but to adorne vertue, and procure her Lovers; then
which there cannot be a worthier designe, and more becomming
115   noble Poesy.

In that you make so small account of the example of almost all the
approuved Poets, ancient and moderne, who thought fit in the
beginning, and some times also in the progresse of their Poems, to
invoke a Muse, or some other Deitye, that should dictate to them,
120   or assist them in their writings, they that take not the lawes of Art,
from any reason of their owne, but from the fashion of precedent
times, will perhaps accuse your singularity. For my part, I neither
subscribe to their accusation, nor yet condemne that Heathen
custome, otherwise then as accessary to their false Religion. For
125   their Poets were their Divines; had the name of Prophets; Excercised
amongst the People a kind of spirituall Authority; would be thought
to speake by a divine spirit; have their workes which they writte in
Verse (the divine stile) passe for the word of God, and not of man;
and to be hearkened to with reverence. Do not our Divines (excepting
130   the stile) do the same, and by us that are of the same Religion cannot
justly be reprehended for it? Besides, in the use of the spirituall
calling of Divines, there is danger sometimes to be feared, from want
of skill, such as is reported of unskillfull Conjurers, that mistaking
the rites and ceremonious points of their art, call up such spirits, as
135   they cannot at their pleasure allay againe; by whom stormes are
raysed, that overthrow buildings, and are the cause of miserable
wrackes at sea. Unskillful divines do oftentimes the like, For when
they call unseasonably for *Zeale* there appeares a spirit of *Cruelty*;
and by the like error insteed of *Truth* they rayse *Discord*; insteed of
140   *Wisedome*, *Fraud*; insteed of *Reformation*, *Tumult*; and *Controversie*
insteed of *Religion*. Whereas in the Heathen Poets, at least in those
whose workes have lasted to the time wee are in, there are none
of those indiscretions to be found, that tended to subversion, or

136 overthrow '50b– '73; overthrough '50a

disturbance of the Commonwealthes wherein they lived. But why
a Christian should thinke it an ornament to his Poeme; either to   145
profane the true God, or invoke a false one, I can imagine no cause,
but a reasonlesse imitation of custome; of a foolish custome; by
which a man enabled to speake wisely from the principles of nature,
and his owne meditation, loves rather to be thought to speake by
inspiration, like a Bagpipe.   150

Time and education begets experience; Experience begets
memory; Memory begets Judgement, and Fancy; Judgement begets
the strength and structure; and Fancy begets the ornaments of a
Poeme. The Ancients therefore fabled not absurdly, in making
memory the mother of the Muses. For memory is the World (though   155
not really, yet so as in a looking glasse) in which the Judgment the
severer Sister busieth her selfe in grave and rigide examination of all
the parts of Nature, and in registring by Letters, their order,
causes, uses, differences and resemblances; Whereby the Fancy,
when any worke of Art is to be performed, findes her materials at   160
hand and prepared for use, and needes no more then a swift motion
over them, that what she wants, and is there to be had, may not lye
too long unespied. So that when she seemeth to fly from one *Indies*
to the other, and from Heaven to Earth, and to penetrate into the
hardest matter, and obscurest places, into the future, and into her   165
selfe, and all this in a point of time, the voyage is not very great, her
selfe being all she seekes; and her wonderfull celerity, consisteth not
so much in motion, as in copious Imagery discreetly ordered, and
perfectly registred in the memory; which most men under the name
of Philosophy have a glimpse of, and is pretended to by many that   170
grossely mistaking her embrace contention in her place. But so
farre forth as the Fancy of man, has traced the wayes of true
Philosophy, so farre it hath produced very marvellous effects to the
benefit of mankind. All that is bewtifull or defensible in buildinge;
or mervaylous in Engines and Instruments of motion; Whatsoever   175
commodity men receave from the observation of the Heavens, from
the description of the Earth, from the account of Time, from walk-
ing on the Seas; and whatsoever distinguisheth the civility of *Europe*,
from the Barbarity of the *American* sauvages, is the workemanship
of Fancy, but guided by the Precepts of true Philosophy. But where   180
these precepts fayle, as they have hetherto fayled in the doctrine of

Morall vertue, there the Architect (*Fancy*) must take the Philoso-
phers part upon herselfe. He therefore that undertakes an Heroique
Poeme (which is to exhibite a venerable and amiable Image of
185 Heroique vertue) must not onely be the Poet, to place and connect,
but also the Philosopher, to furnish and square his matter, that is, to
make both body and soule, coulor and shaddow of his Poeme out
of his owne store: which how well you have performed I am now
considering.

190   Observing how few the persons be you introduce in the begin-
ninge, and how in the course of the actions of these (the number
increasinge) after severall confluences, they run all at last into the
two principall streames of your Poeme, *Gondibert* and *Oswald*, me
thinkes the Fable is not much unlike the Theater. For so, from
195 severall and farre distant Sources, do the lesser Brookes of *Lombardy*,
flowing into one another, fall all at last into the two mayne Rivers,
the *Po*, and the *Adice*. It hath the same resemblance also with a
mans veines, which proceeding from different parts, after the like
concourse, insert themselves at last into the two principall veynes of
200 the Body. But when I considered that also the actions of men, which
singly are inconsiderable, after many conjunctures, grow at last
either into one great protecting power, or into two destroying
factions, I could not but approve the structure of your Poeme,
which ought to be no other then such as an imitation of humane
205 life requireth.

In the streames themselves I find nothing but settled Valour,
cleane Honor, calme Counsell, learned diversion and pure Love;
save onely a torrent or two of Ambition, which (though a fault) has
somewhat Heroique in it, and therefore must have place in an
210 Heroique Poeme. To shew the reader in what place he shall find
every excellent picture of vertue you have drawne, is too long. And
to shew him one, is to prejudice the rest; yet I cannot forbeare to
point him to the Description of Love in the person of *Birtha*, in the
seventh *Canto* of the second Booke. There has nothing bene sayd of
215 that subject neither by the Ancient nor moderne Poets comparable
to it. Poets are Paynters: I would faine see another Painter draw so
true perfect and natural a Love to the Life, and make use of nothing
but pure lines, without the helpe of any the least uncomely shaddow,
as you have done. But let it be read as a piece by it selfe, for in the
220 almost equall height of the whole, the eminence of partes is Lost.

202 into two] into '*51b*

There are some that are not pleased with fiction, unlesse it be bold; not onely to exceed the *worke*, but also the *possibility* of nature, they would have impenetrable Armors, Inchanted Castles, invulnerable bodies, Iron men, flying Horses, and a thousand other such thinges, which are easily fayned by them that dare. Against 225 such I defend you (without assenting to those that condemne either *Homer* or *Virgil*) by dissenting onely from those that thinke the Beauty of a Poeme consisteth in the exorbitancy of the fiction. For as truth is the bound of Historicall, so the Resemblance of truth is the utmost limit of Poeticall Liberty. In old time amongst the 230 Heathen such strange fictions, and Metamorphoses, were not so remote from the Articles of their faith, as they are now from ours, and therefore were not so unpleasant. Beyond the actuall workes of nature a Poet may now go; but beyond the conceaved possibility of nature never. I can allow a Geographer to make, in the Sea, a fish 235 or a ship, which by the scale of his mappe would be two or three hundred mile long, and thinke it done for ornament, because it is done with out the precincts of his undertaking; but when he paynts an Elephant so, I presently apprehend it as ignorance, and a playne confession of *Terra incognita*. 240

As the Description of Great men and Great Actions is the constant designe of a Poet; so the Descriptions of worthy circomstances are necessary accessions to a Poeme, and being well performed are the Jewels and most pretious ornaments of Poesy. Such in *Virgil* are the Funerall games of *Anchises*, The duel of *Æneas* and *Turnus*, &c. 245 and such in yours are *The Hunting, The Battayle, The Citty Morning, The Funerall, The House of Astragon, The Library, and the Temples*, equall to his, or those of *Homer* whom he imitated.

There remaynes now no more to be considered but the Expression, in which consisteth the countenance and coulour of a 250 bewtifull Muse; and is given her by the Poet out of his owne provision, or is borrowed from others. That which he hath of his owne, is nothing but experience and knowledge of Nature, and specially humane nature; and is the true, and naturall Colour. But that which is taken out of Bookes (the ordinary boxes of Counterfeit Complex- 255 ion) shewes well or ill, as it hath more or lesse resemblance with the naturall, and are not to be used (without examination) unadvisedly. For in him that professes the imitation of Nature, (as all Poets do)

246 *Battayle*, Ed: *Battayle*. '50a: *Battel*. 150b: *Bataile*. '51a: *Battel*, '51b: *Battaile*, '73   247 *Temples*] *Temple* '51a–b   258 (as '51b, '73, as '50a, '51a: , (as '50b

8124201   G

what greater fault can there be, then to bewray an ignorance of
260 nature in his Poeme; especially having a liberty allowed him, if he
meete with any thing he cannot master, to leave it out?

That which giveth a Poeme the true and naturall Colour consis-
teth in two things, which are; *To know well*, that is, to have images of
nature in the memory distinct and cleare; and *To know much.* A
265 signe of the first is perspicuity, property, and decency; which delight
all sortes of men, either by instructing the ignorant, or soothing the
learned in their knowledge. A signe of the later is novelty of ex-
pression, and pleaseth by excitation of the mind; for novelty causeth
admiration, and admiration, curiosity, which is a delightfull
270 appetite of knowledge.

There be so many wordes in use at this day in the English tongue,
that, though of magnifique sound, yet (like the windy blisters of a
troubled water) have no sense at all; and so many others that loose
their meaning, by being ill coupled, that it is a hard matter to avoyd
275 them; for having bene obtruded upon youth in the Schooles (by
such as make it, I thinke, their businesse there (as t'is exprest by the
best Poet)

With termes to charme the weake and pose the wise,

Gondi-
280   bert. lib.
                                           II. Cant. 5.

they grow up with them, and gaining reputation with the ignorant,
are not easily shaken off.

To this palpable darknesse, I may also adde the ambitious
285 obscurity of expressing more then is perfectly conceaved; or perfect
conception in fewer words then it requires. Which Expressions,
though they have had the honor to be called strong lines, are in deed
no better then Riddles, and not onely to the Reader, but also (after
a little time) to the Writer himselfe darke and troublesome.

290 To the property of Expression I referre, that clearenesse of
memory, by which a Poet when he hath once introduced any person
whatsoever, speaking in his Poeme, mainteyneth in him to the end
the same character he gave him in the beginning. The variation
whereof, is a change of pace, that argues the Poet tired.

295 Of the Indecencyes of an Heroique Poem, the most remarquable
are those that shew disproportion either betweene the persons and
their actions, or betweene the manners of the Poet and the Poeme.

267 later] latter '51a–'73   281 II *Ed*: I '50a–'73

Of the first kind, is the uncomlinesse of representing in great persons the inhumane vice of Cruelty, or the sordide vices of Lust and Drunkenesse. To such parts as those the Ancient approved 300 Poets, thought it fit to suborne, not the persons of men, but of monsters and beastly Giants, such as *Polyphemus, Cacus*, and the *Centaures*. For it is supposed a Muse, when she is invoked to sing a song of that nature, should maidenly advise the Poet, to set such persons to sing their owne vices upon the stage; for it is not so un- 305 seemely in a *Tragedy*. Of the same kind it is to represent scurrility, or any action or languadge that moveth much laughter. The delight of an *Epique* Poeme consisteth not in mirth, but admiration. Mirth and laughter is proper to *Comedy* and *Satyre*. Great persons that have their mindes employed on great designes, have not leasure 310 enough to laugh, and are pleased with the contemplation of their owne power and vertues, so as they need not the infirmities and vices of other men to recommend themselves to their owne favor by comparison, as all men do when they laugh. Of the second kind, where the disproportion is betweene the Poet, and the Persons of his 315 Poeme, one is in the Dialect of the Inferior sort of People which is allwayes different from the language of the Court. Another is to derive the Illustration of anything, from such metaphores or comparisons as cannot come into mens thoughts, but by meane conversation, and experience of humble or evill Artes, which the persons of 320 an *Epique* Poeme cannot be thought acquainted with.

From *Knowing much*, proceedeth the admirable variety and novelty of metaphors and similitudes, which are not possibly to be lighted on, in the compasse of a narrow knowledge. And the want whereof compelleth a Writer to expressions that are either defac'd 325 by time, or sullied with vulgar or long use. For the Phrases of Poesy, as the ayres of musique with often hearing become insipide, the Reader having no more sense of their force, then our Flesh is sensible of the bones that susteine it. As the sense we have of bodies, consisteth in change and variety of impression, so also does the sense of 330 languadge in the variety and changeable use of words. I meane not in the affectation of words newly brought home from travaile, but in new (and with all significant) translation to our purposes, of those that be already received; and in farre fetch't (but withall, apt, instructive, and comely) similitudes. 335

Having thus (I hope) avoyded the first Exception, against the

320 persons] person '51a–b, '73   323 possibly] possible '51a–b, '73

incompetency of my Judgement, I am but little moved with the second, which is of being bribed by the honor you have done me, by attributing in your Preface somewhat to my Judgment. For I
340 have used your Judgment no lesse in many thinges of mine, which comming to light will thereby appeare the better. And so you have your bribe againe.

Having thus made way for the admission of my Testimony, I give it briefly thus; I never yet saw Poeme, that had so much shape
345 of Art, health of Morality, and vigour and bewty of Expression as this of yours. And but for the clamour of the multitude, that hide their Envy of the present, under a Reverence of Antiquity I should say further, that it would last as long as either the *Æneid*, or *Iliad*, but for one Disadvantage. And the Disadvantage is this: The lan-
350 guages of the *Greekes* and *Romanes* (by their Colonies and Conquests) have put off flesh and bloud, and are become immutable, which none of the moderne tongues are like to be. I honor Antiquity, but that which is commonly called *old time*, is *yong time*. The glory of Antiquity is due, not to the Dead, but to the Aged.
355   And now, whilest I thinke on't, give me leave with a short discord to sweeten the Harmony of the approaching close. I have nothing to object against your Poeme; but dissent onely from something in your Preface, sounding to the prejudice of Age. Tis commonly sayd, that old Age is a returne to childhood. Which me thinkes you insist on so
360 long, as if you desired it should be beleeved. That's the note I meane to shake a litle. That saying, meant onely of the weakenesse of body, was wrested to the weaknesse of minde, by froward children, weary of the controulment of their parents, masters, and other admonitors. Secondly the dotage and childishnesse they ascribe to
365 age is never the effect of Time, but sometimes of the excesses of youth, and not a returning to, but a continuall stay with childhood. For they that wanting the curiosity of furnishing their memories with the rarities of nature in their youth, and passe their time in making provision onely for their ease, and sensuall delight, are
370 children still, at what yeres soever; as they that comming into a populous citty, never going out of their Inne, are strangers still, how longsoever they have bene there. Thirdly, there is no reason for any man to think himselfe wiser to day then yesterday,

---

349 Disadvantage '*51a*: Disauantage '*50a*   361-2 weaknesse of body, '*50a MS*,
'*50b*, '*51a–b*, '*73*: weaknesse, of body '*50a*   371 going '*51a–'73*: go '*50a–b*   their
'*51a–'73*: their owne '*50a–b*

which does not equally convince he shall be wiser to morrow then 375
to day.

Fourthly, you will be forced to change your opinion, hereafter
when you are old; and in the meane time you discredit all I have
sayd before in your commendation, because I am old already. But
no more of this.   380

I beleeve (Sir) you have seene a curious kind of perspective, where,
he that lookes through a short hollow pipe, upon a picture con-
teyning diverse figures, sees none of those that are there paynted,
but some one person made up of their partes, conveighed to the eye
by the artificiall cutting of a glasse. I find in my imagination an 385
effect not unlike it from your Poeme. The vertues you distribute
there amongst so many noble Persons, represent (in the reading) the
image but of one mans vertue to my fancy, which is your owne; and
that so deepely imprinted, as to stay for ever there, and governe all
the rest of my thoughts, and affections in the way of honoring and 390
serving you, to the utmost of my power, that am (SIR) Your most
humble and obedient servant, THOMAS HOBBES.

Paris Jan. 10. 1650.

GONDIBERT:

AN HEROICK

POEM,

WRITTEN BY

S WILLIAM D'AVENANT.

LONDON,

Printed by *Tho. Newcomb* for *John Holden,* and are to
be fold at his Shop at the fign of the Anchor in the
NEVV-EXCHANGE, 1651.

GONDIBERT

THE FIRST BOOK
Canto the First

The ARGUMENT

Old ARIBERT'S *great race, and greater mind*
Is sung, with the renown of RHODALIND.
Prince OSWALD *is compar'd to* GONDIBERT,
And justly each distinguish'd by desert:
Whose Armies are in Fame's fair Field drawn forth,
To shew by discipline their Leaders worth.

1. Of all the *Lombards*, by their Trophies knowne,
   Who sought Fame soon, and had her favor long,
   King *Aribert* best seem'd to fill the Throne;
   And bred most bus'nesse for Heroick Song.

2. From early Childhoods promising estate,
   Up to performing Manhood, till he grew
   To fayling Age, he Agent was to Fate,
   And did to Nations Peace or War renew.

3. War was his study'd Art; war, which the bad
   Condemn, because even then it does them awe
   When with their number lin'd, and purple clad,
   And to the good more needful is then Law.

4. To conquer Tumult, Nature's sodain force,
   War, Arts delib'rate strength, was first devis'd;
   Cruel to those whose rage has no remorse,
   Least civil pow'r should be by Throngs surpris'd.

Arg. 1 ARIBERT'S *'51a MS, '51b, '73*: ARIBERTS *'51a*   *Arg.* 5 forth,
'51a MS, '51b, '73: forth *'51a*   1: 1 *Lombards, '51a MS, '51b, '73*: Lombards *'51a*
1: 2 long, *'51a MS, '51b, '73*: long *'51a*

5. The feeble Law rescues but doubtfully
   From the Oppressors single Arme our right;
   Till to its pow'r the wise war's help apply;
   Which soberly does Man's loose rage unite.

6. Yet since on all War never needful was,
   Wise *Aribert* did keep the People sure
   By Laws from little dangers; for the Laws
   Them from themselves, and not from pow'r secure.

7. Else Conquerors, by making Laws, o'recome
   Their own gain'd pow'r, and leave mens fury free;
   Who growing deaf to pow'r, the Laws grow dumb;
   Since none can plead where all may Judges bee.

8. Prais'd was this King for war, the Laws broad shield;
   And for acknowledg'd Laws, the art of Peace;
   Happy in all which Heav'n to Kings does yeild,
   But a successor when his cares shall cease.

9. For no male Pledg, to give a lasting name,
   Sprung from his bed, yet Heaven to him allow'd
   One of the gentler sex, whose Story Fame
   Has made my Song, to make the *Lombards* proud.

10. Recorded *Rhodalind*! whose high renown
    Who miss in Books, not luckily have read;
    Or vex'd by living beauties of their own
    Have shunn'd the wise Records of Lovers dead.

11. Her Fathers prosp'rous Palace was the Sphear
    Where she to all with Heav'nly order mov'd;
    Made rigid vertue so benigne appear
    That 'twas without Religion's help belov'd.

12. Her looks like Empire shew'd, great above pride;
    Since pride ill counterfeits excessive height;
    But Nature publish'd what she fain would hide;
    Who for her deeds, not beauty, lov'd the light.

13. To make her lowly mindes appearance less,
    She us'd some outward greatness for disguise;

6: 3 little '73: lesser '51a–b   9: 1 lasting '51a cor, '51b Errata, '73: lusty '51a u,
51b

Esteem'd as pride the Cloyst'ral lowliness,
And thought them proud who even the proud despise.

14. Her Father (in the winter of his age)
Was like that stormy season froward grown;
Whom so her youthful presence did asswage,
That he her sweetness tasted as his own.

15. The pow'r that with his stooping age declin'd,
In her transplanted, by remove increas'd;
Which doubly back in homage she resign'd;
Til pow'rs decay, the Thrones worst sickness, ceas'd.

16. Oppressors big with pride, when she appear'd
Blush'd, and beleev'd their greatness counterfeit;
The lowly thought they them in vain had fear'd;
Found vertue harmless, and nought else so great.

17. Her minde (scarce to her feeble sex a kinn)
Did as her birth, her right to Empire show;
Seem'd careless outward when imploy'd within;
Her speech, like lovers watch'd, was kind and low.

18. She shew'd that her soft sex containes strong mindes,
Such as evap'rates through the courser Male,
As through course stone Elixer passage findes,
Which scarce through finer Christal can exhale.

19. Her beauty (not her own but Nature's pride)
Should I describe; from ev'ry Lovers eye
All Beauties this original must hide,
Or like scorn'd Copies be themselves laid by;

20. Be by their Poets shunn'd, whom beauty feeds;
Who beauty like hyr'd witnesses protect,
Officiously averring more then needs,
And make us so the needful truth suspect.

21. And since fond Lovers (who disciples bee
To Poets) think in their own loves they find
More beauty then yet Time did ever see,
Time's Curtain I will draw o're *Rhodalind*;

14: 3 youthful '73: springs fresh '51a–b   17: 1 a] of '51b   19: 2 eye
'51a MS, '51b, '73: ey '51a

22. Least shewing her, each see how much he errs,
    Doubt since their own have less, that they have none;
    Beleeve their Poets perjur'd Flatterers,
    And then all Modern Maids would be undone.

23. In pity thus, her beauty's just renown
    I wave for publique Peace, and will declare
    To whom the King design'd her with his Crown;
    Which is his last and most unquiet care.

24. If in allayance he does greatnesse prise,
    His Minde grown weary, need not travail farre;
    If greatnesse be compos'd of Victories,
    He has at home many that Victors are.

25. Many whom blest successe did often grace
    In Fields where they have seeds of Empire sown;
    And hope to make, since born of princely race,
    Even her (the harvest of those toyls) their own.

26. And of those Victors Two are chiefly fam'd,
    To whom the rest their proudest hopes resigne;
    Though young, were in their Fathers batails nam'd,
    And both are of the *Lombards* Royall Line.

27. *Oswald* the great, and greater *Gondibert*!
    Both from successfull conqu'ring Fathers sprung;
    Whom both examples made of Warr's high art,
    And farr out-wrought their patterns being young.

28. Yet for full fame (as Time Fame's Judg reports)
    Much to Duke *Gondibert* Prince *Oswald* yields;
    Was lesse in mighty mysteries of Courts,
    In peacefull Cities, and in fighting Fields.

29. In Court Prince *Oswald* costly was and gay,
    Finer then near vain Kings their Fav'rites are;
    Outshin'd bright Fav'rites on their Nuptiall day;
    Yet were his Eyes dark with ambitious care.

30. Duke *Gondibert* was still more gravely clad,
    But yet his looks familiar were and clear;

28: 1 Time *'51a cor*, *'51b* Errata: *Trine '51a u, '51b, '73*

As if with ill to others never sad,
Nor tow'rds himself could others practise fear.

31. The Prince, could Porpoise-like in Tempests play,
And in Court storms on shipwrack'd Greatnes feed;
Not frighted with their fate when cast away,
But to their glorious hazards durst succeed.

32. The Duke would lasting calmes to Courts assure,
As pleasant Gardens we defend from windes;
For he who bus'nesse would from Storms procure,
Soon his affairs above his mannage findes.

33. *Oswald* in Throngs the abject people sought
With humble looks; who still too late will know
They are Ambitions Quarry, and soon caught
When the aspiring Eagle stoops so low.

34. The Duke did these by stedy Vertue gain;
Which they in action more then precept tast;
Deeds shew the Good, and those who goodnesse feign
By such even through their vizards are out-fac't.

35. *Oswald* in warr was worthily renown'd;
Though gay in Courts, coursly in Camps could live;
Judg'd danger soon, and first was in it found;
Could toyl to gain what he with ease did give.

36. Yet toyls and dangers through ambition lov'd;
Which does in warr the name of Vertue own;
But quits that name when from the warr remov'd,
As Rivers theirs when from their Channels gon.

37. The Duke (as restless as his fame in warre)
With martial toyl could *Oswald* weary make;
And calmly do what he with rage did dare,
And give so much as he might deign to take.

38. Him as their Founder Cities did adore;
The Court he knew to steer in storms of State;
In Fields a Battle lost he could restore,
And after force the Victors to their Fate.

38: 3 Fields] Field '51b

39. In Camps now chiefly liv'd, where he did aime
    At graver glory then Ambition breeds;
    Designes that yet this story must not name,
    Which with our *Lombard* Authors pace proceeds.

40. The King adopts this Duke in secret thought
    To wed the Nations wealth, his onely child,
    Whom *Oswald* as reward of merit sought,
    With Hope, Ambition's common Baite, beguild.

41. This as his souls chief secret was unknowne,
    Least *Oswald* that his proudest Army led
    Should force possession ere his hopes were gone,
    Who could not rest but in the royal bed.

42. The Duke discern'd not that the King design'd
    To chuse him Heir of all his victories;
    Nor guess'd that for his love fair *Rhodalind*
    Made sleep of late a stranger to her Eies.

43. Yet sadly it is sung that she in shades
    Mildly as mourning Doves love's sorrows felt;
    Whilst in her secret tears her freshness fades
    As Roses silently in Lymbecks melt.

44. But who could know her love, whose jealous shame
    Deny'd her Eyes the knowledge of her glass;
    Who blushing thought Nature her self too blame
    By whom Men guess of Maids more then the face.

45. Yet judge not that this Duke (though from his sight
    With Maids first fears she did her passion hide)
    Did need love's flame for his directing light,
    But rather wants Ambition for his Guide.

46. Love's fire he carry'd, but no more in view
    Then vital heat which kept his heart still warm;
    This Maids in *Oswald* as love's Beacon knew;
    The publick flame to bid them flye from harm.

47. Yet since this Duke could love, we may admire
    Why love ne'r rais'd his thoughts to *Rhodalind*;

43: 1 sung *'51a MS*, *'51b*, *'73*: song *'51a*

But those forget that earthly flames aspire,
Whilst Heav'nly beames, which purer are, descend.

48. As yet to none could he peculiar prove,
But like an universal Influence
(For such and so sufficient was his love)
To all the Sex he did his heart dispence.

49. But *Oswald* never knew love's ancient Laws,
The awe that Beauty does in lovers breed,
Those short breath'd fears and paleness it does cause
When in a doubtful Brow their doom they read.

50. Not *Rhodalind* (whom then all Men as one
Did celebrate, as with confed'rate Eies)
Could he affect but shining in her Throne;
Blindly a Throne did more then beauty prise.

51. He by his Sister did his hopes prefer;
A beautious pleader who victorious was
O're *Rhodalind*, and could subdue her Ear
In all requests but this unpleasant cause.

52. *Gartha*, whose bolder beauty was in strength
And fulness plac'd, but such as all must like;
Her spreading stature talness was, not length,
And whilst sharp beauties peirce, hers seem'd to strike.

53. Such goodly presence ancient Poets grace,
Whose songs the worlds first manliness declare;
To Princes Beds teach carefulness of Race;
Which now store Courts, that us'd to store the warre.

54. Such was the Palace of her Minde, a Prince
Who proudly there, and still unquiet lives;
And sleep (domestick ev'ry where) from thence,
To make Ambition room, unwisely drives.

55. Of manly force was this her watchful mind,
And fit in Empire to direct and sway;
If she the temper had of *Rhodalind*,
Who knew that Gold is currant with allay.

56. As Kings (oft slaves to others hopes and skill)
    Are urg'd to war to load their slaves with spoyles,
    So *Oswald* was push'd up Ambition's hill,
    And so some urg'd the Duke to martial toyles.

57. And these who for their own great cause so high
    Would lift their Lords Two prosp'rous Armies are,
    Return'd from far to fruitful *Lombardy*,
    And paid with rest, the best reward of warre.

58. The old neer *Brescia* lay, scarce warm'd with Tents;
    For though from danger safe, yet Armies then
    Their posture kept 'gainst warring Elements,
    And hardness learn'd against more warring Men.

59. Neer *Bergamo* encamp'd the younger were,
    Whom to the Franks distress the Duke had led;
    The other *Oswald's* lucky Ensigns bear,
    Which lately stood when proud *Ovenna* fled.

60. These that attend Duke *Gondibert's* renown
    Were Youth whom from his Fathers Campe he chose,
    And them betimes transplanted to his own;
    Where each the Planters care and judgment shows.

61. All hardy Youth, from valiant Fathers sprung;
    Whom perfect honor he so highly taught,
    That th'Aged fetch'd examples from the young,
    And hid the vain experience which they brought.

62. They danger met diverted less with fears
    Then now the dead would be if here again,
    After they know the price brave dying bears;
    And by their sinnless rest finde life was vain.

63. Temp'rate in what does needy life preserve,
    As those whose Bodies wait upon their Mindes;
    Chaste as those Mindes which not their Bodies serve;
    Ready as Pilots wak'd with sodain Windes.

64. Speechless in diligence, as if they were
    Nightly to closse surprise and Ambush bred;

57: 2 Armies are, *'51a MS*, *'73*: Armies; are *'51a*: Armies, are *'51b*

Their wounds yet smarting mercifull they are,
And soon from victory to pity led.

65. When a great Captive they in fight had ta'ne,
(Whom in a Filiall duty some fair Maid
Visits, and would by tears his Freedom gain)
How soon his Victors were her Captives made?

66. For though the Duke taught rigid Discipline,
He let them beauty thus at distance know;
As Priests discover some more Sacred Shrine,
Which none must touch, yet all may to it bow.

67. When thus as Sutors mourning Virgins passe
Through their clean Camp, themselves in form they draw,
That they with Martiall reverence may grace
Beauty, the Stranger, which they seldome saw,

68. They vayl'd their Ensignes as it by did move,
Whilst inward (as from Native Conscience) all
Worship'd the Poets Darling Godhead, Love,
Which grave Philosophers did Nature call.

69. Nor there could Maids of Captive Syres dispaire,
But made all Captives by their beauty free;
Beauty and Valor native Jewels are,
And as each others only price agree.

70. Such was the Duke's young Camp by *Bergamo*,
But these near *Brescia* whom fierce *Oswald* led,
Their Science to his famous Father owe,
And have his Son (though now their Leader) bred.

71. This rev'rend Army was for age renown'd;
Which long through frequent dangers follow'd Time;
Their many Trophies gain'd with many'a wound,
And Fame's last Hill, did with first vigour climbe.

72. But here the learned *Lombard* whom I trace
My forward Pen by slower Method stays;
Least I should them (less heeding time and place
Then common Poets) out of season praise.

66: 3 more Sacred '73: especiall '51a–b   70: 1 by] near '51b

73. Think onely then (couldst thou both Camps discern)
     That these would seem grave Authors of the warre,
     Met civilly to teach who e're will learn,
     And those their young and civil Students are.

74. But painful vertue of the war ne'r pays
     It self with consciousness of being good,
     Though Cloyster vertue may beleeve even praise
     A sallary which there should be withstood.

75. For many here (whose vertue's active heat
     Concurs not with cold vertue which does dwell
     In lasie Cells) are vertuous to be great,
     And as in pains so would in pow'r excell.

76. And *Oswald's* Faction urg'd him to aspire
     That by his height they higher might ascend;
     The Dukes to glorious Thrones access desire,
     But at more awful distance did attend.

77. The royal *Rhodalind* is now the Prize
     By which these Camps would make their merit known;
     And think their Gen'rals but their Deputies
     Who must for them by Proxy wed the Crown.

78. From forreign Fields (with toyling conquest tyr'd,
     And groaning under spoiles) came home to rest;
     But now they are with emulation fyr'd,
     And for that pow'r they should obey, contest.

79. Ah how perverse and froward is Mankinde!
     Faction in Courts does us to rage excite;
     The Rich in Cities we litigious finde,
     And in the Field th'Ambitious make us fight:

80. And fatally (as if even soules were made
     Of warring Elements as Bodies are)
     Our Reason our Religion does invade,
     Till from the Schools to Camps it carry warre.

Canto the Second

The ARGUMENT

The hunting which did yearly celebrate
The LOMBARDS *glory and the* VANDALES *Fate.*
The Hunters prais'd; how true to love they are,
How calm in Peace, and Tempest-like in warre.
The Stagg is by the num'rous Chace subdu'd,
And strait his Hunters are as hard pursu'd.

1. Small are the seeds Fate does unheeded sow
   Of slight beginnings to important ends;
   Whilst wonder (which does best our rev'rence show
   To Heav'n) all Reason's sight in gazing spends.

2. For from a Daies brief pleasure did proceed
   (A day grown black in *Lombard* Histories)
   Such lasting griefs as thou shalt weep to read,
   Though even thine own sad love had drain'd thine Eies.

3. In a fair Forrest neer *Verona's* Plain,
   Fresh as if Nature's Youth chose there a shade,
   The Duke with many Lovers in his Train,
   (Loyal, and young) a solemn hunting made.

4. Much was his Train enlarg'd by their resort
   Who much his Grandsire lov'd, and hither came
   To celebrate this Day with annual sport,
   On which by battel here he earn'd his Fame.

5. And many of these noble Hunters bore
   Command amongst the Youth at *Bergamo*;
   Whose Fathers gather'd here the wreaths they wore,
   When in this Forrest they interr'd the Foe.

6. Count *Hurgonil*, a Youth of high descent,
   Was lifted here, and in the story great;
   He follow'd Honor when tow'rd's Death it went;
   Fierce in a charge but temp'rate in retreat.

5: 3 wreaths] wreath '*51b*

7. His wondrous beauty which the world approv'd
   He blushing hid, and now no more would own
   (Since he the Duke's unequal'd Sister lov'd)
   Then an old wreath when newly overthrown.

8. And she, *Orna* the shy! Did seem in life
   So bashful too to have her beauty shown,
   As I may doubt her shade with Fame at strife,
   That in these vicious times would make it known.

9. Not less in publick voice was *Arnold* here;
   He that on *Tuscan* Tombs his Trophys rais'd;
   And now love's pow'r so willingly did beare,
   That even his arbitrary raign he prais'd.

10. *Laura*, the Duke's fair Niece inthrall'd his heart;
    Who was in Court the publick morning Glass
    Where those who would reduce Nature to art,
    Practis'd by dress the conquests of the Face.

11. And here was *Hugo* whom Duke *Gondibert*
    For stout and stedfast kindness did approve;
    Of stature small but was all over heart,
    And though unhappy all that heart was love.

12. In gentle sonnets he for *Laura* pin'd;
    Soft as the murmures of a weeping spring;
    Which ruthless she did as those murmures mind:
    So ere their death sick Swans unheeded sing.

13. Yet whilst she *Arnold* favour'd, he so griev'd
    As loyall Subjects quietly bemone
    Their Yoke, but raise no warr to be reliev'd,
    Nor through the envy'd Fav'rite wound the Throne.

14. Young *Goltho* next these Rivals we may name,
    Whose manhood dawn'd early as Sommer light;
    As sure and soon did his fair day proclame,
    And was no less the joy of publick sight.

15. If Love's just pow'r he did not early see,
    Some small excuse we may his error give;
    Since few (though learn'd) know yet blest Love to be
    That secret vitall heat by which we live:

16. But such it is; and though we may be thought
    To have in Childhood life, ere Love we know,
    Yet life is useless till by reason taught,
    And Love and Reason up together grow.

17. Nor more, the Old shew they out-live their Love,
    If when their Love's decay'd, some signes they give
    Of life, because we see them pain'd and move,
    Then Snakes, long cut, by torment shew they live.

18. If we call living, Life, when Love is gone,
    We then to Souls (Gods coyne) vain rev'rence pay;
    Since Reason (which is Love, and his best knowne
    And currant Image) Age has worne away.

19. And I that Love and Reason thus unite,
    May, if I old Philosophers controule,
    Confirme the new by some new Poets light;
    Who finding Love, thinks he has found the Soule.

20. From *Goltho*, to whom Love yet tastlesse seem'd,
    We to ripe *Tybalt* are by order led;
    Tybalt, who Love and Valor both esteem'd,
    And he alike from eithers wounds had bled.

21. Publique his valor was, but not his love,
    One fill'd the world, the other he contain'd;
    Yet quietly alike in both did move,
    Of that ne'r boasted, nor of this complain'd.

22. With these (whose speciall names Verse shall preserve)
    Many to this recorded hunting came;
    Whose worth authentick mention did deserve,
    But from Time's deluge few are sav'd by Fame.

23. Now like a Giant Lover rose the Sunne
    From th'Ocean Queen, fine in his fires and great;
    Seem'd all the Morne for shew, for strength at Noone;
    As if last Night she had not quench'd his heate!

24. And the Sunn's Servants who his rising waite,
    His Pensioners (for so all Lovers are,
    And all maintain'd by him at a high rate
    With daily fire) now for the Chace prepare.

25. All were like Hunters clad in cheerfull green,
    Young Natures Livery, and each at strife
    Who most adorn'd in favours should be seen,
    Wrought kindly by the Lady of his life.

26. These Martiall Favours on their Wasts they weare,
    On which (for now they Conquest celebrate)
    In an imbroader'd History appeare
    Like life, the vanquish'd in their feares and fate.

27. And on these Belts (wrought with their Ladys care)
    Hung Semyters of *Akons* trusty steele;
    Goodly to see, and he who durst compare
    Those Ladies Eies, might soon their temper feele.

28. Cheer'd as the Woods (where new wak'd Quires they meet)
    Are all; and now dispose their choice Relays
    Of Horse and Hounds, each like each other fleet;
    Which best when with themselvs compar'd we prais;

29. To them old Forrest Spys, the Harborers
    With hast approach, wet as still weeping Night,
    Or Deer that mourn their growth of head with tears,
    When the defenceless weight does hinder flight.

30. And Doggs, such whose cold secrecy was ment
    By Nature for surprise, on these attend;
    Wise temp'rate Lime-Hounds that proclaim no scent;
    Nor harb'ring will their Mouths in boasting spend.

31. Yet vanlier farr then Traytors boast their prise
    (On which their vehemence vast rates does lay,
    Since in that worth their treasons credit lies)
    These Harb'rers praise that which they now betray.

32. Boast they have lodg'd a Stagg, that all the Race
    Out-runs of *Croton* Horse, or *Regian* Hounds;
    A Stagg made long since Royall in the Chace,
    If Kings can honor give by giving wounds.

33. For *Aribert* had pierc't him at a Bay,
    Yet scap'd he by the vigour of his Head;
    And many a sommer since has wonne the day,
    And often left his *Regian* Foll'wers dead.

    32: 3 long *Ed*: long, '51a–b, '73

34. His spacious Beame (that even the Rights out grew)
    From *Antlar* to his *Troch* had all allow'd
    By which his age the aged Woodmen knew;
    Who more then he were of that beauty prowd.

35. Now each Relay a sev'ral Station findes,
    Ere the triumphant Train the Copps surrounds;
    Relays of Horse, long breath'd as winter windes,
    And their deep Cannon Mouth'd experienc'd Hounds.

36. The Huntsmen (Busily concern'd in showe
    As if the world were by this Beast undone,
    And they against him hir'd as Nature's Foe)
    In haste uncouple, and their Hounds outrunne.

37. Now winde they a Recheat, the rows'd Dear's knell;
    And through the Forrest all the Beasts are aw'd;
    Alarm'd by Ecchoe, Nature's Sentinel,
    Which shews that Murdrous Man is come abroad.

38. Tirranique Man! Thy subjects Enemy!
    And more through wantoness then need or hate;
    From whom the winged to their Coverts flie;
    And to their Dennes even those that lay in waite.

39. So this (the most succesful of his kinde,
    Whose Foreheads force oft his Opposers prest,
    Whose swiftness left Persuers shafts behinde)
    Is now of all the Forrest most distrest!

40. The Heard deny him shelter, as if taught
    To know their safety is to yield him lost;
    Which shews they want not the results of thought,
    But speech, by which we ours for reason boast.

41. We blush to see our politicks in Beasts,
    Who Many sav'd by this one Sacrifice;
    And since through blood they follow interests,
    Like us when cruel should be counted wise.

42. His Rivals that his fury us'd to fear
    For his lov'd Female, now his faintness Shunne;
    But were his season hot, and she but neer,
    (O mighty Love!) his Hunters were undone.

43. From thence, well blown, he comes to the Relay;
    Where Man's fam'd reason proves but Cowardise,
    And only serves him meanly to betray;
    Even for the flying, Man, in ambush lies.

44. But now, as his last remedy to live,
    (For ev'ry shift for life kinde Nature makes,
    Since life the utmost is which she can give)
    Coole *Adice* from the swoln Banke he takes.

45. But this fresh Bath the Doggs will make him leave;
    Whom he sure nos'd as fasting Tygers found;
    Their scent no North-east winde could e're deceave
    Which dries the ayre, nor Flocks that foyle the Ground.

46. Swift here the Flyers and Persuers seeme;
    The frighted Fish swim from their *Adice*,
    The Doggs persue the Deer, he the fleet streme,
    And that hasts too to th'*Adriatic* Sea.

47. Refresh'd thus in this fleeting Element,
    He up the stedfast Shore did boldly rise;
    And soon escap'd their view, but not their scent;
    That faithful Guide which even conducts their Eies.

48. This frail relief was like short gales of breath
    Which oft at Sea a long dead calme prepare;
    Or like our Curtains drawn at point of death,
    When all our Lungs are spent, to give us ayre.

49. For on the Shore the Hunters him attend;
    And whilst the Chace grew warm as is the day
    (Which now from the hot *Zenith* does descend)
    He is imbos'd, and weary'd to a Bay.

50. The Jewel, Life, he must surrender here;
    Which the world's Mistris, Nature, does not give,
    But like drop'd Favours suffers us to weare,
    Such as by which pleas'd Lovers think they live.

51. Yet life he so esteems, that he allows
    It all defence his force and rage can make;

46: 4 too to th'*Adriatic* '73: swiftly to the *Adrian* '51a–b

And to the eager Dogs such fury shows
As their last blood some unreveng'd forsake.

52. But now the Monarch Murderer comes in,
Destructive Man! whom Nature would not arme,
As when in madness mischief is foreseen
We leave it weaponless for fear of harme.

53. For she defencelesse made him that he might
Lesse readily offend; but Art armes all,
From single strife makes us in Numbers fight;
And by such art this Royall Stagg did fall.

54. Now weeps till grief does even his Murd'rers pierce;
Grief which so nobly through his anger strove,
That it deserv'd the dignity of verse,
And had it words as humanly would move.

55. Thrice from the ground his vanquishd Head he rear'd,
And with last looks his Forrest walks did view;
Where Sixty Sommers he had rul'd the Heard,
And where sharp *Dittany* now vainly grew:

56. Whose hoary Leaves no more his wounds shall heale;
For with a Sigh (a blast of all his breath)
That viewlesse thing call'd Life, did from him steale;
And with their Bugle Hornes they winde his death.

57. Then with their annuall wanton sacrifice
(Taught by old Custome, whose decrees are vaine,
And we like hum'rous Antiquaries prise
Age though deform'd) they hastne to the Plaine.

58. Thence homeward bend as westward as the Sun;
Where *Gondibert's* Allys prowd Feasts prepare,
That day to honor which his Grandsire won;
Though Feasts the Eves to Fun'ralls often are.

59. One from the Forrest now approach'd their sight,
Who them did swiftly on the Spurr persue;
One there still resident as Day and Night,
And knowne as th'eldest Oke which in it grew.

51: 3 eager Dogs '73: *Regian* Race '51a–b

60. Who with his utmost breath, advancing cries
    (And such a vehemence no Art could feigne)
    Away, happy the Man that fastest flies;
    Flie famous Duke, flie with thy noble Traine!

61. The Duke reply'd, though with thy feares disguis'd,
    Thou do'st my Syres old Rangers Image beare,
    And for thy kindnesse shalt not be despis'd;
    Though Councels are but weak which come from feare.

62. Were Dangers here, great as thy love can shape;
    (And love with fear can danger multiplie)
    Yet when by flight, thou bidst us meanly scape,
    Bid Trees take wings, and rooted Forrests flie.

63. Then said the Ranger, you are bravely lost,
    (And like high anger his complexion rose)
    As little know I fear, as how to boast;
    But shall attend you through your many Foes.

64. See where in ambush mighty *Oswald* lay;
    And see, from yonder Lawne he moves apace,
    With Launces arm'd to intercept thy way,
    Now thy sure Steeds are weary'd with the Chace.

65. His purple Banners you may there behold,
    Which (proudly spred) the fatall Raven beare;
    And full five hundred I by Ranke have told,
    Who in their guilded Helmes his Colours weare.

66. The Duke this falling storme does now discern;
    Bids little *Hugo* fly! but 'tis to view
    The Foe, and timely their first count'nance learne,
    Whilst firme he in a square his Hunters drew.

67. And *Hugo* soone (light as his Coursers Heeles)
    Was in their Faces troublesome as winde;
    And like to it (so wingedly he wheeles)
    No one could catch, what all with trouble finde.

68. But ev'ry where the Leaders and the Led
    He temp'rately observ'd, with a slow sight;
    Judg'd by their looks how hopes and feares were fed,
    And by their order their successe in fight.

69. Their Number ('mounting to the Rangers guesse)
    In Three Divisions evenly was dispos'd;
    And that their Enemies might judg it lesse,
    It seem'd one Grosse with all the Spaces clos'd.

70. The Vann fierce *Oswald* led, where *Paradine*
    And Manly *Dargonet* (both of his blood)
    Outshin'd the Noone, and their Mindes stock within
    Promis'd to make that outward glory good.

71. The next, bold, but unlucky *Hubert* led;
    Brother to *Oswald*, and no lesse ally'd
    To the ambitions which his Soule did wed;
    Lowly without, but lin'd with Costly pride.

72. Most to himself his valor fatall was,
    Whose glorys oft to others dreadfull were;
    So Commets (though suppos'd Destruction's cause)
    But waste themselves to make their Gazers feare.

73. And though his valor seldom did succeed,
    His speech was such as could in Storms perswade;
    Sweet as the Hopes on which starv'd Lovers feed,
    Breath'd in the whispers of a yeilding Mayde.

74. The Bloody *Borgio* did conduct the Rere;
    Whom sullen *Vasco* heedfully attends;
    To all but to themselves they cruel were,
    And to themselves chiefly by mischief Friends.

75. Warr, the worlds Art, Nature to them became;
    In Camps begot, born, and in anger bred;
    The living vex'd till Death, and then their Fame;
    Because even Fame some life is to the Dead.

76. Cities (wise States-men's Folds for civil sheep)
    They sack'd, as painful Sheerers of the wise;
    For they like careful Wolves would lose their sleep,
    When others prosp'rous toyls might be their prise.

77. *Hugo* amongst these Troops spy'd many more
    Who had, as brave Destroyers, got renown;
    And many forward wounds in boast they wore;
    Which if not well reveng'd, had ne'r bin shown.

77: 4 ne'r bin '*51a MS*: ne'r been '*51b*, '*73*: neer bin '*51a*

78. Such the bold Leaders of these Launceers were,
    Which of the *Brescian Vet'rans* did consist;
    Whose practis'd age might charge of Armies beare,
    And claim some ranck in Fame's eternal List.

79. Back to his Duke the dext'rous *Hugo* flies;
    What he observ'd he cheerfully declares;
    With noble pride did what he lik'd despise;
    For wounds he threatned whilst he prais'd their skarrs.

80. Lord *Arnold* cry'd, vain is the Bugle Horn,
    Where Trumpets Men to Manly work invite!
    That distant summons seems to say in skorn,
    We Hunters may be hunted hard ere night.

81. Those Beasts are hunted hard that hard can fly,
    Reply'd alow'd the noble *Hurgonil*;
    But we not us'd to flight, know best to dy;
    And those who know to die, know how to kill.

82. Victors through number never gain'd applause;
    If they exceed our compt in Armes and Men,
    It is not just to think that ods, because
    One Lover equals any other Ten.

Canto the Third

The ARGUMENT

The Ambush is become an interview;
And the Surpriser proves to honor true;
For what had first, ere words his fury spent,
Been murder, now, is but brave killing ment.
A Duel form'd where Princes Seconds are,
And urg'd by Honor each to kill his share.

1. The Duke observ'd (whilst safe in his firm Square)
   Whether their front did change whom *Oswald* led;
   That thence he shifts of figure might prepare,
   Divide, or make more depth, or loosely spred.

1: 2 front '73: form '51a–b

2. Though in their posture closs, the Prince might guess
   The Duke's to his not much in number yield;
   And they were leading Youth who would possess
   This Ground in Graves, rather then quit the Field.

3. Thus (timely certain of a standing Foe)
   His form'd Divisions yet reveal'd no space
   Through haste to charge; but as they neerer grow,
   They more divide, and move with slower pace.

4. On these the Duke attends with watchful Eye;
   Shap'd all his Forces to their Triple strength;
   And that their Launces might pass harmless by,
   Widens his Ranks, and gave his Files more length.

5. At distance *Oswald* does him sharply view,
   Whom but in Fame he met till this sad hower;
   But his fair fame, Vertue's known Image, knew;
   For Vertue spreds the Owner more then pow'r.

6. In Fields far sever'd both had reap'd renown;
   And now his envie does to surfeit feed
   On what he wish'd his Eies had never known;
   For he begins to check his purpos'd deed.

7. And though Ambition did his rage renew;
   Yet much he griev'd (mov'd with the Youthful Train)
   That Plants which so much promis'd as they grew,
   Should in the Bud be ere performance slain.

8. With these remorseful thoughts, he a fair space
   Advanc'd alone, then did his Troops command
   To halt; the Duke th'example did embrace,
   And gives like order by his lifted hand.

9. Then when in easie reach of eithers voice
   Thus *Oswald* spake. I wish (brave *Gondibert*)
   Those wrongs which make thee now my angers choice,
   Like my last fate were hidden from my heart.

10. But since great Glory does allow small rest,
    And bids us jealously to honour wake,
    Why at alarms given hot even at my brest,
    Should I not arm, but think my Scouts mistake?

11. 'Tis lowd in Camps, in Cities, and in Court,
    (Where the important part of Mankind meets)
    That my adoption is thy Faction's sport,
    Scorn'd by hoarse Rymers in *Verona* Streets.

12. Who is renown'd enough but you or I
    (And think not when you visit Fame, she lesse
    Will welcome you for my known Companie)
    To hope for Empire at our Kings decease?

13. The Crowne he with his Daughter has design'd;
    His favour (which to me does frozen prove)
    Growes warme to you as th'eies of *Rhodalind*,
    And she gives sacred Empire with her love.

14. Whilst you usurp thus, and my claime deride,
    If you admire the veng'ance I intend,
    I more shall wonder where you got the pride
    To think me one you safely may offend.

15. Nor judg it strange I have this Ambush laid;
    Since you (my Rivall) wrong'd me by surprise;
    Whose darker vigilance my love betrai'd;
    And so your ill example made me wise.

16. But in the Schoole of glory we are taught,
    That greatness and success should measure deeds;
    Then not my great revenge nor your great fault,
    Can be accus'd when eithers act succeeds.

17. Opinions stamp does vertue currant make;
    But such small Money (though the Peoples Gold
    With which they trade) great Dealers skorne to take,
    And we are greater then one world can hold.

18. Now *Oswald* paws'd, as if he curious were
    Ere this his Foe (the People's Fav'rite) dy'd,
    To know him as with Eies, so with his Eare;
    And to his speech thus *Gondibert* reply'd:

19. Successfull Prince! since I was never taught
    To court a Threatning Foe, I will not pay

12: 3 my] mine '*51b*   19: 2 Threatning '*73*: Threating '*51a–b*

For all the Trophys you from war have brought
A single wreath, though all these woods were Bay!

20. Nor would I by a total silence yeild
My honor ta'ne, though I were Pris'ner made;
Least you should think we may be justly kill'd,
And sacred justice by mistake invade.

21. You might perceive (had not a distant warre
Hindred our Breasts the use of being knowne)
My small ambition hardly worth your care;
Unless by it you would correct your owne.

22. The King's objected love is but your dreame,
As false as that I strive for *Rhodalind*
As Valor's hyre; these sickly visions seeme
Which in Ambitions Feaver vex your minde.

23. Nor wonder if I vouch, that 'tis not brave
To seek war's hire, though war we still pursue;
Nor censure this a proud excuse, to save
These who no safety know, but to subdue.

24. Your misbelief my hirelesse valour scorns;
But your hir'd valour were your faith reclaim'd,
(For faith reclaim'd to highest vertue turns)
Will be of bravest sallary asham'd.

25. Onely with fame valor of old was hir'd;
And love was so suffic'd with its own taste,
That those intemp'rate seem'd, who more desir'd
For love's reward, then that it self should last.

26. If love, or lust of Empire breed your pain,
Take what my prudent hope hath still declin'd,
And my weak vertue never could sustain,
The Crown, which is the worst of *Rhodalind*.

27. 'Tis she who taught you to increase renown,
By sowing Honor's field with noble deeds;
Which yeilds no harvest when 'tis over-grown
With wilde Ambition, the most rank of weeds.

28. Go reconcile the windes faln out at Sea
    With these tame precepts, (*Oswald* did replie)
    But since thou dost bequeath thy hopes to me,
    Know Legacies are vain till Givers die.

29. And here his rage ascended to his Eies
    From his close Brest, which hid till then the flame;
    And like stirr'd fire in sparkles upward flies;
    Rage which the Duke thus practis'd to reclaim.

30. Though you design'd our ruine by surprise,
    Though much in useful Armes you us exceed,
    And in your number some advantage lies,
    Yet you may finde you such advantage need.

31. If I am vallew'd as th'impediment
    Which hinders your adoption to the Crown;
    Let your revenge onely on me be spent,
    And hazard not my Party, nor your own.

32. Ambition else would up to Godhead grow,
    When so profanely we our anger prise,
    That to appease it we the blood allow
    Of whole offencelesse Herds for sacrifice.

33. *Oswald* (who Honor's publick pattern was,
    Till vain ambition led his heart aside)
    More temp'rate grew in mannage of his cause,
    And thus to noble *Gondibert* reply'd.

34. I wish it were not needful to be great;
    That Heav'ns unenvy'd pow'r might Men so awe
    As we should need no Armies for defeat,
    Nor for protection be at charge of Law.

35. But more then Heav'ns, Men, Man's authoritie
    (Though envy'd) use, because more understood;
    For but for that Life's Utensils would be,
    In Markets, as in Camps the price of blood.

36. Since the Worlds safety we in greatness finde,
    And pow'r divided is from greatness gone,
    Save we the world, though to our selves unkinde,
    By both indang'ring to establish one.

        35: 3 For . . . that] For, but for that, '73

37. Not these, who kindle with my wrongs their rage,
    Nor those bold Youth who warmly you attend,
    Our distant Camps by action shall ingage;
    But we our own great cause will singly end.

38. Back to your noble Hunters strait retire,
    And I to those who would those Hunters chace;
    Let us perswade their fury to expire,
    And give obediently our anger place.

39. Like unconcern'd Spectators let them stand,
    And be by sacred vow to distance bound;
    Whilst their lov'd Leaders by our strict command,
    Only as witnesses, approach this ground.

40. Where with no more defensive Armes then was
    By Nature ment us, who ordain'd Men Friends,
    We will on foot determine our great cause;
    On which the *Lombards* doubtful peace depends.

41. The Duke at this did bow, and soon obay,
    Confess'd his honor he transcendent findes,
    Said he their persons might a meaner way
    With ods have aw'd, but this subdues their Mindes.

42. Now wing'd with Hope they to their Troops return,
    Oswald his old grave *Brescians* makes retire,
    Least if too neer, though like slow Match they burn,
    The Duke's rash Youth like Powder might take fire.

43. First with their noble Chiefs they treat aside,
    Plead it humanity to bleed alone,
    And tearm it needless cruelty and pride
    With others Sacrifice to grace their owne.

44. Then to their Troopes gave their resolv'd command
    Not to assist, through anger nor remorse;
    Who seem'd more willing patiently to stand,
    Because each side presum'd their Champion's force.

45. Now neer that ground ordain'd by them and Fate
    To be the last where one or both must tread,
    Their chosen Judges they appoint to waite;
    Who thither were like griev'd Spectators led.

39: 4 Only as '73: As patient '51a–b   41: 1 at this '73: full low '51a–b

46. These from the distant Troops far sever'd are;
    And neer their Chiefs divided Stations take;
    Who strait uncloath, and for such deeds prepare,
    By which strip'd Soules their fleshy Robes forsake.

47. But *Hubert* now advanc'd, and cry'd alow'd,
    I will not trust uncertain Destinie,
    Which may obscurely kill me in a Crowd,
    That here have pow'r in publick view to die.

48. *Oswald* my Brother is! If any dare
    Think *Gondibert's* great name more Kingly sounds,
    Let him alight, and he shall leave the care
    Of chusing Monarchs, to attend his wounds!

49. This *Hurgonill* receiv'd with greedy Ear,
    Told him his summons boldly did expresse,
    That he had little judgement whom to fear,
    And in the choice of Kings his skill was lesse.

50. With equall haste they then alight and met,
    Where both their Chiefs in preparation stood;
    Whilst *Paradine* and furious *Dargonet*
    Cry'd out, we are of *Oswald's* Princely blood.

51. Are there not yet two more so fond of fame,
    So true to *Gondibert*, or Love's commands;
    As to esteem it an unpleasant shame
    With idle Eies to look on busie hands?

52. Such haste makes Beauty when it Youth forsakes,
    And day from Travellers when it does set,
    As *Arnold* to proud *Paradine* now makes,
    And little *Hugo* to tall *Dargonet*.

53. The bloudy *Borgio*, who with anguish stay'd,
    And check'd his rage, till these of *Oswald's* Race,
    By wish'd example their brave Challenge made,
    Now like his curb'd Steed foaming, shifts his place.

54. And thus (with haste and choller hoarse) he spake;
    Who e're amongst you thinks we destin'd are
    To serve that King your Courtly Camp shall make,
    Falsly he loves, nor is his Lady faire!

55. This scarce could urge the temp'rate *Tybalt's* fire,
Who said, When Fate shall *Aribert* remove,
As ill then wilt thou judge who should aspire,
As who is fair, that art too rude to love.

56. But scarce had this reply reach'd *Borgio's* Eare,
When *Goltho* louder cri'd, what ere he be
Dares think her foul who hath a Lover here,
Though Love I never knew, shall now know me!

57. Grave *Tybalt*, who had laid an early'r claime
To this defiance, much distemper'd grows,
And *Goltho's* forward Youth would sharply blame,
But that old *Vasco* thus did interpose.

58. That Boy who makes such haste to meet his fate,
And fears he may (as if he knew it good)
Through others pride of danger come too late,
Shall read it strait ill written in his blood.

59. Let Empire fall, when we must Monarchs choose,
By what unpractis'd Childhood shall approve;
And in tame peace let us our Manhood loose,
When Boyes yet wet with milk discourse of Love.

60. As bashful Maids blush, as if justly blam'd,
When forc'd to suffer some indecent Tongue,
So *Goltho* blush'd (whom *Vasco* made asham'd)
As if he could offend by being young.

61. But instantly offended bashfulnesse
Does to a brave and beauteous anger turn,
Which he in younger flames did so expresse,
That scarce old *Vasco's* Embers seem'd to burn.

62. The Princes knew in this new kindled rage,
Opinion might (which like unlucky winde
Sate right to make it spread) their Troops ingage;
And therefore *Oswald* thus proclaim'd his minde.

63. Seem we already dead, that to our words
(As to the last requests men dying make)
Your love but Mourners short respect affords,
And ere interr'd you our commands forsake?

62: 2 which] have '73

64. We chose you Judges of your needfull strife,
    Such whom the world (grown faithlesse) might esteem
    As weighty witnesses of parting life,
    But you are those we dying must condemn.

65. Are we become such worthlesse sacrifice,
    As cannot to the *Lombards* Heav'n atone,
    Unlesse your added blood make up the price,
    As if you thought it worthier then our own?

66. Our fame which should survive, before us dy!
    And let (since in our presence disobay'd)
    Renown of pow'r, like that of beauty fly
    From knowledge, rather then be known decay'd!

67. This when with rev'rence heard, it would have made
    Old Armies melt, to mark at what a rate
    They spent their Hearts and Eies, kindly afraid
    To be omitted in their Gen'ral's fate.

68. *Hubert* (whose Princely qualitie more frees
    Him then the rest, from all command, unless
    He finde it such as with his will agrees)
    Did nobly thus his firm resolve express.

69. All greatness bred in blood be now abas'd!
    Instinct, the inward Image, which is wrought
    And given with Life, be like thaw'd wax defac'd!
    Though that bred better honor then is taught;

70. And may impressions of the common ill
    Which from street Parents the most low derives,
    Blot all my minds fair book if I stand still
    Whilst *Oswald* singly for the Publick strives:

71. A Brothers love all that obedience stays,
    Which *Oswald* else might as my Leader claime;
    Whom as my love, my honor disobays,
    And bids me serve our greater Leader, Fame.

72. With gentle looks *Oswald* to *Hubert* bowes,
    And said, I then must yeild that *Hubert* shall

64: 1 Your '73: our '51a-b   66: 1 survive, . . . us '73: survive . . . us, '51a-b

(Since from the same bright Sun our lustre growes)
Rise with my Morne, and with my Ev'ning fall!

73. Bold *Paradine* and *Dargonet* reviv'd
Their suit, and cry'd, we are *Astolpho's* sons!
Who from your highest spring his blood deriv'd,
Though now it down in lower Channels runs.

74. Such lucky seasons to attain renown,
We must not lose, who are to you ally'd;
Others usurp, who would your dangers own,
And what our duty is, in them is pride.

75. Then as his last Decree thus *Oswald* spake;
You that vouchsafe to glory in my blood,
Shall share my doom, which for your merits sake,
Fate, were it bad, would alter into good.

76. If any others disobedient rage,
Shall with uncivill love intrude his aid,
And by degrees our distant Troops ingage,
Be it his Curse still to be disobay'd!

77. War's Orders may he by the slow convay
To such as only shall dispute them long;
An ill peace make, when none will him obay,
And be for that, when old, judg'd by the yong.

78. This said, he calmly bid the Duke provide
Such of his bloud, as with those chosen Three
(Whilst their adoption they on foot decide)
May in brave life or death fit Partners bee.

79. Though here (reply'd the Duke) I finde not now
Such as my blood with their alliance grace,
Yet Three I see, to whom your stock may bow,
If Love may be esteem'd of heav'nly Race.

80. And much to me these are by love ally'd;
Then *Hugo*, *Arnold*, and the Count drew neere;
Count *Hurgonill* woo'd *Orna* for his Bride,
The other Two in *Laura* Rivals were.

81. But *Tybalt* cry'd (as swiftly as his voice
 Approach'd the Duke) forgive me mighty Chief,
 If justly I envy thy noble choice,
 And disobey thee in wrong'd Love's relief.

82. If rev'renc'd love be sacred Myst'ry deem'd,
 And mysteries when hid to value grow,
 Why am I lesse for hidden love esteem'd?
 To unknown Godhead, wise Religions bow

83. A Maid of thy high linage much I love,
 And hide her name till I can merit boast,
 But shall I here (where I may worth improve)
 For prising her above my self, be lost?

84. The Duke's firm bosom kindly seem'd to melt
 At *Tybalt's* grief, that he omitted was;
 Who lately had Love's secret conquest felt,
 And hop'd for publick triumph in this cause.

85. Then he decreed, *Hugo* (though chose before
 To share in this great work) should equally
 With *Tybalt* be expos'd to Fortune's pow'r,
 And by drawn Lots their wish'd election try.

86. *Hugo* his dreaded Lord with chearfull awe
 Us'd to obey, and with implicit love;
 But now he must for certain honor draw
 Uncertain Lots, seems heavily to move.

87. And here they trembling reach'd at Honor so,
 As if they gath'ring Flow'rs a Snake discern'd;
 Yet fear'd Love only whose rewards then grow
 To Lovers sweetest, when with danger earn'd:

88. From this brave fear, lest they should danger scape,
 Was little *Hugo* eas'd, and when he drew
 The Champion's lot, his joy inlarg'd his shape,
 And with his lifted minde he taller grew.

89. But *Tybalt* stoop'd beneath his sorrows waight;
 Goltho and him kindly the Duke imbrac'd;

81: 1 as swiftly '73: and swiftly '51a–b   82: 4 Religions] Religious '73

Then to their station sent; and *Oswald* straight
His fo injoyn'd, and with like kindnesse grac'd.

90. When cruel *Borgio* does from *Tybalt* part,
Vasco from *Goltho*, many a look they cast
Backward in sullen message from the heart,
And through their eies their threat'ning anger wast.

Canto the Fourth

The ARGUMENT

The Duel where all rules of artful strife,
To rescue or indanger Darling-life,
Are by reserves of strength and courage shown;
For killing was long since a Science grown.
Th'event by which the Troops ingaged are,
As privat rage too often turns to warre.

1. By what bold passion am I rudely led,
Like Fame's too curious and officious Spie,
Where I these Rolls in her dark Closet read,
Where Worthies wrapp'd in Time's disguises lie?

2. Why should we now their shady Curtains draw,
Who by a wise retirement hence are freed,
And gon to Lands exempt from Nature's Law,
Where love no more can mourn, nor valor bleed?

3. Why to this stormy world from their long rest,
Are these recall'd to be again displeas'd,
Where during Nature's reign we are opprest,
Till we by Death's high priviledg are eas'd?

4. Is it to boast that Verse has Chymick pow're,
And that its rage (which is productive heat)
Can these revive, as Chymists raise a Flowre,
Whose scatter'd parts their Glasse presents compleat?

5. Though in these Worthies gon, valor and love
Did chastly as in sacred Temples meet,
Such reviv'd Patterns us no more improve,
Then Flowres so rais'd by Chymists make us sweet.

6. Yet when the souls disease we desp'rate finde,
   Poets the old renown'd Physitians are,
   Who for the sickly habits of the minde,
   Examples as the ancient cure prepare.

7. And bravely then Physitians honor gain,
   When to the world diseases curelesse seem,
   And they (in Science valiant) ne'r refrain
   Art's war with Nature, till they life redeem.

8. But Poets their accustom'd task have long
   Forborn, (who for Examples did disperse
   The *Heroes* vertues in Heroick Song)
   And now think vertue sick, past cure of verse.

9. Yet to this desp'rate cure I will proceed,
   Such patterns shew as shall not fail to move;
   Shall teach the valiant patience when they bleed,
   And haplesse Lovers constancy in love.

10. Now Honor's chance, the Duke with *Oswald* takes,
    The Count his great Stake, Life, to *Hubert* sets;
    Whilst his to *Paradin's*, Lord *Arnold* stakes,
    And little *Hugo* throwes at *Dargonets*.

11. These Four on equall ground those Four oppose;
    Who wants in strength, supplies it with his skill;
    So valiant that they make no haste to close;
    They not apace, but handsomly would kill.

12. And as they more each others courage found,
    Each did their force more civilly expresse,
    To make so manly and so fair a wound,
    As loyall Ladies might be proud to dresse.

13. But vain, though wond'rous, seems the short event
    Of what with pomp and Noise we long prepare:
    One hour of battail oft that force hath spent,
    Which Kings whole lives have gather'd for a war.

14. As Rivers to their ruine hasty be,
    So life (still earnest, low'd, and swift) runs post
    To the vaste Gulf of Death, as they to Sea,
    And vainly travailes to be quickly lost.

15. And now the Fates (who punctually take care
    We not escape their sentence at our birth)
    Writ *Arnold* down where those inroled are
    Who must in Youth abruptly leave the Earth.

16. Him *Paradine* into the Brow had pierc't;
    From whence his blood so overflow'd his Eies,
    He grew to blinde to watch and guard his brest,
    Where wounded twice, to Death's cold Court he flies.

17. And Love (by which Life's name does valew finde,
    As Altars even subsist by ornament)
    Is now as to the Owner quite resign'd,
    And in a sigh to his dear *Laura* sent.

18. Yet Fates so civil were in cruelty
    As not to yeild that he who conquer'd all
    The *Tuscan* Vale, should unattended dy,
    They therefore doom that *Dargonet* must fall.

19. Whom little *Hugo* dext'rously did vex
    With many wounds in unexpected place,
    Which yet not kill, but killingly perplex;
    Because he held their number a disgrace.

20. For *Dargonet* in force did much exceed
    The most of Men, in valor equal'd all;
    And was asham'd thus diversly to bleed,
    As if he stood where showres of Arrows fall.

21. At once he ventures his remaining strength
    To *Hugo's* nimble skill, who did desire
    To draw this little war out into length,
    By motions quick as Heav'n's fantastick fire!

22. This fury now is grown too high to last
    In *Dargonet*; who does disorder all
    The strengths of temp'rance by unruly haste,
    Then down at *Hugo's* feet does breathless fall.

23. When with his own Storm sunk, his Foe did spie
    Lord *Arnold* dead, and *Paradine* prepare
    To help Prince *Oswald* to that victory,
    Of which the Duke had yet an equal share

16: 4 flies '73: hies '51a–b   22: 4 at . . . feet '73: to Death's low Calm '51a–b

24. Vain Conqueror (said *Hugo* then) returne!
    Instead of Laurel which the Victor weares,
    Go gather *Cypress* for thy Brother's Urne,
    And learn of me to water it with Tears.

25. Thy Brother lost his life attempting mine;
    Which cannot for Lord *Arnold's* loss suffice:
    I must revenge (unlucky *Paradine*)
    The blood his death will draw from *Laura's* Eies.

26. We Rivals were in *Laura*, but though she
    My griefs derided, his with sighs approv'd;
    Yet I (in Love's exact integritie)
    Must take thy life for killing him She lov'd.

27. These quick alike, and artfully as fierce,
    At one sad instant give and take that wound,
    Which does through both their vital Closets pierce;
    Where Life's smal Lord does warmly sit enthron'd.

28. And then they fell, and now neer upper Heaven,
    Heav'ns better part of them is hov'ring still,
    To watch what end is to their Princes given,
    And to brave *Hubert*, and to *Hurgonil*.

29. In progress thus to their eternal home,
    Some method is observ'd by Destinie,
    Which at their Princes setting out did doom,
    These as their leading Harbingers to die.

30. And fatal *Hubert* we must next attend,
    Whom *Hurgonil* had brought to such distress,
    That though Life's stock he did not fully spend,
    His glory that maintain'd it is grown less.

31. Long had they strove, who first should be destroy'd;
    And wounds (the Marks of Manhood) gave and took,
    Which though like honor'd Age, we would avoyd,
    Yet make us when possess'd for rev'rence look.

32. O Honor! Frail as Life thy Fellow Flower!
    Cherish'd and watch'd, and hum'rously esteem'd,
    Then worn for short adornments of an hower;
    And is when lost no more then life redeem'd.

33. This fatall *Hubert* findes, if honor be
    As much in Princes lost, when it grows lesse,
    As when it dies in men of next degree:
    Princes are only Princes by excesse.

34. For having twice with his firm Opposite
    Exchang'd a wound, yet none that reach'd at life,
    The adverse sword his Arms best sinew hit,
    Which holds that strength, which should uphold their strife.

35. When thus his dear defence had left his Hand,
    Thy life (said *Hurgonil*) rejoyce to weare
    As *Orna's* favour, and at her command,
    Who taught the mercy I will practise here.

36. To which defencelesse *Hubert* did reply,
    My life (a worthlesse Blank) I so despise,
    Since Fortune laid it in her Lotary,
    That I'me asham'd thou draw'st it as a Prise.

37. His grief made noble *Hurgonill* to melt,
    Who mourn'd in this a Warrior's various fate;
    For though a Victor now, he timely felt
    That change which pains us most by coming late.

38. But *Orna* (ever present in his thought)
    Prompts him to know, with what successe for fame
    And Empire, *Gondibert* and *Oswald* fought;
    Whilst *Hubert* seeks out death, and shrinks from shame.

39. Valor, and all that practise turns to art,
    Alike the Princes had and understood;
    For *Oswald* now is cool as *Gondibert*;
    Such temper he has got by losing blood.

40. Calmly their temper did their art obay;
    Their stretch'd Arms regular in motion prove;
    And force with as unseen a stealth convay,
    As noyselesse Howres by hands of Dials move.

41. By this new temper *Hurgonill* believ'd
    That *Oswald's* elder vertues might prevail;
    To think his own help needful much he griev'd;
    But yet prepar'd it lest the Duke should fail.

42. Small wounds they had, where as in Casements sate
    Disorder'd Life; who seem'd to look about,
    And fain would be abroad, but that a Gate
    She wants so wide, at once to sally out.

43. When *Gondibert* saw *Hurgonill* draw near,
    And doubly arm'd at conquer'd *Hubert's* cost,
    He then, who never fear'd, began to fear
    Lest by his help his honor should be lost.

44. Retire said he; for if thou hop'st to win
    My sisters love by aiding in this strife;
    May Heav'n (to make her think thy love a sin)
    Ecclipse that beauty which did give it life.

45. Count *Hurgonill* did doubtfully retire,
    Fain would assist yet durst not disobay;
    The Duke would rather instantly expire,
    Then hazard Honor by so mean a way.

46. Alike did *Oswald* for dispatch prepare;
    And cries since *Hubert* knew not to subdue;
    Glory farewel, that art the Soldiers care!
    More lov'd then Woman, lesse then Woman true!

47. And now they strive with all their sudden force
    To storm Life's Cittadil, each others Brest;
    At which could Heav'ns chief Eye have felt remorse,
    It would have wink'd, or hast'ned to the West.

48. But sure the Heav'nly Movers little care
    Whither our motion here be false or true;
    For we proceed, whilst they are regular,
    As if we Dice for all our actions threw.

49. We seem surrender'd to indiff'rent Chance;
    Even Death's great work looks like fantastick play;
    That Sword which oft did *Oswald's* fame advance
    In publique war, fails in a privat fray.

45: 4 Honor . . . way '73: Honor's death, by death's delay '51a–b   48: 2 Whith-
er] Whether '51b   49: 2 great '73: grave '51a–b

50. For when (because he ebbs of blood did feel)
    He levell'd all his strength at *Gondibert*,
    It clash'd and broke against the adverse steel,
    Which travail'd onward till it reach'd his heart.

51. Now he that like a stedfast statue stood
    In many Batails registerd by Fame;
    Does fall depriv'd of language as of blood;
    Whilst high the Hunters send their Victor's name.

52. Some shout alowd, and others winde the Horn!
    They mix the Cities with the Field's applause;
    Which *Borgio* soon interprets as their scorn,
    And will revenge it ere he mourn the cause.

53. This the cold Evening warm'd of *Vasco's* age;
    He shin'd like scorching Noon in *Borgio's* looks;
    Who kindled all about him with his rage;
    And worse the triumph then the Conquest brooks.

54. The Troops (astonish'd with their Leaders fate)
    The horror first with silence entertain;
    With lowd impatience then for *Borgio* waite,
    And next with one confusion all complain.

55. Whom thus he urg'd! Prince *Oswald* did command
    We should remove far from the Combat's list;
    And there like unconcern'd Spectators stand;
    Justly restrain'd to hinder or assist.

56. This (Patient Friends!) we dully have obay'd;
    A temp'rance which he never taught before;
    But though alive he could forbid our ayd,
    Yet dead, he leaves revenge within our pow'r.

Canto the Fifth

The ARGUMENT

The Batail in exact though little shape;
Where none by flight, and few by fortune scape;
Where even the vanquish'd so themselves behave,
The Victors mourn for all they could not save:
And fear (so soon is Fortune's fulness wayn'd)
To lose in one, all that by all they gain'd.

1. Now *Hubert's* Page assists his wounded Lord
   To mount that Steed, he scarce had force to guide;
   And wept to see his hand without that sword
   Which was so oft in busy Batails try'd.

2. Those who with *Borgio* saw his want of blood,
   Cry'd out, If of thy strength enough remain,
   Though not to charge, to make thy conduct good;
   Lead us to add their living to our slain.

3. *Hubert* reply'd, now you may justly boast,
   You Sons of war, that *Oswald* was your Sire;
   Who got in you the honor I have lost;
   And taught those deeds our Ladies songs admire.

4. But he (war's Ancestor, who gave it birth,
   The Father of those fights we *Lombards* fought)
   Lies there imbracing but his length of Earth,
   Who for your use the world's vast Empire sought.

5. And cold as he lies noble *Dargonet*,
   And *Paradine*, who wore the Victors Crown;
   Both swift to charge, and slow in a retreat;
   Brothers in blood, and Rivals in renown.

6. This said, their Trumpets sound Revenge's praise;
   The Hunters Horns (the terror of the wood)
   Reply'd so meanly, they could scarcely raise
   Eccho so loud as might be understood.

1: 3 wept *'51a MS*, *'51b*, *'73*: weep'd *'51a*   1: 4 Batails *Ed*: Batail *'51a*:
Battails *'73*: Battel *'51b*   5: 3 slow *'73*: lame *'51a–b*   6: 2 the terror *'73*:
though terror *'51a–b*

7. The Duke (his fit of fury being spent,
   Which onely wounds and opposition bred)
   Does weep ore the brave *Oswald*, and lament
   That he so great in life, is nothing dead.

8. But cry'd, when he the speechless Rivals spy'd,
   O worth above the ancient price of Love!
   Lost are the living, for with these love dy'd;
   Or if immortal fled with them above.

9. In these we the intrinsick vallew know
   By which first Lovers did love currant deem;
   But Love's false Coyners will allay it now,
   Till men suspect what next they must contemn.

10. Not less young *Hurgonil* resents their chance,
    Though no fit time to practise his remorse,
    For now he cries (finding the Foe advance)
    Let Death give way to life! to horse! to horse!

11. This sorrow is to soft for deeds behinde;
    Which I (a mortal Lover) would sustain;
    So I could make your sister wisely kinde,
    And praise me living, not lament me slain.

12. Swift as *Armenians* in the Panthers chace
    They fly to reach where now their Hunters are;
    Who sought out danger with too bold a pace,
    Till thus the Duke did them alow'd prepare.

13. Impatient Friends, stand that your strength may last!
    Burn not in blaze, rage that should warm you long!
    I wish to Foes the weaknesses of haste,
    To you such slownesse as may keep you strong.

14. Not their scorns force should your fix'd patience move;
    Though scorn does more then bonds free minds provoke:
    Their flashy rage shal harmles lightning prove,
    Which but fore-runs our Thunder's fatall stroke.

15. For when their fury's spent, how weak they are
    With the dull weight of antick *Vandall* Arms?

7: 3–4 ore the brave . . ./That he '73: on faded . . ./What was '51a–b   11: 3 So
I could '73: So as to '51a–b   14: 2 provoke: '51aMS, '51b: provoke '51a, '73

Their work but short, and little is in war,
Whom rage within, and Armor outward warms.

16. When you have us'd those arts your patience yields,
Try to avoid their cowched Launces force
By dext'rous practise of *Croatian* Fields,
Which turns to lazy Elephants their Horse.

17. When false retreat shall scatter you in flight,
As if you back to Elements were fled;
And no lesse faith can you again unite,
Then recollects from Elements the dead,

18. Make Chacers seem by your swift Rallys, slow;
Whilst they your swifter change of figures fear,
Like that in Batails which t'amuse the Foe
My Grandsire taught, as war's Philosopher.

19. Think now your valor enters on the Stage,
Think Fame th'Eternal *Chorus* to declare
Your mighty mindes to each succeeding age,
And that your Ladys the Spectators are.

20. This utter'd was with such a haughty grace,
That ev'ry heart it empty'd, and did raise
Life's chiefest blood in valor to the Face,
Which made such beauty as the Foe did praise.

21. Yet 'twas Ambition's praise, which but approves
Those whom through envy it would fain subdue;
Likes others honor, but her own so loves,
She thinks all others Trophys are her due.

22. For *Hubert* now (though void of strength as feare)
Advanc'd the first Division fast and farre;
Bold *Borgio* with the next attends his Reare,
The Third was left to *Vasco's* stedy care.

23. The Duke still watch'd when each Divisions space
Grew wide, that he might his more open spred;
His own brave conduct did the foremost grace,
The next the Count, the Third true *Tybalt* led.

17: 4 dead, '*51a*, '*73*: dead. '*51b*   20: 1 such a haughty '*73*: so supream a '*51a- b*

24. A forward fashion he did wear awhile,
    As if the Charge he would with fury meet;
    That he their forward fury might beguile,
    And urge them past redemption by retreat.

25. But when with Launces cowch'd they ready were,
    And their thick Front (which added Files in-large)
    With their ply'd spurs kept time in a Carere,
    Those soon were vanish'd whom they ment to charge.

26. The Duke by flight, his Manhood thus and force
    Reserv'd, and to his skill made valor yield,
    Did seem to blush, that he must lead his Horse
    To lose a little ground, to gain the Field.

27. Yet soon he ralleys and revives the warre;
    Hubert pursues the Rear of *Hurgonill*;
    And *Borgio's* Rear with Chace so loos'ned are,
    That them the Count does with close order kill.

28. And that which was erewhile the Duke's firm Van,
    Before old *Vasco's* Front vouchsafe to fly,
    Till with their subtle Rallys they began
    In small Divisions hidden strength to try;

29. Then cursing *Borgio* cry'd, whence comes his skill,
    Who men so scatter'd can so firmly mix?
    The living Metal, held so volatile
    By the dull world, this Chymick Lord can fix!

30. He press'd where *Hurgonill* his fury spends,
    As if he now in *Orna's* presence fought;
    And with respect his brave approach attends,
    To give him all the dangers which he sought.

31. So bloody was th'event of this new strife,
    That we may here applauded valor blame;
    Which oft too easily abandons Life,
    Whilst Death's the Parent made of noble Fame.

25: 2 in-large '*51a MS*: in large '*51a–b*: inlarge '*73*   27: 1 he ralleys and revives
'*73*: with Rallys he reviv'd '*51a–b*   28: 3 their subtle '*73*: *Croatian* '*51a–b*
31: 4 Death's the '*73*: Death is '*51a–b*

K

32. For many now (belov'd by both) forsake
　　In their pursuit of flying Fame, their breath;
　　And through the world their valor currant make,
　　By giving it the ancient stamp of Death.

33. Young *Hurgonil's* renowned self had bought
　　Honor of *Borgio* at no less a rate,
　　Had not the Duke dispatch'd with those he fought,
　　And found his aid must fly or come too late.

34. For he advancing saw (which much him griev'd)
　　That in the fairest Region of the Face,
　　He two wide wounds from *Borgio* had receiv'd;
　　His beautyes blemish, but his valor's grace.

35. Now cry'd the Duke, strive timely for renowne!
　　Thy Age will kiss those wounds thy Youth may loath;
　　Be not dismay'd to think thy beauty gone;
　　My Sister's thine, who has enough for both.

36. Then soon the Youth, Death as an honor gave
　　To one that Strove to rescue *Borgio's* life;
　　Yet *Borgio* had dispatch'd him to his grave,
　　Had *Gondibert* stood neutral in the Strife:

37. Who with his sword (disdaining now to stay
　　And see the blood he lov'd so rudely spilt)
　　Pierc't a bold *Lombard* who would stop his way;
　　Even till his heart did beat against his Hilt.

38. Timely old *Vasco* came to *Borgio's* aid;
　　Whose long experienc'd Arme wrought sure and faste;
　　His rising oppositions level laid,
　　And miss'd no execution by his haste.

39. And timely where the bleeding Count now fought,
　　And where the Duke with Number was opprest,
　　Resistless *Tybalt* came, who *Borgio* sought,
　　But here with many *Borgios* did contest.

40. As Tydes that from their sev'ral Channels haste,
　　Assemble rudely in th'*Ubœan* Bay,

37: 3 would stop '73: imbarr'd '51a–b

And meeting there to indistinction waste,
Strive to proceed, and force each others stay:

41. So here the valiant who with swift force come,
With as resistless valor are ingag'd;
Are hid in anger's undistinguish'd Fome,
And make less way by meeting so inrag'd!

42. But room for *Goltho* now! Whose valor's fire,
Like lightning, did unlikely passage make;
Whose swift effects like Light'nings they admire,
And even the harms it wrought with rev'rence take.

43. *Vasco* he seeks, who had his Youth disdain'd;
And in that search he with irreveren'd rage,
Revengefully, from younger Foes abstain'd,
And deadly grew where he encounter'd Age.

44. And *Vasco* now had felt his *Gothick* steel,
But that Duke *Gondibert* (through Helm and Head)
Gave the last stroke which *Vasco* ere shall feel
And sent him down an honour to the dead.

45. Here *Borgio* too had faln, but bravely then
The Count so much reveng'd the wounds he gave,
As *Gondibert* (the Prop of falling Men)
Such sinking greatness could not chuse but save.

46. When *Vasco* was remov'd, the Count declin'd
His bashful Eies; the Duke thought sodain shame
(From sense of luckless wounds) possess'd his mind;
Which thus he did reform, and gently blame.

47. Now thy complexion lasting is, and good!
As when the Sun sets red, his Morning Eies
In glory wake, so now thou setst in blood,
Thy parting beauty will in honor rise.

48. These scarrs thou need'st not from my Sister hide;
For as our Father, in brave batail lost,
She first did name with sorrow, then with pride,
Thy beauty's loss she'l mourn and after boast.

40: 4 stay: *'51a cor*, *'73*: stay. *'51a u*, *'51b*   41: 4 inrag'd! *51a cor*, *'73*:
inrag'd *'51a u*: inrag'd. *'51b*   44: 3–4 Gave . . . to *'73*: The last dire stroke . . . /
Did give, and sent him to adorn *'51a–b*

49. Mine are but Love's false wounds (said *Hurgonil*)
    To what you *Vasco* gave; for I must grieve
    My strength of honor could not *Vasco* kill,
    That honor lost, yet I have strength to live.

50. But now behold vex'd *Hubert*, who in all
    This Batail was by ready conduct known,
    And though unarm'd, and his spent force so small
    He could to none bring death, yet sought his own:

51. And ev'ry where, where Rallies made a Grosse
    He charg'd; and now with last reserves he try'd
    His too slow fate from *Gondibert* to force,
    Where he was Victor and where *Vasco* dy'd.

52. The Duke (in Honor's School exactly bred)
    Would not that this defenceless Prince should be
    Involv'd with those, whom he to dying led,
    Therefore ordain'd him still from slaughter free.

53. And now his pow'r did gently make him know,
    That he must keep his life, and quit the cause;
    More Pris'ner to himself then to his Foe,
    For life within himself in Prison was.

54. His fierce Assistants did not quit the Field,
    Till forward marks declar'd they fairly fought;
    And then they all with sullen slowness yield;
    Vex'd they have found what vain Revenge had sought.

55. In the renown'd destruction of this day,
    Four Hundred Leaders were by valor's pride
    Led to blest shades, by an uncertain way,
    Where lowliness is held the surest Guide.

56. And twice the Tierce of these consists of those
    Who for Prince *Oswald's* love of Empire bled;
    The Duke does thus with thanks and praise dispose
    Both of the worthy living, and the dead.

57. Binde all your wounds, and shed not that brave life,
    Which did in all by great demeanor past,
    (Teaching your Foes a wiser choice of strife)
    Deserve a Lease of Nature that may last.

51: 3 too '*51b*, '*73*: two '*51a*   54: 1 Assistants] Assistance '*51b*

58. Love warm'd you with those sparks which kindled me;
    And form'd *Ideas* in each Lovers thought
    Of the distress of some beloved she,
    Who then inspir'd and prais'd you whilst you fought.

59. You nobly prompt my passion to desire,
    That the rude Crowd who Lovers softness scorn,
    Might in fair field meet those who love admire,
    To try which side must after Batail mourn.

60. O that those rights which should the good advance,
    And justly are to painful valor due,
    (Howe're misplac'd by the swift hand of Chance)
    Were from that Crowd defended by those few!

61. With this great Spectacle we should refresh
    Those Chiefs, who (though preferr'd by being dead)
    Would kindly wish to fight again in flesh:
    So all that lov'd, by *Hurgonill* were led.

62. This gracious mention from so great a Lord,
    Bow'd *Hurgonill* with dutious homage down,
    Where at his feet he lay'd his rescu'd Sword;
    Which he accepts, but he returns his own.

63. By this and thine, said gentle *Gondibert*,
    In all distress of various Courts and warre,
    We interpledg and binde each others heart,
    To strive who shall possess griefs greatest share.

64. Now to *Verona* haste, and timely bring
    Thy wounds unto my tender sister's care;
    This Days sad story to our dreaded King,
    And watch what veng'ance *Oswald's* Friends prepare.

65. Brave *Arnold*, and his Rival strait remove;
    Where *Laura* shall bestrew their hallow'd Ground;
    Protectors both, and Ornaments of Love;
    This said, his Eies outwep'd his widest wound.

66. Tell her now these (Love's faithful Saints) are gon,
    The beauty they ador'd, she ought to hide;
    For vainly will Love's Miracles be shown,
    Since Lovers faith with these brave Rivals dy'd.

       58: 1 sparks '73: hints '51a–b

67. Say little *Hugo* never more shall mourn
    In noble Numbers, her unkind disdain;
    Who now not seeing beauty, feels no scorn;
    And wanting pleasure, is exempt from pain.

68. When she with Flowres Lord *Arnold's* Grave shall strew,
    And hears why *Hugo's* life was thrown away,
    She on that Rival's Hearse will drop a few;
    Which merits all that *April* gives to *May*.

69. Let us forsake for safety of our Eies,
    Our other loss; which I will strait inter
    And raise a Trophy where each Body lies;
    Vain marks, how those alive the Dead prefer!

70. If my full Breast, my wounds that empty be,
    And this Days toil (by which my strength is gon)
    Forbid me not, I *Bergamo* will see
    Ere it beholds the next succeeding Sun.

71. Thither convay thy soul's consid'rate thought,
    How in this cause the Court and Camp's inclin'd;
    What *Oswald's* Faction with the King has wrought,
    And how his losse prevails with *Rhodalind*.

72. The Count and *Tybalt* take their lowly leaves;
    Their slain they sadly, with consuming hearts,
    Bear tow'rds *Verona*, whilst the Duke perceives
    Prince *Hubert's* grief, and thus his tears diverts.

73. Afflicted Prince! in an unpleasant hower
    You and your living (by blinde valor led)
    Are Captives made to such an easie Pow'r,
    Shall you as little vex, as Death your dead.

74. The Dead can ne'r by living help return
    From that darke Land, which life could ne'r disclose;
    But these alive (for whom the Victors mourn)
    To thee I give, thee to thine own dispose.

75. Be not with Honor's guilded Baites beguild;
    Nor think Ambition wise, because 'tis brave;
    For though we like it, as a forward Child,
    'Tis so unsound, her Cradle is her Grave.

76. Study the mighty *Oswald* vainly gone!
    Fierce *Paradine*, and *Dargonet* the stout!
    Whose Threds by destiny were slowly spunne,
    And by Ambition rashly ravell'd out.

77. But *Hubert's* grief no precept could reform;
    For great grief councel'd, does to anger grow;
    And he provided now a future Storm,
    Which did with black revenge o'recast his Brow.

78. *Borgio* and he from this dire Region haste;
    Shame makes them sightless to themselves and dumb;
    Their thoughts fly swift as Time from what is past;
    And would like him demolish all to come.

79. Strait they inter th'inferior of their slain;
    Their nobler Tragick load their grief attends
    Tow'rds *Brescia*, where the Camp they hope to gain,
    Then force the Court by faction of their Friends.

80. To *Bergamo* the gentle Duke does turn
    With his surviving Lovers, who in kinde
    Remembrance every step look back, and mourn
    Their fellow Lovers Death has stay'd behinde.

81. Some lost their quiet Rivals, some their dear
    Love's Brother, who their hopes with help approv'd;
    Some such joy'd Friends, as even to morrow were
    To take from *Hymen* those they dearest lov'd.

82. But now to *Gondibert* they forward look,
    Whose wounds, ere he could waste Three League of way,
    So wast him, that his speech him quite forsook;
    And Nature calls for Art to make life stay.

83. His Friends in torment least they should forsake
    Delightful him, for whom alone they live;
    Urge Heav'n uncivilly for calling back
    So soon such worth, it does so seldom give.

76: 3 Threds . . . were '73: Thirds by patient *Parcæ* '51a–b: Thrids by patient
Parcae '51b *Errata*   76: 4 And . . . Ambition '73: Ambition's hast has '51a–b

Canto the Sixth

The ARGUMENT

The Victor is (when with his wounds subdu'd)
By such deform'd and dismal Troopes persu'd,
That he thinks Death, then which they uglier seem,
No ill expedient to escape from them.
But ULFIN *guides him to sage* ASTRAGON,
By the last Raies of the descending Sun.

1. Scarce on their Duke their fears kind fit was spent,
    When strait a thick arm'd Squadron clouds their sight;
    Which cast so dark a shade, as if it ment
    Without the Sun's slow leave, to bring in night.

2. This threatning Squadron did consist of Horse,
    And by old *Ulfin* they were bravely led,
    Whose mind was sound, nor wants his Body force,
    Though many Winters Snow had cool'd his Head.

3. The sad remainder who with *Hubert* went,
    Did misse his reach, when they to *Brescia* turn'd,
    And now (as if his haste destruction ment)
    He chac'd these who the Duke's spent valor mourn'd.

4. Whose posture being loose, their number few,
    His Scouts grow scornful as they forward come;
    He makes his Squadron halt, and neer he drew;
    Then asks aloud, what are you, and for whom?

5. The noble *Goltho* (whose great deeds to day
    Prevented Manhood in his early youth)
    Believ'd him *Oswald's* Friend, yet scorn'd the way
    To shelter life, behind abandon'd Truth.

6. For he to *Ulfin* boldly thus reply'd;
    This second Ambush findes us here in vain;
    We have no treasure left that we would hide,
    Since *Gondibert* is reckon'd with the slain.

2: 2 bravely '73: gravely '51a–b

7. Duke *Gondibert* we vouch to be our Lord,
   To whose high vertue's Sov'raignty we bow;
   Oswald sunk low, as death, beneath his Sword,
   Though him superior Fate will vanquish now.

8. Scarce empty Eagles stooping to their Prey,
   Could be more swift then *Ulfin* to alight,
   And come where *Gondibert* expiring lay;
   Now pleasing those whom he did newly fright.

9. For scarce that rev'rence which a Monarch draws,
   Who seldome will be seen, though often sought;
   Who spends his carefull age in making Laws,
   To rule those lands for which in youth he fought:

10. Nor that respect which People pay those Kings,
    Whose peace makes rich, whom civil war made wise,
    Can equall this which aged *Ulfin* brings
    The gentle Duke, to whom he prostrate lies.

11. His Eyes (not us'd to tears) bathe ev'ry wound;
    Which he salutes as things he chiefly lov'd;
    And when expence of spirits he had found,
    To gain him air, his Mourners he remov'd.

12. Make way, said he, and give Experience room;
    The Confident of age, though Youth's scorn'd guide;
    My wounds, though past, out-number yours to come,
    You can but hope the knowledg I have try'd.

13. His Hilts round Pommel he did then unskrew,
    And thence (which he from ancient Precept wore)
    In a small Christall he a Cordial drew,
    That weary life could to her walks restore.

14. This care (amazing all it does delight)
    His ruines, which so reverend appear,
    With wonder not so much surprise their sight,
    As a strange object now his Troops draw near.

15. In whom such death and want of limbs they finde,
    As each were lately call'd out of his Tombe,
    And left some members hastily behinde;
    Or came when born abortive from the Wombe.

16. Yet this defect of Legs, or Arms, or Hands,
    Did wondring valor not disturb, but please;
    To see what divers weapons each commands
    With arts hard shifts, till custome gave them ease.

17. But the uncomely absence of an Eye,
    And larger wants, which ev'ry visage mourn'd,
    (Where black did over-vail, or ill supply)
    Was that which wonder into horror turn'd.

18. And *Ulfin* might be thought (when the rude wind
    Lifting their Curtains, left their ruines bare)
    A formal Antiquary, gravely kind
    To Statues, which he now drew out to aire.

19. The Duke (whose absent knowledg was call'd back
    By Cordials pow'r) his wonder did increase
    So much, that he agen did knowledg lack,
    Till thus old *Ulfin* made his wonder cease.

20. Auspicious Prince! recorded be this day,
    And sung by Priests of each ensuing age;
    On which thou mayst receive, and I may pay
    Some debts of duty, as thy Grandsires Page.

21. That mighty Chief I serv'd in youth's first strength,
    Who our short Scepter meant to stretch so far,
    Till Eastern Kings might grieve theirs wanted length
    Whose Maps scarce teach where all their Subjects are.

22. Full many stormy Winters we have seen,
    When mighty valor's heat was all our fire;
    Else we in stupid Frosts had fetter'd been,
    By which soft sinews are congeal'd to wire.

23. And many scorching Summers we have felt,
    Where Death relieves all whom the sword invades;
    And kindly thence (where we should toyling melt)
    Leads us to rest beneath eternal shades.

24. For aid of action he obedience taught,
    And silent patience for afflictions cure;
    He prais'd my courage when I boldly fought,
    But said they conquer most, that most endure.

22: 2 mighty '73: kindled '51a–b

25. The toyls of diligence as much approv'd
    As Valor's self, or th'Arts her practise gaines;
    The care of Men, more then of glory lov'd,
    Success rewarded, and succesless paines.

26. To joyful Victors quenching water sent,
    Delightful wine to their lamenting slaves;
    For Feasts have more brave lives then famine spent,
    And temp'rance more then Trench or Armor saves.

27. Valor his Mistris, Caution was his Friend;
    Both to their diff'rent seasons he appli'd;
    The first he lov'd, on th'other did depend;
    The first made worth uneasie by her pride.

28. He to submiss devotion more was given
    After a batail gain'd, then ere 'twas fought;
    As if it nobler were to thank high Heav'n
    For favours past, then bow for bounty sought.

29. And thus through smarting heat, and aking cold,
    Till Heav'ns perpetual Travailer, had more
    Then Thirty journies through the *Zodiack* told,
    I serv'd thy Grandsire, whom I now adore.

30. For Heav'n in his too ripe and weary age,
    Call'd him where peacefully he rules a Star;
    Free'd from low Ele'ments continu'd rage,
    Which last like Monarchs pow'r by needful war.

31. Strait thy lamented Father did succeed
    To his high place, by *Aribert's* consent,
    Our Ensignes through remoter Lands to lead:
    Him too I follow'd till he upward went.

32. Till that black day on which the *Hunns* may boast
    Their own defeate, and we our conquest hyde;
    For though we gain'd, and they the batail lost,
    Yet then thy brave victorious Father dyde.

33. And I am stay'd unwillingly behind;
    Not caught with wealth, Life's most intangling snare;
    Though both my Masters were in giving kinde,
    As joyful Victors after Batail are.

30: 3 low Ele'ments continu'd *'73*: the lower Ele'ments ceaseless *'51a-b*

34. Whilst thus this aged Leader does express
    His and their Story whom this bounty feeds,
    His Hands the Duke's worst order'd wounds undress
    And gently binde; then strait he thus proceeds.

35. West from those Hills till you *Cremona* reach,
    With an unmingled right I gather rent;
    By their great Guift who did such precepts teach
    In giving, as their wealth is ne'r misspent.

36. For as their plenteous pity fills my thought,
    So their example was not read in vain;
    A Thousand, who for them in batail fought,
    And now distress'd with Maimes, I intertain:

37. Not giving like to those, whose gifts though scant
    Pain them as if they gave with gowty hand;
    Such vex themselves and ease not others want;
    But we alike injoy, a like command.

38. Most spaciously we dwell, where we possess
    All sinless pleasures Nature did ordain;
    And who that all may have, yet will have less,
    Wiser then Nature, thinks her kindness vain.

39. A sad resolve, which is a wise-mans vow,
    From Cities noise, and Courts unpity'd care
    Did so divorce me, it would scarce allow
    I ere should take one League of distant ayre.

40. But that Alarms from each adjacent part
    Which borders my abode, disturb'd my rest,
    With dreadful newes that gratious *Gondibert*
    By *Oswald's* Faction was in fight opprest.

41. Then it had given your wonder cause to last,
    To see the vex'd mistakes this summons wrought
    In all my Maim'd Domesticks, by their haste;
    For some tie on the Limbs which others sought.

42. Just such mistakes audatious *Ethnicks* say
    Will happen where the Righteous busy are,
    Through glad and earnest hast in the last day;
    Whilst others slowly to their doom prepare.

34: 2 this] his '*51b Errata*   35: 2 unmingled '*51b*, '*73*: unmingled, '*51a*

43. And this had Anger, anger noise had bred,
And Noise, the Enemy of useful Thought,
Had them to more mistakes then blindness led,
But that our awful Camps had silence taught.

44. Silence did mem'ry, Mem'ry order make;
Order to each did his mist wood restore;
For some, who once were stedfast Foot, mistake,
And snatch those limbs which only Horsemen wore.

45. Like swift Pursuers on *Arabian* Horse,
These with their needfull Instruments of hold
(Which give their strange adapted weapons force)
I mounted strait; Five Hundred fully told.

46. These from the *Lombards* highly have deserv'd,
In Conquests where thy Father did command;
Whom they for Science and affection serv'd;
And lost their Limbs to gain our Scepter Land.

47. Which yet are noble though unsightly signes,
That each in active courage much abounds;
And many a widow'd Mother now repines,
They cannot shew the Men who gave those wounds.

48. For dearly did the *Hunns* for honor pay,
When they deform'd them in a fatall fight;
Since though they strongly struggled for the day,
Yet all they got, was everlasting Night.

49. And *Oswald's* Friends, were they not timely gon
(Though all the Faction in one Army were)
Should mourn this act against their Gen'ral's son;
Who was to Soldiers more then Triumph dear.

50. For these to Conquest us'd, Retreats dislike;
They beauty want, to others Beauty's cost;
With envious rage still at the Face they strike;
And punish Youth, for what in youth they lost.

51. Thus, though the Duke's amazement be remov'd,
It now returns, gladly on him to gaze
Who feeds those Fighters whom his Father lov'd;
A gratitude would Vertue's self amaze.

52. Thou art, said he, (then melted whilst he spake)
    So ripe in what high Heav'n does dearly love,
    That Heav'ns remorse for Earth we should mistake,
    To think it will forbear thee long above.

53. As if thy sent for Soule already were
    Upon her Wings, so much I give thee gon;
    And wish thee left in some Successor here,
    That might receive the kindness thou hast shown.

54. Old *Ulfin* now (but meltingly as he)
    T'inrich him, gives the Jewell of his sight;
    For strait, with Fatherly authoritie,
    He bids his sonn, young *Ulfinor*, alight!

55. Take him (said he) whose duty I release;
    In whom all Heav'ns rewards included are,
    For all my Justice in corrupted peace,
    And for my mercy in revengefull warre.

56. The fruit Heav'n sent me by my loyall wife,
    In age, the gloomy Eve of endless night;
    Which eas'd in me the pain of latter life,
    And frustrates death, by fresh succession's sight.

57. The Duke with passion did this Youth embrace;
    Then luckie *Goltho* he call'd forth in view;
    Who was this day in Fortune's speciall grace,
    For though no blood he lost, yet much he drew.

58. Him he with *Ulfinor* does strait unite;
    Bids neither strive the other to precede,
    Unless when danger doth them both invite,
    But be, even in nice Rivalship agreed.

59. Bids both their Breasts be eithers open book,
    Where nought is writ too hard for sodain Eies;
    But thought's plain Text grows easie by a look:
    Study breeds doubts, where reading should suffice.

60. But these to joyn, Nature no Councel needs;
    Whom Sympathy, her secret Priest, does wed;
    Much fam'd will be their loves, and Martial Deeds;
    Which fill all Books that are of *Lombards* read.

52: 2 high '73: nice '51a–b   54: 3 Fatherly '73: Father's grave '51a–b

61. With gracious Eies, and Body lowly bent,
    The Duke his Fathers rev'rend Troops salutes;
    To *Bergamo* he holds his first intent;
    Which to oppose, old *Ulfin* thus disputes.

62. Thou seest (my Prince) the faint decays of Light;
    How hastily the Sun's hot Steeds begin
    To mend their pace, as if their longing sight
    Had newly spy'd their usuall Western Inn.

63. Too far is pleasant *Bergamo* from hence,
    Since Day has reach'd so neer his journies end;
    Dayes strength and yours are at their last expence;
    Do not whilst both are wasting, both misspend.

64. You and your wounded must with Nature strive,
    Till all (whose few hours sway to day excels
    Their elder Foes long raign in Camps) arrive
    Where *Astragon* the wise and wealthy dwells.

65. Rich is that Lord, and rich in learnings wealth;
    Art flies his test, he all Art's test endures;
    Our Cities send their sick to him for health,
    Our Camps the wounded for their certain cures.

66. Though cautious Nature, check'd by Destiny,
    Has many secrets she would ne'r impart;
    This fam'd Philosopher is Nature's Spie,
    And hireless gives th'intelligence to Art.

67. The Duke with vertue (antiquated now)
    Did rev'rence Councel, and to Age did bend;
    His first Course altars, and does this allow;
    Then *Ulfin* as their Guide they all attend.

68. Soon they the Pallace reach'd of *Astragon*;
    Which had its beauty hid by envious Night;
    Whose Cypress Curtain drawn before the Sun,
    Seem'd to performe the Obsequies of light.

69. Yet lights last Rays were not intirely spent;
    For they discern'd their passage through a Gate,
    Whose height and space shew'd ancient ornament,
    And Ancients there in careful Office sate.

67: 3 altars] alters '*51b*

70. Who by their Weights and Measures did record
    Such num'rous Burthens as were thither brought
    From distant Regions, to their learned Lord;
    On which his Chymicks and Distillers wrought.

71. But now their common bus'ness they refrain,
    When they observe a quiet sullenness
    And bloody marks in such a civil Train;
    Which shew'd at once their worth and their distress.

72. The voyce of *Ulfin* they with gladness knew,
    Whom to this house long neighborhood indeer'd;
    Approaching Torches perfected their view,
    And taught the way till *Astragon* appear'd.

73. Who soon did *Ulfin* cheerfully imbrace;
    The visits cause by whispers he receiv'd;
    Which first he hop'd was ment him as a grace,
    But being known with manly silence griev'd.

74. And then with gestures full of grave respect,
    The Duke he to his own Apartment led;
    To each distinct retirements did direct,
    And all the wounded he ordain'd to Bed.

75. Then thin digestive food he did provide,
    More to enable fleeting strength to stay;
    To wounds well search'd he cleansing wines apply'd,
    And so prepar'd his rip'ning Balsoms way.

76. Balm of the Warriour's herbe, *Hypericon*!
    To warriour's as in use, in form decree'd;
    For through the leaves transparent wounds are shown;
    And rudly touch'd, the Golden Flower does bleed.

77. For sleep they juice of pale *Nymphæa* took,
    Which grows (to shew that it for sleep is good)
    Neer sleep's abode, in the soft murm'ring Brook:
    This cools, the yellow Flower restraines the Blood:

78. And now the weary world's great Med'cin, Sleep,
    This learned Host dispenc'd to ev'ry Guest;
    Which shuts those wounds where injur'd Lovers weep,
    And flies Oppressors to relieve th'Opprest.

73: 4 known] known, '51*b*

79. It loves the Cotage, and from Court abstaines,
    It stills the Sea-man though the Storm be high;
    Frees the griev'd Captive in his clossest Chaines,
    Stops wants lowd Mouth, and blinds the treach'rous Spie!

80. Kinde Sleep, Night's welcome Officer, does cease
    All whom this House containes till day return;
    And me, Grief's Chronicler, does gently ease,
    Who have behind so great a task to mourn.

The End of the First Book

79: 3 clossest *'51a MS*; closet *'51a*: closest *'51b*, *'73*   80: 1 cease] seise *'51b*
Errata

GONDIBERT

THE SECOND BOOK
Canto the First

The ARGUMENT

VERONA *by the Poet's Pencil drawn;*
Where HURGONIL *did meet the early dawn:*
Her wealth shown by each Dwellers early'r care;
Which sown by others peace, she reap'd by warre.
The slain, whose life her safety was and pride,
Are now in death their Fun'ral Rites deny'd.

1. Neer to his Evening Region was the sun,
   When *Hurgonil* with his lamented Load,
   And faithful *Tybalt* their sad march begun
   To Fair *Verona*, where the Court aboad.

2. They slowly rod till Night's dominion ceast;
   When Infant Morn (her scarce wak'd beames displai'd)
   With a scant face peep'd shylie through the East,
   And seem'd as yet of the black world afraid.

3. But by increase of swift expansive light,
   The lost Horizon was apparent growne,
   And many Tow'rs salute at once their sight;
   The distant glories of a Royal Towne.

4. *Verona*, sprung from noble *Vera's* name;
   Whom careless Time (still scatt'ring old Records
   Where they are loosly gather'd up by Fame)
   Proclaimes the chief of ancient *Tuscan* Lords.

5. *Verona* borders on that fatal Plaine;
   Whose barren thirst was quench'd with valiant blood,
   When the rough *Cymbrians* by fierce *Marius* slaine,
   Left Hills of Bodies where their Ensignes stood.

1: 1 Neer to '73: SUNK neer '51a–b   3: 4 glories . . . Royal '73: boasts of an
Imperial '51a–b

6. So safely prowd this Towne did now appeare,
   As if it but immortal Dwellers lack'd;
   As if *Theodorick* had ne'r been there,
   Nor *Attila* her wealth and beauty sack'd.

7. Here *Hurgonill* might follow with his Eie
   (As with deep streame it through the City pass'd)
   The fruitfull and the frighted *Adice*,
   Which thence from noise and Nets to sea does haste.

8. And on her peopled Banke they might behold
   The toyels of conquest paid with workes of pride;
   The Pallace of King *Agilulf* the old,
   Or Monument, for ere 'twas built he dyde.

9. To it that Temple joynes, whose lofty Head
   The prospect of a swelling Hill commands;
   In whose coole wombe the City springs are bred:
   On *Dorique* Pillers this tall Temple stands.

10. This to sooth Heav'n the bloody *Clephes* built;
    As if Heav'ns King so softe and easie were,
    So meanly hows'd in Heav'n, and kinde to guilt,
    That he would be a Tyrants Tenant here.

11. And now they might arrest their wandring sight
    With that which makes all other Objects lost;
    Makes *Lombard* greatness flat to *Roman* height,
    And Modern Builders blush, that else would boast;

12. An Amphytheater which has controll'd
    Unheeded conquests of advancing Age,
    Windes which have made the trembling World look old,
    And the fierce Tempests of the *Gothick* rage.

13. This great *Flaminius* did in youth erect,
    Where Cities sat to see whole Armies play
    Death's serious part: but this we may neglect
    To mark the bus'ness which begins with day.

14. As Day new op'ning fills the *Hemisphear*,
    And all at once; so quickly ev'ry street
    Does by an instant op'ning full appear,
    When from their Dwellings busy Dwellers meet.

12: 4 fierce . . . *Gothick '73*: uncivil *Goth*'s malicious '*51a–b*

15. From wider Gates Oppressors sally there;
    Here creeps th'afflicted through a narrow Dore;
    Groans under wrongs he has not strength to bear,
    Yet seeks for wealth to injure others more.

16. And here the early Lawyer mends his pace;
    For whom the earlier Cliant waited long;
    Here greedy Creditors their Debtors chace,
    Who scape by herding in th'indebted Throng.

17. Th'advent'rous Merchant whom a Storm did wake,
    (His Ships on *Adriatick* Billowes tost)
    Does hope of Eastern windes from Steeples take,
    And hastens there a Currier to the Coast.

18. Here through a secret Posterne issues out
    The skar'd Adult'rer, who out-slept his time;
    Day, and the Husbands Spie alike does doubt,
    And with a half hid face would hide his crime.

19. There from sick mirth neglectful Feasters reel,
    Who cares of want in wine's false *Lethe* steep.
    There anxious empty Gamsters homeward steal,
    And fear to wake, ere they begin to sleep.

20. Here stooping Lab'rers slowly moving are;
    Beasts to the Rich, whose strength grows rude with ease;
    And would usurp, did not their Rulers care,
    With toile and tax their furious strength appease.

21. There th'Aged walk, whose needless carefulness
    Infects them past the Mindes best med'cin, sleep;
    There some to Temples early vows address,
    And for th'ore busie world most wisely weep.

22. To this vast Inn, where Tydes of strangers flow,
    The Morne and *Hurgonil* together came;
    The Morn, whose Dewy wings appear'd but slow,
    When Men the motion mark'd of swifter Fame.

23. For Fame (whose journys are through ways unknown,
    Tracelesse and swift, and changing as the winde)
    The Morne and *Hurgonil* had much outgone,
    Whilst Truth mov'd patiently within behinde.

23: 4 Truth . . . within '73: temp'rate Truth mov'd patiently '51a–b

24. For some the Combat (to a Bataile growne)
    Did apprehend in such prodigious shape,
    As if their living to the Dead were gone,
    And only Fame did by her Wings escape.

25. Some said this hunting falsely was design'd,
    That by pretence both Factions might prepare
    Their Armys to contest for *Rhodalind*;
    The Crown's chief Jewel, and Reward of Warre.

26. And some report (so far they range from Truth
    Who for intelligence must follow Fame)
    That then from *Bergamo* th'incamped Youth,
    With *Gondibert*, to this dire hunting came.

27. And some, that *Oswald* had inlarg'd his Traine
    With the old Troopes by his bold Father led;
    And that of these the nobler half were slaine;
    The rest were to their Camp at *Brescia* fled.

28. And as dire Thunder rowling o're Heaven's vault,
    By murmur threatens, ere it kills allowd;
    So was this fatall newes in whisper brought,
    Which menac'd, ere it struck the list'ning Crowd.

29. But Rumor soon to high extreames does move;
    For first it *Oswald* nam'd with dreadful voice,
    Then said that Death had widow'd Truth and Love,
    By making *Gondibert* the second choice.

30. And to all hearts so dear was *Gondibert*,
    So much did Pity, *Oswald's* Valor prise,
    That strait their early bus'nesse they desert,
    And fix on wounded *Hurgonil* their Eies.

31. Him when by perfect day they sadly knew,
    Through hidden wounds, whose blood his beauty stain'd,
    Even from the Temples, Angels soon withdrew;
    So sawcely th'afflicted there complain'd.

32. The People strait united clamor gave,
    Shriek'd lowd like Sea-men split on a strange Coast;
    As if those Pow'rs were deaf who should them save,
    And Pray'rs no lowder then the windes were lost.

33. Now, with impatience urg'd, he does declare
    Whom he so mournfully in Fun'ral brought;
    The publick losses of a private warre,
    Who living, love, and dying, valour taught.

34. For he does *Hugo* and *Arnoldo* name;
    To these (said he) *Verona* Cradles gave,
    And since in forraign Fields they rais'd her Fame,
    They challenge here, though much too soon, a Grave.

35. Bring sprinklings, Lamps, and th'Altar's precious breath;
    All Rites which Priests have prudently devis'd;
    Who gratefully a rev'rence teach to death;
    Because they most by dying men are pris'd.

36. But though our loss we justly may complain;
    Though even by Priests Authority we grieve;
    Yet Heav'n's first bounty, Life, let none disdain,
    Since *Gondibert*, our chief Delight, does live.

37. This heard, as Sea-men neer a Shore unknown,
    Who their North Guide lose in a Stormy night,
    His absence with distracted silence moan,
    And lowdly welcome his return to sight:

38. So when their great Conductor seem'd to be
    Retir'd to endless shades amongst the slain,
    With silent grief they seem'd as dead as he,
    But with new life welcom'd his life again.

39. And now that cold remainder Valor left
    Of these whom Love had lost, and Fate forsook;
    The Two that were of all but Fame bereft,
    From *Hurgonil* the weeping People took.

40. Whilst of them both sad *Hurgonil* takes leave,
    Till th'universal meeting Faith provides;
    The Day when all shall publickly receave
    Those Bodies, Death does not destroy, but Hides.

41. Then to his Palace he retires by stealth;
    His wounds from his lov'd Mistris to conceal;

33: 4 dying, valour '73: valor, dying '51a-b   35: 1 sprinklings '51b, '73
spinklings '51a   35: 2 Priests '51aMS, '51b, '73: Priest '51a

On whose dear joys so much depends his health,
The wounds her Tears should touch would never heal.

42. To the chief Temple strait the People bear
The valiant Rivals, who for love were slain;
Whom all the peaceful Priests behold with fear,
And griev'd such Guests they durst not entertain.

43. For soon the Prior of their Brotherhood
(Who long serv'd Heav'n with praise, the world with pray'r)
Cry'd out, this holy House is shut to blood,
To all that die in combat or dispair.

44. These by their bloody marks in Combat di'de;
Through anger, the disease of Beasts untam'd;
Whose wrath is hunger, but in Men 'tis pride,
Yet theirs is cruelty, ours courage nam'd.

45. Here the neglected Lord of peace does live;
Who taught the wrangling world the rules of love;
Should we his dwelling to the wrathful give,
Our Sainted Dead would rise, and he remove.

46. Well by his precepts may we punish strife;
Whose pity knew that Famine, Plague, and Time,
Are Enemies enough to humane life;
None need o'er-charge Death's Quiver with a crime.

47. To unfrequented Fields bear then your slain;
Where neither Dirge nor Requiem shall be giv'n;
To those who by usurp'd Revenge disdain
To take from Men, neglects they put on Heav'n.

48. But now the People's passions run too farre;
Their untaught love, artless extremes does wed;
Of times they like the past, and since they are
Opprest still by the living, love the Dead:

49. And now resolve these Rivals shall not lose
The Rites of Sprinkling, Incense, Lights, and Song:
Then, as the voice of all their Minds, they chuse
An Orator, of rude, but ready Tongue:

50. Who at the Temple Gate thus pleads alowd!
We know, though Priests are Pensioners of Heav'n,
Your Flock which yeilds best rent, is this dull Crowd;
The learn'd examine why their Fleece is giv'n.

51. Though by the Rich first shorn, to you they bear
A second tribute, and by zeal support
Temples, which Kings for glory raise, and where
The Rich for fame, the Learn'd as Spies resort.

52. Temples are yours, not God's lov'd Palaces;
Where Off'rings make not his, but your own Feasts;
Where you most wisely live, because at ease,
And entertain your Founders as your Guests:

53. With ease you take, what we provide with care;
And we (who your Legation must maintain)
Finde all your Tribe in the Commission are;
And none but Heav'n could send so large a Train.

54. But being all Ambassadors from thence,
The growing charge will soon exceed our rent,
Unless you please to treat at his expence
Who sent you; not at ours, where you are sent.

55. The ancient Laws liv'd in the Peoples voice;
Rites you from Custom, not from Canon draw;
They are but fashions of a graver choice,
Which yeild to Laws, and now our voice is Law.

56. This *Tybalt* heard with sorrow and disdain,
(Who here with *Hurgonil* a Mourner came)
And strait the peaceful Fathers strives to gain,
And thus the Peoples Orator reclaim.

57. Most usefull Fathers! some trace secret things
Even to his Closet, who is hid in Heav'n;
Vainly as *Nilus* to his hidden springs,
And not enjoy, but censure what is given.

58. You with such temper their intemp'rance beare,
To shew your solid science does rely
So on it self, as you no trial feare;
For Arts are weake that are of Scepticks shy.

59. Though in your Office humane safety lies,
    Which op'ns that Hell the vicious vulgar feare,
    Yet never can the People Priesthood prise;
    As if from Heav'n your daily errands were.

60. Not that your message, Truth, they disesteem,
    Or think it comes from any other way,
    But that they Taxes hate, and Truth does seem
    Brought as a Tax, when they the Bringers pay.

61. Thus we to Beasts fall from our noble kinde,
    Making our Pastur'd Bodies all our care;
    Allowing no subsistence to the Minde;
    For Truth we grudg her as a costly fare.

62. But if they feare (since daily you renew
    Disputes) your Oracles are doubtfull still
    As those of old; yet more reward is due
    To paines, where so uneasy is the skill.

63. Or if no skill they think it, but suppose
    'Tis Faith (and Faith ne'r thinks Heav'n's height too high)
    Yet Faiths so sev'ral be, that few are those
    Can chuse right wings when they to Heav'n would fly.

64. Or if they think, Faith humane help transcends,
    And to your science is so strict a bound
    As Death to Valor is, where daring ends;
    And none are farthest in that Progresse found;

65. Yet in our walk to our last home design'd,
    'Tis safe by all the study'd Guides to goe;
    Least we in death, too late, the knowledge finde
    Of what in life 'twas possible to know.

66. Your splendid Pomp, by which your Pow'r indures,
    Though costly, costs much less then Camps or Laws;
    And more then both, Religion us secures;
    Since Hell (your Prison) more then dying awes.

67. For though the plain Judg, Conscience, makes no showe,
    But silently to her dark Session comes,

Not as red Law does to arraignment goe,
Or Warr to Execution with lowd Drums;

68. Though she on Hills sets not her *Gibbets* high,
Where frightful Law sets hers; nor bloody seems
Like War in Colours spred, yet secretly
She does her work, and many Men condemns.

69. Chokes in the seed, what Law till ripe ne'r sees;
What Law would punish, Conscience can prevent;
And so the world from many Mischiefs frees;
Known by her Cures, as Law by punishment.

70. The weaker sighted ever look too nigh;
But their disputes have made your Charter good;
As doubted Tenures, which long pleadings trie,
Authentick grow by being much withstood.

71. These Chiefs, for whom we holy Rites desire,
By well fought Fields begot this City's peace;
Oft with their blood have quench'd intestine fire;
And oft our Famines chang'd into excesse.

72. Their Rites let not the people be deny'd,
Though by untutor'd kindness rudely sought;
Nor think they have in privat Combate dyde,
Where *Gondibert* and mighty *Oswald* fought:

73. Both Princes of the *Lombards* royal blood;
For whom full Thrice Three Hunder'd number'd are,
Whose anger strove to make their anger good:
Number gives strife th'authentick name of War.

74. This said, Warrs cause these Priests no more debate;
They knew, Warr's Justice none could ere decide;
At that more specious name they open strait,
And sacred Rites of fun'ral they provide.

75. How vain is Custom, and how guilty Pow'r?
Slaughter is lawful made by the excess;
Earth's partial Laws, just Heav'n must needs abhor,
Which greater crimes allow, and damn the less.

68: 4 many Men '*73*: many'a Man '*51a–b*   71: 4 into '*73*: to glad '*51a–b*

Canto the Second

The ARGUMENT

Fame's progress through VERONA, *when she brings*
Ill news inlarg'd, as her extended wings.
The Combat's cause shakes ARIBERT'S *great mind;*
And the effect more conquers RHODALIND.
Meek ORNA'S *fears, proud* GARTHA'S *bold disdain;*
And LAURA *kindly dying for the Slain.*

1. To Streets (the People's Region) early Fame
   First brought this grief, which all more tragick make;
   And next, to the triumphant Court she came,
   Where prosp'rous Pow'r sleeps long, though Sutors wake;

2. But yet the early King (from Childhood bred
   To dangers, toyls, and courser wants of warre)
   Rose up to rule, and left soft Love in bed,
   Could conquer Lands and Love, but stoopt to care.

3. Care, that in Cloysters onely seales her Eies,
   Which Youth thinks folly, Age as wisdom owns;
   Fooles by not knowing her, outlive the wise;
   She visits Cities, but she dwells in Thrones.

4. Care, which King *Aribert* with Conquest gain'd,
   And is more sure to him then Realms intail'd;
   Wak'd him to know why Rumor thus complain'd,
   Or who in batail bled, or who prevail'd?

5. Young *Hurgonil* (who does his wounds conceal,
   Yet knew it did his dutious care import
   That some just witness should his cause reveal)
   Sent *Tybalt* to appease, and tast the Court.

6. To that proud Palace which once low did lie
   In *Parian* Quarries, now on Columes stands;
   Ionique Props that bear their Arches high,
   With ample treasure rais'd by *Tuscan* Hands.

Arg. 4 *effect* '73: *effects* '51a–b   6: 4 With . . . by '73: Which conquer'd
treasure rais'd with '51a–b

7. So vast of height, to which such space did fit
   As if it were o're-cyz'd for Modern Men;
   The ancient Giants might inhabit it;
   And there walk free as windes that passe unseen.

8. The *Monarch's* wealth this shew'd in all the parts;
   But his strong numerous Guards denote him wise;
   Who on the weather of his Peoples hearts,
   For a short Course, not voyages, relies.

9. Through many Guards (all watchful, calm, and bold)
   Tybalt did passe the first magnifick Square;
   And through ascents does enter to behold,
   Where the States Head and Eies assembled are.

10. There sat the King, on whose consid'rate Brow
    Sixty experienc'd Sommers he discern'd,
    Which made him ripe, and all of Conduct know
    That from successe is own'd, from losses learn'd.

11. Neer him the Empire's strict Surveyors sate;
    Whose universal sight no object lose;
    Who see not crimes too soon, nor worth too late;
    Finde dangers seed, and choke it ere it grows.

12. He wealth nor birth preferr'd to Councels place;
    For Councel is for use, not ornament;
    Soules are alike, of rich and ancient Race;
    Though Bodies claim distinctions by descent.

13. Here boyling Youth, nor frozen Age can sit:
    It would in Subjects scorne of ruling Breed,
    If that great work should such small ayds admit,
    And make them hope that they no Rulers need.

14. Nature too oft by birthright does preferr
    Less perfect Monarchs to an anxious Throne;
    Yet more then her, Courts by weak Counc'lers err,
    In adding Cyphers where she made but one.

8: 2 his strong numerous '73: the attendant '51a–b   14: 2 an anxious '73: a
busie '51a–b

15. To this wise King, sage *Tybalt* did relate
    The Combats cause, with truth's severe extent;
    Reveales that fire which kindl'd *Oswald's* hate;
    For which such precious valor was misspent.

16. Gives *Gondibert* a just record of praise;
    First how unwilling, then how bold in fight;
    And crownes the Conquer'd with the Victor's Baies,
    When Manhood bids him do their valor right:

17. At last recounts the wounded and the slaine;
    And how Prince *Hubert* and the Duke retir'd;
    From nothing brave or great he did refraine,
    But his own deeds, which doing were admir'd.

18. This *Arribert* with outward patience heares,
    Though wounded by the cause for which they fought;
    With mod'rate joy the death of *Oswald* beares;
    Yet justly to extremes it inward wrought.

19. *Tybalt* he now with peaceful lookes discharg'd;
    And then his thoughts (imprison'd in his breast)
    He strait by liberty of Tongue inlarg'd;
    Which thus unto his Councel he addrest.

20. With what a diff'rence Nature's pallat tasts
    The sweetest draught which Art provides her, Pow'r:
    Since Pow'r, Pride's Wine, but high in relish lasts
    Whilst fuming new, for Time does turne it sowre?

21. Yet Pow'r, Earth's tempting Fruit, Heav'n first did plant
    From Man's first Serpent safe, Ambition's reach;
    Else *Eden* could not serve Ambition's want;
    Whom no command can rule, nor councel teach.

22. Pow'r is that luscious wine, which does the bold,
    The wise, and noble most intoxicate;
    Ads time to Youth, and takes it from the old;
    Yet I by surfeit this Elixer hate.

23. I curse those Wars that make my glory last;
    For which the *Tuscan* Widows curse me more;

21: 1 Earth's '51b, '73: Eatrh's '51a   21: 4 councel '73: precept '51a–b
22: 3 and '51b, 73: aud '51a   22: 4 by '51b, '73: by by '51a

The barren Fields where I in Arms did fast,
That I might surfeit on luxurious pow'r.

24. Thou *Hermegild*, who art for valor Crown'd,
For honor trusted, and for wisdom heard;
And you whom Councel has no less renown'd,
Observe how vertue against peace has err'd.

25. Still I have fought, as if in Beauty's sight,
Out-suffer'd patience, bred in Captives Breasts;
Taught fasts, till Bodys like our Souls grew light;
Outwatch'd the jealous, and outlabour'd Beasts.

26. These were my merits, my reward is Pow'r;
An outward Trifle, bought with inward peace;
Got in an Age, and rifled in an how'r;
When Feav'rish love, the People's Fit, shall cease.

27. For did not pow'r on their fraile love depend,
Prince *Oswald* had not treated with that love;
Whose glory did in hasty darkness end;
A sparke which vanish'd, as it upward strove.

28. By scorne of dangers and of ease, he sought
The *Lombards* hearts, my *Rhodalind*, and Crowne;
And much his youth had by his practise wrought,
Had *Gondibert* not levell'd his renowne:

29. Had *Gondibert* not staid the Peoples Eies
(Whose vertue stept 'twixt *Oswald* and their sight)
Who knows but *Rhodalind* had bin his Prise,
Or war must have secur'd Paternal right.

30. Sad and uneasy is a long kept Throne;
Not that the People think long pow'r unjust;
But that for change, they wish best Monarchs gone;
Fond change, the Peopel's soon repented lust!

31. I did advance (though with some jealous paine)
A forward vertue to my subjects love;
Least one less temp'rat should their favour gaine;
Whom their unstudy'd choice would more approve.

23: 4 surfeit '*51b*, '*73*: sufeit '*51a*   25: 4 and '*51b*, '*73*: nnd '*51a*

32. To thee sage *Hermegild* my self I leave,
My fame and pow'r: Thee action cannot waste;
Caution retard, nor promptitude deceave;
Slowness belate, nor Hope drive on too faste.

33. Think *Hubert* Heir to *Oswald's* bold pretence;
To whom the Camp at *Brescia* is inclin'd;
The Duke at *Bergamo* will seek defence;
And these are seeds of war for *Rhodalind.*

34. This said, his Councel he dismiss'd; who spy'd
A growing rage, which he would fain conceal;
They durst but nicely search, what he would hide;
Least they inflame the wound that else might heal.

35. They haste to sev'ral Cares; some to allay
Court's hectick Feaver, Faction (which does raign
Where Luxury, the Syre of Want, does sway)
Some to appease th'Alliance of the slain.

36. But Order now bids us again persue
Th'unweary'd Motion of unhappy Fame;
From Fields to Streets, from Streets to Court she flew;
Where first she to the Kings Apartment came.

37. Thence through the Palace she her wings did air;
And as her Wings, her Tongue too never ceas'd;
Like restless Swallows in an Evening fair:
At last does on a peaceful dwelling rest.

38. Where Sleep does yet that gentle Sex possesse,
Who ne'r should more of Care's rude wakings know,
But what may help sad Lovers to successe;
Or imp loves wings when they are found too slow.

39. There Lovers seek the Royal *Rhodalind*;
Whose secret brest was sick for *Gondibert*;
And *Orna*, who had more in publick pin'd
For *Hurgonil*, the Monarch of her heart.

40. And there the killing *Laura* did reside;
She, of whose Eies the *Lombard* Youth Complain;
Yet often she for noble *Arnold* dide;
And knew not now, here Murderer was slain.

38: 4 they . . . too '73: *Hymen* thinks them '51a–b

41. Nor *Hugo*, who was all with love indu'd:
    Whom still with teares the *Lombard* Ladies name.
    Esteeming Modern Lovers false, and rude,
    And Poets falser when they sing their fame.

42. These Beauties (who could soften Tyrant Kings)
    Sleep now conceal'd within their Curtains shade;
    Till rudely Fame, by shaking lowd her wings,
    Disturb'd their Eies, and their wak'd hearts dismay'd.

43. They heard in parcels by imperfect sound,
    A Tale too dismal to be understood;
    That all their Lovers lay in hallow'd ground;
    Temples their Bodies hid, the Fields their blood.

44. That this dire Morn to sad *Verona* brought
    The Duke and *Oswald*, of lov'd life depriv'd;
    And that of all who their fierce batail fought,
    Onely the mangled *Hurgonil* surviv'd.

45. This Tale, Fame's course, officious Friends convay'd,
    (Which are attendant Slaves, and Palace Grooms)
    Who by the Lover of some busy Mayd,
    From outward Courts sent it to inward Rooms.

46. Such horror brought, where love had onely us'd,
    Did yet breed more amazement then belief;
    Whilst *Orna* now, and *Laura* fly confus'd
    To *Rhodalind*, Truth's Altar, for relief.

47. There with disorder'd voices they compare,
    And then derive what each has loosly learn'd;
    Each hope applies, where others most despaire;
    As doubting all but where her self's concern'd.

48. This weeping conf'rence had not lasted long,
    When *Tybalt*, free from *Aribert's* commands,
    Scapes the assembling Court's inquiring Throng,
    And enters here; where first he doubtful stands.

49. For Pitty, when he ruin'd *Laura* spi'de,
    Bids his discretion artfully complain;
    And shew far off, what Truth not long can hide:
    Death at a distance seen, may ease fears pain.

50. Their bus'ness now he can no more forbear;
    For who on their urg'd patience can prevail,
    Whose expectation is provok'd with fear?
    He therefore thus their patience did assail.

51. Kinde Heav'n that gave you vertue, give you peace;
    Delightful as your Beauties, be your Mindes;
    Still may your Lovers your renown increase,
    Though he who honor seeks, first danger findes!

52. Still may your beauty bear that ancient rate,
    When beauty was chaste Honors Merchandice;
    When Valor was chief Factor in Love's State;
    Danger, Love's stamp, and Beautie's currant price.

53. Renown'd be *Oswald*, who in high belief
    Of *Rhodalind*, her love with danger sought;
    In Love's Records be *Gondibert* the chief,
    Who for her right, not for his own has fought.

54. Though these for mighty mindes deserve Fame's voice;
    Yet *Orna* needs must boast of *Hurgonill*;
    Whose dangers well have justifi'd her choice,
    And might alone Fame's publick Trumpet fill.

55. Enlarg'd be Honor's Throne, that *Arnold* there
    And *Hugo* may for ever sit and rest,
    Free from their Valor's toyle, and *Laura's* feare;
    Which more then wounds disorder'd eithers Breast.

56. This said, he paws'd; findes each distrusts his art;
    For Hope and Doubt came and return'd apace,
    In chang'd Complexion from th'uncertain heart,
    Like frighted Scowtes for Tidings to the Face.

57. His Eie seem'd most imploy'd on *Rhodalind*;
    Whose love above her bashful caution sways;
    For naming *Gondibert*, he soon did finde,
    Her secret Soul shew'd pleasure at his praise.

58. Yet when she found her comforts did not last,
    And that as Oracles the future taught,
    He hid Truth's Face, and darkned what was past;
    Thus Truth through all her mourning Vailes she sought.

55: 3 toyle '*73*: toyles '*51a–b*

59. Why in these Ladies doe you lengthen paine,
    By giving them Grief's common med'cin, doubt?
    Ease those with death whose Lovers now are slaine;
    Life's fire a Feaver is, when Love's is out.

60. Yet think not that my cares peculiar are;
    Perhaps I from religious pitty learn'd,
    In Vertu's publick loss to take some share;
    For there, all but the vicious are concern'd.

61. Your prudence, Royal Maid (he strait replies)
    More then your birth, may claim the *Lombards* Crowne;
    Whoe're in conquest of your favour dies;
    For short lifes loss, shall finde a long renowne.

62. Then happy *Oswald* who is sure to gaine,
    Even by Ambition that undoes the wise;
    Great was th'attempt for which he's nobly slaine;
    And gets him praise, though he has mist the Prise.

63. But happier *Gondibert*, who does survive
    To begg your Mercy, that he thus hath dar'd
    To own that cause, for which the world might strive;
    And conqu'ring, takes his wounds for his reward.

64. Be *Hurgonil* long distant from his Grave,
    Whose life was so important in this cause;
    Who for each wound he took, a wider gave,
    And lives t'enjoy the pleasure of applause.

65. To say, how *Hugo* and Lord *Arnold* strove
    For victorie, and mention their event,
    Were to provide such fun'ral rites for Love,
    As Death would be closse Mourner, and repent.

66. Now *Laura's* blood back to her Liver fled;
    True Beautie's Mint: For by her Heart, Love's Throne,
    Beautie's call'd in, like Coyn when Kings are dead;
    As if not currant now her Lover's gone.

67. And like her beauty, she had darkned life,
    But that with sprinkled water they restore
    (By sodain cold, with sodain heat at strife)
    Her spirits to those walks they us'd before.

61: 4 short . . . loss '73: life's lost Inch '51a–b

68. She *Arnold* cals, then lost that name againe;
    Which *Rhodalind*, and *Orna's* tears bemone,
    Who busilie would her spent strength sustaine,
    Though Hope has scarcely yet brought back their owne.

69. Now they her Temples chaf'd, and strait prepare
    Hot Eastern Fumes to reach her Brains cool'd sence;
    With Wine's fierce spirits these extracted are,
    Which warme but slowly, though of swift expence.

70. Yet now again she breath'd Lord *Arnold's* name;
    Which her apt Tongue through custom best exprest;
    Then to stay Life, that so unwilling came,
    With Cordial Epithems they bath'd her breast.

71. Th'attendant Maids, by *Tybalt's* ready ayde,
    To stop her Mourners teares, convey her now
    Where she may ease in her own Curtain's shade
    Her weary heart, and grief more Tongue allow.

72. No sooner thus was pity'd *Laura* gon,
    But *Oswald's* sister, *Gartha* the renown'd!
    Enters, as if the World were overthrown,
    Or in the teares of the afflicted drown'd.

73. Unconquer'd as her beauty was her minde;
    Which wanted not a spark of *Oswald's* fire;
    Ambition lov'd, but ne'r to Love was kinde;
    Vex'd Thrones did more then quiet shades desire.

74. Her Garments now in loose neglect she wore,
    As suted to her wilde dishevel'd haire;
    Men in her shape might Nature's work adore,
    Yet ask, why Art's nice dresse was absent there?

75. But soon they found what made this change appear;
    For meeting Truth, which slowly follows Fame,
    Rage would not give her leasure for a Teare
    To quench (ere thus she spake) her passion's flame.

76. Blasted be all your beauties *Rhodalind*,
    Till you a shame, and terror be to light;
    Unwing'd be Love, and slow as he is blind,
    Who with your Looks poyson'd my Brothers sight!

77. Low and neglected be your Father's Throne,
Which like your beauty, *Oswald* did o're-rate;
Let lucklesse war take Lands from his light Crown,
Till those high cares he want that give it weight!

78. Let Pow'rs consumption be his long disease,
(Heav'n's vexing Curb, which makes wilde Monarchs tame)
And be he forc'd in froward age to please
His Favour's Monster, who devoures his Fame.

79. May you soon feel (though secret in your love,
As if your love were Sin) the publick scorn!
May *Gondibert*, who is your glory, move
Your pittie, when none else but you shall mourn!

80. To the dark Inne (where weary Valor, free
From thankless dangers rests) brave *Oswald's* gone!
But *Hubert* may, though vanquish'd, live to see
Your Victor with his victory undone!

81. This said, she mounts (with a tempestuous Brow)
The Chariot her *Calabrian* Coursers drew;
Lifted by Slaves (who still about her bow)
As if with wings of swift revenge she flew.

82. To *Brescia's* Camp her course she had design'd;
And bids her *Tuscan* Char'ioter drive on,
As if his steeds were dieted with winde!
Slow seems their speed whose thoughts before them run.

83. The pav'd Streets kindle with her Chariot wheeles!
The Omen of war's fire, the City spies,
Which with those sparks struck by her Coursers heels,
Shine not so much as rage does in her Eies.

84. Those that observ'd her anger, grief, and haste,
With a dejected melancholy mourn;
She seem'd their Cities Genius as she pass'd,
Who by their Sins expell'd, would ne'r return.

85. The gentle Ladies, she has left in tears,
Who no example need nor cause to melt;

84: 2 a dejec.ed '7 2: ancient *Roman* '51a–b

For soon even grief's Alarms, our foremost fears,
Kill those whose pain by Love's quick sence is felt

86. And *Rhodalind* her fatal love does blame,
Because she findes it now by *Gartha* spy'd;
And does lament Love's fire, which bashful shame
Cannot reveal, nor her discretion hide.

87. She would not have it wast, nor publick grow;
But last conceal'd like that in *Tullia's* Urne;
Or that which prosp'rous *Chymists* nicely show;
Which as it thrives, must more in private burn.

88. Yet strait (grown valiant with her Victors fate)
She would have *Hymen* hold his Torches high;
And Love's fire pris'd, as Vestals theirs did rate;
Which none durst quench, though free to ev'ry Eie.

89. Resolves her love whilst this new valor lasts,
Shall undisguis'd her Father's sight endure;
And *Orna* now to her dear Lover hastes;
Whose outward wounds stay for her inward cure.

90. But here a wonder may arrest our thought,
Why *Tybalt* (of his usual pitty void)
To such soft Eares these direful sorrows brought,
Since to the King he onely was imploy'd?

91. But these are Ridles of misterious Love!
Tybalt in private long for *Laura* pin'd;
And try'd how *Arnold* would her passion move
In death, who living ever fill'd her minde?

92. And by this trial how she *Arnold* us'd,
He wisely ment to urge or stay his heart;
But much by Love the Cautious are abus'd,
Who his wilde Ridles would reduce to Art.

85: 3 fears] tears '*51b*   92: 2 wisely '*73*: gravely '*51a–b*

Canto the Third

The ARGUMENT

Dead OSWALD *to his Camp by* HUBERT *brought;*
The Camp from pity, are to fury wrought;
Yet finde, when GARTHA'S *lookes does them surprise,*
Their forward Hands diverted by their Eies:
Till with her voice new urg'd, they deeds persue
Which even Revenge would, had it Eies, eschew.

1. When from the fatal Forrest *Hubert* rod,
   To *Brescia* he and *Borgio* bent their way;
   That their though dead, yet much important Load,
   They might with horror to the Camp convay.

2. Revenge, impatient *Hubert* proudly sought!
   Revenge, which even when just the wise deride;
   For on past wrongs we spend our time and thought,
   Which scarce against the future can provide.

3. But Fame before him came where those are bred
   Who to her dismal Tales, faint credit give;
   Who could not think their mighty *Oswald* dead,
   Whilst they unconquer'd and unwounded live.

4. Nor could Fame hope to make this Camp her Seate;
   Her Tales, the talking, idle, fearful, heare;
   But these are silent as in stolne retreate,
   Busy as life, and like the Dead past feare.

5. Neer *Mela's* flowry Banke this Army lay;
   Which *Oswald's* Syre, and *Oswald* oft had led
   Against the *Vandales* King; and twice the Day
   They gain'd, whilst he from them and Empire fled.

6. From Youth expos'd, like Cattell in the Field;
   And not taught warmth, as City Infants are;
   But colds and fasts, to kill or to be kill'd;
   Like th'Elements their birth began with Warre.

3: 2 her '*51a MS*, '*51b*, '*73*: his '*51a*

7. So rev'rend now, and strong in age appeare,
   As if maintain'd by more then humane breath;
   So grave, as if the Councelors they were,
   Not Executioners of Tyrant Death.

8. With silence (order's help, and marke of care)
   They chide that noyse which heedless youth affect;
   Still course for use, for health they cleanly weare,
   And save in well fix'd Armes, all niceness check'd.

9. They thought, those that unarm'd expos'd fraile life,
   But naked Nature valiantly betrai'd;
   Who was though naked, safe, till pride made strife;
   But made defence must use, now danger's made.

10. And those who toyle of Armor cannot byde,
    Lose Nature's force, which these in custom finde;
    And make (since strength's but Nature hourly try'd)
    The Body weake by softness of the Minde.

11. They seem'd so calme, and with their age so grave,
    So just and civil in their killing trade,
    As if all life were crime but what they save;
    Or Murder were by method lawful made.

12. Yet now that Manhood which those Victors makes
    (So weake is Man, where most he may be prowd)
    Pity, the tender'st of affections, shakes,
    And they become from order, loose, and lowd.

13. For when they saw the Brother of their Chief
    Led to their Camp by a defeated Traine,
    They soon to late scorn'd Rumor gave belief,
    And then by *Hubert's* wounds thought *Oswald* slaine.

14. But when disguis'd in death they *Oswald* saw,
    In a slow Chariot brought, with fun'ral pace;
    Themselves in an united Croud they draw;
    And give all grief one universal Face.

15. Wonder (which growes unactive by excesse)
    A while did their unruly passion stay;

8: 2 chide '73: chid '51a–b   8: 3 weare '73: were '51a–b   13: 3 soon . . .
belief] soon, too . . . Rumour, . . . '51b

The object lasting, made their wonder lesse,
Which fled to give their grief and anger way.

16. Yet first their grief (which Manhood should restraine)
They vent in woemens sighs, with teares allay'd;
As if those woemen taught them to complaine
Who by their Swords are weeping Widows made.

17. As Icy Rockes which frosts together binde,
Stand silent, till as silently they melt,
But when they meet in Currents unconfin'd,
Swell, and grow loud, as if they freedom felt;

18. So these, unmov'd before, melt quietly
In their first grief, till grief (when tears meet tears,
And sighs meet sighs from ev'ry breast and Eie)
Unruly grows, and danger's visage bears.

19. When hastily they heard by whose dire hand
Their Gen'ral fell, they think it cold to pause
Till anger may be guided by command;
And vain to ask of cureless Death the cause.

20. Some would to *Bergamo* their Ensignes bear,
Against those Youth which *Gondibert* had led;
Whom they in sacrifice would offer there,
T'appease the living, and revenge the dead.

21. And some (to shew their rage more eminent)
Would to *Verona* march, and there do deeds
Should make the shining Court in blacks lament,
And weep, whilst the Victorious Faction bleeds.

22. *Hubert* (who saw Revenge advance so faste,
Whilst Prudence, slower pac'd, was left behinde)
Would keep their anger bent, yet slack their haste;
Because the rash fall oftner then the blinde.

23. He first their melting pitty kindly prais'd,
Which water'd Anger's forge, and urg'd their fire;
That like to Meteors lasts by being rais'd,
But when it first does sink, does strait expire.

21: 3 shining '51b, '73: shining '51a

24. Commends their anger, yet that flame he prays
    May keep the temp'rate Chymicks equal heat;
    That they in furie might not need allays,
    Nor charge so rashly as to want retreat.

25. Begs they this dismal night would there remain,
    And make the hopeful Morn their Guide; whilst Grief
    (Which high Revenge, as tamenesse should disdain)
    Sleep shall conceal, and give his wounds relief.

26. He *Vasco*, *Paradine*, and *Dargonet*,
    With *Oswald*, to the red *Pavilion* sent;
    (Death's equal Pris'ners now for Nature's debt)
    And then retires with *Borgio* to his Tent.

27. This is the night the *Brescians* so bemoan'd;
    Who left their beds, and on their walls appear'd;
    As if th'oppressed World in Earthquakes groan'd,
    Or that some ruin'd Nation's sighs they heard;

28. Admir'd what in that Camp such griefs could raise,
    Where serious Death so oft had been abus'd,
    When even their sportive Fencers Monthly Plays
    Profan'd that shape, which States for terror us'd.

29. Yet this lowd mourning will no wonder breed,
    When we with life lay *Oswald's* errors by,
    And use him as the Living use the Dead;
    Who first allow men vertue when they dy.

30. Still lib'ral of his life, of wealth as free;
    By which he chief in fighting Crowds became;
    Who must their Leaders Valors often see;
    And follow them for bounty more then fame.

31. This gen'ral mourning was to lowdnesse rais'd,
    By shewing Guifts he gave, and wounds he took;
    They chid at last his life which they had prais'd,
    Because such vertue it so soon forsook.

32. Now Night, by Grief neglected, hastes away!
    And they the Morne's officious Usher spy,
    The closse Attendant on the Lord of Day;
    Who shews the warmer of the World is nigh.

33. And now the Drums, the Camps low Thunder, make
    War's thick united noise from ev'ry Guard;
    Though they *Reveillees* scorn, whom grief does wake,
    And sleep, think Nature's curse, not toyls reward.

34. All night proud *Borgio* (chief in *Hubert's* trust)
    With haughty hopes, the Camp does waking keep:
    Ambition is more vigilant then Lust,
    And in hope's feaver is too hot to sleep.

35. Now Day, and *Hubert* haste to publick view;
    His wounds (unlucky more then dangerous)
    Are so refresh'd, that he the Army drew
    To a wide Grosse, and urg'd their Anger thus.

36. Friends to my Father! In whose wounds I see
    The envy'd Merit whence his triumphs came;
    And Fathers to my Brother, and to me;
    For onely you adopted us to Fame!

37. Forgive me that I there have feebly fought,
    Where *Oswald* in your cause did nobly strive;
    Whence of his blood these veines so much have brought,
    As makes me blush that I am still alive!

38. Your valiant Youth is gone, whom you have bred
    From milkie Childhood to the years of blood!
    By whom you joy'd so often to be led,
    Where firme as now your Trophys, then you stood!

39. Gon is he now, who still with low regard
    Bow'd to your age, your wounds as beauty kist;
    Knew Age was of your temp'rance the reward;
    And Courts in beauty by your skarrs subsist.

40. Yet was he not for mean pretensions slaine,
    Who for your int'rest, not his own has fought;
    Vex'd that the Empire which your wounds did gaine,
    Was by a young unwounded Army sought!

41. For *Gondibert* (to whom the Court must bow,
    Now War is with your Fav'rite overthrowne)
    Will by his Camp of Boys at *Bergamo*,
    Wed her, who to your Valor owes the Crowne.

    38: 1 Your . . . gone '73: Gon is your fighting Youth '51a-b

42. Blame not your Chief for his ambitious fire;
 Who was but temp'rate, when he understood
 He might the Empire in your right require;
 The scant reward of your exhausted blood.

43. Thus *Hubert* spake; but now so fierce they grow,
 That *Borgio* strove to quench whom *Hubert* warm'd;
 To *Bergamo*, they cry'd, to *Bergamo*!
 And as they soon were vex'd, as soon are arm'd.

44. For to distinct and spacious Tents they hie,
 Where quick as Vests of *Persia* shifted are,
 Their Arms (which there in cleanly order lie)
 They take from moving Wardrobes of the warre.

45. Arm'd soon as *Porquepines*! as if like those,
 Their very rage them with defence supplies;
 As borne with it, and must have winged Foes,
 That stoop from Heav'n, to harme them by surprise.

46. With Ensignes now display'd, their Force they draw
 To hasty order, and begin to move;
 But are amus'd by something that they saw,
 Which look'd like all that ere they heard of love.

47. Unusual to their Camp such objects were,
 Yet this no ill effect from wonder wrought;
 For it appeas'd them by approaching neer,
 And satisfi'd their Eies in all they sought.

48. And this was *Gartha* in her Chariot drawn;
 Who through the swarthy Region of the Night
 Drove from the Court; and as a second dawn
 Breaks on them, like the Mornes Reserve of Light.

49. Through all the Camp she moves with Fun'rall pace,
 And still bowes meekly down to all she saw;
 Her grief gave speaking beauty to her Face;
 Which lowly look'd, that it might pity draw.

50. When by her Slaves, her name they understood,
 Her Lines of feature heedfully they view;
 In her complexion track their Gen'ral's blood,
 And finde her more, then what by fame they knew.

48: 1 Chariot '*73*: Chari'ot '*51a–b*

51. They humbly her to that Pavilion guide,
    Where *Hubert* his bold Chiefs with fury fir'd;
    But his ambition, when he *Gartha* spy'd
    (To give his sorrow place) a while retir'd.

52. With his respectfull help she does descend;
    Where they, with dear imbraces, mingle Tears,
    But now her Male Revenge would grief suspend;
    Revenge, through Grief, too feminine appears.

53. But when her dear Allies, dead *Paradine*,
    And *Dargonet* she saw; that Manlinesse
    Which her weak Sex assum'd, she does decline;
    As bred too soft, to mannage griefs excesse.

54. Then soon return'd, as loath to shew her Eies
    No more of *Oswald* then she must forsake;
    But sorrow's moisture, heat of anger dries;
    And mounted in her Chariot, thus she spake:

55. If you are those of whom I oft have heard
    My Father boast, and that have *Oswald* bred;
    Ah, where is now that rage our Tyrant fear'd;
    Whose Darling is alive, though yours be dead?

56. The Court shines out at *Rhodalind's* commands,
    To me (your drooping Flowre) no beam can spare;
    Where *Oswald's* name, new planted by your hands,
    Withers, as if it lost the Planters care.

57. From *Rhodalind* I thus disorder'd flie;
    Least she should say, thy Fate unpity'd comes!
    Goe sing, where now thy Fathers Fighters lie,
    Thy Brothers requiem, to their conqu'ring Drums!

58. The happy Fields by those grave Warriors fought,
    (Which from the Dictates of thy aged Syre,
    Oswald in high Victorious Numbers wrot)
    Thou shalt no more sing to thy silenc'd Lyre!

59. Such scorns, pow'r on unlucky vertue throws,
    When Courts with prosp'rous vices wanton are;
    Who your Authentick age despise for those,
    Who are to you but Infants of the warre.

58: 4 sing] sign '73

60. Thus though she spake, her looks did more perswade;
    Like vertuous anger did her colour rise,
    As if th'injurious world it would invade,
    Whilst tears of rage not pitty drown her Eies.

61. The Sun did thus to threatned Nature show
    His anger red, whilst guilt look'd pale in all;
    When Clouds of Floods did hang about his Brow,
    And then shrunk back to let that anger fall.

62. And so she turn'd her Face, not as to grieve
    At ruine, but to lisence what she rais'd;
    Whilst they (like common Throngs) all Tongues beleeve
    When Courts are tax'd, but none when they are prais'd.

63. Like Commets, Courts afflict the Vulgar Eie;
    And when they largest in their glory blaze,
    People through ignorance think plagues are nie,
    And till they waste with mourning wonder gaze.

64. These scorn the Courts dissertion of their age;
    The Active, ease impos'd, like pain endure;
    For though calm rest does Age's pains asswage,
    Yet few the sickness own to get the cure.

65. To Heav'n they lift their looks! whose Sun ne'r saw
    Rage so agreed, as now he does behold;
    Their shining Swords all at an instant draw,
    And bad him judge next day if they were old!

66. And of *Verona* wish'd him take his leave;
    Which ere his third return they will destroy,
    Till none shall guesse by ruines where to grieve,
    No more then *Phrygians* where to weep for *Troy*.

67. Thus *Bergamo* is soon forgot, whilst all
    Alowd, *Verona* cry! *Verona* must
    (That reach'd the Clouds) low as her Quarries fall!
    The Court they'll bury in the Cities dust.

Canto the Fourth

The ARGUMENT

At OSWALD'S *Camp arrives wise* HERMEGILD;
Whose presence does a new diversion yield;
In Councel he reveals his secret Breast;
Would mingle Love with Empires interest:
From rash revenge, to peace the Camp invites,
Who OSWALD'S *Fun'ral grace with Roman Rites.*

1. In this distemper whilst the humors strive
   T'assemble, they again diverted are;
   For tow'rds their Trenches Twenty Chariots drive,
   Swiftly as *Syrians* when they charge in warre.

2. They *Hermegild* with Court Attendants spy'd;
   Whose haste to *Hubert* does advice intend;
   To warn him that just Fate can ne'r provide
   For rash beginnings a succesful end.

3. But fate for *Hermegild* provided well;
   This Story else (which him the wise does call)
   Would here his private ruine sadly tell,
   In hastning to prevent the publick Fall.

4. His noble blood obscurely had been shed,
   His undistinguish'd Limbs torn and unknown,
   As is the dust of Victors long since dead,
   Which here and there, by every wind is blown.

5. Such was their rage when on *Verona's* way
   (With his rich Train) they saw from Court he came;
   Till some did their impetuous fury stay;
   And gave his life protection for his fame,

6. Told them his valor had been long allow'd;
   That much the *Lombard's* to his conduct ow;
   And this preserv'd him, for the very Crowd
   Felt honor here, and did to valor bow.

Arg. 5 to] lo *'51b*   *Arg.* 6 Rites. *'51b, '73*: Rites, *'51a*   3: 4 In] I *'73*
4: 4 here . . . is *'73*: *March* in *April's* watry Eies has *'51a–b*

7. Vain Wrath! Deform'd, unquiet Child of Pride!
   Which in a few the People madness call;
   But when by Number they grow dignify'd,
   What's rage in some is liberty in all.

8. Through dangers of this lawless liberty,
   He like Authentick pow'r does boldly passe;
   And with a quiet and experienc'd Eie,
   Through Death's foul Vizard, does despise his face.

9. At *Hubert's* Tent alights, where *Hubert* now
   With *Gartha* of this Torrent does advise;
   Which he believes does at the highest flow,
   And must like Tides, sink when it cannot rise.

10. When *Hermegild* he saw, he did disperse
    Those cares assembled in his looks, and strove
    (Though to his Master, and the Court perverse)
    To shew him all the civil signes of Love.

11. For him in stormy war he glorious knew;
    Nor in calme Councels was he less renown'd;
    And held him now to *Oswald's* Faction true,
    As by his love, the world's first Tenure, bound.

12. For he (though wasted in the ebb of blood,
    When Man's Meridian tow'rds his Evening turnes)
    Makes against Nature's law, Love's Charter good,
    And as in raging Youth for *Gartha* burnes.

13. Who did his sute not only disapprove,
    Because the summer of his life was paste;
    And she fresh blowne; but that even highest love
    Growes tastless to Ambition's higher taste.

14. Yet now in such a great and single cause,
    With nice Ambition, nicer Love complies;
    And she (since to revenge he usefull was)
    Perswades his hope with Rhet'rique of her Eies.

15. A closse division of the Tent they strait
    By outward Guards secure from all resort;
    Then *Hermegild* does thus the cause relate,
    Which to the Camp dispatch'd him from the Court.

7: 3 grow '51a *MS*: grew '51a–b, '73   7: 4 some '73: one '51a–b

16. Important Prince! who justly dost succeed
    To *Oswald's* hopes, and all my loyal ayde;
    Vertue as much in all thy wounds does bleed,
    As love in me, since wounded by that Mayde.

17. Long have I sayl'd through Times vexatious sea;
    And first set out with all that Youth is worth;
    The *Tropicks* pass'd of bloods hot bravery,
    With all the Sayles, gay Flags, and Streamers forth!

18. But as in hotter voyages, Ships most
    Weare out their trim, yet then they chiefly gaine
    By inward stowage, what is outward lost;
    So Men, decays of youth, repaire in braine.

19. If I experience boast when Youth decays,
    Such vanitie may *Gartha's* pity move,
    Since so I seek your service by selfe praise,
    Rather then seem unuseful where I love.

20. And never will I (though by Time supply'd
    With such discretion as does Man improve)
    To shew discretion, wiser Nature hide,
    By seeming now asham'd to say I Love.

21. For love his pow'r has in gray Senates shown,
    Where he, as to green Courts, does freely come;
    And though lowd youth, his visits makes more known,
    With graver Age he's privatly at home.

22. Scarce *Greece*, or greater *Rome* a Victor showes,
    Whom more Victorious Love did not subdue;
    Then blame not me who am so weake to those;
    Whilst *Gartha* all exceeds, that ere they knew.

23. Hope (Love's first food) I ne'r till now did know;
    Which Love, as yet but temp'ratly devours;
    And claimes not love for love, since *Gartha* so
    For *Autumne* Leaves, should barter Summer Flowres.

24. I dare not vainly wish her to be kinde,
    Till for her love, my Arts and Pow'r bestow
    The Crowne on thee, adorn'd with *Rhodalind*;
    Which yet for *Gartha* is a price too low.

16:2 *Oswald's*] '*51b*; Oswalds '*51a*, '*73*   18:2 Weare out] '*73*; decay '*51a–b*

25. This said, he paws'd; and now the hectick heate
    Of *Oswald's* blood, doubled their Pulces pace;
    Which high, as if they would be heard, did beate,
    And hot Ambition shin'd in eithers face.

26. For *Hermegild* they knew could much outdoe
    His words, and did possess great *Aribert*,
    Not in the Courts cheap Glasse of outward showe,
    But by a study'd Tenure of the heart.

27. Whilst this try'd truth does make their wishes sure,
    Hubert on *Gartha* lookes, with sueing Eies
    For *Hermegild*; whose love she will endure,
    And make Ambition yeild what Youth denies.

28. Yet in this bargain of her self, she knowes
    Not how to treat; but all her chief desires,
    Bids *Hubert*, as the Twinns of his, dispose
    To glory and revenge; and then retires.

29. But with such blushes *Hermegild* she leaves,
    As the unclouded Evening's Face adorn;
    Nor much he for her parting glory grieves,
    Since such an Evening bodes a happy Morn.

30. Now *Hermegild* by vows does *Hubert* binde,
    (Vowes by their fate in *Lombard* Story known)
    He *Gartha* makes the price of *Rhodalind*,
    And *Aribert* his Tenant to the Crown.

31. He bids him now the Armies rage allay;
    By rage (said he) only they Masters are
    Of those they chuse, when temp'rate, to obay:
    Against themselves th'impatient chiefly warre.

32. We are the Peoples Pilots, they our winds;
    To change by Nature prone; but Art Laveers,
    And rules them till they rise with Stormy Mindes;
    Then Art with danger against Nature Steers.

33. Where calms have first amus'd, Storms most prevail;
    Cloze first with Calms the Courts suspitious Eies;
    That whilst with all their trim, they sleeping sail,
    A sodain Gust may wrack them by surprise.

26: 3 outward '73: civil '51a–b

34. Your Army will (though high in all esteem
 That ever rev'renc'd Age to action gave)
 But a small Party to *Verona* seem;
 Which yearly to such Numbers yeilds a Grave.

35. Nor is our vaste Metropolis, like those
 Tame Towns, which peace has soft'ned into fears;
 But Death deform'd in all his Dangers knows;
 Dangers, which he like frightful Vizards wears.

36. From many Camps, who forraign winters felt,
 Verona has her conqu'ring Dwellers ta'ne;
 In War's great Trade, with richest Nations delt;
 And did their Gold and Fame with Iron gain.

37. Yet to the mighty *Aribert* it bowes;
 A King out-doing all the *Lombard* Line!
 Whose Court (in Iron clad) by coursnesse showes
 A growing pow'r, which fades when Courts grow fine.

38. Scorn not the Youthful Camp at *Bergamo*;
 For they are Victors, though in years but young;
 The War does them, they it by action know,
 And have obedient Minds, in Bodies strong.

39. Be slow, and stay for aides, which haste forsakes!
 For though Occasion still does Sloth out-go,
 The Rash, who run from help, she ne'r o're-takes,
 Whose hast thinks Time, the Post of Nature, slow.

40. This is a cause which our Ambition fills;
 A cause, in which our strength we should not waste,
 In vain like Giants, who did heave at Hills;
 'Tis too unwildy for the force of haste.

41. A cause for graver Minds that learned are
 In mistick Man; a cause which we must gain
 By surer methods then depend on Warre;
 And respite valor, to imploy the Brain.

42. In the King's Scale your merits are too light;
 Who with the Duke, weighs his own partial heart;
 Make then the guift of Empire publick right,
 And get in *Rhodalind* the Peoples part.

37: 2 *Lombard*] Lombards '51b   40: 3 In vain '73: Vainly '51a–b

43. But this rough Tyde, the meeting Multitude,
    If we oppose, we make our voyage long;
    Yet when we with it row, it is subdu'd;
    And we are wise, when Men in vain are strong.

44. Then to the People sue, but hide your force;
    For they beleeve the strong are still unjust;
    Never to Armed Sutors yield remorse;
    And where they see the pow'r, the right distrust.

45. Assault their pity as their weakest part;
    Which the first Plaintiff never failes to move;
    They search but in the face to finde the heart;
    And grief in Princes, more then triumph love.

46. And to prepare their pity, *Gartha* now
    Should in her sorrows height with me return;
    For since their Eies at all distresses flow,
    How will they at afflicted beauty mourn?

47. Much such a pledge of Peace will with the King
    (Urg'd by my int'rest here) my pow'r improve;
    And much my power will to your int'rest bring,
    If from the watchful Court you hide my Love.

48. If *Gartha* deignes to love, our love must grow
    Unseen, like *Mandrakes* wedded under ground;
    That I (still seeming unconcern'd) may know
    The King's new depths, which length of trust may sound!

49. Thus *Hermegild* his study'd thoughts declar'd;
    Whilst *Hubert* (who beleev'd, discover'd love
    A solid Pledg for hidden faith) prepar'd
    To stay the Camp, so furious to remove.

50. And now their rage (by correspondence spred)
    Borgio allays, that else like sparks of fire
    (Which drops at first might drowne) by matter fed,
    At last to quench the flame may seas require.

51. As with the Sun they rose in wrath, their wrath
    So with his heat increas'd; but now he hastes
    Down Heav'ns steep Hill, to his *Atlantick* Bath;
    Where he refreshes till his Feaver wastes.

43: 4 when '73: where '51a–b   48: 2 wedded] weeded '51b

52. With his (by *Borgio's* help) their heat declin'd;
So soon lov'd Eloquence does Throngs subdue;
The common Mistress to each private Minde;
Painted and dress'd to all, to no Man true.

53. To Court his *Gartha*, *Hermegild* attends;
And with old Lovers vaine poetick Eies,
Markes how her beauty, when the Sun descends,
His pitty'd Evening povertie supplies.

54. The Army now to Neighb'ring *Brescia* bear,
With dismal pomp, the slaine: In hallow'd ground
They *Paradine*, and *Dargonet* interr;
And *Vasco* much in painful war renoun'd.

55. To *Oswald* (whose illustrious *Roman* minde
Shin'd out in life, though now in dying hid)
Hubert these *Roman* fun'ral rites assign'd;
Which yet the World's last law had not forbid.

56. Thrice is his Body clean by bathing made;
And when with Victor's Oyle anointed or'e,
'Tis in the Pallace Gate devoutly layd'e,
Clad in that Vest which he in Bataile wore.

57. Whilst seven succeeding Suns passe sadly by,
The Palace seems all hid in Cypresse Boughs;
From ancient Lore, of Man's mortalitie
The Type, for where 'tis lopp'd it never grows.

58. The publick fun'ral voyce, till these expire,
Crys out; here Greatness, tir'd with honor, rests!
Come see what Bodies are, when Souls retire;
And visit death, ere you become his Guests!

59. Now on a Purple Bed the Corps they raise;
Whilst Trumpets summon all the common Quire
In tune to mourn him, and disperse his praise;
And then move slowly tow'rds the Fun'ral fire!

60. They beare before him Spoiles they gain'd in warre;
And his great Ancestors in Sculpture wrought;
And now arrive, where *Hubert* does declare
How oft and well, he for the *Lombards* fought.

61. Here, in an Altar's form, a Pile is made
    Of Unctious Firr, and Sleepers fatal Ewe;
    On which the Body is by Mourners laid,
    Who there sweet Gummes (their last kinde Tribute) threw.

62. *Hubert* his Arme, westward, aversly stretch'd;
    Whilst to the hopefull East his Eies were turn'd;
    And with a hallow'd Torch the Pyle he reach'd;
    Which seen, they all with utmost clamor mourn'd.

63. Whilst the full Flame aspires, *Oswald* (they cry)
    Farewell! we follow swiftly as the Houres!
    For with Time's wings, tow'rds Death, even Cripples flie!
    This said, the hungry Flame its food devoures.

64. Now Priests with Wine the Ashes quench, and hide
    The Rev'renc'd Reliques in a Marble Urne.
    The old dismissive *Ilicet* is cry'd
    By the Towne voice, and all to Feasts returne.

65. Thus Urnes may Bodies shew; but the fled Minde
    The Learn'd seek vainly; for whose Quest we pay,
    With such success as cousen'd Shepheards finde,
    Who seek to Wizards when their Cattel stray.

Canto the Fifth

The ARGUMENT

The House of ASTRAGON; *Where in distress*
Of Nature, GONDIBERT *for Art's redress*
Was by old ULFIN *brought: where Art's hard strife,*
In studying Nature for the aid of Life,
Is by full wealth and conduct easy made;
And Truth much visited, though in her shade.

1. From *Brescia* swiftly o're the bord'ring Plain,
   Return we to the House of *Astragon*;
   Where *Gondibert*, and his succesful Train,
   Kindly lament the Victory they won.

61: 4 there] their '73

2. But though I Fame's great Book shall open now,
  Expect a while, till she that *Decad* reads,
  Which does this Dukes eternal Story show,
  And aged *Ulfin* cites for special deeds.

3. Where Friendship is renown'd in *Ulfinore*;
  Where th'ancient musick of delightful verse,
  Does it no lesse in *Goltho's* Breast adore,
  And th'union of their equal hearts reherse.

4. These weary Victors the descending Sun
  Led hither, where swift Night did them surprise;
  And where, for valiant toiles, wise *Astragon*,
  With sweet rewards of sleep, did fill their Eies.

5. When to the needy World Day did appear,
  And freely op'd her Treasurie of light,
  His House (where Art and Nature Tennants were)
  The pleasure grew, and bus'nesse of their sight.

6. Where *Ulfin* (who an old Domestick seems,
  And rules as Master in the Owners Breast)
  Leads *Goltho* to admire what he esteems;
  And thus, what he had long observ'd, exprest.

7. Here Art by such a diligence is serv'd,
  As does th'unwearied Planets imitate;
  Whose motion (life of Nature) has preserv'd
  The world, which God vouchsaf'd but to create.

8. Those heights, which els Dwarf Life could never reach,
  Here, by the wings of diligence they climbe;
  Truth (skar'd with Terms from canting Schools) they teach;
  And buy it with their best sav'd Treasure, Time.

9. Here all Men seem Recov'rers of time past;
  As busy as intentive *Emmets* are;
  As alarm'd Armies that intrench in haste,
  Or Cities, whom unlook'd-for sieges skare.

10. Much it delights the wise Observers Eie,
  That all these toiles direct to sev'ral skills;
  Some from the Mine to the hot Furnace hie,
  And some from flowry Fields to weeping Stills.

11. The first to hopeful *Chymicks* matter bring,
    Where Med'cine they extract for instant cure;
    These bear the sweeter burthens of the Spring;
    Whose vertues (longer known) though slow, are sure.

12. See there wet *Divers* from *Fossone* sent!
    Who of the Seas deep Dwellers knowledge give;
    Which (more unquiet then their Element)
    By hungry war, upon each other live.

13. Pearl to their Lord, and Cordial Coral these
    Present; which must in sharpest liquids melt;
    He with *Nigella* cures that dull disease
    They get, who long with stupid Fish have dwelt.

14. Others through Quarries dig, deeply below
    Where Desart Rivers, cold, and private run;
    Where Bodies conservation best they know,
    And Mines long growth, and how their veines begun.

15. He shews them now Tow'rs of prodigious height,
    Where Natures Friends, Philosophers, remain,
    To censure Meteors in their cause and flight;
    And watch the Wind's authority on Rain.

16. Others with Optick Tubes the Moons scant face
    (Vaste Tubes, which like long Cedars mounted lie)
    Attract through Glasses to so neer a space,
    As if they came not to survey, but prie.

17. Nine hasty Centuries are now fulfill'd,
    Since Opticks first were known to *Astragon*;
    By whom the Moderns are become so skill'd,
    They dream of seeing to the Maker's Throne.

18. And wisely *Astragon*, thus busy grew,
    To seek the Stars remote societies;
    And judge the walks of th'old, by finding new;
    For Nature's law, in correspondence lies.

19. Man's pride (grown to Religion) he abates,
    By moving our lov'd Earth; which we think fix'd;
    Think all to it, and it to none relates;
    With others motion scorn to have it mix'd:

20. As if 'twere great and stately to stand still
    Whilst other Orbes dance on; or else think all
    Those vaste bright Globes (to shew God's needless skill)
    Were made but to attend our little Ball.

21. Now neer a sever'd Building they discern'd
    (Which seem'd, as in a pleasant shade, retir'd)
    A Throng, by whose glad diligence they learn'd,
    They came from Toyles which their own choice desir'd.

22. This they approach, and as they enter it
    Their Eies were stay'd, by reading or'e the Gate,
    Great Nature's Office, in large letters writ;
    And next, they mark'd who there in office sate.

23. Old busy Men, yet much for wisdome fam'd;
    Hasty to know, though not by haste beguil'd;
    These fitly, Nature's Registers were nam'd;
    The Throng were their Intelligencers stil'd:

24. Who stop by snares, and by their chace o'retake
    All hidden Beasts the closser Forrest yeilds;
    All that by secret sence their rescue make,
    Or trust their force, or swiftness in the Fields.

25. And of this Throng, some their imployment have
    In fleeting Rivers, some fix'd Lakes beset;
    Where Nature's self, by shifts, can nothing save
    From trifling Angles, or the swal'wing Net.

26. Some, in the spacious Ayre, their Prey o'retake,
    Cous'ning, with hunger, Falcons of their wings;
    Whilst all their patient observations make,
    Which each to Nature's Office duely brings.

27. And there of ev'ry Fish, and Foule, and Beast,
    The wiles these learned *Registers* record,
    Courage, and feares, their motion and their rest;
    Which they prepare for their more learned Lord.

28. From hence to Nature's Nursery they goe;
    Where seems to grow all that in *Eden* grew;
    And more (if Art her mingled *Species* show)
    Then th'Hebrew King, Nature's Historian, knew.

21: 4 desir'd. '51b: desir'd '51a, '73

29. Impatient *Simplers* climbe for Blossomes here;
 When Dews (Heav'n's secret milk) in unseen showres
 First feed the early Childhood of the yeare;
 And in ripe Summer, stoop for Hearbs and Flowres.

30. In Autumn, Seeds, and Berries they provide;
 Where Nature a remaining force preserves;
 In Winter digg for Roots, where she does hide
 That stock, which if consum'd, the next Spring sterves.

31. From hence (fresh Nature's flourishing Estate!)
 They to her wither'd Receptacle come;
 Where she appears the loathsome Slave of Fate;
 For here her various Dead possess the Room.

32. This dismall Gall'ry, lofty, long, and wide;
 Was hung with *Skelitons* of ev'ry kinde;
 Humane, and all that learned humane pride
 Thinks made t'obey Man's high immortal Minde.

33. Yet on that Wall hangs he too, who so thought;
 And she dry'd by him, whom that He obay'd;
 By her an *El'phant* that with Heards had fought,
 Of which the smallest Beast made her afraid.

34. Next it, a whale is high in Cables ty'd,
 Whose strength might Herds of Elephants controul;
 Then all, (in payres of ev'ry kinde) they spy'd
 Which Death's wrack leaves, of Fishes, Beasts, and Fowl.

35. These *Astragon* (to watch with curious Eie
 The diff'rent Tenements of living breath)
 Collects, with what far Travailers supplie;
 And this was call'd, The Cabinet of Death.

36. Which some the *Monument of Bodies*, name;
 The Arke, which saves from Graves all dying kindes;
 This to a structure led, long knowne to Fame,
 And cald, The Monument of vanish'd Mindes.

37. There, when they thought they saw in well sought Books,
 Th'assembled soules of all that Men held wise,
 It bred such awfull rev'rence in their looks,
 As if they saw the bury'd writers rise.

37: 1 There '51a *cor*: Where '51a *u*, '51b, '73

38. Such heaps of written thoughts (Gold of the Dead,
    Which Time does still disperse, but not devour)
    Made them presume all was from Deluge free'd,
    Which long-liv'd Authors writ ere *Noah's* Showr.

39. They saw *Egyptian* Roles, which vastly great,
    Did like faln Pillars lie, and did display
    The tale of Natures life, from her first heat,
    Till by the Flood o're-cool'd, she felt decay.

40. And large as these (for Pens were Pencils then)
    Others that *Egypts* chiefest Science show'd;
    Whose River forc'd Geometry on Men,
    Which did distinguish what the *Nyle* o're-flow'd.

41. Neer them, in Piles, *Chaldean* Cous'ners lie;
    Who the hid bus'nesse of the Stars relate;
    Who make a Trade of worship'd Prophesie;
    And seem to pick the Cabinet of Fate.

42. There *Persian Magi* stand; for wisdom prais'd;
    Long since wise Statesmen, now *Magicians* thought;
    Altars and Arts are soon to fiction rais'd,
    And both would have, that miracles are wrought.

43. In a dark Text, these States-men left their Mindes;
    For well they knew, that Monarch's Mistery
    (Like that of Priests) but little rev'rence findes,
    When they the Curtain op'e to ev'ry Eie.

44. Behinde this Throng, the talking *Greeks* had place;
    Who Nature turn to Art, and Truth disguise,
    As skill does native beauty oft deface;
    With *Termes* they charm the weak, and pose the wise.

45. Now they the *Hebrew*, *Greek*, and *Roman* spie;
    Who for the Peoples ease, yoak'd them with Law;
    Whom else, ungovern'd lusts would drive awry;
    And each his own way frowardly would draw.

46. In little Tomes these grave first Lawyers lie,
    In Volumes their Interpreters below;
    Who first made Law an Art, then Misterie;
    So cleerest springs, when troubled, cloudy grow.

46: 1 Tomes *'51a MS*, *'51b*, *'73*: Tombs *'51a*

47. But here, the Souls chief Book did all precede;
    Our Map tow'rds Heav'n; to common Crowds deny'd;
    Who proudly aim to teach, ere they can read;
    And all must stray, where each will be a Guide.

48. About this sacred little Book did stand
    Unwieldy Volumes, and in number great;
    And long it was since any Readers hand
    Had reach'd them from their unfrequented Seat.

49. For a deep Dust (which Time does softly shed,
    Where only Time does come) their Covers beare;
    On which, grave Spyders, streets of Webbs had spred;
    Subtle, and slight, as the grave Writers were.

50. In these, Heav'ns holy fire does vainly burn;
    Nor warms, nor lights, but is in Sparkles spent;
    Where froward Authors, with disputes, have torn
    The Garment seamless as the Firmament.

51. These are the old *Polemicks*, long since read,
    And shut by *Astragon*; who thought it just,
    They, like the Authors (Truth's Tormentors) dead,
    Should lie unvisited, and lost in dust.

52. Here the *Arabian's* Gospel open lay,
    (Men injure Truth, who Fiction nicely hide)
    Where they the *Monk's* audacious stealths survay,
    From the World's first, and greater second Guide.

53. The Curious much perus'd this, then, new Book;
    As if some secret ways to Heav'n it taught;
    For straying from the old, men newer look,
    And prise the found, not finding those they sought.

54. We, in Tradition (Heav'n's dark Mapp) descrie
    Heav'n worse, then ancient Mapps farr *India* show;
    Therefore in new, we search where Heav'n does lie,
    The Mind's sought *Ophir*, which we long to know.

55. Or as a Planter, though good Land he spies,
    Seeks new, and when no more so good he findes,
    Doubly esteems the first; so Truth men prise;
    Truth, the discov'ry made by trav'ling Mindes.

56. And this false Book, till truly understood
    By *Astragon*, was openly display'd,
    As counterfeit; false Princes rather shou'd
    Be shewn abroad, then in closse Prison lay'd.

57. Now to the old *Philosophers* they come;
    Who follow'd Nature with such just despaire,
    As some doe Kings farr off; and when at home,
    Like Courtiers, boast, that they deep secrets share.

58. Neer them are grave dull *Moralists*, who give
    Counsell to such, as still in publick dwell;
    At sea, in Courts, in Camps, and Cities live;
    And scorn experience from th'unpractis'd Cell.

59. *Esop* with these stands high, and they below;
    His pleasant wisdome mocks their gravitie;
    Who Vertue like a tedious Matron show,
    He dresses Nature to invite the Eie.

60. High skill their *Ethicks* seemes, whilst he stoops down
    To make the People wise; their learned pride
    Makes all obscure, that Men may prise the Gown;
    With ease he teaches, what with pain they hide.

61. And next (as if their bus'ness rul'd Mankinde)
    Historians stand, bigg as their living looks;
    Who thought, swift Time they could in fetters binde;
    Till his Confessions they had ta'ne in Books:

62. But Time oft scap'd them in the shades of Night;
    And was in Princes Closets oft conceal'd,
    And hid in Batails smoke; so what they write
    Of Courts and Camps, is oft by guess reveal'd.

63. Neer these, *Physitians* stood; who but reprieve
    Life like a Judge, whom greater pow'r does awe;
    And cannot an Almighty pardon give;
    So much yeilds Subject Art to Nature's Law.

64. And now weak Art, but Nature we upbrayd,
    When our frail essence proudly we take ill;
    Think we are robb'd, when first we are decay'd,
    And those were murder'd whom her law did kill.

63: 2 Life like] Like life '73

65. Now they refresh, after this long survay,
    With pleasant *Poets*, who the Soule sublime;
    Fame's *Heraulds*, in whose Triumphs they make way;
    And place all those whom Honor helps to climbe.

66. And he who seem'd to lead this ravish'd Race,
    Was Heav'n's lov'd *Laureat*, that in *Jewry* writ;
    Whose Harp approach'd Gods Ear, though none his Face
    Durst see, and first made inspiration, wit.

67. And his Attendants, such blest Poets are,
    As make unblemish'd Love, Courts best delight;
    And sing the prosp'rous Batails of just warre;
    By these the loving, Love, and valiant, fight.

68. O hyreless Science! and of all alone
    The Liberal! Meanly the rest each State
    In pension treats, but this depends on none;
    Whose worth they rev'rendly forbear to rate.

Canto the Sixth

The ARGUMENT

How ASTRAGON *to Heav'n his duty pays*
In Pray'r, and Penitence, but most in Praise:
To these he sev'ral Temples dedicates;
And ULFIN *their distinguish'd use relates.*
Religion's Rites, seem here, in Reasons sway;
Though Reason must Religion's Laws obay.

1. The noble Youths (reclaim'd by what they saw)
   Would here unquiet war, as pride, forsake;
   And study quiet Nature's pleasant Law;
   Which Schools, through pride, by Art uneasy make.

2. But now a sodain Showt their thoughts diverts!
   So cheerfull, general, and lowd it was,
   As pass'd through all their Ears, and fill'd their Hearts;
   Which lik'd the joy, before they knew the cause.

68: 2 State *'51b*, *'73*: Statc *'51a*   68: 3 In *'51b*, *'73*: Iu *'51a*

3. This *Ulfin*, by his long Domestick skill
   Does thus explain. The Wise I here observe,
   Are wise tow'rds God; in whose great service still,
   More then in that of Kings, themselves they serve.

4. He who this Building's Builder did create,
   Has an Apartment here Triangular;
   Where *Astragon*, Three Fanes did dedicate,
   To daies of *Praise*, of *Penitence*, and *Pray'r*.

5. To these, from diff'rent motives, all proceed;
   For when discov'ries they on Nature gain,
   They praise high Heav'n which makes their work succeed,
   But when it fails, in Penitence complain.

6. If after *Praise*, new blessings are not giv'n,
   Nor mourning *Penitence* can ills repair,
   Like practis'd Beggers, they solicite Heav'n,
   And will prevail by violence of *Pray'r*.

7. The Temple built for *Pray'r*, can neither boast
   The Builder's curious Art, nor does declare,
   By choice Materials he intended cost;
   To shew, that nought should need to tempt to *Pray'r*.

8. No Bells are here! Unhing'd are all the Gates!
   Since craving in distresse is naturall,
   All lies so op'e that none for ent'rance waites;
   And those whom Faith invites, can need no call.

9. The Great have by distinction here no name;
   For all so cover'd come, in grave disguise,
   (To shew none come for decency or fame)
   That all are strangers to each others Eies.

10. But *Penitence* appears unnaturall;
    For we repent what Nature did perswade;
    And we lamenting Man's continu'd fall,
    Accuse what Nature necessary made.

11. Since the requir'd extream of Penitence
    Seems so severe, this Temple was design'd,
    Solemn and strange without, to catch the sense,
    And dismal shew'd within, to awe the mind.

7: 1 neither '*51a MS*, '*51b*, '*73*: never '*51a*

12. Of sad black Marble was the outward Frame,
    (A Mourning Monument to distant sight)
    But by the largenesse when you neer it came,
    It seem'd the Palace of Eternal Night.

13. Black beauty (which black *Meroens* had prais'd
    Above their own) gravely adorn'd each part;
    In Stone, from *Nyle's* hard Quarries, slowly rais'd,
    And slowly'er polish'd by *Numidian* Art.

14. Hither a lowd Bells tole, rather commands,
    Then seems t'invite the persecuted Eare;
    A summons Nature hardly understands;
    For few, and slow are those who enter here.

15. Within a dismall Majesty they find!
    All gloomy great, all silent does appear!
    As *Chaos* was, ere th'Elements were design'd;
    Man's evil fate seems hid and fashion'd here.

16. Here all the Ornament is rev'rend black;
    Here, the check'd Sun his universal Face
    Stops bashfully, and will no entrance make;
    As if he spy'd Night naked through the Glasse.

17. Black Curtains hide the Glasse; whilst from on high
    A winking Lamp, still threatens all the Room;
    As if the lazy flame just now would die:
    Such will the Sun's last light appear at Doom!

18. This Lamp was all, that here inform'd all Eies;
    And by reflex, did on a Picture gain
    Some few false Beames, that then from *Sodome* rise;
    Where Pencils feigne the fire which Heav'n did rain.

19. This on another Tablet did reflect,
    Where twice was drawn the am'rous *Magdaline*;
    Whilst beauty was her care, then her neglect;
    And brightest through her Tears she seem'd to shine.

20. Neer her, seem'd crucifi'd, that lucky Thief
    (In Heav'n's dark Lot'ry prosp'rous, more then wise)
    Who groap'd at last, by chance, for Heav'n's relief,
    And Throngs undoes with Hope, by one drawn Prise.

13: 3 hard] head '*51b*   14: 4 here. '*51b*: here, '*51a*, '*73*   18: 3 then '*73*: thence '*51a–b*

21. In many Figures by reflex were sent,
    Through this black Vault (instructive to the minde)
    That early, and this tardy Penitent;
    For with *Obsidian* stone 'twas chiefly lin'd.

22. The Seats were made of *Ethiopian* wood,
    Abstersive Ebony, but thinly fill'd;
    For none this place by nature understood;
    And practise, when unpleasant, makes few skill'd.

23. Yet these, whom Heav'n's misterious choice fetch'd in,
    Quickly attain Devotion's utmost scope;
    For having softly mourn'd away their sin,
    They grow so certain, as to need no Hope.

24. At a low Dore they enter'd, but depart
    Through a large Gate, and to fair Fields proceed;
    Where *Astragon* makes Nature last by Art,
    And such long Summers shews, as ask no seed.

25. Whilst *Ulfin* this black Temple thus exprest
    To these kinde Youths, whom equal soule endeers;
    (*Goltho*, and *Ulfinore*, in friendship blest)
    A second gen'ral shout salutes their Ears.

26. To the glad House of *Praise* this shout does call!
    To *Pray'r* (said he) no Summons us invites,
    Because distress does thither summon all;
    As the loud tole to *Penitence* excites.

27. But since, dull Men, to gratitude are slow;
    And joy'd consent of Hearts is high Heav'ns choyce;
    To this of Praise, shouts summon us to goe;
    Of Hearts assembled, the unfeigned Voyce.

28. And since, wise *Astragon*, with due applause,
    Kinde Heav'n, for his success, on Nature pays;
    This day, Victorious Art, has given him cause,
    Much to augment Heav'n's lov'd reward of praise.

29. For this effectual day his Art reveal'd,
    What has so oft Made Nature's spies to pine,
    The Loadstones mistick use, so long conceal'd
    In closs allyance with the courser Mine.

22: 1 *Ethiopian* '73: *Ethiops* swarthy '51a–b

30. And this, in sleepy Vision, he was bid
    To register in Characters unknown;
    Which Heav'n will have from Navigators hid,
    Till *Saturne's* walk be Twenty Circuits grown.

31. For as Religion (in the warm East bred)
    And Arts (which next to it most needful were)
    From Vices sprung from their corruption, fled;
    And thence vouchsaf'd a cold Plantation here;

32. So when they here again corrupted be,
    (For Man can even his Antidotes infect)
    Heav'n's reserv'd World they in the West shall see;
    To which this stone's hid vertue will direct.

33. Religion then (whose Age this world upbraids,
    As scorn'd deformitie) will thither steer;
    Serv'd at fit distance by the Arts, her Maids;
    Which grow too bold, when they attend too neer.

34. And some, whom Traffique thither tempts, shal thence
    In her exchange (though they did grudg her shrines,
    And poorly banish'd her to save expence)
    Bring home the Idol, Gold, from new found Mines.

35. Till then, sad Pilots must be often lost,
    Whilst from the Ocean's dreaded Face they shrink;
    And seeking safety neer the cous'ning Coast,
    With windes surpris'd, by Rocky Ambush sink.

36. Or if successe rewards, what they endure,
    The World's chief Jewel, Time, they then ingage
    And forfeit (trusting long the *Cynosure*)
    To bring home nought but wretched Gold, and Age.

37. Yet when this plague of ignorance shall end,
    (Dire ignorance, with which God plagues us most;
    Whilst we not feeling it, him most offend)
    Then lower'd Sayles no more shall tide the Coast.

38. They with new *Tops* to *Formasts* and the *Main*,
    And *Misens* new, shall th'Ocean's Breast invade;
    Stretch new Sayles out, as Armes to entertain
    Those windes, of which their Fathers were afraid.

37: 4 tide] tie '*51b*

39. Then (sure of either Pole) they will with pride,
    In ev'ry storm, salute this constant Stone!
    And scorn that Star, which ev'ry Cloud could hide;
    The Seamen's spark! which soon, as seen, is gone!

40. 'Tis sung, the Ocean shall his Bonds untie,
    And Earth in half a Globe be pent no more;
    Typhis shall sayle, till *Thule* he discry,
    But a domestick step to distant Shore!

41. This *Astragon* had read; and what the *Greek*,
    Old *Cretias*, in *Egyptian* Books had found;
    By which, his travail'd soule, new Worlds did seek,
    And div'd to finde the old *Atlantis* droun'd.

42. Grave *Ulfin* thus discours'd; and now he brings
    The Youths to view the Temple built for *Praise*;
    Where *Olive*, for th'*Olimpian* Victor Springs;
    Mirtle, for Love's; and for War's triumph, *Bayes*.

43. These, as rewards of *Praise*, about it grew;
    For lib'rall praise, from an aboundant Minde,
    Does even the Conqueror of Fate subdue;
    Since Heav'n's good King is Captive to the Kinde.

44. Dark are all Thrones, to what this Temple seem'd;
    Whose Marble veines out-shin'd Heav'n's various Bow;
    And would (eclipsing all proud *Rome* esteem'd)
    To Northern Eies, like Eastern Mornings, show.

45. From *Paros* Isle, was brought the milkie white;
    From *Sparta*, came the Green, which cheers the view;
    From *Araby*, the blushing *Onychite*,
    And from the *Misnian* Hills, the deeper Blew.

46. The Arched Front did on vaste Pillars fall;
    Where all harmonious Instruments they spie
    Drawn out in Bosse; which from the *Astrigall*
    To the flat *Frise*, in apt resemblance lie.

47. Toss'd *Cymbals* (which the sullen Jewes admir'd)
    Were figur'd here, with all of ancient choice
    That joy did ere invent, or breath inspir'd,
    Or flying Fingers touch'd into a voice.

48. In Statue o're the Gate, God's Fav'rite-King
(The Author of Celestiall praise) did stand;
His Quire (that did his sonnets set and Sing)
In *Niches* rang'd, attended either Hand.

49. From these, old *Greeks* sweet Musick did improve;
The Solemn *Dorian* did in Temples charm,
The softer *Lydian* sooth'd to Bridal Love,
And warlick *Phrygian* did to Batail warm!

50. They enter now, and with glad rev'rence saw
Glory, too solid great to taste of pride;
So sacred pleasant, as preserves an awe;
Though jealous Priests, it neither praise nor hide.

51. Tapers and Lamps are not admitted here;
Those, but with shadowes, give false beauty grace;
And this victorious glory can appear
Unvayl'd before the Sun's Meridian Face:

52. Whose Eastern Lusture rashly enters now;
Where it his own mean Infancy displays;
Where it does Man's chief obligation show,
In what does most adorn the House of Praise;

53. The great Creation by bold Pencils drawn;
Where a feign'd Curtain does our Eies forbid,
Till the Sun's Parent, Light, first seems to dawn
From quiet *Chaos*, which that Curtain hid.

54. Then this all-rev'renc'd Sun (God's hasty Spark
Struck out of *Chaos*, when he first struck Light)
Flies to the Sphears, where first he found all dark,
And kindled there th'unkindled Lamps of Night.

55. Then Motion, Nature's great Preservative,
Tun'd order in this World, Life's restless Inn;
Gave Tydes to Seas, and caus'd stretch'd Plants to live;
Else Plants but seeds, and Seas but Lakes had bin.

56. But this Fourth *Fiat*, warming what was made,
(For light ne'r warm'd, till it did motion get)
The Picture fills the World with woody shade;
To shew how Nature thrives by Motion's heat.

50: 4 hide. *Ed*: hide, *'51a–b, '73*

57. Then to those Woods the next quick *Fiat* brings
    The Feather'd kinde; where merrily they fed,
    As if their Hearts were lighter then their Wings;
    For yet no Cage was fram'd, nor Net was spred.

58. The same Fifth voyce does Seas and Rivers Store;
    Then into Rivers Brooks the Painter powres,
    And Rivers into Seas; which (rich before)
    Return their gifts, to both, exhal'd in Showrs.

59. This voice (whose swift dispatch in all it wrought,
    Seems to denote the Speaker was in hast,
    As if more worlds were framing in his thought)
    Adds to this world one *Fiat*, as the last.

60. Then strait an universal Herd appears;
    First gazing on each other in the shade;
    Wondring with levell'd Eies, and lifted Ears,
    Then play, whilst yet their Tyrant is unmade.

61. And Man, the Painter now presents to view;
    Haughty without, and busy still within;
    Whom, when his Furr'd and Horned Subjects knew,
    Their sport is ended, and their fears begin.

62. But here (to cure this Tyrant's sullennesse)
    The Painter has a new false Curtain drawn,
    Where, Beauty's hid Creation to expresse;
    From thence, harmlesse as light, he makes it dawn.

63. From thence breaks lov'ly forth, the World's first Maid;
    Her Breast, Love's Cradle, where Love quiet lies;
    Nought yet had seen so foule, to grow afraid,
    Nor gay, to make it cry with longing Eies.

64. And thence, from stupid sleep, her Monarch steals;
    She wonders, till so vain his wonder growes,
    That it his feeble sov'raignty reveales;
    Her Beauty then, his Manhood does depose.

65. Deep into shades the Painter leads them now;
    To hide their future deeds; then storms does raise
    Or'e Heav'n's smooth face, because their life does grow
    Too black a story for the House of *Praise*.

66. A noble painted Vision next appears;
    Where all Heav'n's Frowns in distant prospect waste;
    And nought remains, but a short showre of Teares,
    Shed, by its pity, for Revenges past.

67. The World's one ship, from th'old to'a new World bound;
    Fraighted with Life (chief of uncertain Trades!)
    After Five Moons at drift, lies now a ground;
    Where her frail Stowage, she in haste unlades.

68. On *Persian Caucasus* the Eight descend;
    And seem their trivial beings to deplore;
    Griev'd to begin this World in th'others end;
    And to behold wrack'd Nations on the Shore.

69. Each humbled thus, his Beasts led from aboard,
    As fellow Passengers, and Heirs to breath;
    Joynt Tennants to the World, he not their Lord;
    Such likeness have we in the Glass of Death.

70. Yet this humility begets their joy;
    And taught, that Heav'n (which fully sin survays)
    Was partial where it did not quite destroy;
    So made the whole World's Dirge their song of praise.

71. This first redemption to another led,
    Kinder in deeds, and nobler in effects;
    That but a few did respit from the Dead,
    This all the Dead, from second death protects.

72. And know, lost Nature! this resemblance was
    Thy franke Redeemer, in ascension shown;
    When Hell he conquer'd in thy desp'rate cause;
    Hell, which before, Man's common Grave was grown.

73. By Pencills this was exquisitely wrought;
    Rounded in all the Curious would behold;
    Where life *Came out*, and *Met* the Painters thought;
    The *Force* was *tender*, though the strokes were *bold*.

74. The holy Mourners, who this Lord of life
    Ascending saw, did seem with him to rise;
    So well the Painter drew their passions strife,
    To follow him with Bodys, as with Eies.

68: 2 beings '73: essence '51a–b   68: 4 Shore. '51b: Shore, '51a, '73
73: 1 Pencills . . . exquisitely '73: an Imperial Pencil this was '51a–b

75. This was the chief which in this Temple did
    By Pencils Rhetorique, to praise perswade;
    Yet to the living here, compar'd, seems hid;
    Who shine all painted Glory into shade.

76. Lord *Astragon* a Purple Mantle wore,
    Where Nature's story was in Colours wrought;
    And though her ancient Text seem'd dark before,
    'Tis in this pleasant Comment clearly taught.

77. Such various Flowry Wreaths th'Assembly weare,
    As shew'd them wisely proud of Nature's pride;
    Which so adorn'd them, that the coursest here
    Did seem a prosp'rous Bridegroom, or a Bride.

78. All shew'd as fresh, and faire, and innocent,
    As Virgins to their Lovers first survay;
    Joy'd as the Spring, when *March* his sighs has spent,
    And *April's* sweet rash Teares are dry'd by *May*.

79. And this confed'rate joy so swell'd each Breast,
    That joy would turn to pain without a vent;
    Therefore their voyces Heav'n's renown exprest;
    Though Tongues ne'r reach, what Minds so nobly ment.

80. Yet Musick here, shew'd all her Art's high worth;
    Whilst Virgin-Trebles, seem'd, with bashfull grace,
    To call the bolder marry'd Tenor forth;
    Whose Manly voyce challeng'd the Giant Base.

81. To these the swift soft Instruments reply;
    Whisp'ring for help to those whom winds inspire;
    Whose lowder Notes, to Neighb'ring Forrests flie,
    And summon Nature's Voluntary Quire.

82. These *Astragon*, by secret skill had taught,
    To help, as if in artfull Consort bred;
    Who sung, as if by chance on him they thought,
    Whose care their careless merry Fathers Fed.

83. Hither, with borrow'd strength, Duke *Gondibert*
    Was brought, which now his rip'ning wounds allow;
    And high Heav'ns praise in musick of the heart,
    He inward sings, to pay a victor's vow.

75: 2 Rhetorique *Ed*: Rhetrique *'51a*, *'73*: Rhethorick *'51b*   76: 4 Comment
'51a MS, *'51b*, *'73*: Commet *'51a*

84. *Praise*, is devotion fit for mighty Mindes!
    The diff'ring World's agreeing Sacrifice;
    Where Heav'n divided Faiths united findes;
    But Pray'r in various discord upward flies.

85. For *Pray'r* the Ocean is, where diversly
    Men steer their Course, each to a sev'ral Coast;
    Where all our int'rests so discordant be,
    That half beg windes by which the rest are lost.

86. By *Penitence*, when we our selves forsake,
    'Tis but in wise design on pitious Heav'n;
    In Praise we nobly give, what God may take,
    And are without a Beggers blush forgiv'n.

87. Its utmost force, like Powder's is unknown!
    And though weak Kings excess of Praise may fear,
    Yet when tis here, like Powder, dang'rous grown,
    Heav'n's Vault receives, what would the Palace tear.

Canto the Seventh

The ARGUMENT

The Duke's wish'd health in doubtful wounds assur'd;
Who gets new wounds before the old are cur'd:
Nature in BIRTHA, *Art's weak help derides;*
Which strives to mend, what it at best but hides;
Shews Nature's courser works, so hid, more course;
As Sin conceal'd, and unconfess'd, growes worse.

1. Let none our *Lombard* Author rudely blame,
   Who from the Story has thus long digrest;
   But for his righteous paines, may his fair Fame
   For ever travail, whilst his Ashes rest.

2. Ill could he leave Art's Shop of Nature's Store;
   Where she the hiden Soul would make more known;
   Though Common faith seeks Souls, which is no more
   Then long Opinion to Religion grown.

3. A while then let this sage Historian stay
   With *Astragon*, till he new wounds reveales,
   And such (though now the old are worn away)
   As *Balm*, nor juice of *Pyrol*, never heales.

4. To *Astragon*, Heav'n for succession gave
   One onely Pledge, and *Birtha* was her name;
   Whose Mother slept, where Flowers grew on her Grave;
   And she succeeded her in Face, and Fame.

5. Her beauty, Princes, durst not hope to use,
   Unless, like Poets, for their Morning Theam;
   And her Mindes beauty they would rather chuse,
   Which did the light in Beautie's Lanthorn seem.

6. She ne'r saw Courts, yet Courts could have undone
   With untaught looks, and an unpractis'd heart;
   Her Nets, the most prepar'd, could never shunne;
   For Nature spred them in the scorn of Art.

7. She never had in busy Cities bin;
   Ne'r warm'd with hopes, nor ere allay'd with fears;
   Not seeing punishment, could guesse no Sin;
   And Sin not seeing, ne'r had use of tears.

8. But here her Father's precepts gave her skill,
   Which with incessant bus'nesse fill'd the Howres;
   In spring, she gather'd Blossoms for the Still,
   In Autumn, Berries; and in Sommer, Flowres.

9. And as kinde Nature with calm diligence
   Her own free vertue silently imploys,
   Whilst she, unheard, does rip'ning growth dispence,
   So were her vertues busie without noise.

10. Whilst her great Mistris, Nature, thus she tends,
    The busy Houshold waites no lesse on her;
    By secret law, each to her beauty bends;
    Though all her lowly Minde to that prefer.

11. Gratious and free, she breaks upon them all
    With Morning looks; and they when she does rise,
    Devoutly at her dawn in homage fall,
    And droop like Flowres, when Evening shuts her Eies.

4: 1 succession] snccession '51a   11: 4 Eies. *Ed*: Eyes. '51b, '73: Eies '51a

12. The sooty *Chymist* (who his sight does waste,
    Attending lesser Fires) she passing by,
    Broke his lov'd Lymbick, through enamour'd haste,
    And let, like common Dew, th'Elixer fly.

13. And here the grey Philosophers resort,
    Who all to her, like crafty Courtiers, bow;
    Hoping for secrets now in Nature's Court;
    Which only she (her fav'rite Mayd) can know.

14. These, as the Lords of science, she respects;
    And with familiar Beams their age she chears;
    Yet all those civil formes seem but neglects
    To what she shewes, when *Astragon* appears.

15. For as she once from him her being took,
    She howrly takes her Law; reads with swift sight
    His will, even at the op'ning of his look,
    And shews, by haste, obedience her delight.

16. She makes (when she at distance to him bowes)
    His int'rest in her Mother's beauty known;
    For that's th'*Orig'nal* whence her *Copy* growes;
    And neer *Orig'nalls*, *Copys* are not shown.

17. And he, with dear regard, her gifts does weare
    Of Flowres, which she in mistick order ties;
    And with the sacrifice of many'a teare
    Salutes her loyal Mother in her Eies.

18. The just Historians, *Birtha* thus express;
    And tell how by her Syres Example taught,
    She serv'd the wounded Duke in Life's distress,
    And his fled Spirits back by Cordials brought.

19. Black melancholy Mists, that fed dispair
    Through wounds long rage, with sprinkled *Vervin* cleer'd;
    Strew'd Leaves of *Willow* to refresh the air,
    And with rich Fumes his sullen sences cheer'd.

20. He that had serv'd great Love with rev'rend heart,
    In these old wounds, worse wounds from him endures;
    For Love, makes *Birtha* shift with Death, his Dart,
    And she kills faster then her Father cures.

21. Her heedless innocence as little knew
    The wounds she gave, as those from Love she took;
    And Love lifts high each secret Shaft he drew;
    Which at their Stars he first in triumph shook!

22. Love he had lik'd, yet never lodg'd before;
    But findes him now a bold unquiet Guest;
    Who climbes to windows, when we shut the Dore;
    And enter'd, never lets the Master rest.

23. So strange disorder, now he pines for health,
    Makes him conceal this Reveller with shame;
    She not the Robber knows, yet feels the stealth;
    And never but in Songs had heard his name.

24. Yet then it was, when she did smile at Hearts
    Which Country Lovers wear in bleeding Seals;
    Ask'd where his pretty Godhead found such Darts,
    As make those wounds that onely *Hymen* heals.

25. And this, her ancient Maid, with sharp complaints
    Heard, and rebuk'd; shook her experienc'd Head;
    With teares besought her not to jest at Saints,
    Nor mock those Martyrs, Love had Captive led.

26. Nor think the pious Poets e're would waste
    So many Teares in Ink, to make Maids mourn,
    If injur'd Lovers had in ages paste
    The lucky Mirtle, more then Willow worn.

27. This grave rebuke, Officious Memory
    Presents to *Birtha's* thought; who now believ'd
    Such sighing Songs, as tell why Lovers dy,
    And prais'd their faith, who wept, when Poets griev'd.

28. She, full of inward questions, walks alone,
    To take her heart aside in secret Shade;
    But knocking at her Breast, it seem'd, or gone,
    Or by confed'racie was useless made;

29. Or else some stranger did usurp its room;
    One so remote, and new in ev'ry thought,
    As his behaviour shews him not at home;
    Nor the Guide sober that him thither brought.

30. Yet with this forraign Heart, she does begin
    To treat of Love, her most unstudy'd Theame;
    And like young Conscienc'd Casuists, thinks that sin,
    Which will by talk and practise lawfull seeme.

31. With open Eares, and ever-waking Eies,
    And flying Feet, Love's fyre she from the sight
    Of all her Mayds does carry, as from Spys;
    Jealous, that what burns her, might give them light.

32. Beneath a Mirtle Covert she does spend
    In Mayds weak wishes, her whole stock of thought;
    Fond Mayds! who love, with Mindes fine stuff would mend,
    Which Nature purposely of Bodys wrought.

33. She fashions him she lov'd of Angels kinde;
    Such as in holy Story were imploy'd
    To the first Fathers, from th'Eternal Minde;
    And in short vision onely are injoy'd.

34. As Eagles then, when neerest Heav'n they flie,
    Of wild impossibles soon weary grow;
    Feeling their bodies finde no rest so high,
    And therefore pearch on Earthly things below:

35. So now she yields; him she an Angel deem'd
    Shall be a Man; the Name which Virgins fear;
    Yet the most harmless to a Maid he seem'd,
    That ever yet that fatal name did bear.

36. Soon her opinion of his hurtlesse heart,
    Affection turns to faith; and then Loves fire
    To Heav'n, though bashfully, she does impart;
    And to her Mother in the Heav'nly Quire.

37. If I do love, (said she) that love (O Heav'n!)
    Your own Disciple, Nature, bred in me;
    Why should I hide the passion you have given,
    Or blush to shew effects which you decree?

38. And you, my alter'd Mother (grown above
    Great Nature, which you read, and rev'renc'd here)
    Chide not such kindnesse, as you once call'd Love,
    When you as mortal as my Father were.

32: 1 she '73: now '51a–b

39. This said, her Soul into her Breast retires!
    With Love's vain diligence of heart she dreams
    Her self into possession of desires,
    And trusts unanchor'd Hope in fleeting Streams.

40. Already thinks, the Duke her own spous'd Lord,
    Cur'd, and again from bloody Batail brought;
    Where all false Lovers perish'd by his sword;
    The tru to her for his protection sought.

41. She thinks, how her imagin'd Spouse and she,
    So much from Heav'n, may by her vertues gain;
    That they by Time shall ne'r o'retaken be,
    No more then Time himself is overta'ne.

42. Or should he touch them as he by does passe,
    Heav'n's favour may repay their Sommers gone,
    And he so mix their sand in a slow Glasse,
    That they shall live, and not as *Two*, but *One*.

43. She thinks of *Eden*-life; and no rough winde,
    In their pacifique Sea shall wrinkles make;
    That still her lowliness shall keep him kinde,
    Her cares keep him asleep, her voice awake.

44. She thinks, if ever anger in him sway
    (The Youthful Warrior's most excus'd disease)
    Such chance her Teares shall calm, as showres allay
    The accidental rage of Windes and Seas.

45. She thinks that Babes proceed from mingling Eies,
    Or Heav'n from Neighbourhood increase allows,
    As *Palm*, and the *Mamora* fructefies;
    Or they are got, by closse exchanging vows.

46. But come they (as she hears) from Mothers pain,
    (Which by th'unluky first-Maids longing, proves
    A lasting curse) yet that she will sustain,
    So they be like this Heav'nly Man she loves.

47. Thus to her self in day-dreams *Birtha* talks;
    The Duke (whose wounds of war are healthful grown)
    To cure Love's wounds, seeks *Birtha* where she walks;
    Whose wandring Soul, seeks him to cure her own.

43: 2 In *Ed*: Jn '51a   43: 4 cares] eares '73

48. Yet when her solitude he did invade,
    Shame (which in Maids is unexperienc'd fear)
    Taught her to wish Night's help to make more shade,
    That Love (which Maids think guilt) might not appear.

49. And she had fled him now but that he came
    So like an aw'd, and conquer'd Enemy,
    That he did seem offencelesse, as her shame;
    As if he but advanc'd for leave to fly.

50. First with a longing Sea-mans look he gaz'd,
    Who would ken Land, when Seas would him devour;
    Or like a fearful Scout, who stands amaz'd
    To view the Foe, and multiplies their pow'r.

51. Then all the knowledge which her Father had
    He dreams in her, through purer Organs wrought;
    Whose Soul (since there more delicately clad)
    By lesser weight, more active was in thought.

52. And to that Soul thus spake, with tremb'ling voice;
    The world wil be (O thou, the whole world's Mayd!)
    Since now tis old enough to make wise choice,
    Taught by thy minde, and by thy beauty sway'd.

53. And I a needless part of it, unless
    You think me for the whole a Delegate,
    To treat for what they want, of your excesse,
    Vertue to serve the universal State.

54. Nature (our first example, and our Queen,
    Whose Court this is, and you her Minion Mayd)
    The World thinks now, is in her sickness seen,
    And that her noble influence is decay'd.

55. And the Records so worn of her first Law,
    That Men, with Art's hard shifts, read what is good;
    Because your beauty many never saw,
    The Text by which your Minde is understood.

56. And I with the apostate world should grow,
    From sov'raigne Nature, a revolted Slave,
    But that my lucky wounds, brought me to know,
    How with their cure my sicker minde to save.

53: 3 treat . . . want . . . excesse, '51a MS: . . . success, '51a cor: treat, . . . want,
. . . success; '51a u: . . . excess, '51b, '73   54: 1 and our '51b, '73: and onr '51a

57. A minde still dwelling idly in mine Eies,
    Where it from outward pomp could ne'r abstain;
    But even in beauty, cost of Courts did prise,
    And Nature, unassisted, thought too plain.

58. Yet by your beauty now reform'd, I finde
    All other only currant by false light;
    Or but vain Visions of a feav'rish minde;
    Too slight to stand the test of waking sight.

59. And for my healthfull Minde (diseas'd before)
    My love I pay; a gift you may disdain,
    Since Love to you, Men give not, but restore;
    As Rivers to the Sea pay back the Rain.

60. Yet Eastern Kings, who all by birth possess,
    Take gifts, as gifts, from vassals of the Crown;
    So think in love, your propertie not less,
    By my kinde giving what was first your own.

61. Lifted with Love, thus he with Lovers grace,
    And Love's wilde wonder, spake; and he was rais'd
    So much with rev'rence of this learned place,
    That still he fear'd to injure all he prais'd.

62. And she in love unpractis'd and unread,
    (But for some hints her Mistress, Nature, taught)
    Had it, till now, like grief with silence fed;
    For Love and grief are nourish'd best with thought.

63. But this closse Diet, Love endures not long;
    He must in sighs, or speech, take ayre abroad;
    And thus, with his Interpreter, her Tongue,
    He ventures forth, though like a stranger aw'd.

64. She said, those vertues now she highly needs,
    Which he so artfully in her does praise,
    To check (since vanitie on praises feeds)
    That pride which his authentick words may raise.

58: 2 false '51a MS, '51b, '73: fase '51a   59: 4 pay back '73: restore '51a–b
60: 2 from '51b, '73: ftom '51a   64: 2 artfully in her does '73: pow'rfully does
in her '51a–b

65. That if her Pray'rs, or care, did ought restore
Of absent health, in his bemoan'd distress;
She beg'd, he would approve her duty more,
And so commend her feeble vertue less.

66. That she the payment he of love would make
Less understood, then yet the debt she knew;
But coynes unknown, suspitiously we take,
And debts, till manifest, are never due.

67. With bashfull Looks she sought him to retire,
Least the sharp Ayre should his new health invade;
And as she spake, she saw her rev'rend Syre
Approach to seek her in her usual shade.

68. To whom with fillial homage she does bow;
The Duke did first at distant duty stand,
But soon imbrac'd his knees; whilst he more low
Does bend to him, and then reach'd *Birtha's* hand.

69. Her Face, o'recast with thought, does soon betray
Th'assembled spirits, which his Eies detect
By her pale look, as by the Milkie way,
Men first did the assembled Stars suspect.

70. Or as a Pris'ner, that in Prison pines,
Still at the utmost window grieving lies;
Even so her Soule, imprison'd, sadly shines,
As if it watch'd for freedome at her Eies!

71. This guides him to her Pulse, th'Alarum Bell,
Which waits the insurrections of desire;
And rings so fast, as if the *Cittadell*,
Her newly conquer'd Breast, were all one fire!

72. Then on the Duke, he casts a short survay;
Whose Veines, his Temples, with deep purple grace;
Then Love's dispaire gives them a pale allay;
And shifts the whole complexion of his Face.

73. Nature's wise Spy does onward with them walk;
And findes, each in the midst of thinking starts;
Breath'd short, and swiftly in disorder'd talk,
To cool, beneath Love's Torrid Zone, their hearts.

67: 1 she sought '73: besought '51a–b   73: 1 onward '51a cor, '73: outward
'51a u, 51b

74. When all these Symptomes he observ'd, he knows
    From *Alga*, which is rooted deep in Seas,
    To the high Cedar that on Mountains grows,
    No sov'raign hearb is found for their disease.

75. He would not Nature's eldest Law resist,
    As if wise Nature's Law could be impure;
    But *Birtha* with indulgent Looks dismist,
    And means to counsel, what he cannot cure.

76. With mourning *Gondibert* he walks apart,
    To watch his Passions force; who seems to bear
    By silent grief, Two Tyrants o're his Heart,
    Great Love, and his inferior Tyrant, Fear.

77. But *Astragon* such kinde inquiries made,
    Of all which to his Art's wise cares belong,
    As his sick silence he does now disswade,
    And midst Lov's fears, gives courage to his Tongue.

78. Then thus he spake with Love's humility;
    Have pitty Father! and Since first so kinde,
    You would not let this worthlesse Body dy,
    Vouchsafe more nobly to preserve my Minde!

79. A Minde so lately lucky, as it here
    Has Vertues Mirror found, which does reflect
    Such blemishes as Custom made it weare,
    But more authentick Nature does detect.

80. A Minde long sick of Monarchs vain disease;
    Not to be fill'd, because with glory fed;
    So busy it condemn'd even War of ease,
    And for their uselesse rest despis'd the Dead.

81. But since it here has Vertue quiet found,
    It thinks (though Storms were wish'd by it before)
    All sick at least at Sea, that scape undrown'd,
    Whom Glory serves as winde to leave the shore.

82. All Vertue is to yours but fashion now,
    Religion, Art; Internals are all gon,
    Or outward turn'd, to satisfie with show,
    Not God, but his inferiour Eie, the Sun.

83. And yet, though vertue be as fashion sought,
     And now Religion rules by Art's prais'd skill;
     Fashion is Vertue's Mimmick, falsely taught;
     And Art, but Nature's Ape, which plays her ill.

84. To this blest House (great Nature's Court) all Courts
     Compar'd, are but dark Closets for retreat
     Of private Mindes, Batails but Childrens sports;
     And onely simple good, is solid great.

85. Let not the Minde, thus freed from Error's Night,
     (Since you repriev'd my Body from the Grave)
     Perish for being now in love with light,
     But let your Vertue, Vertue's Lover save.

86. *Birtha* I love; and who loves wisely so,
     Steps far tow'rds all which Vertue can attain;
     But if we perish, when tow'rds Heav'n we go,
     Then have I learnt that Vertue is in vain.

87. And now his Heart (extracted through his Eies
     In Love's Elixer, Tears) does soon subdue
     Old *Astragon*; whose pity, though made wise
     With Love's false *Essences*, likes these as true.

88. The Duke he to a secret Bowre does lead,
     Where he his Youths first Story may attend;
     To guesse, ere he will let his love proceed;
     By such a dawning, how his day will end.

89. For Vertue, though a rarely planted Flowre,
     Was in the seed by this wise *Florist* known;
     Who could foretell, even in her springing howre,
     What colours she shall wear when fully blown.

89: 2 *Florist*] '*51a cor*, '*73*; Florist '*51a u*, '*51b*

Canto the Eighth

The ARGUMENT

BIRTHA her first unpractis'd Love bewailes,
Whilst GONDIBERT on ASTRAGON prevailes,
By shewing, high Ambition is of use,
And Glory in the Good needs no excuse.
GOLTHO a grief to ULFINORE reveales,
Whilst he a greater of his own conceales.

1. *Birtha* her griefs to her Apartment brought,
    Where all her Maids to Heav'n were us'd to raise
    Their voices, whilst their busy Fingers wrought
    To deck the Altar of the House of Praise.

2. But now she findes their Musick turn'd to care;
    Their looks allay'd, like beauty overworn;
    Silent and sad as with'ring Fav'rites are,
    Who for their sick indulgent Monarch mourn.

3. *Thula* (the eldest of this silenc'd Quire)
    When *Birtha* at this change astonish'd was,
    With hasty whisper, begg'd her to retire;
    And on her Knees, thus tells their sorrows cause.

4. Forgive me such experience, as too soon,
    Shew'd me unlucky Love; by which I guesse
    How Maids are by their innocence undon,
    And trace those sorrows that them first oppresse.

5. Forgive such passion as to speech perswades,
    And to my Tongue my observation brought;
    And then forgive my Tongue, which to your Maids,
    Too rashly carry'd, what Experience taught.

6. For since I saw this wounded stranger here,
    Your inward musick still untun'd has been;
    You who could need no hope, have learnt to fear,
    And practis'd grief, e're you did know to Sin.

7. This, being love, to *Agatha* I told;
Did on her Tongue, as on still Death rely;
But winged Love, she was too young to hold,
And, wanton-like, let it to others fly.

8. Love, who in whisper scap'd, did publick grow;
Which makes them now their time in silence waste;
Makes their neglected Needles move so slow,
And through their Eies, their Hearts dissolve so faste.

9. For oft, dire tales of Love has fill'd their Heads;
And while they doubt you in that Tyrant's pow'r,
The Spring (they think) may visit Woods and Meads,
But scarce shall hear a Bird, or see a Flow'r.

10. Ah how (said *Birtha*) shall I dare confesse
My griefs to thee, Love's rash, impatient Spie?
Thou (*Thula*) who didst run to tell thy guesse,
With secrets known, wilt to confession flie.

11. But if I love this Prince, and have in Heav'n
Made any Friends by vowes, you need not fear
He will make good the feature, Heav'n has given;
And be as harmless as his looks appear.

12. Yet I have heard, that Men whom Maids think kinde,
Calm, as forgiven Saints, at their last Hour,
Oft prove like Seas, inrag'd by ev'ry winde,
And all who to their Bosoms trust, devour.

13. Howe're, Heav'n knows, (the witness of the Minde)
My heart bears Men no malice, nor esteems
Young Princes of the common cruel kinde,
Nor Love so foul as it in Story seems.

14. Yet if this Prince brought Love, what e're it be,
I must suspect, though I accuse it not;
For since he came, my medc'nal Huswiffrie,
Confections, and my Stills, are all forgot.

15. *Blossoms* in windes, *Berries* in Frosts may fall!
And *Flowers* sink down in Rain! For I no more
Shall Maids to woods, for early gath'rings call,
Nor haste to Gardens to prevent a showre.

8: 3 Needles '*51a cor*, '*51b Errata*, '*73*: Beedles '*51a u*, '*51b*   12: 4 who to] to
who '*73*

16. Then she retires; and now a lovely shame
     That she reveal'd so much, possess'd her Cheeks;
     In a dark Lanthorn she would bear Love's flame,
     To hide her self, whilst she her Lover seeks.

17. And to that Lover let our Song return:
     Whose Tale so well was to her Father told,
     As the Philosopher did seem to mourn
     That Youth had reach'd such worth, and he so old.

18. Yet *Birtha* was so precious in his Eies,
     And her dead Mother still so neer his minde
     That farther yet he thus his prudence tries,
     Ere such a Pledg he to his trust resign'd.

19. Whoe're (said he) in thy first story looks,
     Shall praise thy wise conversing with the Dead;
     For with the Dead he lives, who is with Books,
     And in the Camp (Death's moving Palace) bred.

20. Wise Youth, in Books and Batails early findes
     What thoughtless lazy Men perceive too late;
     Books shew the utmost conquests of our Mindes;
     Batails, the best of our lov'd Bodys fate.

21. Yet this great breeding, joyn'd with Kings high blood
     (Whose blood Ambition's feaver over heats)
     May spoile digestion, which would else be good,
     As stomachs are deprav'd with highest Meats.

22. For though Books serve as Diet of the Minde;
     If knowledg, early got, self vallew breeds,
     By false digestion it is turn'd to winde;
     And what should nourish, on the Eater feeds.

23. Though Wars great shape best educates the sight,
     And makes small soft'ning objects less our care;
     Yet War, when urg'd for glory, more then right,
     Shews Victors but authentick Murd'rers are.

24. And I may fear that your last Victories
     Were Glory's Toyles, and you will ill abide

16: 1 Then she retires '73: This said, retires '51a–b   18: 2 And her dead '73:
Her vanish'd '51a–b   24: 2 Were] Where '51b, '73

(Since with new Trophys still you feed your Eies)
Those little objects which in Shades we hide.

25. Could you, in Fortunes smiles, foretell her frowns,
Our old Foes slain, you would not hunt for new;
But Victors, after wreaths, pretend to Crowns;
And such think *Rhodalind* their Valor's due.

26. To this the noble *Gondibert* replies;
Think not Ambition can my duty sway;
I look on *Rhodalind* with Subjects Eies,
Whom he that conquers, must in right obay.

27. And though I humanly have heretofore
All beauty lik'd, I never lov'd till now;
Nor think a Crown can raise his valew more,
To whom already Heav'n does Love allow.

28. Though, since I gave the *Hunns* their last defeat,
I have the *Lombards* Ensignes onward led,
Ambition kindled not this Victor's heat,
But 'tis a warmth my Fathers prudence bred.

29. Who cast on more then Wolvish Man his Eie,
Man's necessary hunger judg'd, and saw
That caus'd not his devouring Maledy;
But like a wanton whelp he loves to gnaw.

30. Man still is Sick for pow'r, yet that disease
Nature (whose Law is temp'rance) ne'r inspires;
But 'tis a humor, which fond Man does please,
A luxury, fruition only tires.

31. And as in persons, so in publick States,
The lust of Pow'r provokes to cruel Warre;
For wisest Senates it intoxicates,
And makes them vain, as single persons are.

32. Men into Nations it did first divide;
Whilst place, scarce distant, gives them diff'rent stiles;
Rivers, whose breadth Inhabitants may stride,
Parts them as much as Continents, and Isles.

24: 3 feed '*51a cor*: fed '*51a u*, '*51b*, '*73*   25: 3 to '*73*: at '*51a–b*   26: 1
noble '*73*: gentle '*51a–b*   29: 4 but '*51b*, '*73*: Bnt '*51a*   30: 3 which . . . does
'*73*: does his Manship '*51a–b*

33. On equal, smooth, and undistinguish'd Ground,
    The lust of pow'r does libertie impair,
    And limits by a Border and a Bound,
    What was before as passable as Air.

34. Whilst change of Languages oft breeds a warre,
    (A change which Fashion does as oft obtrude
    As womens dresse) and oft Complexions are,
    And diff'rent names, no less a cause of feud.

35. Since Men so causelesly themselves devour;
    (And hast'ning still, their else too hasty Fates,
    Act but continu'd Massacres for pow'r,)
    My Father ment to chastise Kings, and States.

36. To overcome the world, till but one Crown
    And universal Neighbourhood he saw;
    Till all were rich by that allyance grown;
    And want no more should be the cause of Law.

37. One Family the world was first design'd;
    And though some fighting Kings so sever'd are,
    That they must meet by help of Seas and winde,
    Yet when they fight 'tis but a civil warre.

38. Nor could Religion's heat, if one rul'd all,
    To bloody War the unconcern'd allure;
    And hasten us from Earth, ere Age does call,
    Who are (alas) of Heav'n so little sure.

39. Religion, ne'r till divers Monarchys,
    Taught that almighty Heav'n needs Armys ayd;
    But with contentious Kings she now complies,
    Who seem for their own cause, of God's afraid.

40. To join all sever'd Powr's (which is to end
    The cause of War) my Father onward fought;
    By War the *Lombard* Scepter to extend
    Till peace were forc'd, where it was slowly sought.

41. He lost in this attempt his last dear blood;
    And I (whom no remoteness can deterr,
    If what seems difficult, be great and good)
    Thought his Example could not make me err.

42. No place I merit in the Book of Fame!
    Whose leaves are by the *Greeks* and *Romans* fill'd;
    Yet I presume to boast, she knows my name,
    And she has heard to whom the *Hunns* did yeild.

43. But let not what so needfully was done,
    Though still pursu'd, make you ambition feare;
    For could I force all Monarchys to one,
    That Universal Crown I would not weare.

44. He who does blindly soar at *Rhodalind*,
    Mounts like seel'd Doves, stil higher from his ease;
    And in the lust of Empire he may finde,
    High Hope does better then Fruition please.

45. The Victor's solid recompence is rest;
    And 'tis unjust, that Chiefs who pleasure shunn,
    Toyling in Youth, should be in Age opprest
    With greater Toyles, by ruling what they wonn.

46. Here all reward of conquest I would finde;
    Leave shining Thrones for *Birtha* in a shade;
    With Nature's quiet wonders fill my minde;
    And praise her most, because she *Birtha* made.

47. Now *Astragon* (with joy suffic'd) perceiv'd
    How nobly Heav'n for *Birtha* did provide;
    Oft had he for her parted Mother griev'd,
    But can this joy, less then that sorrow hide.

48. With teares, bids *Gondibert* to Heav'n's Eie make
    All good within, as to the World he seems;
    And in gain'd *Birtha* then from *Hymen* take
    All youth can wish, and all his age esteems.

49. Strait to his lov'd Philosophers he hies,
    Who now at Nature's Councel busy are
    To trace new Lights, which some old Gazer spies;
    Whilst the Duke seeks more busily his Starre.

50. But in her search, he is by *Goltho* stay'd;
    Who in a closs dark Covert foldes his Armes;
    His Eies with thought grow darker then that shade,
    Such thoughts as yielding Breasts with study warmes.

42: 3 boast *'51a cor*, *'51b*, *'73*: hoast *'51a u*   47: 3 parted *'73*: vanish'd *'51a–b*
50: 4 thoughts . . . Breasts *'73*: thought as Brow and Breast *'51a–b*

51. Fix'd to unheeded object is his Eie!
His sences he calls in, as if t'improve
By outward absence, inward extacie,
Such as makes Prophets, or is made by Love.

52. Awake (said *Gondibert*) for now in vain
Thou dream'st of sov'raignty, and War's success;
Hope, nought has left, which Worth should wish to gain;
And all Ambition is but Hope's excess.

53. Bid all our Worthys to unarm, and rest!
For they have nought to conquer worth their care;
I have a Father's right in *Birtha's* Breast,
And that's the peace for which the wise make warre.

54. At this starts *Goltho*, like some Army's Chief,
Whom unintrench'd, a midnight Larum wakes;
By pawse then gave disorder'd sence relief,
And this reply with kindled passion makes.

55. What means my Prince to make so low a boast,
Whose merit may aspire to *Rhodalind*?
For who could *Birtha* miss if she were lost,
That shall by worth the others treasure find?

56. When your high blood, and conquests shall submit
To such mean joys, in this unminded shade,
Let Courts, without Heav'n's Lamps, in darkness sit,
And War become the lowly Shepheard's Trade.

57. *Birtha*, (a harmless Cottage Ornament!)
May be his Bride, that's born himself to serve;
But you must pay that blood your Army spent,
And wed that Empire which our wounds deserve.

58. This brought the Duke's swift anger to his Eies;
Which his consid'rate Heart rebuk'd as faste;
He *Goltho* chid, in that he nought replies;
Leaves him, and *Birtha* seeks with Lovers haste.

59. Now *Goltho* mourns, yet not that *Birtha's* fair;
Or that the Duke shuns Empire for a Bride;
But that himself must joyn love to dispair;
Himself who loves her, and his love must hide.

53: 4 peace ... make '*51aMS*ᵇ, '*51b*, '*73*: peace ... may '*51a cor*: place ... may
'*51a u*: place ... make '*51a u MS*ᵃ   55: 1 make '*73*: learn '*51a–b*

60. He curs'd that him the wounded hither brought
    From *Oswald's* Field; where though he wounds did scape
    In tempting Death, and here no danger sought,
    Yet here met worse then Death in Beauty's shape.

61. He was unus'd to love, as bred in warres;
    And not till now for beauty leasure had;
    Yet bore Love's load, as Youth bears other Cares;
    Till new dispair makes Love's old weight too sad.

62. But *Ulfinore*, does hither aptly come,
    His second Breast, in whom his griefs excesse
    He may ebb out, when they o'reflow at home;
    Such griefs, as thus in Throngs for utt'rance press.

63. Forgive me that so falsly am thy Friend!
    No more our Hearts for kindnesse shall contest;
    Since mine I hourly on another spend,
    And now imbrace thee with an empty Brest.

64. Yet pard'ning me, you cancel Nature's fault;
    Who walks with her first force in *Birtha's* shape;
    And when she spreads the Net to have us caught,
    It were in youth presumption to escape.

65. When *Birtha's* grief so comly did appear,
    Whilst she beheld our wounded Duke's distresse;
    Then first my alter'd Heart began to fear,
    Least too much Love should friendship dispossesse;

66. But this whilst *Ulfinore* with sorrow hears,
    Him *Goltho's* busier sorrow little heeds;
    And though he could replie in sighs and tears,
    Yet governs both, and *Goltho* thus proceeds.

67. To Love's new dangers I have gone unarm'd;
    I lack'd experience why to be afraid;
    Was too unlearn'd to read whom Love had harm'd;
    But have his will as Nature's law obay'd.

68. Th'obedient and defencelesse, sure, no law
    Afflicts, for law is their defence, and pow'r;
    Yet me, Loves sheep, whom rigour needs not aw,
    Wolf-Love, because defencelesse, does devour:

60: 4 met] meet '73   67: 3 whom . . . harm'd '51a MSª, '51b *Errata,* '73:
home . . . arm'd '51a: home . . . harm'd '51a MSᵇ: how . . . harm'd '51b

69. Gives me not time to perish by degrees,
    But with dispair does me at once destroy;
    For none who *Gondibert* a Lover sees,
    Thinks he would love, but where he may enjoy.

70. *Birtha* he loves; and I from *Birtha* fear
    Death that in rougher Figure I despise!
    This *Ulfinore* did with distemper hear,
    Yet with dissembled temp'rance thus replies.

71. Ah *Goltho*! who Love's Feaver can asswage?
    For though familiar seems that old disease;
    Yet like Religion's fit, when People rage,
    Few cure those evils which the Patient please.

72. Natures Religion, Love, is still perverse;
    And no commerce with cold discretion hath,
    For if Discretion speak when Love is fierce,
    'Tis wav'd by Love, as Reason is by Faith.

73. As *Gondibert* left *Goltho* when he heard
    His Saint profan'd, as if some Plague were nie;
    So *Goltho* now leaves *Ulfinore*, and fear'd
    To share such veng'ance, if he did not flie.

74. How each at home o're-rates his miserie,
    And thinks that all are musical abroad,
    Unfetter'd as the Windes, whilst onely he
    Of all the glad and licens'd world is aw'd?

75. And as Cag'd Birds are by the Fowler set
    To call in more, whilst those that taken be,
    May think (though they are Pris'ners in the Net)
    Th'incag'd, because they sing, sometimes are free.

76. So *Goltho* (who by *Ulfinore* was brought
    Here where he first Love's dangers did perceive
    In Beauty's Field) thinks though himself was caught,
    Th'inviter safe, because not heard to grieve.

77. But *Ulfinore* (whom Neighbourhood led here)
    Impressions took before from *Birtha's* sight;
    Ideas which in silence hidden were,
    As Heav'n's designes before the birth of Light.

75: 4 sing, sometimes '73: ne'r complain, '51a–b

78. This from his Father *Ulfin* he did hide,
Who, strict to Youth, would not permit the best
Reward of worth, the Bosome of a Bride,
Should be but after Vertuous toyles possest.

79. For *Ulfinore* (in blooming honor yet)
Though he had learnt the count'nance of the Foe,
And though his courage could dull Armys whet,
The care o're Crouds, nor Conduct could not know;

80. Nor varie Batails shapes in the Foes view;
But now in forraigne Fields meanes to improve
His early Arts, to what his Father knew,
That merit so might get him leave to love.

81. Till then, check'd passion, shall not venture forth:
And now retires with a disorder'd Heart;
Griev'd, least his Rival should by early'r worth
Get Love's reward, ere he can gain desert.

82. But stop we here, like those who day-light lack;
Or as misguided Travailers that rove,
Oft finde their way by going somewhat back;
So let's return, thou ill Conductor Love!

83. Thy little wanton Godhead as my Guide
I have attended many'a Winter night;
To seek whom Time for honor's sake would hide,
Since in mine age sought by a wasted light:

84. But ere my remnant of Life's Lamp be spent,
Whilst I in Lab'rinths stray amongst the Dead;
I mean to recollect the paths I went,
And judge from thence the steps I am to tread.

85. Thy walk (though as a common Deitie
The Croud does follow thee) misterious grows:
For *Rhodalind* may now closs Mourner die,
Since *Gondibert*, too late, her sorrow knows.

86. Young *Hurgonil* above dear light prefers
Calm *Orna*, who his highest Love outloves;
Yet envious Clouds in *Lombard* Registers
O'recast their Morn, what e're their Evening proves.

87. For fatall *Laura*, trusty *Tybalt* pines;
    For haughty *Gartha*, subtle *Hermegild*;
    Whilst she her beauty, youth, and birth declines;
    And as to Fate, does to Ambition yeild.

88. Great *Gondibert*, to bashful *Birtha* bends;
    Whom she adores like Vertue in a Throne;
    Whilst *Ulfinore*, and *Goltho* (late vow'd Friends
    By him) are now his Rivals, and their owne.

89. Through ways thus intricate to Lovers Urnes,
    Thou lead'st me Love, to shew thy Trophys past;
    Where Time (less cruel then thy Godhead) mournes
    In ruines which thy pride would have to last.

90. Where I on *Lombard* Monuments have read
    Old Lovers names, and their fam'd Ashes spy'd;
    But less can learn by knowing they are dead,
    And such their Tombes; then how they liv'd, and dy'd.

91. To *Paphos* flie! and leave me sullen here!
    This Lamp shall light me to Records which give
    To future Youth, so just a cause of feare,
    That it will Valor seem to dare to live!

The End of the Second Book

GONDIBERT

THE THIRD *BOOK

Canto the First

*Written by
the Author
During his
Imprison-
ment.

The ARGUMENT

The People, left by GARTHA, *leave to mourn;*
And worship HERMEGILD *for her return.*
The wounded HURGONIL *by* ORNA *cur'd;*
Their loyal loves by mariage plight assur'd.
In LAURA'S *hasty change, Love's pow'r appears,*
And TYBALT *seeks the kindness which he fears.*

1. When sad *Verona* saw in *Gartha's* shape
   Departed Peace brought back, the Court they prais'd;
   And seem'd so joy'd as Citys which escape
   A siege, even by their own brave Sallys rais'd.

2. And *Hermegild*, to make her triumph long,
   Through all the streets his Chariot slowly drove;
   Whilst she endures the kindness of the Throng,
   Though rude, as was their rage, is now their love.

3. On *Hermegild* (so longingly desir'd
   From *Hubert's* Camp) with Childish Eies they gaze;
   They worship now, what late they but admir'd,
   And all his Arts to mighty Magick raise.

4. On both they such abundant Blessings throw,
   As if those num'rous Priests who here reside,
   (Loath to out-live this joy) assembled now
   In haste to bless the Laytie e're they dyde.

5. Thus dignify'd, and Crown'd through all the Streets
   To Court they come; where them wise *Aribert*
   Not weakly with a publick passion meets;
   But in his open'd Face conceal'd his heart.

1: 4 even] that '73   2: 1 her '51a MS, '51b, '73: their '51a

6. With mod'rate joy he took this Pledge of Peace,
    Because great joys infer to judging Eies
    The minde distress'd before; and in distress,
    Thrones, which are jealous Forts, think all are Spies.

7. Yet, by degrees, a Soul delighted showes
    To *Gartha*, whom he leads to *Rhodalind*;
    And soon to *Hermegild* as artless grows
    As Maids, and like succesful Lovers kind.

8. And *Rhodalind*, though bred to daily sight
    Of Courts feign'd Faces, and pretended hearts,
    (In which disguises Courts take no delight,
    But little mischiefs shun by little Arts.)

9. She, when she *Gartha* saw, no kindness faign'd;
    But faithfully her former rage excus'd;
    For now she others sorrows entertain'd,
    As if to love, a Maid's first sorrow us'd,

10. Yet did her first with cautious gladness meet;
    Then soon from grave respect to fondness grew;
    To kisses in their taste and odour sweet,
    As *Hybla* Hony, or *Arabian* Dew.

11. And *Gartha* like an Eastern Monarch's Bride,
    This publick love with bashful homage took;
    For she had learn'd from *Hermegild* to hide
    A rising Heart, behinde a falling Look.

12. Thus, mask'd with meekness, she does much intreat
    A pardon for that Storm her sorrow rais'd;
    Which *Rhodalind* more sues she would forget,
    Unless to have so just a sorrow prais'd.

13. Soon is this joy through all the Court dispers'd;
    So high they vallew peace, who daily are
    In Prides invasions, private faction, vers'd;
    The small, but fruitful seed of publick warre.

14. Whilst thus sweet Peace had others joys assur'd,
    Orna with hopes of sweeter Love was pleas'd;
    For of war's wounds brave *Hurgonil* was cur'd;
    And those of love, which deeper reach'd, were eas'd.

15. In both these cures her Sov'raign help appears,
    Since as her double Patient he receiv'd
    For bloody wounds, Balm, from her precious tears,
    And bloodless wounds of love her vowes reliev'd.

16. She let no medc'nal Flowre in quiet grow,
    No Art lie hid, nor Artist ease his thought,
    No Fane be Shut, no Priest from Altars goe,
    Nor in Heav'n's Quire no Saint remain unsought,

17. Nor more her Eies could ease of sleep esteem
    Then sleep can the world's Eie, the Sun, conceal;
    Nor breath'd she but in vows to Heav'n, or him,
    Till Heav'n, and she, his diff'rent wounds did heal.

18. But now she needs those ayds she did dispence;
    For scarce her cures were on him perfect grown,
    E're shame afflicts her for that diligence,
    Which Love had in her fits of pitty shown.

19. When she (though made of cautious bashfulness)
    Whilst him in wounds a smarting Feaver burn'd,
    Invok'd remotest aydes to his redress,
    And with a lowd ungovern'd kindness mourn'd.

20. When o're him then, whilst parting life She ru'd,
    Her kisses faster (though unknown before)
    Then Blossomes fall on parting Spring, she strew'd;
    Then Blossomes sweeter, and in number more.

21. But now when from her busy Maid she knew
    How wildly Grief had led her Love abroad,
    Unmask'd to all, she her own Pris'ner grew;
    By shame, a Virgin's Native Conscience, aw'd.

22. With undirected Eies which careless rove,
    With thoughts too singly to her self confin'd,
    She blushing starts at her remember'd love,
    And grievs the world had Eies, when that was blind.

23. Sad darkness, which does other Virgins fright,
    Now boldly and alone, she entertain'd;

15: 3–4 For . . . reliev'd '73: For War's wounds, Balm, dropp'd in her precious tears,
/And Love's, her more accepted vows, reliev'd '51a–b   19: 1 cautious '73: shunning
'51a–b   22: 4 Eies '51a cor: Eys '51a u: Eyes '51b, '73

And shuns her Lover, like the Traytor, light,
Till he her curtains drew, and thus complain'd.

24. Why, bashful Maid, will you your beauty hide
Because your fairer Mind, your Love, is known?
So Jewellers conceal with artful pride
Their second wealth, after the best is shown.

25. In pitty's passion you unvaild your minde;
Let him not fall, whom you did help to climbe;
Nor seem by being bashful, so unkinde
As if you think your pitty was a crime.

26. O useless shame! Officious bashfulness!
Vertues vain signe, which onely there appears
Where Vertue grows erroneous by excess,
And shapes more sins, then frighted Conscience fears.

27. Your Blushes, which to meer complexion grow,
You must as nature, not as vertue own;
And for your open'd Love, you but blush so
As guiltless Roses blush that they are blown.

28. As well the Morn (whose essence Poets made,
And gave her bashful Eies) we may beleeve
Does blush for what she sees through Night's thinn shade,
As that you can for love discover'd grieve.

29. Arise! and all the Flowres of ev'ry Mead
(Which weeping through your Stills my health restor'd)
Bring to the Temple to adorn your Head,
And there where you did worship, be ador'd.

30. This with a low regard (but voyce rais'd high
By joys of Love) he spake; and not less kind
Was now (ent'ring with native harmony,
Like forward spring) the bloomy *Rhodalind*:

31. Like Summer, goodly *Gartha*, fully blown;
Laura, like Autumn, with as ripe a look;
But shew'd, by some chill griefs, her Sun was gon,
Arnold, from whom she Life's short glory took.

29: 4 where '51a u MS, '51 a cor, '51b, '73: wuere '51a u   30: 2 kinde '51a MS:
kinde, '51a   30: 4 forward . . . bloomy '51a cor MS: forward . . . blooming '51a u
MS, '51b, '73: foward . . . bloomy '51a cor: foward . . . blooming '51a u

32. Like Winter, *Hermegild*; yet not so gray
    And cold, but that his fashion seem'd to boast,
    That even weak Winter is allow'd some day,
    And the Ayre cleer, and healthfull in a Frost.

33. All these, and *Tybalt* too (unless a Spy
    He be, watching who thrives in *Laura's* sight)
    Came hither, as in kinde conspiracy,
    To hasten *Orna* to her mariage plight.

34. And now the Priests prepare for this high vow
    All Rites that to their Lawes can add a grace;
    To which the sequent knot they not allow,
    Till a spent Moon recovers all her Face.

35. And now the streets like Summer Meads appear!
    For with sweet strewings Maids left Gardens bare,
    As Lovers wish their sweeter Bosomes were,
    When hid unkindly by dishevel'd Haire.

36. And *Orna* now (importun'd to possess
    Her long wish'd joys) breaks through her blushes so
    As the fair Morn breaks through her rosyness;
    And from a like guilt did their blushes grow.

37. She thinks her Love's high sickness now appears
    A fit so weak, as does no med'cine need;
    So soon societie can cure those feares
    On which the Coward, Solitude, does feed.

38. They with united joy blest *Hurgonil*
    And *Orna* to the sacred Temple bring;
    Whilst all the Court in triumph shew their Skil,
    As if long bred by a triumphant King.

39. Such days of joy, before the mariage day,
    The *Lombards* long by custome had embrac't;
    Custom, which all, rather then Law obay,
    For Lawes by force, Customes, by pleasure last.

40. And wisely Ancients by this needfull snare
    Of guilded joys, did hide such bitterness
    As most in mariage swallow with that care,
    Which bashfully the wise will ne'r confess.

34: 4 Moon '51a MS, '51b Errata: Morn '51a, '51b, '73

41. 'Tis Statesmens musick, who States Fowlers be,
    And singing Birds, to catch the wilder, set;
    So bring in more to tame societie;
    For wedlock, to the wilde, is the States Net.

42. And this lowd joy, before the mariage Rites,
    Like Batails Musick which to fights prepare,
    Many to strife and sad success invites;
    For mariage is too oft but civil warre.

43. A truth too amply known to those who read
    Great *Hymen's* Roles; though he from Lovers Eies
    Hides his most Tragick stories of the Dead,
    Least all, like *Goths*, should 'gainst his Temples rise.

44. And thou (what ere thou art, who dost perchance
    With a hot Reader's haste, this Song pursue)
    Mayst finde, too soon, thou dost too far advance,
    And wish it all unread, or else untrue.

45. For it is sung (though by a mourning voyce)
    That in the *Ides* before these Lovers had,
    With *Hymens* publick hand, confirm'd their choyce,
    A cruell practise did their peace invade.

46. For *Hermegild*, too studiously foresaw
    The Counts allyance with the Duke's high blood,
    Might from the *Lombards* such affection draw,
    As could by *Hubert* never be withstood.

47. And he in haste with *Gartha* does retire,
    Where thus his Breast he opens to prevent,
    That *Hymen's* hallow'd Torch may not take fire,
    When all these lesser lights of joy are spent.

48. High Heav'n (from whose best Lights your beauty grows,
    Born high, as highest Mindes) preserve you still
    From such, who then appear resistless Foes,
    When they allyance joyn to Armes and Skill!

49. Most by conjunction Planets harmfull are;
    So Rivers joyning overflow the Land,
    And Forces joyn'd make that destructive warre,
    Which else our common conduct may withstand.

45: 4 cruell '*51a cor*, '*51b*, '*73*: cruest '*51a u*   48: 1 grows, '*51a cor*, '*51b*, '*73*:
grows. '*51a u*

50. Their Knees to *Hurgonil* the People bow
    And worship *Orna* in her Brothers right;
    They must be sever'd, or like Palms will grow,
    Which planted neer, out-climbe their native hight.

51. As Windes, whose violence out-does all art,
    Act all unseen; so we as secretly
    These Branches of that Cedar *Gondibert*
    Must force till his deep Root in rising dy.

52. If we make noise whilst our deep workings last,
    Such rumour through thick Towns unheeded flies,
    As winds through woods, and we (our great work past)
    Like winds will silence Tongues, and scape from Eies.

53. E're this dark lesson she was clearer taught,
    His enter'd Slaves place at her rev'renc'd Feet
    A spacious Cabinet, with all things fraught,
    Which seem'd for wearing artful, rich, and sweet.

54. With leisurely delight, she by degrees
    Lifts ev'ry Till, does ev'ry Drawer draw;
    But nought which to her Sex belongs she sees;
    And for the Male all nice adornments saw.

55. This seem'd to breed some strangeness in her Eies;
    Which like a wanton wonder there begen;
    But strait she in the Lower Closet spies
    Th'accomplish'd dress, and Garments of a Man.

56. Then starting, she her Hand shrunk nicely back;
    As if she had been stung, or that she fear'd
    This Garment was the Skin of that old Snake,
    Which at the fatal Tree like Man appear'd.

57. Th'ambitious Mayd at scornful distance stood;
    And bravely seem'd of Love's low vices free;
    Though vicious in her minde, not in her blood:
    Ambition is the Mindes immodestie!

58. He knew great mindes disorder'd by mistake,
    Defend through pride, the errors they repent;
    And with a Lovers fearfulness he spake
    Thus humbly, that extremes he might prevent.

59. How ill (delightfull Mayd!) shall I deserve
    My Life's last flame, fed by your beauty's fire,
    If I shall vex your vertues, that preserve
    Others weak vertues, which would else expire.

60. How, more then death, shall I my life despise,
    When your fear'd frowns, make me your service fear;
    When I scarce dare to say, that the disguise
    You shrink to see, you must vouchsafe to wear.

61. So rude a Law your int'rest will impose;
    And solid int'rest must not yeild to shame:
    Vain shame, which fears you should such honor lose
    As lasts but by intelligence with Fame.

62. Number, which makes opinion Law, can turn
    This shape to fashion, which you scorn to use,
    Because not by your Sex as fashion worn;
    And fashion is but that which Numbers chuse.

63. If you approve what Numbers lawfull think,
    Be bold, for Number cancels bashfulness;
    Extremes, from which a King would blushing shrink,
    Unblushing Senates act as no excess.

64. Thus he his thoughts (the picture of his minde)
    By a dark Vayle to sodain sight deny'd;
    That she might prise, what seem'd so hard to finde;
    For Curtains promise worth in what they hide.

65. He said her Manhood would not strange appear
    In Court, where all the fashion is disguise;
    Where *Masquerades* are serious all the year;
    None known but strangers, nor secure but Spies.

66. All rules he reads of living great in Courts;
    Which some the Art of wise dissembling call;
    For Pow'r (born to have Foes) much weight supports
    By their false strength who thrust to make it fall.

67. He bids her wear her beauty free as light;
    By Eares as open be to all endeer'd;
    For the unthinking Croud judge by their sight;
    And seem half eas'd, when they are fully heard.

62: 4 chuse. '51b: chuse, '51a, '73

68. He shuts her Breast even from familiar Eies;
    For he who secrets (Pow'r's chief Treasure) spends
    To purchase Friendship, friendship dearly buys:
    Since Pow'r seeks great Confed'rates, more then Friends.

69. And now with Councels more perticular,
    He taught her how to wear tow'rdes *Rhodalind*
    Her looks; which of the Minde false pictures are;
    And then how *Orna* may believe her kinde.

70. How *Laura* too may be (whose practis'd Eies
    Can more detect the shape of forward love)
    By treaty caught, though not by a surprise;
    Whose ayd would precious to her faction prove.

71. But here he ends his Lecture, for he spy'd
    (Adorn'd, as if to grace Magnifique Feasts)
    Bright *Rhodalind*, with the elected Bride;
    And with the Bride, all her selected Guests.

72. They *Gartha* in their civil pity sought;
    Whom they in midst of triumphs mist, and feare
    Least her full Breast (with *Huberts* sorrows fraught)
    She, like a Mourner, came to empty here.

73. But she, and *Hermegild*, are wilde with hast,
    As Traytors are whom Visitants surprise;
    Decyph'ring that which fearfully they cast
    In some dark place, where viler Treason lies.

74. So open they the fatal Cabinet,
    To shut things slighter with the Consequent;
    Then soon their rally'd looks in posture set;
    And boldly with them to their triumphs went.

75. *Tybalt*, who *Laura* gravely ever led,
    With ceaseless whispers laggs behinde the Train;
    Trys, since her wary Governour is dead,
    How the fair Fort he may by Treaty gain.

76. For now unhappy *Arnold* she forsakes;
    Yet is he blest that she does various prove,
    When his spent heart for no unkindness akes,
    Since from the Light as sever'd as from Love.

73: 2 Traytors *'51a MS*, *'51b*, *'73*: Tyrants *'51a*   73: 3 Decyph'ring *'73*:
Dechyphring *'51a*: Decyphring *'51b*   73: 4 viler *'73*: worser *'51a–b*

77. Yet as in storms and sickness newly gon,
    Some Clouds awhile, and strokes of faintness last;
    So, in her brow, so much of grief is shown,
    As shews a Tempest, or a sickness past.

78. But him no more with such sad Eies she seeks,
    As even at Feasts would make old Tyrants weep;
    Nor more attempts to wake him with such shreeks,
    As threatned all where Death's deaf Pris'ners sleep.

79. *Hugo* and him, as Leaders now she names,
    Not much as Lovers does their fame approve;
    Nor her own fate, but chance of batail blames;
    As if they dy'd for honor, not for love.

80. This *Tybalt* saw, and findes that the turn'd Stream
    Came fairly flowing to refresh his heart;
    Yet could he not forget the kinde esteem
    She lately had of *Arnold's* high desert.

81. Nor does it often scape his memory,
    How gravely he had vow'd, that if her Eies,
    After such Showres of Love, were quickly drie,
    He would them more then Lamps in Tombs despise.

82. And Whilst he watch'd like an industrious Spy
    Her Sexes changes, and revolts of youth;
    He still reviv'd this vow as solemnly,
    As Senates Count'nance Laws or Synods, Truth.

83. But Men are frail, more Glasse then Women are!
    Tybalt who with a stay'd judicious heart
    Would love, grows vain amidst his gravest care:
    Love free by nature, scorns the Bonds of Art!

84. *Laura* (whose Fort he by approach would gain)
    With a weak sigh blows up his Mine, and Smiles;
    Gives fire but with her Eie, and he is slain;
    Or treats, and with a whisper him beguiles.

85. Nor force of Arms or Arts (ô Love!) endures
    Thy mightynesse; and since we must discern
    Diseases fully e're we study cures;
    And our own force by others weaknesse learn;

82: 2 revolts] revolt '51b   85: 4 others] othes, '51b

86. Let me to Courts and Camps thy Agent be,
    Where all their weakness and diseases spring
    From their not knowing, and not hon'ring thee
    In those who Nature in thy triumphs sing.

Canto the Second

The ARGUMENT

Whilst BIRTHA *and the Duke their joyes persue*
In conqu'ring Love, Fate does them both subdue
With triumphs, which from Court young ORGO *brought;*
And have in GOLTHO *greater triumphs wrought:*
Whose hopes the quiet ULFINORE *does bear*
With patience feign'd, and with a hidden fear.

1. The prosp'rous *Gondibert* from *Birtha* gains
   All bashful plights a Maids first bounties give;
   Fast vows, which binde Love's Captives more then chains,
   Yet free Love's Saints in chosen bondage live.

2. Few were the daies, and swiftly seem'd to waste,
   Which thus he in his mindes fruition spent;
   And least some envious Cloud should overcast
   His Love's fair Morn, oft to his Camp he sent:

3. To *Bergamo*, where still intrenched were
   Those Youth, whom first his Father's Army bred;
   Who ill the rumor of his wounds did bear,
   Though he that gave them, of his own be dead.

4. And worse those haughty threat'nings they abhor,
   Which Fame from *Brescia's* ancient Fighters brought;
   Vain Fame, the Peoples trusted Orator,
   Whose speech (too fluent) their mistakes has wrought.

5. Oft *Goltho* with his temp'rate Councels went,
   To quench whom Fame to dang'rous fury warm'd;
   Till temp'rately his dangers they resent,
   And think him safest in their patience arm'd.

6. And safe now is his love, as love could be,
   If all the World like old *Arcadia* were;
   Honor the Monarch, and all Lovers free
   From jealousy, as safety is from fear.

7. And *Birtha's* heart does to his civil Breast
   As much for ease and peace, as safety come;
   For there 'tis serv'd and treated as a Guest,
   But watch'd, and taught, and often chid at home.

8. Like great and good Confed'rates, whose designe
   Invades not others but secures their own,
   So they in just and vertuous hopes combine,
   And are, like new Confed'rates, busy grown.

9. With whisper earnest, and now grave with thought;
   They walk consulting, standing they debate;
   And then seek shades, where they in vaine are sought
   By servants who intrude and think they waite.

10. In this great League, their most important care
    Was to dispatch their Rites; yet so provide,
    That all the Court might think them free as ayre,
    When fast as faith, they were by *Hymen* ty'd.

11. For if the King (said he) our love surprise,
    His stormy rage will it rebellion call;
    Who claims to chuse the Brides of his Allys;
    And in that storm our joys in blossome fall.

12. Our love, your cautious Father, onely knows
    (On whose safe prudence, Senates may depend)
    And *Goltho*, who to time few reck'nings owes,
    Yet can discharge all duties of a Friend.

13. Such was his minde, and hers (more busy) shows
    That bonds of love does make her longer fast
    Then *Hymen's* knot, as plain Religion does,
    Longer then Rites (Religion's fashions) last.

14. That her discretion somewhat does appeare,
    Since she can Love, her minds chief beauty, hide;
    Which never farther went then *Thula's* Eare,
    Who had (alas) but for that secret di'de.

15. That she already had disguises fram'd,
    And sought out Caves where she might closs reside;
    As being, nor unwilling nor asham'd
    To live his Captive, so she die his Bride.

16. Full of themselves, delight them onward leads,
    Where in the Front was to remoter view
    Exalted Hills, and neerer prostrate Meads,
    With Forrests flanck'd, where shade to darkness grew.

17. Beneath that shade, Two Rivers slily steal,
    Through narrow walks, to wider *Adice*,
    Who swallows both, till proudly she does swel,
    And hasts to shew her beauty to the Sea.

18. And here, whilst forth he sends his ranging Eie,
    Orgo he spies; who plies the spur so fast,
    As if with newes of Vict'ry he would flie
    To leave swift Fame behinde him by his haste.

19. If (said the Duke) because this Boy is come
    I second gladness shew, doe not suppose
    I spread my Breast to give new Comforts roome,
    That were to welcome rain where *Nylus* flowes.

20. Though the unripe appearance of a Page
    For weighty trust, may render him too weak,
    Yet this is he, who more then cautious Age,
    Or like calm Death, will bury what we speak.

21. This, *Birtha*, is the Boy, whose skilless face
    Is safe from jealousie of oldest spies;
    In whom, by whisper, we from distant place
    May meet, or wink our meaning to his Eies.

22. More had he said to gain him her esteem,
    But *Orgo* enters speechless with his Speed;
    And by his looks more full of haste did seem,
    Then when his spurs provok'd his flying steed.

23. And with his first recover'd breath he crys;
    Hayle my lov'd Lord; whom Fame does vallew so,
    That when she swift with your successes flies,
    She feares to wrong the World in being slow.

24. I bring you more then tasts of Fortune's love,
    Yet am afraid I err, in having dar'd
    To think her favours could your gladness move;
    Who have more worth then Fortune can reward.

25. The Duke, with smiles, forewarns his hasty Tongue;
    As loath he should proceed in telling more;
    Kindly afraid to do his kindness wrong,
    By hearing what he thought he knew before.

26. Thy diligence (said he) is high desert;
    It does in Youth supply defects of skil;
    And is of duty the most useful part;
    Yet art thou now but slow to *Hurgonil.*

27. Who hither by the Moons imperfect light
    Came and return'd, without the help of day,
    To tell me he has *Orna's* Virgin plight,
    And that their nuptials for my presence stay.

28. *Orgo* reply'd, though that a triumph be
    Where all false Lovers are, like savage Kings,
    Led Captive after Love's great Victorie,
    It does but promise what your triumph brings.

29. It was the Eve to this your Holy-day!
    And now *Verona* Mistris does appear
    Of *Lombardy*; and all the Flowres which *May*
    E're wore, does as the Countrie's favours wear.

30. The weary Eccho from the Hills makes haste;
    Vex'd that the Bells still call for her replies
    When they so many are, and ring so faste;
    Yet oft are silenc'd by the Peoples cries:

31. Who send to Heav'n the name of *Rhodalind*,
    And then Duke *Gondibert* as high they raise,
    To both with all their publick passion kinde,
    If kindness shine in wishes and in praise.

32. The King this day made your adoption known,
    Proclaim'd you to the Empire next ally'd,
    As heir to all his Conquests and his Crown,
    For royal *Rhodalind* must be your Bride.

33. Not all the dangers valor findes in war,
    Love meets in Courts, or pride to Courts procures,
    When sick with peace they hot in faction are,
    Can make such fears as now the Duke endures.

34. Nor all those fears which ev'ry Maid has found,
    On whose first Guards, Love by surprises steals,
    (Whose sightlesse Arrow makes a curelesse wound)
    Are like to this which doubtful *Birtha* feels.

35. He from his looks wild wonder strives to chace;
    Strives more to teach his Manhood to resist
    Death in her Eies; and then with all the grace
    Of seeming pleasure, *Orgo* he dismist.

36. And *Orgo* being gone, low as her knees
    Could fall, she fell; and soon he bends as low
    With weight of heart; griev'd that no Grave he sees,
    To sink, where love no more can sorrow know.

37. Her sighs as showrs lay windes, are calm'd with tears;
    And parting life seems stay'd awhile to take
    A civil leave, whilst her pale visage wears
    A cleerer Sky, and thus she weeping spake.

38. Since such a Prince has forfeited his pow'r,
    Heav'n give me leave to make my duty lesse,
    Let me my vows, as sodain oathes abhor,
    Which did my passion, not my truth expresse.

39. Yet yours I would not think were counterfeit,
    But rather ill and rashly understood;
    For 'tis impossible I can forget
    So soon, that once you fatally were good.

40. Though cruel now as Beasts where they have pow'r;
    Chusing, like them to make the weakest bleed;
    For weaknesse soon invites you to devour,
    And a submission gives you ease to feed.

41. To fighting Fields, send all your honor back,
    To Courts your dang'rous Tongue and civil shape,
    That Country Maids may Men no more mistake,
    Nor seek dark Death, that they may Love escape.

37: 4 cleerer] clearie '*51b*   40: 2 them] them, '*73*

42. Now soon to Heav'n her Soul had found the way,
    (For there it oft had been in pray'r and praise)
    But that his vows did life with lowdness stay,
    And life's warm help did soon her body raise.

43. And now he gently leads her; for no more
    He lets th'unhallow'd Ground a faln Flowre wear,
    Sweeter then Nature's Bosome ever wore;
    And now these vows sends kindly to her Ear.

44. If (*Birtha*) I am false think none to blame
    For thinking Truth (by which the Soul subsists)
    No farther to be found then in the name;
    Think humane kinde betraid even by their Priests.

45. Think all my Sex so vile, that you may chide
    Those Maids who to your Mothers Nuptials ran;
    And praise your Mother who so early dyde,
    Remembring whom she marry'd was a Man.

46. This great Court miracle you strait receive
    From *Orgo*, and your faith the whole allows;
    Why since you *Orgo's* words so soon believe
    Will you lesse civilly suspect my vowes?

47. My Vowes, which want the Temples seal, will binde
    (Though private kept) surer then publick Laws;
    For Laws but force the Body, but my Minde
    Your Vertue Councels, whilst your beauty draws.

48. Thus spake he, but his mourning looks did more
    Attest his grief, and fear does hers renew;
    Now losing (were he lost) more then before,
    For then she fear'd him false, now thinks him true.

49. As sick Physitians seldome their own Art
    Dare trust to cure their own disease, so these
    Were to themselves quite useless when apart;
    Yet by consult, each can the other ease.

50. But from themselves they now diverted stood;
    For *Orgo's* Newes (which need not borrow wings,
    Since *Orgo* for his Lord believ'd it good)
    To *Astragon* the joyful Houshold brings.

44: 1 to '73: too 51a–b

51. But *Astragon*, with a judicious thought,
    This days glad news took in the dire portent;
    A day which mourning Nights to *Birtha* brought;
    And with that fear, in search of *Birtha* went.

52. And here he findes her in her Lovers Eies,
    And him in hers; both more afflicted grown
    At his approach; for each his sorrow spies;
    Who thus would counsel theirs, and hide his own.

53. Though much this fatall joy to anger moves,
    Yet reasons aydes shall anger's force subdue;
    I will not chide you for your hasty Loves,
    Nor ever doubt (great Prince) that yours is true.

54. In chiding Love, because he hasty was,
    Or urging errors, which his swiftness brings,
    I finde effects, but dare not tax the cause;
    For Poets were inspir'd, who gave him wings.

55. When low I digg, where desart-Rivers run,
    Dive deep in Seas, through Forrests follow windes,
    Or reach with Optick Tubes the ragged Moon,
    My sight no cause of Love's swift motion findes.

56. Love's fatall haste, in yours, I will not blame,
    Because I know not why his Wings were given;
    Nor doubt him true, not knowing whence he came,
    Nor *Birtha* chide, who thought you came from Heav'n.

57. If you lay snares, we err when we escape;
    Since evil practise learns Men to suspect
    Where falshood is, and in your noble shape,
    We should by finding it, our skill detect.

58. Yet both your griefs I'le chide, as ignorance;
    Call you unthankful; for your great griefs show
    That Heav'n has never us'd you to mischance,
    Yet rudely you repine to feele it now.

59. If your contextures be so weak, and nice,
    Weep that this stormy world you ever knew;
    You are not in those Calmes of Paradice,
    Where slender Flowres as safe as Cedars grew.

59: 2 stormy '73: windy '51a–b

60. This which your Youth cals grief, was frowardness
    In flatter'd Infancy, and as you beare
    Unkindly now amidst Youth's joys distress,
    So then unless still rock'd you froward were.

61. Griefs conflicts gave these Haires their silver shine;
    (Torne Ensignes which victorious Age adorne)
    Youth is a Dress too garish and too fine
    To be in foule tempestuous weather worne.

62. Grief's want of use does dang'rous weakness make;
    But we by use of Burdens are made strong;
    And in our practis'd Age can calmely take
    Those sorrows, which like Feavers, vex the young.

63. When you in Lov's fair Books (which Poets keep)
    Read what they hide, his Tragick History,
    You will rejoyce that half your time is sleep,
    And smile at Love when Nature bids you die.

64. Learn then that Love's diseases common are;
    Doe not in sickness known (though new to you)
    Whilst vital heat does last, of cure dispaire;
    Love's vital heat does last, whilst Love is true.

65. Thus spake the kinde and prudent *Astragon*:
    And much their kinde impatience he appeas'd,
    For of his griefs (which heavi'er then their own
    Were born by both) their dutious fears are eas'd.

66. She begs that he would pardon her distress,
    Thought that even sin which did his sorrow move;
    And then with all her Mother's lowliness
    His pardon craves for asking leave to love.

67. The Duke who saw fair Truth so undisguis'd,
    And love in all, but love so unconcern'd,
    Pitty'd the studious world, and all despis'd
    Who did not here unlearn, what they had learn'd.

68. I am reform'd (said he) not that before
    I wanted love, or that my love was ill;

60: 4 then . . . froward] *'51a u*: then, . . . froward, *'51a cor*: then, . . . rock'd, . . .
'51b: then, . . . *'73*   61: 3 garish *'51a cor, '51b, '73*: garnish *'51a u*   66: 2 his]
her *'51b*

But I have learnt to perfect Nature more
By giving innocence a little skill.

69. For 'tis some skill in innocence to bear
With temper the distempers of our Stars;
Not doubling griefs already come by fear
Of more, for fears but hasten threatned Wars.

70. But we will bravely suffer to inure
Our strength to wieghts against the new are laid;
That when 'tis known how much we can endure,
Our sufferings may make our Foes afraid.

71. This Comet Glory shines but in portent;
Which from the Court does send her threatning Beams;
And looks as if it were by malice ment
To hasten *Oswald's* faction to extreams.

72. Since *Hurgonil*, who just fore-ran the Boy
Could not instruct us, we as much may know
Of the first Light, as of these fires of joy;
Which is, that both did out of darkness grow.

73. Yet this the King might hide in Kingly skill,
Wisely to make his bounty more his own:
Kings stoop for Councel, who impart their will;
His Acts, like Heav'ns, make not their Causes known.

74. Yet with as plain a heart as love untaught
In *Birtha* wears, I here to *Birtha* make
A vow that *Rhodalind* I never sought,
Nor now would with her love her greatnesse take.

75. Loves bonds are for her greatness made too straight;
And me Ambition's pleasures cannot please;
Even Priests who on the higher Altar wait,
Think a continu'd rev'rence losse of ease.

76. Let us with secrecy our love protect;
Hiding such precious wealth from publick view;
The proffer'd glory I will first suspect
As false, and shun it when I finde it true.

69: 3 doubling] doubting '*51b*   75: 2 me '*51a cor*, '*51b*, '*73*: we '*51a u*
76: 1 us '*51b*, '*73*: us us '*51a*

77. They now retire because they *Goltho* saw,
Who hither came to watch with *Ulfinore*,
If much the Duke's woo'd Mistris did him awe;
Since love woo'd him, and in the shape of Pow'r.

78. But when he mark'd that he did from them move
With sodain shyness, he suppos'd it shame
Of being seen in chase of *Birtha's* love;
As if above it grown since *Orgo* came.

79. *Goltho* by nature was of Musick made,
Cheerful as Victors warm in their success;
He seem'd like Birds created to be glad,
And nought but love could make him taste distress.

80. Hope, which our cautious Age scarce entertains,
Or as a Flatt'rer gives her cold respect,
He runs to meet, invites her, and complains
Of one hours absence as a years neglect.

81. Hope, the world's welcom, and his standing Guest,
Fed by the Rich, but feasted by the Poor;
Hope, that did come in triumph to his Breast,
He thus presents in boast to *Ulfinore*.

82. Well may I (Friend) auspicious Love adore,
Seeing my mighty Rival takes no pride
To be with *Birtha* seen; and he before
(Thou knowst) injoyn'd that I his love should hide.

83. Nor doe I break his trust when 'tis reveal'd
To thee, since we are now so much the same,
That when from thee, it is from me conceal'd,
For we admit no diff'rence but in name.

84. But be it still from ev'ry other Ear
Preserv'd, and strictly by our mutual vow:
His Laws are still to my obedience dear,
Who was my Gen'ral, though my Rival now.

85. And well thou knowst how much mine Eies did melt
When our great Leader they did first perceive
Love's Captive led; whose sorrows then I felt,
Though now for greater of mine own I grieve.

86. Nor do I now by love in duty err;
   For if I get what he would fain possesse,
   Then he a Monarch is, and I preferr
   Him who undoes the World in being lesse.

87. When Heav'n (which hath preferr'd me to thy Brest
   Where Friendship is inthron'd,) shall make it known
   That I am worth thy love, which is exprest
   By making Heav'nly *Birtha* all mine own,

88. Then at this quiet *Eden* thou wilt call,
   And stay a while, to mark if Love's prais'd Plant
   Have after Spring a ripeness, and a Fall,
   Or never of the first abundance want.

89. And I shall tell thee then if Poets are
   In using Beauty's Pencil false, or blinde;
   For they have *Birtha* drawn but sweet and faire;
   Stiles of her Face, the Curtain of her Minde!

90. And thou at parting shalt her Picture weare,
   For Nature's honor, not to shew my pride;
   Try if her like the teeming World does beare,
   Then bring that Copy hither for thy Bride.

91. And they shall love as quietly as we;
   Their Beauty's pow'r no civil War will raise;
   But flourish, and like neighb'ring Flowres agree;
   Unless they kindly quarrel in our praise.

92. Then we for change will leave such luscious peace;
   In Camps their Favours shall our Helms adorn;
   For we can no way else our joys increase,
   But by beholding theirs at our return.

93. Thus cloth'd in Feathers, he on Steeples walks;
   Not guessing yet, that silent *Ulfinore*,
   Had study'd her of whom he loosly talks,
   And what he likes did solidly adore.

94. But *Ulfinore* with cold discretion aw'd
   His passion, and did grave with Love become;
   Though Youthfully he sent his Eies abroad,
   Yet kept with Manly care, his Tongue at home.

86: 4 Him] Him, *'73*   91: 4 Unless *'51b*, *'73*: Uuless *'51a*

95. These Rival's hopes, he did with patience hear;
    His count'nance not uneasy seem'd, nor strange;
    Yet meant his cares should more like Love appear,
    If in the Duke Ambition bred a change.

96. But as the Duke shun'd them for secrecy,
    So now they from approaching *Orgo* move,
    Made by Discretion (Love's strict Tutor) shy,
    Which is to Lovers painful as their Love.

97. But *Orgo* they did ill suspect, whose Youth
    And nature yeilded Lovers no offence;
    Us'd by his Lord for kindness and for truth;
    Both native in him as his innocence:

98. And her pass'd by in haste, to Court imploy'd,
    That *Birtha* may no more have cause to mourn;
    Full was his little Breast, and overjoy'd
    That much depended on his quick return.

99. Many like *Orgo*, in their Manhoods Morn,
    As Pages did the Noble Duke attend;
    The Sons of Chiefs whom beauty did adorn,
    And fairer Vertue did that beauty mend.

100. These in his *Heroe's* schools he bred (which were
     In Peace his Palace, and in War his Tent)
     As if Time's self had read sage Lectures there
     How he would have his howres (life's Treasure) spent.

101. No action, though to shorten dreaded warre,
     Nor needful Counsels, though to lengthen Peace,
     Nor Love, of which wise Nature takes such care,
     Could from this usefull work his cares release.

102. But with the early Sun he rose, and taught
     These Youths, by growing vertue to grow great;
     Shew'd greatness is without it blindly sought,
     A desp'rate charge which ends in base retreat.

103. He taught them shame, the sodain sence of ill;
     Shame, Nature's hasty Conscience, which forbids
     Weak inclination ere it grows to will,
     And stays rash will, before it grows to deeds.

103: 3 grows] grow '51b   103: 4 grows '73: grow '51a–b

104. He taught them Honor, Vertue's bashfulness;
     A Fort so yeildless, that it fears to treat;
     Like Pow'r, it grows to nothing, growing less;
     Honor, the moral Conscience of the Great!

105. He taught them kindness; Soul's civilitie;
     In which, nor Courts, nor Citys have a part;
     For theirs is fashion, this from falshood free;
     Where Love, and pleasure, know no Lust nor Art.

106. And Love he taught; the Soul's stolne Visit made
     Though froward Age watch hard, and Law forbid;
     Her walks no Spie has trac'd, nor Mountain staide;
     Her friendship's cause, is as the Loadstone's hid.

107. He taught them love of Toyle; Toyle which does keep
     Obstructions from the Minde, and quench the blood;
     Ease but belongs to us like sleep, and sleep
     Like *Opium*, is our Med'cine, not our Food.

108. To Dangers us'd them; which Death's Visards are,
     More uggly then himself, and often chace
     From Batail Coward-life; but when we dare
     His Visard see, we never fear his Face.

Canto the Third

The ARGUMENT

The Poet takes the Wise assyde, to prove
Even them concern'd in all he writes of Love.
The dutious ORGO *from the Court returns*
With joys, at which again fair BIRTHA *mourns.*
The Duke with open Armes does entertain
Those Guests whom he receives with secret pain.

1. Thou, who some Ages hence these Roles dost read
   (Kept as Records by Lovers of Love's pow'r)
   Thou who dost live, when I have long been dead,
   And feed'st from Earth, when Earth does me devowr:

2. Who liv'st, perhaps, amidst some Cities joys,
   Where they would fall asleep with Lazy peace,
   But that their triumphs make so great a noise,
   And their loud Bells cannot for nuptials cease:

3. Thou, who perhaps, proudly thy bloomy Bride
   Lead'st to some Temple, where I wither'd lie;
   Proudly, as if she Age's Frosts defy'd;
   And that thy springing self could never die:

4. Thou, to whom then the cheerful Quire will sing,
   Whilst hallow'd Lamps, and Tapers, brave the Sun
   As a Lay-Light, and Bells in triumph ring,
   As when from sallies the Besiegers run.

5. That when the Priest has ended, if thine Eies
   Can but a little space her Eies forbear,
   To shew her where my Marble Coffin lies;
   Her Virgin Garlands she will offer there:

6. Confess, that reading me she learnt to love;
   That all the good behaviour of her heart,
   Even tow'rds thy self, my doctrin did improve;
   Where Love by Nature is forwarn'd of Art.

7. She will confess, that to her Maiden state
   This Story shew'd such Patterns of great Life,
   As though she then could those but imitate,
   They an Example make her now a Wife.

8. And thy life's fire could she awhile outlive
   (Which were, though lawful, neither kind nor good)
   Then, even her sorrows would examples give;
   And shine to others through dark widowhood.

9. And she will boast, how spite of *Cynick* Age,
   Of bus'ness, which does Pow'r uncivil make,
   Of ruder Cells, where they Love's Fire asswage
   By study'ng Death, and Fear for Vertue take:

10. And spite of Courts (where loving now is made
    An Art, as dying is in Cells) my Laws
    Did teach her how by Nature to perswade,
    And hold by Vertue whom her beauty draws.

5: 1 That '73: Then '51 *a–b*

11. Thus when by knowing me, thou know'st to whom
    Love owes his Eies, who has too long been blinde;
    Then in the Temple leave my Bodies Tomb,
    To seek this Book, the Mon'ment of my Minde.

12. Where thou mai'st read; who with impatient Eies
    For *Orgo* on the guilded *Tarras* stay;
    Which high, and golden shews, and open lies,
    As the Morn's Window when she lets out Day.

13. Whose height Two rising Forrests over-looks;
    And on *Pine*-tops the Eiesight downward casts;
    Where distant Rivers seem bestrided Brooks,
    Churches but Anchor'd Ships, their Steeples, Masts.

14. Hence, by his little *Regian* Courser brought,
    Orgo they spie, with diligence indu'd,
    As if he would o'ertake forerunning Thought;
    And he by many swiftly seem'd pursu'd.

15. But his light speed left those awhile behinde;
    Whilst with rais'd Dust, their swiftness hid the way;
    Yet *Birtha* will, too soon, by *Orgo* finde
    What she by distance lost in this survay.

16. *Orgo* a precious *Casket* did present
    To his dear Lord, of *Podian Saphyr* wrought;
    For which, unknown to *Birtha*, he was sent;
    And a more precious Pledg was in it brought.

17. Then thus proclaim'd his joy! Long may I live!
    Sent still with blessings from the Heav'nly Powers;
    And may their bountys shew what they can give;
    And fall as fast as long expected Showres!

18. Behold the King, with such a shining Traine
    As dazles sight, yet can inform the Blind;
    But there the Rich, and Beautious shine in vaine,
    Unless they distance keep from *Rhodalind*.

19. Me thinks, they through the Middle Region come;
    Their Chariots hid in Clouds of Dust below,
    And o're their Heads, their Coursers scatter'd Fome
    Does seem to cover them like falling Snow.

13: 2 casts] cast '*51b*   17: 1–2 live! . . . Powers; '*51a u*, '73: live, . . . Powers!
'*51a u*: joy, . . . live! . . . '*51b*   17: 4 fall '*51a cor*: full '*51a u*, '*51b*, '73

20. This *Birtha* heard, and she on *Orgo* cast
   A piteous look (for she no anger knew)
   But griev'd he knows not, that he brings too fast
   Such joys, as fain she faster would eschew.

21. So *Gondibert* this Gust of glory took
   As Men whose Sayls are full, more weather take;
   And she so gaz'd on him, as Sea-men look
   On long sought shore, when Tempests drive them back.

22. But now these Glorys more apparent be;
   And justly all their observation claim'd;
   Great, as in greatest Courts less Princes see,
   When entertain'd to be eclips'd, and sham'd.

23. West from *Verona's* Road, through pleasant Meads
   Their Chariots cross, and to the Palace steer;
   And *Aribert* this winged triumph leads
   Which like the Planets Progress did appear.

24. So shin'd they, and so noisless seem'd their speed;
   Like *Spartans*, touching but the silken Reynes,
   Was all the conduct which their Coursers need;
   And proudly to sit still, was all their pains.

25. With *Aribert* sat royal *Rhodalind*;
   Calm *Orna* by the Count; by *Hermegild*
   (Silver'd with time) the Golden *Gartha* shin'd;
   And *Tybalt's* Eies were full by *Laura* fill'd.

26. The lesser Beauties, numberless as Stars,
   Shew'd sickly and far off, to this Noon-day;
   And lagg'd like Baggage Treasure in the Wars;
   Or only seem'd, another *milky way*.

27. The Duke perceav'd, the King design'd to make
   This visit more familiar by surprise;
   And with Court art, he would no notice take
   Of that which Kings are willing to disguise.

28. But as in heedless sleep, the House shall seem
   New wak'd with this Alarm; and *Ulfin* strait
   (Whose fame was precious in the Courts esteem)
   Must, as with casual sight, their entrance wait.

29. To *Astragon* he doubles all his Vows;
    To *Birtha*, through his Eies, his Heart reveal'd;
    And by some civil jealousies he shows
    Her beauty from the Court must be conceal'd.

30. Prays her, from Envy's danger to retire;
    The Palace war; which there can never cease
    Till Beauty's force in age or death expire:
    A War disguis'd in civil shapes of Peace.

31. Stil he the precious Pledg kept from her view;
    Who guess'd not by the *Casket* his intent;
    And was so willing not to fear him true,
    That she did fear to question what it ment.

32. Now hasts she to be hid; and being gon,
    Her Lover thinks the Planet of the day
    So leaves the mourning World to give the Moon
    (Whose Train is mark'd but for their number) way.

33. And entring in her Closet (which took light
    Full in the Palace Front) she findes her Maids
    Gather'd to see this gay unusual sight;
    Which Commet-like, their wondring Eies invades.

34. Where *Thula* would by climbing highest be,
    Though ancient grown, and was in Stature short;
    Yet did protest, she came not there to see,
    But to be hid from dangers of the Court.

35. Their curious longing *Birtha* durst not blame
    (Boldness, which but to seeing did aspire)
    Since she her self, provok'd with Courts great Fame,
    Would fain a little see what all admire.

36. Then through the Casement ventur'd so much Face
    As Kings depos'd, shew when through Grates they peep,
    To see Deposers to their Crowning passe;
    But strait shrink back, and at the triumph weep.

37. Soon so her Eies did too much glory finde;
    For ev'n the first she saw was all; for she
    No more would view, since that was *Rhodalind*;
    And so much beauty could none others be.

6: 2 Grates '*51a MS*, '*51b*, '*73*: Gates '*51a*   36: 3 Crowning] Crowding '*51b*

38. Which with her Vertue wiegh'd (no less renown'd)
    Afflicts her that such worth must fatal prove;
    And be in tears of the Possessor drown'd,
    Or she depose her Lover by her love.

39. But *Thula* (wildly earnest in the view
    Of such gay sights as she did ne'r behold)
    Mark'd not when *Birtha* her sad Eies withdrew;
    But dreamt the world was turn'd again to Gold.

40. Each Lady most, till more appear'd, ador'd;
    Then with rude liking prais'd them all alowd;
    Yet thought them foul and course to ev'ry Lord;
    And civilly to ev'ry Page she bow'd.

41. The objects past, out-sigh'd even those that woo;
    And strait her Mistris at the Window mist;
    Then finding her in grief, out-sigh'd her too;
    And her fair Hands with parting passion kist:

42. Did with a Servants usual art profess
    That all she saw, was to her beauty, black;
    Confess'd their Maids well bred, and knew to dress,
    But said those Courts are poor which painting lack.

43. Thy praise (said *Birtha*) poyson'd is with spite;
    May blisters cease on thy uncivil Tongue,
    Which strives so wickedly to do me right,
    By doing *Rhodalind* and *Orna* wrong.

44. False Fame, thy Mistris, tutor'd thee amiss;
    Who teaches School in streets, where Crowds resort;
    Fame, false, as that their beauty painted is;
    The common Country slander on the Court.

45. With this rebuke, *Thula* takes gravely leave;
    Pretends she'll better judge ere they be gon;
    At least see more, though they her sight deceave;
    Whilst *Birtha* findes, wilde Fear feeds best alone.

46. *Ulfin* receives, and through Art's Palace guides
    The King; who owns him with familiar grace;
    Though Twice seven Years from first observance hides
    Those Marks of valor which adorn'd his Face.

47. Then *Astragon* with hasty homage bows:
And says, when thus his Beams he does dispence
In lowly visits, like the Sun he shows
Kings made for universal influence.

48. Him with renown the King for Science pays,
And Vertue; which Gods likest Pictures bee;
Drawn by the Soul, whose onely hire is praise;
And from such Salary not Heav'n is free.

49. Then kindly he inquires for *Gondibert*;
When, and how far his wounds in danger were?
And does the cautious progress of his Art
Alike with wonder and with pleasure heare.

50. Now *Gondibert* advanc'd, but with delay;
As fetter'd by his love; for he would fain
Dissembled weakness might procure his stay,
Here where his Soul does as in Heav'n remain.

51. Him, Creature like, the King did boldly use
With publick love; to have it understood
That Kings, like God, may chuse whom they wil chuse;
And what they make, judg with their own Eies good.

52. This grace the Duke at bashful distance takes;
And *Rhodalind* so much concern'd is grown,
That his surprisal she her trouble makes;
Blushing, as if his blushes were her own.

53. Now the bright Train with *Astragon* ascend;
Whilst *Hermegild*, with *Gartha* moves behinde;
Whom much this gracious visit did offend;
But thus he practis'd to appease her minde.

54. Judg not you strangely in this visit showe;
As well in Courts think wise disembling new;
Nor think the kindness strange, though to your Foe,
Till all in Courts where they are kinde are true.

55. Why should your closser mourning more be worn?
Poor Priests invented Blacks for lesser cost;
Kings for their Syres in Regal Purple mourn;
Which shews what they have got, not what they lost.

56. Though rough the way to Empire be, and steep,
    You look that I should level it so plain,
    As Babes might walk it barefoot in their sleep;
    But Pow'r is the reward of patient pain!

57. This high Hill Pow'r, whose Bowels are of Gold,
    Shews neer to greedy and unpractis'd sight;
    But many grow in travail to it old,
    And have mistook the distance by the height.

58. If those old Travailers may thither be
    Your trusted Guides, they will your haste reform;
    And give you fears of Voyages by Sea;
    Which are not often made without a storm.

59. Yet short our Course shall prove, our passage faire,
    If in the *Steerage* you will quiet stand,
    And not make storms of ev'ry breath of Aire;
    But think the Helm, safe in the Pilots hand.

60. You like some fatal King (who all Men hears
    Yet trusts intirely none) your trust mistake
    As too much weight for one: one Pillar bears
    Weight that would make a Thousand Shoulders ake.

61. Your Brothers storm I to a calm have turn'd;
    Who lets th's guilded Sacrifice proceed
    To *Hymen's* Altar, by the King adorn'd,
    As Priests give Victims Gerlonds ere they bleed.

62. *Hubert* to triumph would not move so faste;
    Yet you (though but a kinde Spectator) mean
    To give his triumph Laws, and make more haste
    To see it pass, then he does to be seen.

63. With patience lay this Tempest of your heart!
    For you, ere long, this Angels form shall turn
    To fatal Man's; and for that shape of Art,
    Some may, as I for yours of Nature, mourn!

64. Thus by her Love-sick Statesman she was taught;
    And smil'd with joy of wearing Manly shape;
    Then smil'd, that such a smile his Heart had caught;
    Whose Nets Camps break not through, nor Senates scape.

59: 3 breath '73: sigh '51a–b

Canto the Fourth

The ARGUMENT

The King to GONDIBERT *is grown so kinde,*
That he prevents the bounteous RHODALIND
In giving of her love; and GONDIBERT
Laments his Breast holds but a single heart;
Which BIRTHA *grievs her beauty did subdue,*
Since he undoes the world in being true.

1. Full grows the Presence now, as when all know
   Some stranger Prince must be receiv'd with state;
   When Courts shew those, who come to see the *Show*;
   And all gay Subjects like Domesticks waite.

2. Nor *Ulfinore* nor *Goltho* absent were;
   Whose hopes expect what list'ning *Birtha* (hid
   In the adjoyning Closet) feares to heare;
   And beggs kinde Heav'n in pitty would forbid.

3. The King (who never time nor pow'r mis-spent
   In Subjects bashfulness, whiling great deeds
   Like Coward Councels, who too late consent)
   Thus to his secret will aloud proceeds.

4. If to thy fame (brave Youth) I could add wings,
   Or make her Trumpet louder by my voice,
   I would (as an example drawn for Kings)
   Proclaim the cause, why thou art now my choice.

5. But this were to suspect the world asleep;
   Or all our *Lombards* with their envy blinde,
   Or that the *Hunns* so much for bondage weep,
   As their drown'd Eies cannot thy Trophies finde.

6. When this is heard, none dare of what I give
   Presume their equal merit might have shar'd;
   And to say more, might make thy Foes beleeve,
   Thy dang'rous worth is grown above reward.

7. Reward even of a Crown, and such a Crown,
   As by Heav'n's Model ancient Victors wore;
   When they, as by their Coyn, by Laws were known;
   For Laws but made more currant Victors pow'r.

8. A Crown soon taught, by whom Pow'r first was given;
   When Victors (of Dominion cautious made
   By hearing of that old revolt in Heaven)
   Kept Pow'r too high for Subjects to invade.

9. A Crown, which ends by Armies their debate,
   Who question height of Pow'r; who by the Law
   (Till plain obedience they make intricate)
   Would not the People, but their Rulers aw.

10. To Pow'r adoption makes thy title good;
    Preferring worth, as birth gives Princes place;
    And Vertue's claim exceeds the right of blood,
    As Souls extraction does the Bodies Race.

11. Yet for thy Bloods long walk through Princes veins,
    Thou maist with any *Lombard* measure time;
    Though he his hidden house in *Illium* feigns;
    And not step short, when *Hubert's* self would climbe.

12. And *Hubert* is of highest Victors Breed;
    Whose worth I shall for distant Empire chuse;
    If he will learn, that you by Fate precede,
    And what he never had, he cannot lose.

13. His valor shall the *Gothick* conquest keep:
    And would to Heav'n that all your mighty mindes
    As soon were pleas'd, as Infants are with sleep,
    And you had Musick common as the windes.

14. That all the Year your Seasons were like Spring;
    All joy'd as Birds, and all as Lovers kinde;
    That ev'ry famous Fighter were a King,
    And each like you could have a *Rhodalind*.

15. For she is yours, as your adoption, free;
    And in that gift my remnant Life I give;
    But 'tis to you, brave Youth! Who now are she;
    And she that Heav'n where secondly I live.

16. And richer then that Crown (which shall be thine,
    When Life's long Progress I am gone with Fame)
    Take all her love; which scarce forbears to shine
    And own thee, through her Virgin-Curtain, *Shame*.

11: 4 would '51a MS, '51b, '73: could '51a   12: 1 Breed '51a MS, '51b: bred
51a: breed '73

17. Thus spake the King; and *Rhodalind* appear'd
    Through publish'd Love, with so much bashfulness,
    As young Kings shew, when by surprise o're-heard
    Moaning to Fav'rite Eares a deep distress.

18. For Love is a distress, and would be hid
    Like Monarchs griefs, by which they bashful grow;
    And in that shame beholders they forbid;
    Since those blush most, who must their blushes show.

19. And *Gondibert* with dying Eies did grieve
    At her vail'd love (a wound he cannot heal)
    As great Mindes mourn, who cannot then relieve
    The vertuous when through shame they want conceal.

20. And now cold *Birtha's* rosy looks decay;
    Who in Fear's Frost had like her beauty dy'd,
    But that Attendant Hope perswades her stay
    A while, to hear her Duke; who thus reply'd.

21. Victorious King! Abroad your Subjects are
    Like Legats safe; at home like Altars free!
    Even by your fame they conquer as by warre;
    And by your Laws safe from each other be.

22. A King you are o're Subjects, so as wise
    And noble Husbands seem o're Loyal Wives;
    Who claim not, yet confess their liberties,
    And brag to strangers of their happy loves.

23. To Foes a winter storm; whilst your Friends bow
    Like Summer Trees, beneath your bountys load;
    To me (next him whom your great self, with low
    And cheerful duty serves) a giving God.

24. Since this is you, and *Rhodalind* (the Light
    By which her Sex fled vertue finde) is yours;
    Your *Diamond*, which tests of jealous sight,
    The stroke, and fire, and *Oisel's* juice endures;

25. Since she so precious is, I shall appear
    All counterfeit, of Art's disguises made;
    And never dare approach her Lusture neer;
    Who scarce can hold my vallew in the shade.

26. Forgive me that I am not what I seem;
   But falsly have dissembled an excess
   Of all such vertues as you most esteem;
   But now grow good but as I ills confess.

27. Farr in Ambition's Feaver am I gon!
   Like raging Flame aspiring is my Love;
   Like flame destructive too, and like the Sun
   Does round the world tow'rds change of Objects move.

28. Nor is this now through vertuous shame confess'd;
   But *Rhodalind* does force my conjur'd feare,
   As Men whom evil spirits have possess'd,
   Tell all when saintly Votaries appeare.

29. When she will grace the Bridall dignitie,
   It will be soon to all young Monarchs known;
   Who then by posting through the World, will trie
   Who first can at her Feet present his Crown.

30. Then will *Verona* seem the Inn of Kings;
   And *Rhodalind* shall at her Palace Gate
   Smile when great Love these royal Sutors brings;
   Who for that smile would as for Empire waite.

31. Amongst this ruling Race she choyce may take
   For warmth of Valor, coolness of the minde,
   Eies that in Empire's drowsy Calms can wake,
   In storms look out, in darkness dangers finde.

32. A Prince who more inlarges pow'r then lands;
   Whose greatness is not what his Mapp contains;
   But thinks that his, where he at full commands;
   Not where his Coyn does pass, but pow'r remains.

33. Who knows that Pow'r can never be too high
   When by the Good possest; for 'tis in them
   The swelling *Nyle*; from which though People fly,
   They prosper most by rising of the stream.

34. Thus (Princess) you should chuse; and you will finde;
   Even he, since Men are Wolves, must civilize
   (As light does tame some Beasts of savage kinde)
   Himself yet more, by dwelling in your Eies.

35. Such was the Duke's reply; which did produce
    Thoughts of a diverse shape through sev'ral Eares:
    His jealous Rivals mourn at his excuse;
    But *Astragon* it cures of all his feares.

36. *Birtha* his praise of *Rhodalind* bewayles;
    And now her hope a weak Physitian seems,
    For Hope, the common Comforter, prevailes
    Like common Med'cines, slowly in extreams.

37. The King (secure in offer'd Empire) takes
    This forc'd excuse, as troubled bashfulness,
    And a disguise which sodain passion makes,
    To hide more joy then prudence should express.

38. And *Rhodalind* (who never lov'd before,
    Nor could suspect his love was giv'n away)
    Thought not the treasure of his Breast so poore,
    But that it might his debts of honor pay.

39. To hasten the rewards of his desert,
    The King does to *Verona* him command;
    And kindness so impos'd, not all his Art
    Can now instruct his duty to withstand.

40. Yet whilst the King does now his time dispose
    In seeing wonders, in this Palace shown,
    He would a parting kindness pay to those
    Who of their wounds are yet not perfect grown.

41. And by this faire pretence, whilst on the King
    Lord *Astragon* through all the House attends,
    Young *Orgo* does the Duke to *Birtha* bring;
    Who thus her sorrows to his bosome sends.

42. Why should my Storm, your Life's calm voyage vex?
    Destroying wholly vertue's Race in one;
    So by the first of my unlucky Sex.
    All in a single ruine were undone.

43. Make Heav'nly *Rhodalind* your Bride! Whilst I
    Your once lov'd Maid, excuse you, since I know
    That vertuous Men forsake so willingly
    Long cherish'd life, because to Heav'n they go.

44. Let me her servant be! A dignity,
　　Which if your pitty in my fall procures;
　　I still shall vallew the advancement high,
　　Not as the Crown is hers, but she is yours.

45. E're this high sorrow up to dying grew,
　　The Duke the Casket op'ned, and from thence
　　(Form'd like a Heart) a cheerful *Emrauld* drew;
　　Cheerful, as if the lively stone had sence.

46. The Thirti'th *Carract* it had doubled Twice;
　　Not taken from the *Attick* silver Mine,
　　Nor from the Brass, though such (of nobler price)
　　Did on the Necks of *Parthian* Ladies shine:

47. Nor yet of those which make the *Ethiop* proud;
　　Nor taken from those Rocks where *Bactrians* climbe;
　　But from the *Scythian*, and without a *Cloud*;
　　Not *sick* at *fire*, nor *languishing* with time.

48. Then thus he spake! This (*Birtha*) from my male
　　Progenitors, was to the loyal she
　　On whose kinde Heart they did in love prevail,
　　The Nuptial Pledg, and this I give to thee!

49. Seven Centuries have pass'd, since it from Bride
　　To Bride did first succeed; and though tis known
　　From ancient lore, that Gemms much vertue hide,
　　And that the *Emrauld* is the Bridal Stone.

50. Though much renown'd because it chastness loves,
　　And will when worn by the neglected wife,
　　Shew when her absent Lord disloyal proves,
　　By faintness, and a pale decay of life;

51. Though *Emraulds* serve as Spies to jealous Brides,
　　Yet each compar'd to this does councel keep;
　　Like a false Stone, the Husbands fals-hood hides,
　　Or seems born blinde, or feigns a dying sleep.

52. With this take *Orgo*, as a better Spy;
　　Who may in all your kinder fears be sent
　　To watch at Court, if I deserve to dy
　　By making this to fade, and you lament.

51: 3 fals-hood *Ed*: falsh-hood '*51a MS*, '*73*: falshood '*51b*: falsh hood '*51a*
51: 4 sleep. '*51a MS*, '*51b*: sleep, '*73*: sleep '*51a*

53. Had now an artful Pencil *Birtha* drawn
    (With grief all dark, then strait with joy all light)
    He must have fancy'd first, in early dawn,
    A sodain break of beauty out of Night.

54. Or first he must have mark'd what paleness, Fear,
    Like nipping Frost, did to her visage bring;
    Then think he sees, in a cold backward year,
    A Rosy Morn begin a sodain Spring.

55. Her joys (too vaste to be contain'd in speech)
    Thus she a little spake! Why stoop you down,
    My plighted Lord, to lowly *Birtha's* reach,
    Since *Rhodalind* would lift you to a Crown?

56. Or why doe I, when I this plight imbrace,
    Boldly aspire to take what you have given?
    But that your vertue has with Angels place,
    And 'tis a vertue to aspire at Heav'n.

57. And as tow'rds Heav'n all travail on their Knees;
    So I tow'rds you, though Love aspire, will move:
    And were you crown'd, what could you better please
    Then aw'd obedience led by bolder Love?

58. If I forget the depth from whence I rise,
    Far from your bosome banish'd be my heart;
    Or claim a right by beauty to your Eies;
    Or proudly think, my chastity desert.

59. But thus ascending from your humble Maid
    To be your plighted Bride, and then your Wife,
    Will be a debt that shall be hourly paid,
    Till Time my duty cancel with my life.

60. And fruitfully if Heav'n ere make me bring
    Your Image to the World, you then my pride
    No more shall blame, then you can tax the Spring
    For boasting of those Flowres she cannot hide.

61. *Orgo,* I so receive as I am taught
    By duty to esteem what ere you love;
    And hope the joy he in this Jewel brought,
    Will luckyer then his former triumphs prove.

62. For though but Twice he has approach'd my sight,
    He Twice made haste to drown me in my Tears:
    But now I am above his Planets spite,
    And as for sin beg pardon for my fears.

63. Thus spake she; and with fix'd continu'd sight,
    The Duke did all her bashful beauties view;
    Then they with kisses seal'd their sacred plight;
    Like Flowrs still sweeter as they thicker grew.

64. Yet must these pleasures feel, though innocent,
    The sickness of extreames, and cannot last;
    For Pow'r (Love's shun'd Impediment) has sent
    To tell the Duke, his Monarch is in hast:

65. And calls him to that triumph which he fears
    So as a Saint forgiven (whose Breast does all
    Heav'n's joys contain) wisely lov'd Pomp forbears;
    Lest tempted Nature should from blessings fall.

66. He often takes his leave, with Love's delay;
    And bids her hope, he with the King shall finde,
    By now appearing forward to obay,
    A meanes to serve him less in *Rhodalind.*

67. She weeping to her Closet-window hies;
    Where she with teares does *Rhodalind* survay;
    As dying Men, who grieve that they have Eies,
    When they through Curtains spy the rising day.

68. The King has now his curious sight suffis'd
    With all lost Arts, in their revival view'd;
    Which when restor'd, our pride thinks new devis'd:
    Fashions of Mindes, call'd new when but renew'd!

69. The busy Court prepares to move; on whom
    Their sad offended Eies the Country caste;
    Who never see enough where Monarchs come;
    And nothing so uncivil seems as haste.

70. As Men move slow, who know they lose their way,
    Even so the Duke tow'rds *Rhodalind* does move;
    Yet he does dutious fears, and wonder pay,
    Which are the first, and dang'rous signes of Love.

71. All his addresses much by *Goltho* were
    And *Ulfinore* observ'd; who distant stand;
    Not daring to approach his presence neer;
    But shun his Eies to scape from his command:

72. Least to *Verona* he should both require;
    For by remaining here, both hope to light
    Their *Hymen's* Torches at his parting fire;
    And not dispaire to kindle them to night.

73. The King his Golden Chariot now ascends;
    Which neer fair *Rhodalind* the Duke containes;
    Though to excuse that grace he lowly bends;
    But honor so refus'd, more honor gaines.

74. And now their Chariots (ready to take wing)
    Are even by weakest breath, a whisper stay'd;
    And but such whisper as a Page does bring
    To *Laura's* Woman from a Houshold Mayd.

75. But this low voyce did raise in *Laura's* Eare
    An Eccho, which from all redoubled soon;
    Proclaiming such a Country beauty here,
    As makes them look, like Evning to her Noon.

76. And *Laura* (of her own high beauty proud,
    Yet not to others cruel) softly prays,
    She may appear! but *Gartha*, bold, and loud,
    With Eies impatient as for conquest, stays.

77. Though *Astragon* now owns her, and excus'd
    Her presence, as a Mayd but rudely taught,
    Infirm in health, and not to greatness us'd;
    Yet *Gartha* still calls out, to have her brought!

78. But *Rhodalind* (in whose relenting Breast
    Compassion's self might sit at School, and learn)
    Knew bashful Mayds with publick view distrest;
    And in their Glass, themselves with fear discern;

79. She stopt this Challenge which Court Beauty made
    To Country shape; not knowing Nature's hand
    Had *Birtha* dress'd, nor that her self obay'd
    In vain, whom conqu'ring *Birtha* did command.

75: 3 Country '51*b*, '73: Couutry '51*a*   78: 4 themselves '51*b*, '73: themseves '51*a*

80. The Duke (whom vertuous kindness soon subdues)
    Though him his Bonds from *Birtha* highly please,
    Yet seems to think, that lucky he, who sues
    To wear this royal Mayd's, will walk at ease.

81. Of these a brief survay sad *Birtha* takes;
    And *Orgo's* help directs her Eie to all;
    Shews her for whom grave *Tybalt* nightly wakes;
    Then at whose feet wise *Hermegild* does fall.

82. And when calm *Orna* with the Count she saw,
    Hope (who though weak, a willing Painter is,
    And busily does ev'ry Pattern draw)
    By that example could not work amiss.

83. For soon she shap'd her Lord and her so kinde,
    So all of love; till Fancy wrought no more
    When she perceiv'd him sit with *Rhodalind*;
    But froward-Painter-like the Copy tore.

84. And now they move; and she thus robb'd, believes
    (Since with such haste they bear her wealth away)
    That they at best, are but judicious Thieves,
    And know the noble vallew of their Prey.

85. And then she thus complain'd! Why royal Maid!
    Injurious Greatness! Did you hither come
    Where Pow'r's strong Nets of Wyre were never laid?
    But childish Love took Cradle as at home?

86. Where can we safe our harmless blessings keep,
    Since glorious Courts our solitude invade?
    Bells which ring out, when th'unconcern'd would sleep;
    False lights to scare poor Birds in Country shade!

87. Or if our joys their own discov'ry make,
    Envy (whose Tongue first kills whom she devours)
    Calls it our Pride; Envy, the poys'nous snake,
    Whose breath blasts Maids, as innocent as Flowres!

88. Forgive me beautious Greatness, if I grow
    Distemper'd with my fears, and rudely long
    To be secure; or praise your beauty so
    As to beleeve, that it may do me wrong!

88: 1 beautious *'51b*, *'73*: beuatious *'51a*

89. And you my plighted Lord, forgive me too,
    If since your worth and my defects I find,
    I fear what you in justice ought to do;
    And praise your judgment when I doubt you kind.

90. Now sodain fear o'er all her beauty wrought
    The pale appearance of a killing Frost;
    And careful *Orgo*, when she started, thought
    She had her Pledg, the precious *Emrauld*, lost.

91. But that kinde Heart, as constant as her own,
    She did not miss; 'twas from a sodain sence,
    Least in her Lover's heart some change was grown,
    And it grew pale with that intelligence.

92. Soon from her bosome she this *Emrauld* took:
    If now (said she) my Lord my Heart deceaves,
    This Stone will by dead paleness make me look
    Pale as the Snowy skin of Lilly Leaves.

93. But such a cheerful green the Gemm did fling
    Where she oppos'd the Rayes, as if she had
    Been dy'de in the complexion of the Spring,
    Or were by Nimphs of *Brittain* Valleys clad.

94. Soon she with earnest passion kist the Stone;
    Which ne'r till then had suffer'd an eclips;
    But then the Rayes retir'd, as if it shone
    In vain, so neer the Rubies of her Lips.

95. Yet thence remov'd, with publick glory shines!
    She *Orgo* blest, who had this Relique brought;
    And kept it like those Reliques lock'd in shrines,
    By which the latest Miracles were wrought.

96. For soon respect was up to rev'rence grown;
    Which fear to Superstition would sublime,
    But that her Father took Fear's Ladder down;
    Lose steps, by which distress to Heav'n would climbe.

97. He knew, when Fear shapes Heav'nly Pow'r so just,
    And terrible (parts of that shape drawn true)
    It vails Heav'n's beauty, Love; which when we trust
    Our courage honors him to whom we sue!

93: 2 Where '*51b*, '*73*: where '*51a*   96: 4 Lose] Loose '*51b Errata*

Canto the Fifth

The ARGUMENT

The deep Designes of BIRTHA *in distress;*
Her Emrauld's vertue shews her Love's success.
Wise ASTRAGON *with reason cures dispair;*
And the Afflicted chides for partial Pray'r.
With grief the secret Rivals take their leave;
And but dark hope for hidden love receive.

1. To shew the Morn her passage to the East,
   Now *Birtha's* dawn, the Lover's Day, appears!
   So soon Love beats *Revellies* in her Breast;
   And like the Dewy Morn she rose in tears:

2. So much she did her jealous dreams dislike.
   Her Maids strait kindle by her light their Eies;
   Which when to hers compar'd, Poets would strike
   Such sparks to light their Lamps, ere Day does rise.

3. But O vain Jealousie! why dost thou haste
   To finde those evils which too soon are brought?
   Love's frantick Valor! which so rashly faste
   Seeks dangers, as if none would come unsought.

4. As often fairest Morns soon cover'd be,
   So she with dark'ning thoughts is clouded now;
   Looks so, as weaker Eies small objects see,
   Or studious Statesmen who contract the Brow.

5. Or like some thinking *Sybill* that would finde
   The sence of mystick words by Angels given!
   And this fair Politick bred in her minde
   (Restless as Seas) a deep designe on Heav'n.

6. To Pray'rs plain Temple she does hast unseen;
   Which though not grac'd with curious cost for show,
   Was nicely kept; and now must be as clean
   As Tears make those who thence forgiven goe.

4: 1 fairest '51b: fairests '51a, '73

7. For her own Hands (by which best Painters drew
   The Hands of Innocence) will make it shine;
   Penance which newly from her terrors grew;
   And was (alas!) part of her deep designe.

8. And when this holy huswifry was past,
   Her vows she sends to Heav'n, which thither fly
   Intire; not broken by unthinking hast;
   Like Sinners Sparks that in ascending dy.

9. Thence she departs; but at this Temple Gate
   A needy Crowd (call'd by her Summons there)
   With such assurance for her bounty waite,
   As if ne'r failing Heav'n their Debtor were.

10. To these the store of Antick Treasure gave
    (For she no Money knew) Medals of Gold,
    Which curious *Gath'rers* did in travail save,
    And at high worth were to her Mother sold.

11. Figures of fighting Chiefs, born to o'rcome
    Those who without their leave would all destroy;
    Chiefs, who had brought renown to *Athens*, *Rome*,
    To *Carthage*, *Tyre*, and to lamented *Troy*.

12. Such was her wealth, her Mothers Legacy;
    And well she knew it was of special price;
    But she has begg'd what Heav'n must not deny;
    So would not make a common Sacrifice.

13. To the black Temple she her Sorrow bears;
    Where she outbeg'd the tardy begging Thief;
    Made weeping *Magdaline* but poor in Tears,
    Yet Silent as their Pictures was her Grief.

14. Her purpos'd penance she did here fulfil;
    Those Pictures dress'd, and the spent Lamp reliev'd
    With fragrant Oyles, dropp'd from her Silver Still;
    And now for those that there sat mourning, griev'd.

15. Those Penitents, who knew her innocence,
    Wonder what Parents sin she did bemoan;
    And venture (though they goe unpardon'd thence)
    More sighs for her redress then for their own.

16. Now jealousie no more benights her face,
    Her courage beautious grows, and grief decays;
    And with such joy as shipwrack'd Men imbrace
    The Shore, she hastens to the House of Praise.

17. And there the Gemm she from her bosome took,
    (With which till now she trembled to advise)
    So far from pale, that *Gondibert* would look
    Pale if he saw, how it out-shin'd her Eies.

18. These Rayes she to a Miracle prefers;
    And lustre that such beauty so defys,
    Had Poets seen (Love's partial Jewellers,
    Who count nought precious but their Mistress Eies)

19. They would with grief a miracle confess!
    She enters strait to pay her gratitude;
    And could not think her beauty in distress,
    Whilst to her Love, her Lord is still subdu'd.

20. The Altar she with Imagry array'd;
    Where Needles boldly, as a Pencill, wrought
    The story of that humble *Syrian* Mayd,
    Who Pitchers bore, yet Kings to *Juda* brought.

21. And there she of that precious Linnen spreds,
    Which in the consecrated Month is spun
    By *Lombard* Brides; for whom in empty Beds
    Their Bridegrooms sigh till the succeeding Moon.

22. 'Tis in that Moon, bleach'd by her fuller Light;
    And wash'd in Sudds of Amber till it grow
    Clean as this spredders Hands, and those were white
    As rising Lillys, or as falling Snow.

23. The voluntary Quire of Birds she feeds,
    Which oft had here the Virgin-Consort fill'd;
    She diets them with *Aromatick* seeds;
    And quench'd their Thirst with *Rainbow-Dew* distill'd.

24. Lord *Astragon*, whose tender care did waite
    Her progress, since her Morn so cloudy broke,
    Arrests her passage at this Temple Gate,
    And thus, he with a Father's license spoke.

25. Why art thou now, who hast so joyful liv'd
E're love thou knew'st, become with Love so sad?
If thou hast lost fair Vertue, then be griev'd;
Else shew, thou know'st her worth by being glad.

26. Thy love's high soaring cannot be a crime;
Nor can we if a Spinster loves a King,
Say that her love ambitiously does climbe:
Love seeks no honor, but does honor bring.

27. Mounts others value, and her own lets fall!
Kings honor is but little, till made much
By Subjects Tongues! *Elixer*-Love turns all
To pow'rful Gold, where it does only touch.

28. Thou lov'st a Prince above thine own degree:
Degree is monarch's Art, Love, Nature's Law;
In Love's free State all Pow'rs so Levell'd be,
That there, affection governs more then aw.

29. But thou dost love where *Rhodalind* does love;
And thence thy griefs of jealousie begin;
A cause which does thy sorrow vainly move;
Since 'tis thy noble Fate, and not thy Sin.

30. This Vain and voluntary Loade of grief
(For Fate sent Love, thy will does sorrow bear)
Thou to the Temple carry'st for relief;
And so to Heav'n art guided by thy fear.

31. Wilde Fear! Which has a Common-wealth devis'd
In Heav'n's old Realm, and Saints in Senates fram'd;
Such as by which, were Beasts well civilliz'd,
They would suspect their Tamer Man, untam'd.

32. Wilde Fear! which has the *Indian* worship made;
Where each unletter'd Priest the Godhead draws
In such a form, as makes himself afraid;
Disguising Mercy's shape in Teeth and Claws.

33. This false Guide Fear, which does thy Reason sway,
And turns thy valiant vertue to dispair,
Has brought thee here, to offer, and to pray;
But Temples were not built for Cowards pray'r.

34. For when by Fear thy noble Reason's led
    (Reason, not Shape gives us so great degree
    Above our Subjects, Beasts) then Beasts may plead
    A right in Temples helps as well as we.

35. And here, with absent Reason thou dost weep
    To beg success in love; that *Rhodalind*
    May lose, what she as much does beg to keep;
    And may at least an equal audience find.

36. Mark *Birtha*, this unrighteous war of prayer!
    Like wrangling States, you ask a Monarch's aide
    When you are weak, that you may better dare
    Lay claim, to what your passion would invade.

37. Long has th'ambitious World rudely preferr'd
    Their quarrels, which they call their pray'rs, to Heav'n;
    And thought that Heav'n would like themselves have err'd,
    Depriving some, of what's to others given.

38. Thence Modern Faith becomes so weak and blinde,
    Thinks Heav'n in ruling other Worlds imploy'd,
    And is not mindful of our abject Kinde,
    Because all Sutes are not by all enjoy'd.

39. How firm was Faith, when humbly Sutes for need,
    Not choice were made? then (free from all dispair
    As mod'rate Birds, who sing for daily Seed)
    Like Birds, our Songs of Praise included prayer.

40. Thy Hopes are by thy Rival's vertue aw'd;
    Thy Rival *Rhodalind*; whose vertue shines
    On Hills, when brightest Planets are abroad;
    Thine privately, like Miners Lamps, in Mines.

41. The Court (where single Patterns are disgrac'd;
    Where glorious Vice, the weaker Eies admire;
    And Vertue's plainness is by Art out-fac'd)
    She makes a Temple by her Vestal Fire.

42. Though there, Vice sweetly dress'd, does tempt like bliss
    Even Cautious Saints; and single Vertue seem
    Fantastick, where brave Vice in fashion is;
    Yet she has brought plain Vertue in esteem.

37: 3 err'd, *'51b*: err'd. *'51a*, *'73*   41: 2 the weaker *'51a MS*: weak *'51a* *'51b*
'73: our weaker *'51b Errata*

43. Yours is a vertue of inferior rate;
    Here in the dark a Pattern, where 'tis barr'd
    From all your Sex that should her imitate,
    And of that pomp which should her Foes reward:

44. Retyr'd, as weak Monasticks fly from care;
    Or devout Cowards steal to Forts, their Cells,
    From pleasures, which the worlds chief dangers are:
    Hers passes yours, as Valor fear excells.

45. This is your Rival in your sute to Heav'n:
    But Heav'n is partial if it give to you
    What to her bolder Vertue should be given;
    Since yours, pomps, Vertue's dangers, never knew.

46. Your sute would have your love with love repay'd;
    To which Arts conquests, whence all science flowes,
    Compar'd, are Students dreams; and triumphs made
    By glorious Courts and Camps but painted showes.

47. Even Arts Dictators, who give Laws to Schools,
    Are but dead Heads; Statesmen, who Empire move,
    But prosp'rous Spys; and Victors, fighting Fools,
    When they their Trophys rank with those of Love.

48. And when against your fears I thus declame,
    (Yet make your danger more whilst I decry
    Your worth to hers) then wisely fear I blame;
    For fears are hurtfull'st when attempts are high.

49. And you should think your noble dangers less,
    When most my praise does her renown prefer;
    For that takes off your hasty hope's excess;
    And when we litle hope, we nothing fear.

50. Now you are taught your sickness, learn your cure;
    You shall to Court, and there serve *Rhodalind*;
    Trie if her vertue's force you can endure
    In the same Sphear, without eclipse of mind.

51. Your Lord may there your Souls compare; for we,
    Though Souls, like Stars, make not their greatness known;
    May finde which greater then the other be;
    The Stars are measur'd by Comparison!

46: 2 whence *Ed*: when '51a-'73

52. Your plighted Lord, shall you ere long preferr
To neer attendance on this royal Maid:
Quit then officious Fear! The Jealous fear
They are not fearful, when to death afraid.

53. These words he clos'd with kindness, and retir'd;
In which her quick Ei'd Hope three blessings spy'd;
With joy of being neer her Lord, inspir'd,
With seeing Courts, and having Vertue try'd!

54. She now with jealous questions, utter'd faste,
Fils *Orgo's* Ear, which there unmark'd are gone,
As Throngs through guarded Gates, when all make haste,
Not giving Warders time t'examine one.

55. She ask'd if Fame had render'd *Rhodalind*
With favour, or in Truth's impartial shape?
If *Orna* were to humble Vertue kinde,
And beauty could from *Gartha's* envy scape?

56. If *Laura* (whose faire Eies those but invites,
Who to her wit ascribe the Victory)
In conquest of a speechless Mayd delights?
And ere to this prompt *Orgo* could reply,

57. She ask'd, in what consist the Charms of Court?
Whether those pleasures so resistless were
As common Country Travailers report,
And such as innocence had cause to feare?

58. What kinde of Angels shape young Fav'rites take?
And being Angels, how they can be bad?
Or why delight so cruelly to make
Fair Country Mayds, return from Court so sad?

59. More had she ask'd (for study warm'd her brow,
With thinking how her love might prosp'rous be)
But that young *Ulfinore* approach'd her now,
And *Goltho*, warmer with designe then she.

60. Though *Goltho's* hope (in *Indian* Feathers clad)
Was light, and gay, as if he meant to flie;
Yet he no farther then his Rival had
Advanc'd in promise, from her Tongue, or Eie.

56: 1 those but *'51a cor*, *'51b*, *'73*: but those *'51a u*

61. When distant, talk'd, as if he plighted were;
    For hope in Love, like Cowards in the Warr,
    Talks bravely till the enterprise be neer;
    But then discretion dares not venture farr.

62. He never durst approach her watchful Eie
    With studious gazing, nor with sighs her Eare;
    But still seem'd frolick, like a Statesman's Spy;
    As if his thoughtful bus'ness were not there.

63. Still, Superstitious Lovers Beauty paint,
    (Thinking themselves but Devils) so divine,
    As if the thing belov'd, were all a Saint;
    And ev'ry place she enter'd, were a Shrine.

64. And though last Night were the auspitious time
    When they resolv'd to quit their bashful fears;
    Yet soon (as to the Sun when *Eaglets* climbe)
    They stoop'd, and quench'd their daring Eies in tears.

65. And now (for Hope, that formal *Centry*, stands
    All Windes and Showrs, though where but vainly plac'd)
    They to *Verona* beg her dear commands;
    And look to be with parting kindness grac'd.

66. Both dayly journies meant, 'twixt this and Court:
    For taking leave is twice Love's sweet Repast;
    In being sweet, and then in being short;
    Like *Manna*, ready still, but cannot last.

67. Her Favours not in lib'ral looks she gave,
    But in a kinde respectful lowliness,
    Them honor gives, yet did her honor save;
    Which gently thus, she did to both express.

68. High heav'n that did direct your Eies the way
    To chuse so well, when you your friendship made,
    Still keep you joyn'd, that daring Envy may
    Fear such united Vertue to invade!

69. In your safe Breasts, the Noble *Gondibert*
    Does trust the secret Treasure of his love;
    And I (grown Conscious of my low desert)
    Would not, you should that wealth for me improve.

70. I am a Flow'r that merit not the Spring!
    And he (the World's warm Sun!) in passing by
    Should think, when such as I leave flourishing,
    His Beams to Cedars haste, which else would dy.

71. This from his humble Maid you may declare
    To Him, on whom the good of humane kinde
    Depends; and as his greatning is your care,
    So may your early love successes finde!

72. So may that beautious She, whom eithers Heart
    For vertue and delight of life shall chuse,
    Quit in your siege the long defence of Art,
    And Nature's freedom in a treaty lose.

73. This gave cold *Ulfinore* in Love's long Night
    Some hope of Day; as Sea-men that are run
    Far Northward finde long Winters to be light,
    And in the *Cynosure* adore the Sun.

74. It shew'd to *Goltho*, not alone like Day,
    But like a wedding Noon; who now grows strong
    Enough to speak; but that her beauties stay
    His Eies, whose wonder soon arrests his Tongue.

75. Yet something he at parting seem'd to say,
    In pretty Flow'rs of Love's wild Rhetorick;
    Which mov'd not her, though Orators thus sway
    Assemblies, which since wilde, wilde Musick like.

72: 1 She *51a cor*, '*51b*, '*73*: she '*51a u*

Canto the Sixth

The ARGUMENT

Here ULFIN *reads the art to* ULFINORE
Of wisely getting, and increasing Power.
The Rivals to VERONA *haste, and there*
Young GOLTHO'S *frailty does too soon appear.*
Black DALGA'S *fatal beauty is reveal'd;*
But her descent and Story is conceal'd.

1. Old *Ulfin* parting now with *Ulfinore*,
   His study'd thoughts, and of a grave import
   Thus utter'd, as well read in ancient Lore;
   When prudence kept up greatness in the Court.

2. Heav'n guide thee Son, through Honor's slipp'ry way;
   The Hill, which wary painfulness must climbe;
   And often rest, to take a ful survay
   Of ev'ry path trod by Experienc'd Time.

3. Rise glorious with thy Master's hopeful Morn!
   His favour calls thee to his secret Breast;
   Great *Gondibert*! to spacious Empire born;
   Whose careful Head will in thy bosome rest.

4. Be good! and then in pitty soon be great!
   For vertuous men should toile to compass power,
   Least when the Bad possess Dominion's Seat,
   We vainly weep for those whom they devowr.

5. Our vertue without pow'r, but harmless is!
   The Good, who lazily are good at home,
   And safely rest in doing not amiss,
   Fly from the Bad, for fear of Martyrdome!

6. Be in thy greatness easy, and thy Brow
   Still cleer, and comforting as breaking Light;
   The Great, with bus'ness troubled, weakly bow;
   Pow'r should with publick Burdens walk upright!

2: 4 path *'51a MS, '51b*: ph, at *'51a*: path, *'73*

7. We chearfulness, as innocence commend!
   The Great, may with benigne and civil Eies
   The People wrong, yet not the wrong'd offend;
   Who feel most wrong, from those who them despise!

8. Since wrongs must be, Complaints must shew the Griev'd;
   And Favorites should walk still open Ear'd;
   For of the suing Croud, half are reliev'd
   With the innate delight of being heard.

9. Thy greatness be in Armes! who else are great,
   Move but like Pageants in the People's view;
   And in foul weather make a scorn'd retreat;
   The *Greeks*, their painted Gods in Armor drew!

10. Yeild not in storms of State to that dislike
    Which from the People does to Rulers grow;
    Pow'r (Fortune's Sail) should not for threatnings strike;
    In Boats bestorm'd all check at those that row.

11. Courts little Arts contemn! dark Holes to save
    Retreated Pow'r, when fear does Friendship feigne;
    Poor Theeves retire to Woods! Chiefs, great, and brave,
    Draw out their Forces to the open Plaine!

12. Be by thy Vertue bold! when that Sun shines,
    All Art's false lights are with disgrace put out;
    Her straitness shews it self and crooked Lines;
    And her plain Text the *Scepticks* dare not doubt.

13. Revenge (weak Womens Valor! and in Men
    The *Ruffians* Cowardise!) keep from thy Breast!
    The factious Palace is that Serpent's Den;
    Whom Cowards there, with secret slaughter feast.

14. Revenge is but a braver Name for Fear!
    'Tis *Indians* furious fear, when they are fed
    With valiant Foes; whose Hearts their Teeth must tear
    Before they boldly dare believe them dead.

15. When thou giv'st death, thy Banners be display'd!
    And move not till an open Foe appears!
    Courts lurking war, shews Justice is afraid;
    And no broad Sword, but a closs Ponyard wears.

13: 1 Valor! *'51a u*: Valor, *'51a cor*, *'51b*, *'73*   13: 2 Cowardise! *'51a u*;
Cowardise, *'51a cor*, *'51b*, *'73*

16. To kill, shews Fear dares not more fears endure!
    When wrong'd, destroy not with thy Foes thy fame;
    The Valiant by forgiving mischief, cure;
    And it is Heav'n's great conquest to reclame!

17. Be by thy bounty known! for since the needs
    Of life, so rudely press the bold, and wise;
    The bountious heart, all but his God exceeds;
    Whom bounty best makes known to Mortal Eies!

18. And to be bountiful, be rich! for those
    Fam'd *Talkers*, who in Schools did wealth despise,
    Taught doctrine, which at home would Empire lose,
    If not believ'd first by their Enemies.

19. And though in ruling Ministers of State,
    The People wretched povertie adore,
    (Which Fools call innocence, and wise Men hate
    As sloth) yet they rebell for being poore.

20. And to be rich, be diligent! Move on
    Like Heav'ns great Movers that inrich the Earth;
    Whose Moments sloth would shew the world undone,
    And make the Spring strait bury all her birth.

21. Rich are the diligent! who can command
    Time, Nature's stock! and could his Hour-glass fall,
    Would, as for seed of Stars, stoop for the sand;
    And by incessant Labour gather all.

22. Be kinde to Beauty! that unlucky Shrine!
    Where all Love's Thieves come bowing to their Prey;
    And honor steal; which Beauty makes divine:
    Be thou still kinde, but never to betray!

23. Heav'n study more in Nature, then in Schools!
    Let Nature's Image never by thee pass
    Like unmark'd Time; but those unthinking Fools
    Despise, who spie not Godhead through her Glass!

24. These precepts *Ulfinore*, with dutious care,
    In his Hearts Closet lock'd, his faithful Brest!
    And now the Rival-Friends for Court prepare;
    And much their Youth, is by their haste exprest.

17: 3 his '*51a cor*, '*51b*, '*73*: this '*51a u*   18: 3 home '*51a*, '*73*: whom '*51b*
8124201   T

25. They yet ne'r saw *Verona* nor the Court;
    And expectation lengthens much their way;
    Since by that great Inviter urg'd, Report;
    And thither fly on Coursers of Relay.

26. E're to his Western Mines the Sun retir'd;
    They his great Mint for all those Mines behold,
    Verona, which in Towres to Heav'n aspir'd;
    Guilt doubly, for the Sun now guilt their gold.

27. They make their Entry through the Western Gate!
    A *Gothick* Arch! Where, on an *Elephant*
    Bold *Clephes* as the second Founder sate;
    Made to mock life, and onely life did want.

28. Still strange, and divers seem their Objects now;
    And still increase, where e're their Eies they cast;
    Of lazy Pag'ant-Greatness, moving slow,
    And angry bus'ness, rushing on in haste.

29. All strange to them, as they to all appear;
    Yet less like strangers gaz'd then those they see;
    Who this glad day the Duke's Spectators were;
    To mark how with his fame, his looks agree.

30. And guess that these are of his fighting Train,
    Renown'd in Youth; who by their wonder stay'd,
    And by their own, but slowly passage gain;
    But now much more their progress is delay'd:

31. For a black Beauty did her pride display
    Through a large Window, and in Jewels shon,
    As if to please the World, weeping for day,
    Night had put all her Starry Jewels on.

32. This Beauty gaz'd on both, and *Ulfinore*
    Hung down his Head, but yet did lift his Eies;
    As if he fain would see a litle more:
    For much, though bashful, he did beauty prise.

33. *Goltho* did like a blushless Statue stare;
    Boldly her practis'd boldness did out-look;
    And even for fear she would mistrust her snare,
    Was ready to cry out, that he was took!

32: 3 if he fain '51a cor, '51a u MS, '51b, '73: if fain '51a u

34. She, with a wicked Woman's prosp'rous Art,
    A seeming modesty, the Window cloz'd;
    Wisely delay'd his Eies, since of his Heart
    She thought, she had sufficiently dispos'd.

35. And he thus strait complain'd! Ah *Ulfinore*,
    How vainly Glory has our Youth misled?
    The Winde which blowes us from the happy Shore,
    And drives us from the Living to the Dead.

36. To Bloody slaughters, and perhaps of those
    Who might beget such Beauties as this Maid;
    The Sleepy here are never wak'd with Foes;
    Nor are of ought but Ladies frowns afraid.

37. E're he could more lament, a little Page,
    Clean, and perfum'd (one whom this Dame did breed
    To guess at ills, too manly for his age)
    Steps swiftly to him, and arrests his steed.

38. With civil whisper cries, *My Lady Sir!*—
    At this, *Goltho* alights as swiftly post
    As Posters mount; by lingring loath to err,
    As Wind-bound Men, whose sloth their first Wind lost.

39. And when his Friend advis'd him to take care;
    He gravely, as a Man new potent grown,
    Protests he shall in all his Fortunes share;
    And to the House invites him as his own.

40. And, with a Rival's wisdom, *Ulfinore*
    Does hope, since thus blinde Love leads him astray,
    Where a false Saint he can so soon adore,
    That he to *Birtha* ne'r will finde the way.

41. They enter, and ascend; and enter then
    Where *Dalga* with black Eies does Sinners draw;
    And with her voice holds fast repenting Men;
    To whose warm Jett, light *Goltho* is but Straw.

42. Nicely as Bridegrooms, was her Chamber drest,
    Her Bed, as Brides; and richer then a Throne;
    And sweeter seem'd then the *Circania's* Nest,
    Though built in Eastern Groves of *Cinamon*.

40: 4 That he to] That to '73

43. The price of Princes pleasures; who her love
    (Though but false ware) at rates so costly bought;
    The wealth of many, but may hourly prove
    Spoils to some one by whom her self is caught.

44. She, sway'd by sinful Beauty's destenie,
    Findes her Tyrannick pow'r must now expire;
    Who ment to kindle *Goltho* with her Eie,
    But to her Breast has brought the raging fire.

45. Yet even in simple love she uses Art;
    Though weepings are from looser Eies but leaks,
    Yet oldest Lovers scarce would doubt her heart;
    So well she weeps, and thus to *Goltho* speaks.

46. I might, if I should ask your pardon, Sir,
    Suspect that pitty which the noble feel
    When Women fail; but since in this I err
    To all my Sex, I would to Women kneel.

47. Yet happy were our Sex, could they excuse
    All breach of modesty, as I can mine;
    Since 'tis from passion which a Saint might use,
    And not appear less worthy of a Shrine.

48. For my brave Brother you resemble so
    Throughout your shape; who late in Combat fell;
    As you in that an inward vertue show,
    By which to me you all the World excell.

49. All was he which the Good as greatness see,
    Or Love can like! in judgement match'd by none;
    Unless it fail'd in being kinde to me;
    A crime forbid to all since he is gone.

50. For though I send my Eies abroad, in hope
    Amongst the streams of Men still flowing here,
    To finde (which is my passions utmost scope)
    Some one that does his noble Image beare;

51. Yet still I live recluse; unless it seem
    A libertie too rude, that I in you
    His likeness at so high a rate esteem,
    As to believe your heart is kinde and true.

44: 3 with] in *'51b*   45: 3 oldest] eldest *'51b*   46: 1 should] would *'51b*

52. She casts on *Ulfinore* a sodain look;
    Starts like a *Mountebank*, who had forgot
    His Viol, and the cursed poyson took
    By dire mistake before his Antidote.

53. Prays *Goltho* that his Friend may strait forbear
    Her presence; who (she sai'd) resembled so
    Her noble Brother's cruel Murderer,
    As she must now expire, unless he go!

54. *Goltho*, still gravely vain, with formal Face
    Bids *Ulfinore* retire; and does pretend
    Almost to know her Parents, and the place,
    And even to swear her Brother was his Friend.

55. But wary *Ulfinore* (who beautious Truth
    Did never but in plainest dress behold)
    Smiles, and remembers Tales, to forward Youth
    In Winter Nights by Country Matrons told:

56. Of *Witches Towns*, where seeming Beauties dwell,
    All hair, and black within, Maids that can fly!
    Whose Palaces at Night are smoky Hell,
    And in their Beds their slaughter'd Lovers lie.

57. And though, the Sun now setting, he no Lights
    Saw burning blew, nor steam of Sulphur smelt;
    Nor took her Two black *Meroen* Maids for Sprites;
    Yet he a secret touch of honor felt.

58. For not the craft of Rivalship (though more
    Then States, wise Rivals study interest)
    Can make him leave his Friend, till he restore
    Some cold discretion to his burning Breast.

59. Though to his fears this cause now serious shows;
    Yet smiles he at his solemn loving Eie;
    For Lust in reading Beauty solemn grows
    As old *Physitians* in *Anatomie*.

60. *Goltho* (said he) 'tis easie to discern
    That you are grave, and think you should be so;
    Since you have bus'ness here of grave concern;
    And think that you this House and Lady know:

61. You'l stay, and have your sleep with musick fed;
    But little think to wake with *Mandrakes* grones;
    And by a Ghost be to a Garden led
    At midnight, strew'd with simple Lovers Bones:

62. This *Goltho* is inchantment, and so strange,
    So subt'ly false, that whilst I tell it you,
    I fear the spell will my opinion change,
    And make me think the pleasant Vision true.

63. Her dire black Eies are like the *Oxes Eie*,
    Which in the *Indian* Ocean Tempest brings;
    Let's goe! Before our Horses learn to fly,
    Ere she shew cloven Feet, and they get wings!

64. But high rebellious Love, when counsell'd, soon
    As sullen as rebuk'd Ambition grows;
    And *Goltho* would pursue what he should shun,
    But that his happy'r fate did interpose:

65. For at the Garden Gate, a Summons, loud
    Enough, to shew authority, and haste,
    Brought cares to *Dalga's* Brow; which like a Cloud
    Did soon her shining beauty over-cast.

66. Like Thieves surpris'd, whilst they divide their Prise,
    Her Maids run and return through ev'ry Room;
    Still seeming doubtful where their safety lies;
    All speaking with their looks, and all are dumb.

67. She, who to dangers could more boldly wake,
    With words, swift as those errands which her heart
    Sends out in glances, thus to *Goltho* spake:
    My Mother, Sir! Alas! You must depart!

68. She is severe, as dying Confessors,
    As jealous as unable Husbands are,
    She Youth in Men, like age in Maids abhors;
    And has more Spies then any civil Warre.

69. Yet would you but submit to be conceal'd
    I have a Closet, secret as my Brest,
    Which is to Men, nor Day, no more reveal'd,
    Then a closse Swallow in his Winters Nest.

66: 3 doubtful '73: doubtfnl '51a: doubtfull '51b

70. To this good *Goltho* did begin to yeild;
But *Ulfinore* (who doubts that it may tend
To base retreat, unless they quit the Field)
Does by example govern and descend.

71. And now his Eies even ake with longingness,
Ready to break their Strings, to get abroad
To see this Matron, by whose sole access
Dalga in all her furious hopes is aw'd.

72. And as he watch'd her civil *Mercury*,
The hopeful Page; he saw him entrance give,
Not to a Matron, still prepar'd to die,
But to a Youth wholly design'd to live.

73. He seem'd the Heir to prosp'rous Parents toiles;
Gay as young Kings, that woo in forraign Courts;
Or Youthful Victors in their *Persian* spoiles;
He seem'd like Love and Musick made for sports.

74. But wore his clothing loose, and wildly cast,
As Princes high with Feasting, who to wine
Are seldom us'd: shew'd warm, and more unbrac't
Then Ravishers, oppos'd in their designe.

75. This *Ulfinore* observ'd, and would not yet
In civil pitty, undeceive his Friend;
But watch'd the signes of his departing Fit;
Which quickly did in bashful silence end.

76. To the Dukes Palace they inquir'd their way;
And as they slowly rod, a grave excuse
Griev'd *Goltho* frames; vowing he made this stay
For a discov'ry of important use.

77. If Sir, (said he) we heedlesly pass by
Great Towns, like Birds that from the Country come
But to be skar'd, and on to Forrests fly;
Let's be no travail'd Fools, but roost at home.

78. I see (reply'd his Friend) you nothing lack
Of what is painful, curious, and discreet
In Travailers; else would you not look back
So often to observe this House, and Street:

74: 2 wine] win '*51b*   78: 3 back '*51a MS*, '*51b*, '*73*: black '*51a*

79. Drawing your City Mapp with Coasters care;
    Not onely marking where safe Channels run,
    But where the Shelves, and Rocks, and Dangers are;
    To teach weak Strangers what they ought to shun.

80. But, *Goltho,* fly from Lust's experiments!
    Whose heat we quench much sooner then asswage;
    To quench the Furnace-Lust, stop all the vents;
    For give it any air the flames will rage.

FINIS

POSTSCRIPT

To the Reader

I am here arriv'd at the middle of the Third BOOK; which
makes an equal half of the *POEM*; And I was now by degrees to
present you (as I promis'd in the *Preface*) the severall Keys of the
main Building; which should convey you through such short Walks
5 as give an easie view of the whole Frame. But 'tis high time to strike
Sail, and cast Anchor (though I have run but half my Course) when
at the Helme I am threatned with Death; who, though he can visit
us but once, seems troublesome; and even in the Innocent may beget
such a gravitie, as diverts the Musick of Verse. And I beseech thee
10 (if thou art so civill as to be pleas'd with what is written) not to take
it ill, that I run not on till my last gasp. For though I intended in this
POEM to strip Nature naked, and clothe her again in the perfect
shape of Vertue; yet even in so worthy a Designe I shall ask leave
to desist, when I am interrupted by so great an experiment as Dying:
15 and 'tis an experiment to the most experienc'd; for no Man (though
his Mortifications may be much greater then mine) can say, *He has
already Dy'd.*
    It may be Objected by some (who look not on Verse with the
Eies of the Ancients, nor with the reverence which it still preserves
20 amongst other Nations) that I beget a *POEM* in an unseasonable
time. But be not thou, *Reader,* (for thine own sake, as well as mine)

11 till '*51a MS,* '*51b,* '*73:* to '*51a*

a common Spectator, that can never look on great Changes but with tears in his Eies: for if all Men would observe, That Conquest is the Wheels of the World, on which it has ever run, the Victorious would not think they have done so new, and such admirable actions, as 25 must draw Men from the noble and beautifull Arts, to gaze wholly upon them; neither would the Conquer'd continue their wonder till it involve them in sorrow; which is then the Minde's incurable Disease, when the Patient grows so sullein, as not to listen to Remedy: And *Poesie* was that Harp of *David*, which remov'd 30 from *Saul*, the Melancholy Spirit, that put him in a continuall remembrance of the revolution of Empire.

I shall not think I instruct Military Men, by saying, That with *Poesie*, in *Heroick Songs*, the Wiser Ancients prepar'd their Batails; nor would I offend the austerity of such, as vex themselves with the 35 mannage of Civill Affairs, by putting them in minde, that whilst the Plays of Children are punish'd, the plays of Men, are but excus'd under the title of business.

But I will gravely tell thee (*Reader*) he who writes an *Heroick POEM*, leaves an Estate entayl'd; and he gives a greater Gift to 40 Posterity, then to the present Age; for a publique benefit is best measured in the number of Receivers; and our Contemporaries are but few, when reckon'd with those who shall succeed.

Nor could I sit idle, and sigh with such as mourn to hear the Drum; for if this Age be not quiet enough to be taught Vertue a 45 pleasant way, the next may be at leisure: Nor could I (like Men that have civilly slept, till they are old in dark Cities) think War a novelty: For we have all heard, that *Alexander* walk'd after the Drum, from *Macedon* into *India*; and I tell thee (*Reader*) he carry'd *Homer* in his Pocket; and that after *Augustus*, by many Batails, had 50 chang'd the Government of the World, he and *Mecænas* often feasted very peaceably with *Horace*: And that the last wise Cardinall (whilst he was sending Armies abroad, and preparing against civill Invasion) took *Virgill* and *Tasso* aside under the *Louvre* Gallery, and at a great expence of time and Treasure, sent them forth in 55 new Ornaments. And perhaps, if my *POEM* were not so severe a representation of Vertue (undressing Truth even out of those disguises which have been most in fashion throughout the World) it might arrive at fair entertainment, though it make now for a Harbor in a Storm.   60

If thou art a malicious Reader, thou wilt remember, my

PREFACE boldly confess'd, That a main motive to this under-taking, was a desire of Fame; and thou maist likewise say, I may very possibly not live to enjoy it. Truly I have some Years ago consider'd,
65 that Fame, like Time only gets a reverence by long running; and that like a River, tis narrowest where tis bred, and broadest afarr off: but this concludes it not unprofitable; for he whose Writings divert Men from indiscretion and vice, becomes famous as he is an example to others endevours: and exemplary Writers are Wiser
70 then to depend on the gratuities of this World; since the kinde looks and praises of the present Age, for reclaiming a few, are not mentionable with those solid rewards in Heaven, for a long and continuall conversion of Posterity.

If thou (*Reader*) art one of those, who has been warm'd with
75 Poetick Fire, I reverence thee as my Judg, and whilst others tax me with vanity, as if the *PREFACE* argu'd my good opinion of the Work, I appeal to thy Conscience, whether it be more then such a necessary assurance, as thou hast made to thy self in like Under-takings? For when I observe that Writers have many Enemies, such
80 inward assurance (me thinks) resembles that forward confidence in Men of Armes, which makes them to proceed in great Enterprise; since the right examination of abilities, begins with inquiring whether we doubt our selves.

Cowes-Castle in the Isle of
85 Wight, *October* 22
1650

WILL. D'AVENANT.

FINIS

The Seventh Canto of the Third Book

Dedicated to Charles Cotton, Esq.

The ARGUMENT

Wakt by the Duke's Adoption, HUBERT *brings*
BORGIO *beneath the shade of Nights black Wings,*
To dark VERONA: ORNA *is betray'd,*
And HURGONIL, *not Jealous, but dismay'd.*
The CHIEFS *their Passions vent to* Hermegild,
But soon to GARTHA'S *braver Passion yield.*

1. Unlucky Fire, which tho from Heaven deriv'd,
   Is brought too late like Cordials to the Dead,
   When all are of their Sovereign sence depriv'd,
   And Honour which my rage should warm is fled.

2. Dead to Heroick Song this Isle appears,
   The ancient Musick of Victorious Verse:
   They tast no more, than he his Dirges hears,
   Whose useless Mourners sing about his Herse.

3. Yet shall this Sacred Lamp in Prison burn,
   And through the darksom Ages hence invade
   The wondring World, like that in *Tullia's* Urn,
   Which tho by time conceal'd, was not decay'd.

4. And *Charles* in that more civil Century,
   When this shall wholly fill the Voyce of Fame,
   The busie Antiquaries then will try
   To find amongst their Monarchs Coins thy Name.

5. They will admire thy force 'gainst *Gothick* rage,
   Thy Head of *Athens*, and thy Woman breast,
   Which rescu'd these Records in a rude Age,
   When the free Arts were frighted, and opprest.

6. If they who read thy Victories, thus confest,
   Find not thy wreathed Image, their blind Skill
   In gath'ring Monarchs Medals, they'll detest,
   And think they made their long Collections ill.

3: 3 Tullia's *Ed:* Tullie's *1685*   5: 3 in a] in *McM*

7. They'll highly bless thy Vertue, by whose Fire
   I keep my Lawrel warm, which else would fade,
   And thus enclos'd, think me of Nature's Quire
   The chief, who still sing sweetest in the shade.

8. To Fame who rules the World, I lead thee now,
   Whose solid Power the thoughtful understand,
   Whom tho too late, weak Princes to her Bow,
   The People serve, and Poets can command.

9. And Fame the only Guide to Empires past,
   Shall to *Verona* lead thy Fancie's Eyes,
   When Night so black a Robe on Nature cast,
   As Nature seem'd afraid of her Disguise.

10. Ambitious *Hubert* to *Verona* came
    In the dark Reign of Universal Sleep;
    And means no Tears shall quench his Angers flame,
    Tho all the Dwellers must be wak'd to weep.

11. Till Fame had made the Duke's Adoption known,
    He painfully supprest this raging Fire:
    But now it was above his Conduct grown,
    And *Borgio* thus provok'd it to aspire.

12. Thy Wealth, thou painted City, who shall save?
    Black art thou now, and sleep thy business seems;
    Each dark abode is silent as the Grave,
    Thy sleep were perfect Death if Death had Dreams.

13. Thou civil Crowd of soft inhabitants,
    Sleep and forget thy Crimes; may *Adice*
    No more relieve thy thirsty Medows wants,
    But swelling here, thy drowning *Lethe* be.

14. Wake but to kindle lust, and boldly think
    Heaven has no Eyes, but the departed Sun;
    May thy new marri'd at Adult'ries wink,
    Both soon seek Strangers, and each other shun.

15. Sleep you who Ruin States by Trades Encrease,
    Rich Traffickers who fetch those Toyes from far,
    Which soften us at home, you plead for Peace,
    Because our Luxuries we quit in War.

16. Sleep as securely as your Carricks steer,
    When in deep Seas your Gale is from the East,
    You and Your Pilots want the Art to fear
    The suddain Tempest breeding in my Breast.

17. You Statesmen sleep, who States tame Lyons be,
    For you and Lyons sleep with open Eyes,
    And shut 'em when you wake, you seem to see
    Through darkness, and with Wink your sight disguise.

18. Sleep you Oppressors, Monsters quickly bred,
    When private Will is joyn'd to publick Power,
    Like Bears in Winter long by slumber fed,
    You wake with Hunger, that would Herds devour.

19. Sleep all, till waking each with ravisht Mind,
    Shall the strange Glory of new Light admire,
    And thinking 'tis the Morn, Curse when ye find,
    Your City is become your Funeral Fire.

20. *Borgio* did *Hubert's* Fury thus excite,
    Which from his darkn'd thoughts breaks through his Eyes
    As suddainly as Morning breaks from Night,
    Or glorious *Chiefs* from sleep to Battle rise.

21. And now the Morn in suddain Glory rose,
    And to salute the World, shifts from his Face
    Night's Veil, as fast as Brides unmask to those
    Whom they saluting, would with kindness Grace.

22. To restless *Hubert*, *Borgio* leads the way,
    Near *Orna's* Window *Hurgonil* he spies,
    Who there with Musick welcomes Break of Day,
    And as the Lark the East salutes her Eyes.

23. For there at ev'ry dawn with Lovers layes,
    Till this sweet Moon shall end their nuptial Rites,
    And Joyes begin, he love *Reveillees* payes,
    Which made their morning sweet as Lovers nights,

24. Such Aires the untun'd *Borgio* ill abides,
    For Musick which is so the Soul of Love,
    As Love is of our Life, his Soul derides,
    Whom only Drums ambitious Noice could move.

24: 4 ambitious *Ed*: ambitions *Harvard, Folger, McM*

25. He oft sends back, as he does forward pass,
    His fatal Looks, which did the Count less awe
    Than did that Amorous, but more dreadful Face,
    Which he too soon in *Orna's* window saw,

26. For there appear'd, tho but obliquely plac'd,
    As shrunk behind the Glass, a Youth, who seem'd
    Repleat with all those Graces, which have grac'd
    Great Courts, or greater Love has e'er esteem'd.

27. Such seem'd this Amorous Youth, who soon withdrew
    His Looks, and shut the Casement hastily,
    As if he only watch'd to scape from view,
    By stealth would see, and to be seen was shy.

28. A Youth, who thus his Beauty seems to hide,
    So guiltlessly in a suspicious time,
    And in the Chamber of a plighted Bride,
    Might blot the whitest Vertue with a Crime.

29. Yet this as Loves false Fire, the Count did scorn.
    Grave *Tybalt*, who these Rites attended, seems
    So lost in Sleep, as if not yet the Morn
    Were broke, and ranks his Vision with his Dreams.

30. Yet Jealousie, which does by Thoughts subsist,
    As Life by Air; grew stronger by their pause;
    For they their Musick silently dismist,
    And fearing ill Effects, must doubt the Cause.

31. Musick which here at *Oran's* dawn had sung,
    For Love's Morn breaks not in a common Sky;
    But now their Lutes did seem on Willows hung,
    Where near some murmuring Brook dead Lovers lye.

32. Vain Jealousie, thou fruitful little Seed,
    Tho single, and as small as Atoms sown,
    Yet faster riseth than a forward Weed,
    In many Stems soon great and fully blown.

33. 'Tis Love's Alarm Bell too often hung
    Near Lover's Beds, and keeps 'em still awake;
    Yet Noble *Hurgonil*, when first it rung,
    Scarce seem'd to start, and now thus calmly spake.

34. Since Love the valiant Aids I must not dread
    A Shadows force, and I should vain appear,
    To let my Eyes be by a Vision led
    From Her whose Image in my Heart I wear.

35. Such Maiden Stratagems each plighted Bride,
    Rul'd by her Virgin Counsel does devise;
    And thus my Faith in *Orna* must be tri'd,
    Faith's Fort is best attempted by Surprise.

36. She as betroath'd does till this Moon be past,
    And Marriage Laws begin by Custom Sway,
    And now she tempts my Jealousie to taste
    How I will Reign, when she must long obey.

37. That Youth her near Ally, such harmless Art
    Assists, which may to Country Eyes seem bold;
    But Courts *Elixir* Vertue does convert
    The worst and most suspected Coyn to Gold.

38. *Tybalt* repli'd, this Tryal, *Hurgonil,*
    Exalts you both, it proves your love not light,
    And shews that she wants guilt to give her Skill,
    Where to direct her Jealous Tryals right.

39. Your solid healthful Love sweats not away
    At the faint Heat of Jealousies pale Flame,
    Nor even in Death will more than Souls decay,
    Which dye not, but return from whence they came.

40. And since her Tryal is so useless made,
    Her Errour does her Innocence proclaim;
    For as we trace strange Thieves by known Thieves aid,
    So our own Guilt lights us to others Shame.

41. The Guilty often wake, when Jealous grown,
    To watch Love's Treasons in another's Bed;
    Yet after foul Adulteries in their own,
    Sleep as secure from Terrors as the Dead.

42. Thus as they homeward move, they timely draw
    Discretion's Curtain o'r each others Eyes,
    And would not see, what they with Sorrow saw,
    Truth oft more modest seems in a Disguise.

40: 3 Thieves aid, *Harvard, McM*: Thieve aid *Folger*

43. Wise Nature does reprove our Jealousie,
    'Tis Fear, and Fear none willingly express,
    The Jealous shrink like Spies from every Spy,
    And what they find with Honours less confess.

44. But why (misterious Love) to blemish Truth
    In truest Lovers hast thou Art devis'd?
    Even in the Artless Sex, for that fair Youth
    Was *Gartha* in a manly shape disguis'd.

45. Whose Beauty stoop'd to *Hermegild's* advice,
    And she of *Ulpha*, *Orna's* Woman bought
    The Jewel Honour at a common price,
    And was by stealth to *Orna's* Chamber brought.

46. There she in Night's black Bosom lay,
    As in dark Lanthorns Light for Treason lyes,
    And so when she peep'd forth, 'twas to betray,
    As those were made to shine for a Surprise.

47. Calm *Orna* fearless slept, since free from Sin,
    And little did her Womans duty doubt,
    Nor heard when she had took the Traytors in,
    Who through her Windows let her Honour out.

48. And still she slept with as becalm'd a Breast,
    As thoughtless Martyrs in a Monument,
    Whilst *Gartha* (whose Success her Cares encreas'd)
    Shifts her Disguise, and to her Palace went.

49. Where *Hubert* longingly expects that she
    The reason of her Absence should unfold,
    Who big with Plot longs for delivery,
    And thinks Successes lost that are not told.

50. With *Hermegild* she hastily arrives,
    Where when she *Hubert* and bold *Borgio* spi'd,
    Her Anger seem'd to threaten Lovers Lives,
    And at her Frowns has many a Lover dy'd.

51. The two fierce Leaders gravely thoughtful grow
    Like scar'd Astrologers, as griev'd to take
    From this new Comet in her threatening Brow,
    The Empires Doom, and thus her Passion spake.

43: 4 And *Ed.*: Aud *Folger, Harvard, McM*

52. Wild Rumour, which from Court to *Brescia* fled,
    Has brought you here bright in your Angers Flame,
    You, *Hubert*, who in War have others led,
    Now for your own chief Guide chuse common Fame.

53. At *Gondibert's* Success, and new Renown
    Your sick Ambition in a Fever seems;
    Which from the Camp so drives you to the Town,
    As fev'rish men shift Beds to change their Dreams.

54. Back to your Camp, and come not here to boast
    Of numerous Ensigns, which but seldom are
    By Valour gain'd, tho oft by Cowards lost,
    Rags which the Beggar Honour wears in War.

55. Dull force cannot wise Courts with threatnings fright,
    Who breed strong not in Helmets but in Heads,
    Those Battles which you know not why you fight,
    And whilst you frown in Fields, smile in their Beds.

56. More had she said, but studious *Hermegild*
    Begg'd with his Looks, grown pale with Lovers Cares,
    That her bold Passion would to Prudence yield,
    And thus to *Hubert* he his Mind declares.

57. Think not great Prince, that our Designs are slow,
    But think your Courage makes a dang'rous hast;
    The Cures of Inward Wounds then doubtful grow
    To Art, when outwardly they heal too fast.

58. The Duke's Adoption is a tender Wound,
    Which cannot rough and hasty hands endure,
    By gentle search are narrow Arteries found,
    Where we the Spirits closer Walks secure.

59. Think not the Wounds ill searcht, which Artists close,
    Whilst you to open it grow rashly bold;
    As men ill cur'd haste desp'ratly to Blows,
    Because new Wounds may launce and cure the old.

60. Your Station is on Hills, your Glories all
    Watch as a Beacon, that does bid 'em Arm,
    And here your Name but whisper'd, serves to call
    The sleeping Faction like a new Alarm.

61. Retire, tho like the Sun declin'd you keep
    Your Circle still, and give to others Light,
    Since we must wish your Enemies a-sleep,
    Give us betimes the benefit of Night.

62. Preserve your Camp, no Force but of the Mind
    Can make our way, and when such Force you doubt,
    Think then that Giants, loth to die, can bind
    And master Souls with Limbs from going out.

63. *Hubert's* lost Patience, he did thus restore,
    Then *Gartha* with such Reverence he did chide,
    As Indian Priests in Storms check and adore
    Their Idols Rage, but *Hubert* thus repli'd.

64. Who doubts your Wisdom, *Hermegild*, which long
    Has led fierce Armies, and calm Councils taught,
    Must the worlds Mistress, grave Experience wrong,
    As if she wanted Worth, which all have sought.

65. Such who play with Truth, are punisht by
    Derided Anguish, till they serious turn,
    As wanton Scepticks, who Effects deny
    Of Fire, see others smiling whilst they burn.

66. Your Faith to me, your love of *Gartha* binds,
    Which doubting, I her force of Beauty doubt
    A Light held up, when Courts tempestuous Winds
    Threaten to blow Heavens Lamps, the Planets out.

67. Think my Impatience is the Armies Sin,
    And if when *Gartha* with my wrong's is warm'd,
    Your Power can hardly keep her Passions in,
    How should I stop three angry Legions arm'd?

68. Her Anger Heavenly is, for as kind Heaven
    Grieves that our own advantage we decline
    By doing ill; so her Rebukes are given,
    Because she suffers when the Loss is mine.

69. Victorious Maid, I find deep Wounds of Cares
    On your fair Brow; but so by Beauty shown,
    As youthful Victors wear their boasted Scars,
    To make their Vertue more than Beauty known.

70. Tell me the Empire's safe, and tell me where
    You and your Faction have so early met;
    To humble those who are so proud to fear,
    That at your Dawn their Sun must ever set.

71. *Gartha* from each to all now shifts her Eyes,
    As if too wild, and proud to be confin'd,
    So proud with Praise, that she does Praise despise,
    And spreads like Sails swell'd with a prosp'rous Wind.

72. Her Words abound, as Maids first Stories flow,
    When to stoln Lovers they from Parents scape,
    And fast she speaks, as Scouts chas'd by the Foe
    Declare their Number, and their Battles shape.

73. She tells how scarce from man she knew,
    When so audacious made by her Disguise,
    How soon her treble Voyce a Tenour grew,
    Her bashful Looks, bolder than Eagles Eyes.

74. She makes her secret Progress fully known,
    And how false *Ulpha* aided the Success;
    Whose Treason though she scorn'd, she grac'd her own,
    As Traytors Greatness makes their Treason less.

75. Whilst thus her mourning Conquest she reports,
    Their forward hopes shrunk back and seem'd dismaid
    To be instead of Sovereign Gold, with Courts
    Small Plots (the common Coyn of Statesmen) paid.

76. Then thus spake *Hermegild* to highest Heights,
    The lowest Steps must be the first Degrees,
    The strongest stoop to carry greater Weights,
    And from conceal'd small Roots, spring lofty Trees.

77. Nature disguis'd, does oft from Lowness rise,
    To high Effects; so does her Servant Art,
    Courts which by Art subsist, and low Disguise
    Oft dress a King to play a Subject's part.

78. These Clouds which threaten *Hurgonil*, e'r long
    Shall o'r the sleeping Duke a Tempest breed;
    As weaker Winds may suddainly grow strong,
    And split a Mast, which first scarce shook a Reed.

        72: 1 abound, *ed.*: abound,, *Harvard, McM, Folger*

79. The World is not subdu'd by Victories,
    Nor by the Voyce of Publick Councils sway'd,
    'Tis being wild best conquer'd by Surprise,
    And easi'st rul'd, when to the Yoke betray'd.

80. Wise Courts for Man have many a little Snare
    In Cities (now grown wild as Forrests) spread
    To take the useful Beast alive, whom War
    Destroyes, tho he be useless being dead.

81. Now *Borgio*, who with Hopes swell'd Sails had steer'd,
    Grows troublesom, as Sails then strong winds change
    Like Sails he slackn'd, when his Hope laveer'd,
    And seem'd as much a storm, as storms seem strange.

82. Invite, said he, State Student to your Feast
    Of Ruling Councils, an insipid Food.
    When *Canibal* Ambition is your Guest,
    Who is not fed with Precepts, but with Blood.

83. Poorly you make us fall from publick Heights,
    To private Depths; and all your great Designs,
    Are subt'ly shrunk to Lovers little Slights,
    Your *Indian* Voyage was to Copper Mines.

84. The Duke's Adoption by the King is seal'd,
    The Count by Marriage plight to *Orna* ti'd,
    Fast by Confederate the Crown is held,
    And we watch hard to scare a sleeping Bride.

85. Accurs'd be Courts where you, wise Statesmen, make
    Your selves, and not your Master great, you keep
    Your Watch with false Alarms, and only wake
    To breed those Fears, which hinder others sleep.

86. Falshood condemn'd you free from publick good,
    Bind Truth to the Authority of Schools,
    Least in your Priests you should be understood,
    Priests you make false, and they confirm you Fools.

87. Tho humbly first you low as Serpents crawl,
    Yet soon you show your power, which is your Sting.
    Wildly you catch at him, when you must fall
    Who by your Weights grows weak, your govern'd King.

88. Greedy as Lyons o'r your trembling Prey,
    Rowling your Eyes about with Jealous Care,
    For fear some other strong Devourer may
    In what you long have hunted, quickly share.

89. You sell the Peace that with your Blood you bought,
    Then in your Clossets other Quarrels feign
    To break that Peace, for which like Fools we fought
    And make the People purchase it again.

90. At this old *Hermegild* renounc'd his Age,
    For heat of Anger made his Visage young,
    And soon in Words he would let loose his Rage,
    But *Gartha* sooner thus prevents his Tongue.

91. Is this your Lyon *Hubert*, whom you bring
    In terrour from his Canvas Cage, your Tent,
    That by instinct he may to free the King
    Roar, if he find him not of Kings Descent.

92. Or would he cure Courts tame Civility?
    Or must the Ladies yield to him for fear?
    Soon a dispis'd dead Lyon shall he be,
    If he pronounce his Savage Doctrine here.

93. Rebels to Courts, the Force of useful Power,
    Where Statesmen should be safe tho vext with Cares,
    To rescue whom your Fury would devour,
    They breed not War for you, but you for Wars.

94. Courts form'd not War to keep the World alarm'd,
    Or vex the Quiet, but to tame the Rude,
    To Right whom Tumults wrongfully have harm'd,
    And Conquer those who have the good subdu'd.

95. Courts your wise Masters, did invent the odds
    Of Camps o'r Crowds, you muster'd by your wills,
    Would now like Ruffian Giants brave your Gods,
    Who smile in Clouds to see you heave at Hills.

96. How wildly would the World be Rul'd, if left
    By Civil Courts to your uncivil Sway?
    Justice would hardly dare to blush at Theft,
    Nor Priests to sigh, when Priests become their Prey.

97. What are your Battles where Ambition tries
    Those Titles which avoid the Test of Law,
    Battles, the Worlds confused Lotteries,
    Where for the Prize thousands together draw.

98. Like mighty Murtherers you Honour boast,
    Ofener by Chance than Valour give Defeats;
    Vainly like Gamesters count not what you lost,
    But what you won, hiding your base Retreats.

99. By wretched Rapine urg'd to bold Attacks,
    And when a City even by Treaty yields,
    You oft out-do the Fame of *Gothick* Sacks,
    And where they City's left, leave desart Fields.

100. And when your conquering Train comes home quite tir'd
     With emptying Cities, and with filling Graves,
     Your Foreign Vices are at first admir'd,
     'Till low you fall in Riots as your Slaves.

101. Now *Hubert* did arrest her pleading hand,
     Which earnest grew, and did her Tongue out-plead,
     His Looks did *Borgio's* Silence soon command,
     And on her Hand he Tears of kindness shed.

102. And that sweet Pledge with fervent Kisses held,
     As fast as Lovers then that fair Hand hold,
     Which has the long sought Promise newly seal'd,
     When Rivals hopes grow warm, and theirs grow cold.

103. He said she was Heavens private Mirrour wrought,
     For Kings that they might secret Truths discern;
     He prais'd the Court, that her such greatness taught
     As only Courts can teach, and Princes learn.

104. Now with one Mind to several Cares they hie;
     She hastes to Court to hasten *Orna's* shame:
     And both the Chiefs disguis'd to *Brescia* fly,
     Thro Mists returning as in Crowds they came.

105. *Hubert* will wait till her Designs appear
     In larger Growth, for He was bred to sow
     Courts little Fields, and well he knew that there
     Small Rivals oft to mighty Mischiefs grow.

102: 4 cold. *Harvard, McM*: cold *Folger*

106. They look but wrong on Courts who can derive
     No great Effects from outward Littleness;
     Thro Foolish Scorn they turn the Prospective,
     And so contract Courts little things to less.

107. Man's little Heart in narrow space does hide
     Great Thoughts, such as have spacious Empire sway'd
     The little Needle does vast Carricks guide,
     And of small Atoms were the Mountains made.

APPENDICES

TO

Sʳ WILL. D'AVENANT,
Upon his Two first Books of
GONDIBERT,
Finish'd before his Voyage to *AMERICA*

Thus the wise Nightingale that leaves her home,
Her native Wood, when Storms and Winter come,
Pursuing constantly the chearfull Spring
To forraign Groves does her old Musick bring:
   The drooping *Hebrews* banish'd Harps unstrung
At *Babilon*, upon the Willowes hung;
Yours sounds aloud, and tell's us you excell
No lesse in Courage, then in Singing well;
Whilst unconcern'd you let your Country know,
They have impov'rished themselves, not you;
Who with the Muses help can mock those Fates
Which threaten Kingdoms, and disorder States.
   So *Ovid* when from *Cæsar's* rage he fled,
The *Roman* Muse to *Pontus* with him led;
Where he so sung, that We through Pity's Glass,
See *Nero* milder then *Augustus* was.
Hereafter such in thy behalf shall be
Th'indulgent censure of Posteritie.
To banish those who with such art can sing,
Is a rude crime which its own Curse does bring:
Ages to come shall ne'r know how they fought,
Nor how to Love their present Youth be taught.
This to thy Self. Now to thy matchlesse Book,
Wherein those few that can with Judgment look,
May finde old Love in pure fresh Language told,
Like new stampt Coin made out of *Angel-gold*.
Such truth in Love as th'antique World did know,
In such a stile as Courts may boast of now.
Which no bold tales of *Gods* or *Monsters* swell,
But humane Passions, such as with us dwell.
Man is thy theame, his Vertue or his Rage
Drawn to the life in each elaborate Page.
Mars nor *Bellona* are not named here;

But such a *Gondibert* as both might feare.
Venus had here, and *Hebe* been out-shin'd
By thy bright *Birtha*, and thy *Rhodalind*.
Such is thy happy skill, and such the odds
Betwixt thy *Worthies* and the *Grecian Gods*.
Whose Deity's in vain had here come down,
Where Mortall Beauty wears the Soveraign Crown;
Such as of flesh compos'd, by flesh and blood
(Though not resisted) may be understood.

ED. WALLER

TO
Sir WILLIAM D'AVENANT,
Upon his two first Books of GONDIBERT,
Finish'd before his Voyage to *America*

Methinks Heroick Poesy till now,
Like some fantastique Fairy-land did show;
Gods, Devils, Nymphs, Witches, and Giants race,
And all but Man, in Mans best Work had place.
Thou like some worthy Knight, with sacred Arms
Dost drive the *Monsters* thence, and end the Charms:
In stead of those, dost *Men* and Manners plant,
The things which that rich soyl did chiefly want.
But even thy *Mortals* doe their *Gods* excell,
Taught by thy Muse to Fight and Love so well.
  By fatall hands whilst present Empires fall,
Thine from the grave past Monarchies recall.
So much more thanks from human kinde does merit
The Poets Fury, then the Zelots Spirit.
And from the grave thou mak'st this Empire rise,
Not like some dreadfull Ghost t'affright our Eyes,
But with more beauty and triumphant state,
Then when it crown'd at proud *Verona* sate.
So will our God re-build Mans perish'd frame,
And raise him up much better, yet the same:
So God-like Poets doe past things rehearse,
Not change, but heighten Nature with their Verse.
  With shame me thinks great *Italy* must see
Her Conqu'rors call'd to life again by thee;

Call'd by such powerfull Arts, that ancient *Rome*
May blush no less to see her Wit o'rcome.
Some men their Fancies like their Faiths derive;
And count all ill but that which *Rome* does give;
The marks of *Old* and *Catholick* would finde;
To the same Chair would *Truth* and *Fiction* binde.
Thou in these beaten paths disdain'st to tread,
And scorn'st to Live by robbing of the Dead.
Since Time does all things change, thou thinkst not fit
This latter Age should see all new, but *Wit*.
Thy Fancy, like a Flame, her way does make;
And leaves bright tracks for following Pens to take.
Sure 'twas this noble boldness of the *Muse*
Did thy desire to seek new Worlds infuse;
And ne'r did Heaven so much a Voyage bless,
If thou canst Plant but there with like success.

AB. COWLEY

CERTAIN

VERSES

WRITTEN
By severall of the
Authors Friends;

TO BE

RE-PRINTED

WITH THE
Second Edition
OF

GONDIBERT

———————

LONDON,
Printed in the Year, 1653.

Certain VERSES written by severall of the Authors Friends, to be Re-printed with the second Edition of *Gondibert*.

Upon the PREFACE

Room for the best of Poets heroick,
If you'l believe two Wits and a Stoick;
Down go the *Iliads*, down go the *Æneidos*,
All must give place to the *Gondiberteidos*.
For to *Homer* and *Virgill* he has a just Pique,
Because one's writ in Latin, the other in Greek:
Besides an old grudg (our Criticks they say so)
With *Ovid*, because his Sirname was *Naso*.
If Fiction the fame of a Poet thus raises,
What Poets are you that have writ his praises.
But we justly quarrell at this our defeat,
You give us a stomach, he gives us no meat.
A Preface to no Book, a Porch to no house;
Here is the Mountain, but where is the Mouse?
But, oh, *America* must breed up the Brat,
From whence 'twill return a *West Indy* Rat.
For *Will* to *Virginia* is gone from among us,
With thirty two Slaves, to plant *Mundungus*.

Upon the Preface of Gondibert

Mar. Epig.
Lasciva est nobis Pagina vita proba est.

As *Martials* life was grave and sad,
Wanting the mirth his verses had:
Even so, this our long Preface shows,
What ere we want, our Book has nose.

To Sir W. DAVENANT

(1)
After so many sad mis-haps,
Of drinking, riming, and of claps.
I pitty most thy last relaps.

(2)

That having past the Soldiers pains,
The Statesmens Arts, the Seamens gains,
With *Gondibert* to break thy brains.

(3)

And so incessantly to ply it,
To sacrifice thy sleep, thy diet,
Thy business; and what's more, our quiet.

(4)

And all this stir to make a story,
Not much superior to *John Dory*,
Which thus in brief I lay before yee.

(5)

All in the land of *Lombardie*,
A Wight there was of Knights degree,
Sir *Gondibert* ycleap't was he.

(6)

This *Gondibert* (as sayes our Author)
Got the good will of the Kings daughter,
A shame it seems, the Divell ought her.

(7)

So thus succeeded his Disaster,
Being sure of the Daughter of his Master,
He chang'd his Princess for a Playster.

(8)

Of person he was not ungracious,
Grave in Debate, in Fight audacious;
But in his Ale most pervicatious.

(9)

And this was cause of his sad Fate,
For in a Drunken-street-Debate
One Night he got a broken Pate.

(10)

Then being Cur'd, he would not tarry,
But needs this simpling Girle would marry
Of *Astragon* the Apothecary.

(11)

To make the thing yet more Romancie,
Both wife and rich you may him fancie;
Yet he in both came short of *Plancy*.

(12)

And for the Damsel, he did Wooe so,
To say the truth, she was but so-so,
Not much unlike her of *Toboso*.

(13)

Her beauty, though 'twas not exceeding,
Yet what in Face and Shape was needing,
She made it up in Parts and Breeding.

(14)

Though all the Science she was rich in,
Both of the Dairy and the Kitchin:
Yet she had Knowledg more bewitching.

(15)

For she had learnt her Fathers skill,
Both of th'Alimbick and the Still,
The Purge, the Potion, and the Pill.

(16)

But her chief Talent was a Glister,
And such a hand to administer,
As on the Breech it made no blister.

(17)

So well she handled *Gondibert*,
That though she did not hurt that part,
She made a blister on his Heart.

(18)

Into the Garden of her Father:
Garden said I ? or Backside rather
One night she went a Rose to gather.

(19)

The Knight he was not far behinde,
Full soon he had her in the winde:
(For Love can smel though he be blinde)

(20)

Her business she had finisht scarcely,
When on a gentle bed of Parcely
Full fair and soft, he made her Arse-ly. {*Desunt
cætera*

Upon the Continuation of GONDIBERT

THy Verses feet to run so fast,
And thine alas, in fetters plac't;
I always thought, and now I see't,
Thy brain's lesse stable then thy feet.
This 'tis, to be severe to us,
For naming Gods and *Pegasus.*
Couldst thou but such a horse have shap't,
Thou hadst with gallant *Massie* scap't,
Or couldst thou but frame *Gyges* Ring,
Long since (poor *Will*) th'hadst been a Wing,
Thou liest not there for any plot,
But cause a Poet thou art not.
Nor kenst thou *Daphne* how thy rimes should rage
And lift the Poet ore the walled stage;
Tis not a Moat can have the fate or power,
To hold the Muses, nor great *Cæsars* Tower,
Homer and *Virgil* both thy back-friends have
The priviledge to break out of their grave,
And they that slight them must not hope to thrive
But lie confin'd and buried alive.
Nor think it strange thou art not spar'd,
But cast into a Goale unheard.
Those ancient *Bards* no better sped,
Condemn'd by thee though never read:
Naso made *Dedalus* the Seas to cross,
Though the rash *Icarus* were at a loss.
But this our Anti-*Nasos* Muse doth flutter,
Like stubble goose that scarce gets ore the gutter

These colours that they nere may faile,
Were laid in Sack and Northdoune Ale.

The Author upon himself

I am old *Davenant* with my Fustian quill,
  Though skill I have not,
  I must be writing still
    On *Gondibert*,
    That is not worth a fart.

Waller and *Cowly* tis true have prais'd my Book,
  But how untruly
  All they that read may look;
    Nor can old *Hobbs*
    Defend me from dry bobbs.

Then no more I'le dabble, nor pump fancy dry,
  To compose a Fable,
  Shall make *Will Croafts* to cry,
    Oh gentle Knight,
    Thou writ'st to them that shite.

A Letter sent to the good Knight

THou hadst not been thus long neglected,
  But we thy four best friends expected,
Ere this time thou hadst stood corrected.

But since that Planet governs still,
That rules thy tedious Fustian Quill
'Gainst Nature and the Muses will.

When by thy friends advice and care,
'Twas hop'd in time thou woulldst despaire
To give ten pounds to write it faire.

Lest thou to all the world shouldst show it,
We thought it fit to let thee know it,
Thou art a damn'd insipid Poet.

Upon fighting WILL

THe King knights *Will* for fighting on his side,
  Yet when *Will* comes for fighting to be tri'd,
There is not one in all the Armies can
  Say they ere felt, or saw, this fighting man.

Strange that the knight should not be known it'h Field,
A Face wel charg'd, tho nothing in his Shield.
Sure fighting *Will* like Basilisk did ride
Among the Troops, and all that saw *Will* di'de,
Else how could *Will* for fighting be a Knight,
And none alive that ever saw *Will* fight.

In pugnacem Daphnem

Pugnacem Daphnem Rex ordine donat Equestri,
Sed quod pugnasset cum foret ille reus,
Arma virumq; ferum se vel sensisse rogatus,
Vel vid sse quidem Miles utrinq; negat.
Tantum equitis mirer campos latuisse per omnes,
Insignem vultu Parma sit alba licet,
Scilicet aspectu victor Basiliscus obibat
Agmina sub monstro quæ periere novo.
Pugnando haud aliter referet calcaria Daphnis,
Cui pugnæ testis nemo superstes erat.

Ad eundem

De titulo ablato non recte Daphni *quer̂eris*
Facti in te causam Daphni *Senatus habet.*
Jure decus perdis, si vitam jure tueris,
Testis abest culpæ, testis honoris abest.

In Daphnen Causedicum

IT being prov'd that fighting *Will* ne're fought,
The Judges straight for other treasons sought.
On that, point-blank two witnesses did swear,
Such, and such words from his mouth they did hear.
In answer to which by a speech *Will* showes,
Alas, that his words are drawn through his nose.
Through his nose it was the witnesses cry'd,
But *Will* has none, so again they ly'd.
Thus with a lost nose the fame he bears,
To have won both his enemies ears,
And now by his Poetry sure *Will* knows
How to turn those ears again into nose.

The Poet is angry being censured by
one he knowes not

DAphne, in scorn, not knows me. In all shows
More know *Jack puddin then Jack pudding* knows.

Titulus compitis Londini cum
licentia imponendus

A Letter sent out of the Countrey

MOnstrum hic horrendum nomine Daphnin nuperrime captam in Insulas *Barbadas contendentem visui Anglorum, præbeamus natum, uti ex scriptis placet inter Helvetios, valde enim de rebus istorum gestis, (quorum ne pili pendimus) animo æstuat; Londini propugnaculo à Parliamento Angliæ incarceratus, non quidem inter captos, sed ferociorum animalium domiciliis in lucrum Domini* Backster *manet; Philosophorum nonnulli, de forma querentes, nihil nisi illum non esse Elephantem ausi sunt affirmari. Illi enim Proboscis deest, vocem tamen (vix articulatam) non ex ore, sed per nasum trahit, & tamen (proh Deorum miracula) nasum non habet, sed quasi per minima foramina nasutum, Ballenæ instar evomit, quid ni illum Cetum esse ex elogio Germani cujusdam Leviatham satis constat.*

Upon the Author

DEnham come help me to laugh
at old *Daph,*
Whose fancies are higher then Chaffe,
He abuses
All our Muses,
And would it not make a man laugh till he burst,
That he would be thought of all Poets the first,
That is of all Rimers the worst?

Daphne wer't thou not content
For to vent
Thy fancies without our consent,
But hadst the face
In thy Preface
To laugh at all those that had written before,
When we thy best friends to the number of four
Advis'd thee to scribble no more.

Canto 2

RAis'd by a Prince of *Lombard* blood, {*Duke of*
An antick fabrick long hath stood   {*Savoy*
Of *Podian* Flint, and *Parian* Free-stone
Mingled as well as you shall see stone,
A part whereof height *Cripples Region*,
Contains of half-men a whole Legion,
Who still have been *from ancient lore*
For three *swift Centuries* and more,
Friends to the Debtors and the Drinkers,
And foes unto the Smiths and Clinkers.
When in the Churchyard or the Ally,
Occasion serves them, forth they sally,
Both horse and foot, but now I wrong 'um,
There's neither horse nor foot among 'um;
But those that are for horse accounted,
Are on tall woodden Engines mounted,
On which in *Lombard Autors* notion,
They'abuse the *Property of Motion*.
But for the foot 'tis more improper,
For they move not on foot, but Crupper,
And having neither leg nor stump,
Advance themselves on hand and rump.
A stand they make. A stand d'ye cal't?
The word of Art is make a halt.
Then steps forth a *Grave Eastern Cripple*,
One that could fight, and talk, and tipple,
Brave friends, quoth he, *Power is a liquor*,
Makes hands more bold, and wit more quicker,
It is *a tree* whose boughes and branches
Serve us in stead of legs and hanches,
It is a Hill to whose command,
Men *walk by Sea* and *sail by Land*.
But what's our power unlesse we know it?
And knowledge what? unlesse we shew it.
Behold the Knight who late did marry
The daughter of our 'Pothecary,
Hurried to durance like a stinkard,
By *Oswald Smith*, and *Borgia Clinkard*,
And him like to a *Civill sheep*
In Goale (*Nice Statesmens pound*) they'l keep.
This said, you might have seen (for such is
The force of eloquence) their crutches

Indu'd with diligence in th'eys and noses
Of such as had them, flames and roses,
Their *Nerves of Wyer* new heat makes limber,
And rage ev'n animates their timber,
   Then as a pack of *Regian hounds*
Pursuing o're the *Illyrian grounds*
A *Tuscan Stag*, if in the wind
A flock of *Brescian* sheep they find,
Calabrian swine, or *Padan Goats*,
In blood they bath their *Cannon throats*,
And in the trembling entrails hasten
Their *Wel-experienc't* teeth to fasten,
With such *Croatian* rage the stout
Grave Cripples did the Bailiffs rout.
Thus rescuing *Gondibert* they save him,
Then to a *Berkshire Coachman* gave him.
   The Bailiffs being fled, or dead all,
The Knight puls out an *antique meddall*,
On the reverse whereof was graved,
Th'alliance betwixt *Christ* and *David.*   { *Cross*
Quoth he of rescu'd Knighthood carry   { *and*
This just reward, broach of *Canary*,   { *Harp*
Or *Belgian Brandewine* the *Vessell*
Wherewith the *Argonauts* of *Tessell*
When *Mars* and *Neptune* them engages,
Inflame their flegmatick courages.
   He safe return'd, here Joy and mirth a-
bounded twixt *Astragon* and *Byrtha.*
Thus leave we them in humor jolly,
Free from *old Roman Melancholy.*

Thus far in the Authors own words,
Now a little in his own way.

1. Sunk neer his evening Region was the Sun,
(But though the Sun can ne're be said to sink,
Yet when his beams from our dull eyes are run,
He of the Oceans moysture seems to drink.)

(And though the Ocean be as far remote
From him as we, yet such is the false light
Of mortall eye, that though for truth we know't,
We yet believe our own deceiving sight.)

(Nor without cause) (for what our eyes behold
Unto our sense most evident hath been;
But still we doubt of things by others told,
(For Faith's the evidence of things not seen.)

2. When *Gondibert* and *Byrtha* went to bed,
(For it the custome was of *Lombard Brides*,
That on the day when they were married,
They never slept till *Sol* his visage hides.)

(For though bright *Sol* doth never close his eyes,
When he resignes our hemisphere to night,
Bold Ethnicks say, that he with *Thetis* lyes,
And make him but a lay adulterous light.)

3. The posts were of *abstersive Ebony*,
(Though no *abstersiveness* in *Posts* we finde,
In powder tane (the *learned* not deny
It cleanses choler, and in pills, breaks wind.)

(So when a Sword is forg'd of solid steel.
It serves for nothing but to cut and wound,
But when to powder turn'd, *shy virgins* feel
It cures green sickness, & the spleen makes sound.

4. The Curtains in well shadowed colours wrought,
(For though *old Astragon* his child had bred
To his own trade, yet something she was taught
By her *Nice Mother*, (who was *gravely dead.*)

His limbeck though the sooty Chymist broke
As she past by (when out th'elixar flew)
And (though) as a grave modern author spoke)
The power of Potion, Purge, and Pill, she knew.)

(Yet something had she gain'd of female lore,
Though much she was in med'cinal science skild,
She and th'experienc'd maid had samplers store,
And could the needle or the distaff weild.)

5. The sheets so nicely fine, none could have thought
Them spun from course *Batavian Freisters* toyls,
But by the fingers of *Arachne* wrought,
From the most subtile of the *Silkworms spoyls*.

There *Byrtha* lay, but when the knight drew nigh,
She seem'd to fly from what she long'd t'enjoy,
Orna herselfe was not then she more shie,
Gartha more nice, nor *Rodalind* more coy.

But when *great Natures office* was unseald,   { A wo-
Then through *Loves limbeck* his elixar flew   { mans
Motion and heat, things *stiff* as if congeald,   { womb.
Dissolve to *Amber sudds*, and *Rainbow* dew.

To DAPHNE

On his Incomparable Incomprehensible Poem
GONDIBERT

CHear up small Wits; now you shall crowned be,
    Daphne himself is turn'd into a tree.
(Nor think it strange, for our great Author can
Clap stones to *Hirmigil*, and make her Man:)
Goe gather Spriggs, nor can you strip him bare
For all the ancient Wreaths fall to his share.
Poor *Homers* Eyes by his *unshaded Light*
Again put out, who bids the world Goodnight,
And is as much eclips'd by one more blind,
As is his, by our new *Hectors* out-shin'd:
Virgill thou hast no Wit, and *Naso* is
More short of *Will* then is *Wills* Nose of his;
Can silence *Tasso* and the *Fairy-Queen*,
Though all by *Will* unread, and most unseen,
Nor shall we ere hear more of great *Tom-thumb*,
For *Gondibert* and *Oswald* strike all dumb.
Thus then secur'd, thy Babe shall not miscarry,
Since all doe bow to Fames *Fine Secretary*.
So have I heard the great *Leviathan*,
Let me speak true, and not bely-a-man,
Raign in the Deep, and with tyrannick Power
Both Costick *Codd*, and squallid *Sprats* devour.

An Essay in Explanation of Mr.
Hobbs, where he tels the Author,

The Vertues you distribute there among so many Noble persons,
represent the Image but of one Mans Vertue to my Fancy, which
is your own

CANTO 1

1

OF all Ill Poets by their *Lumber* known,
　Who ne'r Fames favors wore, yet sought them long
Sir *Daphne* gives precedency to none,
　　And breeds most business for *abstersive Song*.

2

From untaught Childhood, to mistaking Man,
　An ill-performing Agent to the Stage;
With *Albovin* in *Lumber* he began,
　　With *Gondibert* in *Lumber* ends his rage.

3

Rime was his studyed Art; Rime which was bad;
　Rime meant for charms to keep the Devil in aw;
Rime which with Fustian lin'd, & Nonsence clad,
　　More needfull is, then Finger, Shirt or Straw.

4

To conquer Reason, Natures common gift,
　Feind Art, sophisticated Rime devis'd,
While those who canot their weak Judgments lift
　　To discern, sense, & with hard words surpris'd.

5

Yet Laws of Verse rescue but doubtfully
　From one ill Poet all good Poets fame;
Till against Rime, the wise Rimes help apply,
　　Which soberly tells *Will* he is too blame.

On GONDIBERT

CLose-stools thus made by *Astragon* we have,
　That will both finger, drugs, and Paper save;
On stool of Ebony, O Reader sit,
　　Or else poor *Gondibert* will be beshit:
　　　For things *abstersive* will availe,
　　　As well to purge, as wipe the Taile.

The Poets Hot-Cockles

THus Poets passing time away,
　Like Children at Hot-cockles play;
All strike by turn, and *Will* is strook,
(For he lyes down that writes a Book.)
Have at thee *Will*, for now I come,
Spred thy Hand fair upon thy Bombe;
For thy much insolence, bold Bard,
And little sense, I strike thus hard.
Whose Hand was that? 'twas *Jaspar Mayne*;
Nay, there you'r out, lie down againe.
With *Gondibert*, Preface and all
See where the *Doctor* comes to maul
The Authors hand, 'twill make him reel;
No, *Will* lies still and does not feel;
That Book's so light, 'tis all one whether
You strike with that, or with a Feather.
But room for one new come to Town,
That strikes so hard he'll knock him down:
The hand he knows since it the place
Has toucht more tender then his face:
Important Shrieve, now thou ly'st down,
We'll kiss thy Hands, and clap our own.

Preface, page 25. That his writings are adapted
　to an easie musical Singer, which the Reader
　may judge by these following Verses

OSwald, *Paradin, Rodalind, Hugo, Hubert, Aribert,*
　Hurgonil, Astolpho, Borgia, Goltha, Tibalt,
Croatian, Lumbards, Huns, Vasco, Dargonet, Orna,
　Astragon, Hermogild, Ulfinor, Orgo, Thula.

Epithetes that will serve for any Substantives,
　either in this part or the next.

NIce, *Wise, Important, Eager, Grave, Busy, Recorded,*
　Antient, Abstersive, Shie Roman, *Experienc'd.*

Upon the Authors writing his name, (as in the Title of his Booke) D'Avenant

AS severall Cities made their claime
   Of *Homers* birth to have the fame;
So, after ages will not want
Towns claiming to be *Avenant*:
Great doubt there is where now it lies,
Whether in *Lombard* or the *Skies*.

Some say by *Avenant* no place is meant,
And that this *Lombard* is without descent;
And as by *Bilke* men mean ther's nothing there,
So come from *Avenant*, means from *No-where*
Thus *Will* intending *D'Avenant* to grace
Has made a Notch in's name, like that in's face.
Fitter it were the Author of *Harrigo*,
Had stil'd himselfe *D'aphne D'Avenantigo*.

FINIS

[Charles Cotton's poem] TO| Sir WILLIAM DAVENANT,|
IN| ANSWER| TO THE| Seventh Canto| OF THE| THIRD
BOOK| OF HIS| GONDIBERT,| Dedicated to my Father.

1. O Happy Fire, whose Heat can thus controul
   The Rust of Age, and thaw the Frost of Death;
   That renders Man immortal, as his Soul.
   And swells his Fame with everlasting Breath.

2. Happy that hand, that unto Honours climb;   5
   Can lift the Subject of his living Praise;
   That rescues Frailty from the Scyth of Time,
   And equals Glory to the length of Days.

3. Such, Sir, in you, who uncontroul'd, as Fate
   In the Black Bosom of Oblivions Night;   10
   Can Suns of Immortality create,
   To dazle Envy with prevailing Light.

4. In vain they strive your glorious Lamp to hide
   In this dark Lanthorn, to all Noble Minds;
   Which through the smallest cranny is descry'd,   15
   Whose Force united, no resistance finds.

5. Blest be my Father, who has found his Name
   Among the Heroes, by your Pen reviv'd;
   By Running in Times Wheel, his thriving Fame
   Shall still more youthful grow, and longer liv'd.   20

6. Had *Alexander's* Trophies thus been rear'd,
   And in the Circle of your Story come;
   The spacious Orb full well he might have spar'd,
   And reapt his distant Victories at home.

7. Let men of greater Wealth than Merit, cast   25
   Medals of Gold for their succeeding part;
   That Paper Monument shall longer last,
   Than all the Rubbish of decaying Art.

COMMENTARY

THE PREFACE

6 Building: See line 884 below and *passim*. See Cowley, *Davideis* i. 33–6, where that poem is spoken of as a temple, and Herbert's *The Temple*, as other examples of this concept.

14, 18 Sea-Marks: Davenant uses this conceit again in lines 504–6 below and in *Gondibert* III. vi. 79.

61 Eagle: Cf. 'The Philosophers Disquisition', stanza 21 (*Shorter Poems*, ed. Gibbs; '73, p. 328).

112 *Dante*: On the subject of 17th-century references to Dante see K. C. M. Sills, *MP* iii (1905), 99 (Spingarn, *Critical Essays of the Seventeenth Century*, Oxford, 1908, ii. 331).

125 ff. Both Davenant and Hobbes renounce the preternatural as epic matter. See Davenant's remarks below (lines 173 ff.) on imitation, and Hobbes's remarks in *The Answer* . . . *to* . . . [the] *Preface*, 116 ff. and 221 ff.

144 live equally with them: Cf. Cotton's poem 'To Sir William Davenant', p. 287 above. Cotton expresses the hope that his father's fame will livewith Davenant's.

161 exploded: Clapped out, or clapped off the stage (*OED*).

170 painted History: See *Gondibert* II. vi. 53 ff., a painted history of creation which Davenant himself attempts in words.

175 errors of others: Davenant has one censure for all his predecessors: the use of the supernatural, and yet the supernatural intrudes into Davenant's own story at several points. A dead hero 'rules a star' (I. vi. 30); Astragon has a prophetic dream (II. vi. 30); and Gondibert gives Birtha a magic emerald (III. iv. 45 ff.).

The theory that the supernatural is out of place belongs to Hobbes (*Answer to the Preface*, lines 221 ff., and *Leviathan* I. ii). Spingarn (*Critical Essays of the Seventeenth Century* ii. 332) observes that Davenant 'foreshadows . . . the school of Boileau' and cites Boileau's *Art Poétique* iii. 193. Contrast Dryden's defence of the supernatural in 'Essay of Heroic Plays' (ed. Scott and Saintsbury, iv. 23).

240–343 This discussion of the choice of Christian persons, distant time, and distant place may have been at least partly inspired by Tasso's *Discorsi del Poema Eroico* (Spingarn ii. 332).

307–8 discover their eyes to be weake, etc.: Cf. below, line 845 n.; *Gondibert* III. v. 41; and 'The Philosophers Disquisition', stanza 21 (*Shorter Poems*, ed. Gibbs; '73, p. 328).

228–332 Childhood . . . has: Maynard Mack (the Twickenham Edition of *The Poems of Alexander Pope* iii–1, 88–9) cites several parallels of this conceit: Horace, *Ars Poetica* 158 ff.; Shakespeare, *As You Like It* II. vii. 139 ff.; Sir William Temple i. 249; and others.

388–9 Davenant designed his poem as a 'courtesy book' with the intention of instructing young rulers. Another attempt, on a smaller scale, may be seen in 'Madagascar', which he wrote to encourage Prince Rupert's conquest of the island (see Nethercot, *Sir William D'avenant: Poet Laureate and Playwright-Manager*, pp. 142–7). See also Davenant's pastoral lament for Colonel Goring (*Shorter Poems*, ed. Gibbs; '73, pp. 247–9), stanza 4. Henry Jermyn and Endymion Porter appear under the sobriquets 'Arigo' and 'Endymion' (Nethercot, p. 144).

Later in the *Preface* (lines 915 ff.) Davenant cites examples of the political power of poets and poetry, as he does also in the Postscript to *Gondibert* (pp. 250 ff. below). In *The Seventh Canto* Davenant seems to lament his lack of success (stanza 2).

405–456 The virtue of ambition develops into an important theme in *Gondibert*. See I. i. 2 ff.; II. viii. 26 ff.; II. viii. 55 ff. *The Cruel Brother* (1630) is also full of this theme (*The Dramatic Works of Sir William Davenant*, ed. J. Maidment and W. H. Logan, i. 121, 127). See also Davenant's *Macbeth* (ibid. v. 333); the poem 'To I. W. upon the Death of his Mistress' (*Shorter Poems*, ed. Gibbs; '73, pp. 232–3); and the 'Poem on His Sacred Majestie's Most Happy Return to His Dominions' (ibid., p. 256).

429 *retir'd men*: Perhaps this can be taken as a direct reference to Charles II, in the light of Davenant's convictions about the political power of poets (lines 388–9 n., and 405–56 n. above). Davenant wanted the new king to assert himself.

457–67 Davenant sought to make his poem a discussion of love in its various forms. The plot is a love triangle. Hurgonil and Orna represent chaste lovers, while Goltho's experience with Dalga in III. vi. represents lust. In Goltho and Ulfinor is represented the sexless love of male friends. Hermegild and Gartha represent love for political expediency. Rhodalind provides sophisticated, courtly love, and Birtha, pastoral, idyllic love. See *Gondibert* III. iii. 1–11, where 'The poet takes the wise aside' (III. iii, Arg.) to explain that his poem is the only good guide to love.

477 the *Spartans*: This account may be found in the 'Life of Demetrius' in Plutarch's *Lives*.

487 ff. The idea of using the five-act structure in forms other than drama was older than *Gondibert*. See Thomas May's *The Reign of King Henry the Second* (1633), which includes *The Description of King Henry the Second, with a Short Survey of the Changes in His Reigne*. The 'changes' are likened to five acts, 'for . . . *Tanquam fabula est vita hominis*'. William Prynne's *Histrio-mastix* (1633) is divided into acts and scenes. See also Magendie (ed., *L'Astrée d'Urfé*, Paris, 1929, p. 46): 'Selon Baro, D'Urfé avait conçu l'Astrée comme une "tragi-comédie pastorale"; les cinq tomes correspondaient aux cinq actes, et les douze livres de chaque tome, aux scènes de chaque acte.' Davenant knew d'Urfé's work through Henrietta Maria, who had commissioned him to do *The Platonic Lovers*.

Sir Francis Kynaston's *Leoline and Sydanis* (1642) is a mock-heroic poem consisting of five 'parts' which follow in a very general way the five-act formula. In Part One Leoline is married to Sydanis but, owing to a magical spell, is unable to consummate the marriage; in Part Two the lovers are separated; in Part Three Leoline recovers his potency, and the marriage is consummated, only he does not realize it, because Sydanis has taken another girl's place in the dark; in Part Four Sydanis realizes that she cannot reveal her identity, and the couple are separated again; in Part Five they are reunited, thanks largely to the kindness of certain fairies, goddesses, and druids. This matter of structure, together with certain other similarities between *Gondibert* and the *Leoline* (see the discussion of the sub-plot in *Gondibert* involving Gartha's disguise, pp. xv–xvi above; line 637 n. below; and III. i. 53–7 n. below) suggests that Davenant may have been acquainted with Kynaston's poem.

Cf. Richard H. Perkinson, 'The Epic in Five Acts', *SP* xliii (1946), 465–81.

508–9 The second . . . finishes all the characters: Dalga is not mentioned until III. vi.

532–5 a Bill of fare . . . Guests: Harington uses the same figure in his translation of *Orlando Furioso* (1591), pp. 405–6.

549–72 In connection with Davenant's discussion of his stanza, cf. Hobbes's *Answer*, lines 84–104 below; Dryden's Preface to *Annus Mirabilis*, where Dryden approves of quatrains for heroic verse, but acknowledges the difficulty of composing in them; and the comparison of Dryden's and Davenant's stanzas in *The Works of John Dryden: Poems 1639–1680*, ed. Niles Hooker *et al.* (1965) i. 193–5 and 267–9.

569 sung at Village-feasts: In his aspiration to have his poem sung, Davenant was anticipated by Patrick Hannay. Hannay even provides a musical setting for his *Philomela* (1622) (see George Saintsbury, ed., *Minor Poets of the Caroline Period*, Oxford, 1905, i. 620).

580 ff. With Davenant's remarks about wit, cf. Hobbes's discussion of wit and fancy (*Answer*, lines 151 ff. below); Hobbes's *Leviathan* i. 8 (Michael Oakeshott, ed., Oxford, 1946, p. 43); and Dryden's Preface to *Annus Mirabilis*.

601 loseth all force, etc.: Davenant makes a different use of this figure in *Gondibert* II. vi. 87.

637 The idea of Lapland witches is proverbial (see George Lyman Kittredge, *Witchcraft in Old and New England*, New York, 1929, p. 159). In Kynaston's *Leoline and Sydanis* II. cxxxvii ff., the wizard Morrough ties three knots in a handkerchief, each of which when untied releases a wind—the first two favourable and the third disastrous.

646–76 Hobbes's rebuttal of this slander of old men appears in his *Answer*, below, lines 355 ff.

659 ff. Davenant makes Ulfin express this same concern for youth and beauty in his parting words to his son (*Gondibert* III. vi. 22).

676–7 Ornaments . . . Witte: Cf. Dryden, in the Preface to *Annus Mirabilis*: 'The composition of all poems is, or ought to be, of wit.'

678–9 in . . . bosoms: The phrase seems borrowed from Bacon's dedicatory letter to the Duke of Buckingham, prefixed to his *Essays* (James Spedding, ed., Boston, 1900, xii. 77). Davenant admired Bacon and experimental philosophy. His 'House of Astragon' (*Gondibert* II. v) seems to derive from Bacon's *New Atlantis*. In fact, Davenant's whole rationale in this poem has to do with applying to poetry the methods of the 'new philosophy', and consequently he rejects the supernatural (line 175 above), and he makes free use of terminology proper to sciences, arts, and trades (see lines 755–6 below).

701–3   See Horace, *Epistularum* I. i. 7–9, and Pope's translation (The Twickenham Edition, iv. 279). And see Davenant's 'A Journey into Worcestershire' (*Shorter Poems*, ed. Gibbs; '73 pp. 215–7).

705–7   not to bring home the names, etc.: This intention, again, is in keeping with the spirit of experimental philosophy as opposed to scholastic (see lines 678–9 n. above).

755–6   Nor . . . liberall: Cf. Dryden's defence of 'terms of art' in his 'Account of' *Annus Mirabilis* (Hooker, ed., i. 51 ff.).

767 ff.   On the subject of books and men, cf. Hobbes's *Answer*, below, lines 249–61.

839   Two Colleagues: 'Cowley and Waller, whose commendatory verses on *Gondibert* follow this preface in the original' (Spingarn ii. 332).

840–41   of whom . . . mindes: Cf. *Gondibert* II. v. 36; III. iii. 11; and see Dryden's parody in *MacFlecknoe*, line 82; and, of course, *Areopagitica*, 'a good book is the precious life-blood of a master-spirit . . .'.

845   Eaglets: See Pliny's *Natural History* x. iii (tr. Holland, 1601, i.272). The haliartos, a mixed breed of eagle, beats its unfledged young and forces them to look at the sun. If one blinks, or if its eyes water, it is expelled from the nest. Cf. *Gondibert* III. v. 64 and 'The Philosophers Disquisition', stanza 21 (*Shorter Poems*, ed. Gibbs'; *73*, p. 328).

872   Pellicans: See Browne's *Vulgar Errors* (*Works*, ed. Geoffrey Keynes, 1929) v. i. The legend that the pelican pecked its breast to feed its young was alive enough to require Browne's comment.

919 ff.   Cf. *Orlando* xxxv concerning how poets preserve names of men from obscurity. Davenant again takes up the subject in *Gondibert* II. v. 65; III. iii. 1 ff.; and the *Seventh Canto*, stanzas 1 ff. Cf. also Milton's Sonnet VIII.

959 ff.   These stanzas are 84–7 in every text of the poem. Cf. II. vi. 84–7 n. below.

991   a small Republique: Venice? Her feud with the popes went back to 1581 (T. Okey, *Venice and its Story*, London, 1930, p. 175).

1046   *Phineas*: See Numbers 25: 6–8. Phineas, a priest, took a javelin and chased an Israelite who had brought a Mideanitish woman to the Tabernacle.

1076 ff.   For a contemporary reference to the quarrels of little kings in America see Richard Hakluyt, *The Principal Navigations*, ed. Ernest Rhys (Everyman's Library), vi. 51, 187, and 236.

1104 ff.   See lines 387 ff. above, and 388–9 n. above.

1175–6   Letters on bury'd Marble: The preservation (albeit imperfect) of ancient names would have been a familiar topic of reference, thanks to John Selden's having translated the Arundel Marbles within Davenant's adult life (John Selden, *Marmora Arundelliana*, 1629).

1200 Goverment resembles a Ship: Davenant likes to use this commonplace ingeniously. See *Gondibert* II. iv. 32–3 and III. vi. 10, and 'To the Duke of Richmond, in the Year 1639' (*Shorter Poems*, ed. Gibbs; '73, pp. 293–4,).

1366–8 Glowormes . . . keep the Sunns beames: Browne, in *Pseudodoxia Epidemica* III. xxvii. 12 (ed. Keynes, ii. 262–3), says that the glow-worm glows only so long as he has life. Browne doubts that the light proceeds from another source. Pliny XI. xxviii (tr. Holland, i. 326) says of glow-worms that 'they shine in the night like a spark of fire: and it is no more but the brightnes of their sides and taile . . .'.

1485–6 *Menenius Agrippa*: See Livy ii. 32 (Spingarn, ii. 332).

1492–3 *Epimenides* and *Aratus*: Epimenides in Titus 1 : 12; Aratus in Acts 17 : 28 (Spingarn i. 242).

1540 *Plato*: Plato's *Republic* iii. 398 (Spingarn ii. 332).

1585 in another World: Cowley uses the same metaphor in his Preface to his *Miscellanies* (*Works*, ed. A. R. Waller, 1905, i. 8).

THE ANSWER

48 *Pybrach*: The *Quatrains* 'appeared in 1574' and 'were translated into English by Sylvester' (Spingarn ii. 333).

96–7 verses . . . Winges: Concerning shaped poems see Gregory Smith, *Elizabethan Critical Essays* ii. 95, and note (Spingarn ii. 333). And see Richard Wills, *De Re Poetica* (1573).

133 Conjurers: See *Preface*, line 637 n. above.

151 ff. Cf. Hobbes's discussion in *Leviathan* I. ii–iii.

190–205 The metaphor may have been suggested to Hobbes by *Gondibert* I. iv. 14.

208 Ambition: Cf. *Gondibert* I. i. 29 and note; II. viii. 28 ff.

222 the *possibility* of nature: See *Leviathan* I. ii, on witches and apparitions.

278 *to*: Hobbes misquotes; the poem reads *they*.

308 admiration: Spingarn (ii. 333) cites Gregory Smith, *Elizabethan Critical Essays* i. 392.

308–14 'On Hobbes's theory of laughter, see his *Human Nature*, 1650, ix. 13' (Spingarn ii, 333).

317–21 This may be a rebuke. See *Preface*, above, lines 755–6 and note. Spingarn (ii. 333) cites other documants on this topic, by Dryden, Dennis, and Rymer.

355 ff. Here Hobbes answers Davenant's remark about old men (cf. *Preface*, above, lines 646–76).

GONDIBERT

I. i, Arg. ARIBERT . . . RHODALIND . . . OSWALD . . . GONDI-
BERT: Thomas Rymer notes Davenant's use of description in his charac-
terizations, instead of letting the characters' actions 'speak for them as former
Poets have done' (*Biographia Britannica*, 1747–66, iii, 1607 [H]). It is charac-
teristic of Davenant's style that he depends on illustrative particulars in his
characterizations rather than on generalizations. His method of presentation is
that of the dramatist, to disclose scenes, showing a little, and then drawing the
curtain, as it were, so that some passages read like stage directions, not epic
poetry.

1 These lines are parodied in Denham's (?) 'An Essay in Explanation of
Mr. Hobbes. . .' in *Certain Verses Written by Several of the Author's Friends; to
Be Reprinted with the Second Edition of Gondibert* (London, 1653), pp. 21–2
(Appendix ii, p. 284). Cf. also the opening lines of Dryden's *MacFlecknoe*.

9 For no male Pledg, etc.: Possibly suggested by *Aeneid* vii. 48–57, where
Latinus is described as an old warrior king whose only issue is a daughter.

17–18 Cf. II. vii. 51 below, in description of Birtha's soul.

27 *Oswald*: Cf. *Aeneid* vii. 57 ff.; Turnus is the principal suitor until Aeneas
arrives in Italy. Aeneas is the favourite of heaven and Latinus.

28 Courts . . . Cities . . . Fields: Cf. Davenant's *Platonic Lovers* v (*Dramatic
Works*, ed. Maidment and Logan, ii. 101): Buonateste: 'You have been bred in
cities, courts, and camps.' Hobbes (*Answer*, lines 16–42) divides poetry into three
genres, *Heroique*, *Scommatique*, and *Pastorall*, proper to court, city, and country,
respectively.

29 Yet . . . care: Although Oswald dies early in the poem, his faction repre-
sents ambition as an evil; i.e. as an attribute of the hero's enemies. For the just,
ambition is 'no more than an extraordinary lifting of the feet in the rough ways
of Honor, over the impediments of Fortune' (*Preface*, above, lines 412–15).
See *Preface*, lines 405–56 n.

39 *Lombard* Authors: Davenant's 'Lombard Author' is apparently a fiction.
See Dowlin, *Sir William Davenant's Gondibert*, p. 112; Harbage, *Sir William
Davenant: Poet Venturer*, 1935, p. 186; and p. xii above. Kynaston evidently
used a similar ruse in *Leoline and Sydanis*, which he purported to have taken
from Celtic myth.

54 The brain 'is (as it were) a Privy Counsellor, and Chancellor, to the *Heart*'
and 'the *Heart* as King keeps his Court [in the chest], and by his arteries com-
municates life to the whole body' (Burton's *Anatomy of Melancholy*, ed. A. R.
Shilleto, 1903, I. I. II. IV (vol. i, p. 172). Cf. I. iv. 27 below.

72 less . . . Poets: Before *Gondibert*, which is a heroic poem with the structure
of a drama, the unities of time and place were not of such great concern to the
epic poet. To praise Oswald's troops out of season would be to heed the unities
even less than common poets do.

74 Cloyster vertue: Cf. Milton on 'cloistered virtue' in the *Areopagitica*.

80 Our . . . warre: One of several allusions to contemporary religious developments. See also II. i. 44–75 and II. v. 51 below. Davenant's 'Philosophers Disquisition' and 'Christians Reply' amount to a debate on reason v. unreasoning faith.

I. ii, Arg. Cf. *Aeneid* vii. 481–2, where the first battle on Italian soil is occasioned by Ascanius's killing a stag, and its owners are summoned, by rustic horns, to avenge the injury. See also Denham's *Cooper's Hill*, lines 247–322.

1 seeds . . . sow: Cf. II. vii. 89 below, and Shakespeare's *Macbeth* I. iii. 58–9: 'If you can look into the seeds of time', etc. Davenant's *Macbeth* keeps these lines virtually unaltered.

2 from a Daies brief pleasure, etc.: So in *Aeneid* vii. 475 ff., except that in Virgil it is the malignant supernatural power of Alecto that brings about the trouble.

11 Compare Hugo with Otho in Tasso's *Godfrey of Bulloigne, or the Recovery of Jerusalem* (tr. Fairfax, 1600), VI. 28 ff. Both are small in stature but noblehearted.

15–19 Sexual love is the 'secret vital heat by which we live', and combined with reason makes the man. Cf. Donne's 'Air and Angels' and 'The Extasie' concerning the function of love in the operation of the soul. Donne was not exactly a new poet in 1650, except as 'new' is opposed to ancient, but he does, in a sense, seem to find the soul by 'finding love'. Concerning 'vital heat' see I. iv. 27 below, and note.

27 *Akons* trusty steele: Pliny XXXIV, xiv (tr. Holland, ii. 514) mentions an image, in Rome, 'of *Hercules* all of hard yron or steele, which *Alcon* the famous workman made . . .'. Possibly Alcon is meant instead of 'Akon' in Davenant's lines, but an emendation seems not sufficiently justified, in the absence of a manuscript.

29 Harborers: The office of a harbourer is to trace a deer to its covert (*OED*). Deer that mourn . . . with tears: Proverbial. See Morris Palmer Tilley, *A Dictionary of the Proverbs in England in the Sixteenth and Seventeenth Centuries*, 1950, §D 189.

30 Lime-Hounds: Var. of Lyman-Hound. A blood-hound. Apparently had the reputation of not barking in chase (*OED*).

32 ff. The nobility of the stag is suggested by Pliny VIII. xxxii (tr. Holland, i. 213–14). Here, in an early canto, the stag seems to prefigure symbolically human nobility as represented by Aribert and Gondibert.
Croton: An ancient name for Cotrone, in Calabria, in the 'toe' of Italy. Davenant speaks of Calabrian Coursers in II. ii. 81 below.
Regian Hounds: Perhaps referring to the city of Reggio, in Calabria.

36–8 Cf. 'Tyrant man' in II. vi. 60.

42 Harbage (*Sir William Davenant*, 1935, p. 187) calls this 'the worst stanza in the poem' because of its bathetic 'effort to exalt and dignify physical love'.

45 foyle: 'to run over or cross (the ground, scent, or track) with the effect of baffling the hounds' (*OED*).

49 imbos'd: Imbost; foaming at the mouth from exhaustion (*OED*).

55 *Dittany*: Cf. *Aeneid* xii. 411–15, where Venus plucks dittany to cure Aeneas's wound. Cf. also Tasso XI. lxxii, where the wounded Duke Godfrey is cured of a wound by the use of dittany.

62 Bid . . . flie: See Shakespeare's *Macbeth* v. v. 30 ff., and Davenant's *Macbeth* v. iv: 'If thou speak false I'll send thy soul | To th'other world to meet with moving woods, | And walking forests.'

64 in ambush: Cf. *Aeneid* xi. 522 ff., where Turnus waits in ambush for Aeneas, and *Thebaid* ii. 469, which is modelled on the passage in the *Aeneid*.

65 fatal Raven: The raven was proverbially a harbinger of death, and the epithet *fatal* is common. See Tilley § R 33.

69 Grosse: Of a body of armed men: compact, solid (*OED*).

I. iii, Arg. *For . . . ment*: On the subject of organized killing, cf. I. iv, Arg.; II. i. 44; II. i. 73–4; II. viii. 23. See also I. ii. 36–8 and II. vi. 60.

11 'Tis . . . meets: See I. i. 28 and note.

27 sowing . . . weeds: Perhaps adapted from Shakespeare. See Shakespeare's Sonnet 94; *Romeo and Juliet* II. iii. 1–30; and *Hamlet* I. ii. 135.

31 Let . . . spent: Cf. the battle between Aeneas and Turnus in *Aeneid* xii. 674–952, where the champions have the same humanitarian motive.

32 Ambition . . . grow: Cf. III. iv. 96: 'respect was up to rev'rence grown'; II. v. 19: 'pride grown to religion'; and II. vii. 2: 'opinion to Religion grown'. Davenant seems to be thinking in terms of a sort of Aristotelian mean.

34 I . . . great: This may be an early symptom of the indolence which later causes Gondibert to spurn the throne and Rhodalind. See the *Preface*, lines 405–456 and note.

76–7 For other specimens of the literary curse see II. ii. 76–80 and III. iii. 43–4. These passages would seem to adumbrate the ranting scenes which became conventional in the Heroic Plays of the Restoration (see Allardyce Nicoll's analysis of 'The Rimed Heroic Tragedy: 1664–1677' in *A History of English Drama 1660–1900*, 1955, i. 100–31). J. H. Mozley, in *Ovid: the Art of Love, and Other Poems* (Loeb Classical Library), has an interesting appendix to *Ibis*, wherein he cites many examples of the curse in ancient literature.

87 As . . . discern'd: Davenant repeats this figure in III. i. 56. Cf. *Iliad* iii. 33–7; *Aeneid* ii. 379–82; *Orlando Furioso* xxxix. 32.

I. iv. Arg. See I. iii, Arg., and note.

1–9 On the instructive value of heroic verse, see *Preface*, lines 388 ff. and note.

4 Chymists . . . compleat: See *Shorter Poems*, ed. Gibbs, 'The Christians Reply to the Philosopher', stanza 2 n., for the details of the experiment alluded to.

6 The poet boasts that he can 'minister to the mind diseased'. Davenant shifts rather abruptly from the alchemical figure of 4–5 to the medical figure of 6–9.

8 But . . . Forborn: See *Preface*, lines 388–9 n. When one contrasts the resolute tone of the present passage with the tone of discouragement in *The Seventh Canto*, stanza 2, one suspects that Davenant may have dropped *Gondibert* half-finished because he became disenchanted.

13 Cf. II. ii. 26, where Davenant uses similar terms for a similar discussion.

14 See Hobbes's treatment of this metaphor in his *Answer*, above, lines 190–205.

17 And in . . . sent: See G. B. Evans's *The Plays and Poems of William Cartwright*, 1951, pp. 701–3, concerning the frequency of this theme in poems by Cartwright's contemporaries.

27 vital . . . enthroned: One would assume that the 'vital Closet' is the breast and 'Life's smal Lord' the heart, which Burton calls the Sun and King of the body (*The Anatomy of Melancholy*, ed. A. R. Shilleto, I. I. II. IV). Cf. William Harvey's dedicatory letter to Charles, before his *An Anatomical Disquisition on the Motion of the Heart and Blood in Animals* (1628), tr. Robert Willis: 'The heart of animals is the foundation of their life, the sovereign of everything within them, the sun of their microcosm, that upon which all growth depends, from which all power proceeds. The King, in like manner, is the foundation of his kingdom . . .'. Cf. also the first paragraph of Chapter 15 in the same work: '. . . since death is a corruption which takes place through deficiency of heat, and since all living things are warm, all dying things cold, there must be a particular seat and fountain . . . where . . . fire is stored and preserved . . .'. This concept can be found expressed in Aristotle's *On Life and Death* i. 24. Cf. also I. i. 54 above, and note.

32 Cf. 'The Christians Reply', stanza 9 (*Shorter Poems*, ed. Gibbs; '73, p. 335).

42 Cf. 'The Philosophers Disquisition', stanza 34 (ibid., p. 329), where reason is described as scorning to look out through her prison windows, the eyes.

48–9 Cf. Spenser's *Faerie Queene* II. viii. 1: 'And is there care in Heaven', etc. Davenant's 'heaven' is the sky (stanza 47); Spenser's is Heaven. Copernicus had established the heliocentric cosmology, but it was still thought that the orbits of celestial bodies were based on the perfect circle and hence 'regular'.

49–50 *That Sword . . . steel*. This is practically a translation of *Aeneid* xii. 731–41.

I. v. 7 Cf. *Orlando Furioso* xlii. 19 (tr. Sir John Harington, 1591):

> Save that *Orlando* with compassion mov'd,
> To see him lie so lorne, and so distressed,
> Gate him such needfull things as best behov'd, . .
> And not his foe, a man might him have guessed:
> Such was this Earles good nature, fierce in fight
> But fight once done, from mallice free or spite.

and Harington's Gloss: 'A true praise of a noble mind.'

12 Swift as *Armenians* in the Panthers chace: Pliny VIII. xvii (tr. Holland, i. 203-4) makes 'Syria' the native country of the panther, and he places 'Syria' and 'Armenia' in the same geographical neighbourhood. It is understandable that where panthers existed the natives would be swift in pursuit of them (and the other way round).

18 amuse: To cause to muse or stare, to puzzle (*OED*).

25 in-large: Enlarge (*OED*).
Carere: A short gallop at full speed (*OED*).

44 *Gothick* steel: Gothic: 'Formerly used in extended sense, now expressed by TEUTONIC or GERMANIC' (*OED*). Pliny XXXIV. xiv (tr. Holland, ii. 513-15) says that iron mines in 'Austrich' yield a good quality of steel. The 'barbars' whet with oil for a finer edge than a water grindstone gives.

47 Cf. Tilley §M 1175: 'A red morning foretells a stormy day.' The proverb appears in numerous poetic forms in the 16th and 17th centuries. Davenant uses it again in II. iv. 29.

52 This is a crucial stanza. Much trouble would be avoided in the sequel if Gondibert were 'in Honor's School' less 'exactly bred'.

56 Tierce: A third part (*OED*).

62-3 Evidently Davenant had planned the *Seventh and Last Canto of Book III* early enough for the plot of it to open here, with this pledge of alliance.

76 Threds . . . out: Davenant may be alluding to *Orlando Furioso* xxxiv. 88-91, where Ariosto describes the palace in which the Parcae spin, sort, and lop the threads of life.
Note Davenant's revision in accordance with his principle of keeping the supernatural out of the heroic poem (cf. *Preface*, line 175 and note). This stanza is cited by Thomas Rymer as an instance of the supernatural creeping in (*Biographia Britannica* iii. 1607 [H]).
Thrid and *thred* are forms of the word *thread* (*OED*). *Third* is evidently a printer's error, though it may have arisen because *thrid* is also a form of the word *third* (*OED*).

I. vi. 2 *Ulfin*: Curiously, Ulfin, with his white hair and his good-natured sarcasm, is the most real character in the poem. It is he who guides us through Astragon's laboratories and temples (II. v-vi) and who delivers one of Davenant's most important didactic pronouncements (III. vi. 1-23). Yet he has a minor part in the plot, so far as the poem is completed.

23 And . . . invades: Cf. Shakespeare's *Romeo and Juliet* III. i, where Mercutio dies quickly on a hot day, of a scratch.

28 Cf. II. vi. 43 and 84-7 concerning praise and prayer.

30 Call'd . . . Star: Thomas Rymer (*Biographia Britannica* iii. 1607 [H]) cites this as an intrusion of the supernatural.

35-9 See John Morrison Hobson, *Some Early and Later Houses of Pity*, London, 1926, pp. 168-70. Sir Thomas Sutton (*c.* 1532-1611) established a hospital and free school for eighty pensioners—gentlemen fallen into poverty and veterans of military service, all over fifty years old, though if wounded in action they could be admitted at forty. The school was 'for forty-four poor boys . . .'.

43–4 And this . . . led: Compare Hobbes's habit of putting things in terms of action and reaction (e.g. *Answer*, lines 151 ff.). Davenant seems here to borrow Hobbes's stylistic device.

55 ff. Ulfinor and Goltho, as bosom friends, recall Virgil's Nisus and Euryalus (*Aeneid* ix. 176 ff.) and their many successors in romances.

67 vertue (antiquated now): See the *Preface*, lines 388–9 and notes.

76 *Hypericon*: Cf. Pliny xxvi. viii (tr. Holland, ii. 255). Pliny says that 'it doth incrassat and thicken humors' and describes it as of a red colour.

77 *Nymphaea*: Cf. Pliny xxv. vii (tr. Holland, ii. 222). According to Pliny, Nymphaea is an anaphrodisiac, effective for twelve days. This may explain 'cools . . . the Blood'. Gondibert, however, though cured of his fever, soon falls in love with his nurse, Birtha.

80 cease: *Cease* is a form of the verb *seize* (*OED*).

II. i. 3–21 These verses amount to a 'prospect poem'. Cf. Denham's *Cooper's Hill* and Robert Arnold Aubin's *Topographical Poetry in XVIII-Century England* (New York, 1936), which, however, fails to include Davenant's lines in its summary of antecedents of the 18th-century poems.

4 *Vera*: Verona takes its name from Dietrich von Bern—Theodoric the Goth —who took the city by defeating Odoacer. Can the name Bern have been corrupted to 'Vera'?
Time . . . Fame: Cf. *Orlando Furioso* xxxv, stanzas 11 ff., where Time is represented as an old man scattering papers with names on them, only a few of which are rescued and preserved.

5 When . . . stood: Caius Marius (157–86 B.C.) defeated the Cymbri in a great slaughter on Campi Raudii (101 B.C.).

6 *Attila*: Fought Theodoric and overran Lombardy in the 5th century.

8 Pallace of King *Agilulf*: Paulus Diaconus mentions a palace in *De Gestis Langobardorum* iv. 22, but nothing is said of Agilulf's dying before it was finished. Indeed, according to Paulus, it was his queen, Theudelinda, who built the palace.

10 *Clephes*: Cleph was king of the Lombards A.D. 572–4. He had a bad temper and killed 'with the sword' many of 'the old Roman aristocracy' (Thomas Hodgkin, *Italy and Her Invaders*, Oxford, 1895, v. 182).

13 *Flaminius*: According to Baedeker (*Italy*, First Part: *Northern Italy*, pp. 243 ff.), the Amphitheatre was 'erected under Diocletian about A.D. 290' (p. 249). It is associated with Theodoric (p. 250). Gaius Flaminius, Censor and Consul, erected the Circus Flaminius (200 B.C.), which is not at Verona.

14–21 These verses seem redolent of Juvenal's Third Satire and Donne's Fourth Satire.

21 med'cin, sleep: Cf. I. vi. 78.

23 Fame: Cf. *Aeneid* iv. 173–88, Virgil's famous description of Fama, and Ovid's in *Metamorphoses* ix. 137 and xii. 43 ff. And see II. ii. 36–7 below. *Truth . . . behinde.* Cf. II. ii. 75.

37 Davenant uses this figure in II. vii. 50 and in III. iii. 21. Cf. Tasso's *Jerusalem Delivered* III. 4, where the figure is used in connection with an approach to the city Jerusalem.

40 *Bodies, Death . . . Hides*: See George Williamson, 'Milton and the Mortalist Heresy', *Studies in Philology*, xxxii (1935), 553–79. Davenant would seem to take a middle ground in this important question of whether or not the soul is immortal. Associated with the controversy are names closely associated with Davenant's: Davies, Hobbes, and Milton, not to mention Bacon and Browne.

49 ff. *An Orator*: This rude orator speaks like the voice of the Reformation, anachronistically, for a poem about 8th-century Lombardy.

50–5 Cf. Dryden's sentiments in the Preface to *Religio Laici*, and see *Leviathan*, Part IV, 'Of the Kingdom of Darkness'.

57–73 The tone of these stanzas, and some of the ideas, are echoed in Davenant's 'Philosophers Disquisition' (*Shorter Poems*, ed. Gibbs; '73. p. 326.)

57 *some . . . Heav'n*: This sentiment is again expressed in II. v. 17, where Davenant seems more particularly to asperse the Royal Society—or experiments such as theirs.

63 *Yet . . . fly*: This passage is anachronistic, since the problem of too many faiths arose after the Reformation, not in medieval Lombardy. But cf. Donne's debate over the choice of a faith, in his Third Satire.

73–4 Cf. I. iii, Arg. and note.

II. ii, Arg. *Fame . . . wings*: See II. i. 23; II. ii. 1; and II. ii. 36 ff. The contents of cantos i and ii seem jumbled, since Fame appears in three isolated passages. The argument with the priests (II. i. 49–73) seems digressive and may have been interpolated. Moreover, the order of events suggested by the first three lines of II. ii, Arg. is not the order in which the events occur in the canto. 'Fame's progress' is described (stanzas 36 ff.) after the 'shaking' of 'Aribert's great mind' (stanzas 2–35), and the introduction of Hermegild (II. ii. 32) is abrupt.

2 Aribert is like Charles II, whose virtue flourished in adversity, according to official propaganda.

6 *Parian* Quarries: Quarries in Paros are discussed in Pliny XXXVI. v (tr. Holland, ii. 564 ff.). The marble is especially good.

20–3 There are some witty touches in these stanzas, but together they seem repetitive and disorganized. The metaphor based on wine (20 and 22) is interrupted by the figure based on Eden and the 'tempting fruit' (21), and the idea of surfeit is repetitiously handled in 22 and 23.

26 Cf. I. iv. 13.

36–7 See II. i. 23 and note. Davenant's swallow simile is in neither Ovid nor Virgil.

54 Fame's publick Trumpet: See Chaucer's *House of Fame*, Book III, where Aeolus blows trumpets, one for good fame and one for 'Sclaunder'.

66 liver ... True Beautie's Mint: 'Beautie's Mint' evidently in the sense that the liver makes blood as a mint makes coins. Cf. Burton's *Anatomy of Melancholy*, I. I. II. II: blood is made in the liver, 'and from it *spirits* are first begotten in the heart, which afterwards . . . [go] to the other parts'.

call'd in, like Coyn when Kings are dead: Cf. *The Seventh Canto*, stanza 4. These ought to be allusions to the recalling of Charles's coinage after his death, but I find no comment in historical sources to indicate such a recalling.

68–70 All the remedies mentioned here seem to have their rationale in the theory, which goes back to Aristotle, that death takes place through the loss of heat. (See William Harvey's *An Anatomical Disquisition on the Motion of the Heart and Blood in Animals*, Chapter 15; and Aristotle's *On Life and Death* 479ᵃ.)

70 Epithems. Moist, or soft, external applications (*OED*).

76–80 Concerning the formal curse (here, as in the Restoration heroic play, delivered by the infuriated noblewoman) see I. iii. 76–7 n. above.

81 *Calabrian* Coursers: See I. ii. 32 and note. Italy was foremost in horsemanship schools in 16th-century Europe (*Encyclopaedia Britannica*, 11th edn. XIII. 726), and apparently the district of Calabria represented horsemanship and horses for Davenant.

84 Cities Genius . . . by their Sins expell'd: The concept of the genius or daemon of a locality has been common from antiquity, but I have still to find another instance of a miffed genius leaving because of the sins of the people. However, the Attendant Spirit in *Comus* appears as a rustic who shies away from Comus's revels.

87 *Tullia's* Urne: In *The Seventh Canto*, stanza 3, it is 'Tullie's Urn'. Mr. A. M. Gibbs supplies me the following quotation from Lemprière's *Classical Dictionary*: 'According to a ridiculous story which some of the moderns report, in the age of Pope Paul the Third a monument was discovered on the Appian road, with the inscription of *Tulliolae filiae meae*. The body of a woman was found there, which was reduced to ashes as soon as touched; there was also a lamp burning, which was extinguished as soon as the air gained admission, and which was supposed to have been lighted above 1500 years.' See *The Poems of John Donne*, ed. Grierson, ii. 98. Grierson also cites Browne, *Vulgar Errors*, iii. 21. See also *The Elegies and the Songs and Sonnets of John Donne*, ed. Gardner, p. 180, the note on ll. 5–12 of 'The Undertaking'. Cf. *The Seventh and Last Canto*, stanza 3.

Mr. Gibbs suggests that the second two lines of this stanza are a joking reference to the alchemist's fire of calcination.

II. iii. 2 Revenge ... sought: This is the topic sentence for Hubert's part in the poem.

4 But these are silent: This motif is continued in stanza 8 below. And Ulfin's maimed troops are also silent (I. vi. 43–4).

11 murder . . . lawful made: See I. iii, Arg. and notes.

46 amus'd: See I. v. 18 n.

II. iv. 2–13 These stanzas introduce Hermegild much more appropriately than do the King's offhand remarks in II. ii. 32, which is the first mention of him. It may be that the earlier passage was added as an afterthought. Canto ii above shows other evidence of having been revised (see II. ii, Arg. n.).

9 ff. Cf. the famous quarrel scene between Cassius and Brutus in *Julius Caesar* IV. iii. Davenant is perhaps giving another treatment of this venerable dramatic scene. Lines 3 and 4 of Davenant's stanza suggest *Julius Caesar* IV. iii. 216 ff.: 'There is a tide in the affairs of men . . .'.

18–19 Davenant takes a gentle interest in youth, age, and the process of growth. See his *Preface*, lines 659 ff., where the poet speaks of the enemies of youth and beauty; III. ii. 100–8, where Gondibert's school for young warriors is discussed; III. iii. 1–11, where the poet gently instructs a hypothetical young bride and groom; III. vi. 1–23, where Ulfin instructs his parting son; and III. vi. 31–80, where Goltho and Ulfinor meet Dalga.

29 Since . . . Morn: Cf. I. v. 47 n.

32 Laveers: To beat to windward, to tack (*OED*). So in *The Seventh Canto*, stanza 81, and in the 'Poem to the Earl of Orrery' (*Shorter Poems*, ed. Gibbs; '73, p. 280).

46 For . . . mourn: Davenant makes the common people emotional and shrewd but unreasonable. See II. i. 32, where the people shriek when they see dead Hugo and Arnold; II. i. 48; III. i. 2; and the *Preface*, lines 130–1 and 1021–40.

48 *Mandrakes* wedded under ground: Pliny XXV. xiii (tr. Holland, ii. 235) observes that there are considered to be mandrakes of two sexes, but he says nothing of their 'wedding'. I think Davenant's metaphor more probably has to do with the manner in which the parts of the bifurcated root of a single mandrake twist together (cf. Browne's *Vulgar Errors* II. vi. 1).

55 *Roman* . . . rites: Cf. the funeral rites in *Aeneid* VI. 216 and VI. 156 ff.

57 Cypresse . . . never grows: See Kirchmann, *De Funeribus Romanorum*, Hamburg, 1605, pp. 112 ff. See also Servius's comment on *Aeneid* VI. 216.

64 Ashes . . . *Ilicet*: Cf. Servius on *Aeneid* VI. 216.

II. v, Arg. *The House of* ASTRAGON: Dowlin (*Sir William Davenant's Gondibert*, p. 112) finds the source of this academy in Bacon's *New Atlantis*. But it is just possible that Davenant had in mind William Gilbert (1540–1603), who was physician to Elizabeth and whose house in London was a meeting-place for experimental scientists and the precursor of the Royal Society. Gilbert's *De Magnete Magneticisque Corporibus et de Magno Magnete Tellure Physiologia Nova* (1600) was the result of experiments of the kind celebrated by Davenant in this and the following two cantos. See especially vi. 28–41 below, a hymn to the virtues of the magnet and compass.

Astragon: The King in *The New Atlantis* is generally taken to represent

COMMENTARY 303

James I (Bacon, *The New Atlantis*, ed. H. Gortein, London, 1925, p. 225), and the figure of Astragon may represent the same king, or one of the Charleses, who were patrons of science and learning.

For a suggestion that Astragon and Birtha are partly modelled on Prospero and Miranda in *The Tempest*, *see* A. W. Ward, *A History of English Dramatic Literature*, iii. 169 n.

8 Truth . . . Schools: Cf. ii. v. 44.

11 Paracelsus is supposed to have introduced non-organic remedies (Douglas Guthrie, *A History of Medicine*, 1949, p. 160).

13 Cordial Coral: Herbarius (*De Virtutibus Herbarum*, 1499, Chapter LXVI at the back of the book) does not call coral 'cordial', but powdered coral is supposed to be good for hemorrhage.

Nigella: Herbarius says of Nigella, 'propietas eius est quae aufert febrem flegmaticam & melancolicam', so the herb is evidently a remedy for lethargy.

15 Tow'rs . . . height: Cf. *The New Atlantis* (ed. Gortein, p. 241): 'We have high towers, the highest about half a mile in height, and some . . . upon . . . mountains . . .'.

17 Nine . . . *Astragon*: Thus Astragon is placed about A.D. 750.

18 For . . . lies: This line is practically a versification of a phrase in the *Preface*, lines 1462–3.

19 pride (grown to Religion): See I. iii. 32 and note for other similar passages.

moving our lov'd Earth: Cf. Donne's 'Valediction Forbidding Mourning', line 9, and Grierson's note in *The Poems of John Donne* (Oxford, 1963, ii. 40).

21–68 The allegorical representation of functions (e.g. stanza 23) is somewhat suggestive of the type of treatment in Spenser's House of Alma in the *Faerie Queene* and in Fletcher's *Purple Island*. But, more pointedly, the three cabinets (Nature's Office, the Cabinet of Death, and the Monument of Vanished Minds) contain nature (1) present and (2) past, and 'nature' as (3) the philosophical product of human minds. These are, moreover, according to Davenant's metaphor, a second Noah's Ark, for the 'new philosophy'. Time, in the metaphor, is the 'Flood'.

28 Nature's Nursery: Cf. the orchards and gardens mentioned in Bacon's *New Atlantis* (ed. Gortein, p. 242); and the garden in Logistilla's palace in *Orlando Furioso* x. 63. A more metaphorical variant of the theme can be seen in Spenser's Garden of Adonis.

th'Hebrew King: Probably Solomon, since part of his wisdom consisted of 'plant and animal fables' (*The Interpreter's Bible*, 1957, i. 214a).

29–30 Cf. ii. vii. 8. Birtha, the herbalist girl, is called a 'simpling Girle' in 'To Sir W. Davenant' in *Certain Verses* (1653), pp. 5–7 (see p. 274 above).

32–5 This description of relics bears some similarity to *A Catalogue of All the Chiefest Rarities in the Publick Theatre* [at Leyden University] (1591), but Davenant conceives it a figurative 'Noah's Ark' (stanzas 36 and 38 below). Cf. I. ii. 36–8 and II. vi. 60.

32 all . . . Minde: Man's reckless dominion over nature is a favourite theme with Davenant. See I. iii, Arg. n.

33 she . . . whom . . . He obay'd: The implication would seem to be that these are the skeletons of Adam and Eve.

36 Cf. III. iii. 11 and *Preface* lines 840–1. Dryden parodies the phrase 'monument of vanish'd Mindes' in *MacFlecknoe*, line 82. Cf. *Orlando Furioso* xxxiv. 73 ff., where Orlando's lost wits are found preserved in an urn.

41 *Chaldean* Cous'ners: In Daniel and classical authors the term 'Chaldeans' is used to mean 'astrologers, astronomers' because of 'the celebrated Babylonian works on astrology and divination . . .' (*Encyclopaedia Britannica*, 11th edn., v. 805a).

42 *Persian Magi*: Matthew 2: 1–18.
Altars . . . wrought: See I. iii. 32 and note.

44 *Termes*: See II. v. 8 and the *Answer to the Preface*, line 278.

48–51 Cf. Cowley's 'To the Royal Society':

> Yet still, methinks, we fain would be
> Catching at the forbidden tree—
> We would be like the Deity—
> When truth and falsehood, good and evil, we
> Without the senses' aid, within ourselves would see;
> For 'tis God only who can find
> All Nature in his mind.

50 Garment . . . Firmament: Cf. Davenant's 'Poem upon His Sacred Majesties Most Happy Return to His Dominions' (*Shorter Poems*, ed. Gibbs; '73, p. 256):

> No more shall *sacred Priests* fall from their own
> *Supported Power*, by shrinking from the Throne:
> Nor in *divided shapes* that Garment tear,
> Which their *Great Chief* did *whole* and *seemless* weare.

Cf. Bacon's 'Unity of Religion': 'Men ought to take heed of rending God's church by two kinds of controversies. . . . For as it is noted by one of the fathers, Christ's coat indeed had no seam; but the church's vesture was of divers colours. . . .'

52 *Arabian's* Gospel: One of course thinks of the Koran; but possibly the reference is to Thomas van Erpe's translation of the New Testament from an 8th-century Arabic MS. at Leyden in 1616. The 'Gospel' would have been new in Astragon's time (see II. v. 17), and the translation would have been new in Davenant's.

54 *Ophir*: Unidentified place mentioned in the Old Testament, 'whence fine gold was obtained' (*OED*). Davenant apparently places it in India in this rather 'metaphysical' conceit.

II. vi. 10 It is the 'best of all possible worlds', apparently. Cf. II. v. 7, to the same effect.

13 *Meroens*: Moors. Associated with *Maroon* and *Moor* (*OED*).
Numidian: See Pliny XXXVI. vii–viii (tr. Holland, ii. 572 ff.), concerning black Numidian marble and the cutting and polishing of marble.

18 This lamp was all: Cf. Ariosto's *Orlando Furioso* iii. 8, 14, and 15, a description of Merlin's tomb. The tomb is like a chapel, lit by one light which reflects throughout all the rooms because of the highly polished walls.

22 Cf. *Certain Verses* (1653) pp. 21-4, where Davenant's language in this stanza is ridiculed, in the verses 'An Essay in Explanation of Mr. Hobbes' (p. 284 above), 'On Gondibert' (p. 284 above), and 'Epithets that will serve for any Substantives, either in this part or the next' (p. 285 above).

30 in sleepy vision: Note the supernatural element.

Till *Saturne's* . . . grown: This amounts to about 550 years, since Saturn's period is about 29½ years. If Astragon 'lived' in the 8th century (see II. v. 17 and note), the loadstone would be 'from Navigators hid' until the 13th century. According to the *Encyclopaedia Britannica* (11th edn., vi. 809) a legend arose in the 17th century 'that the compass was invented in the year 1302 by a person to whom was given the fictitious name of Flavio Gioja of Amalfi'.

hid: Cf. *Orlando Furioso* xv, where the route to the New World is to be hidden until the time of Charles V.

36 *Cynosure*: Ursa Minor and the pole-star.

38 *Tops . . . Misens*: Cf. the *Preface*, lines 755-6 n., concerning 'terms of art'.

40 Compare the tone of praise in Dryden's *Annus Mirabilis*, stanzas 155-66; Sprat's Dedication to the King in the *History of the Royal Society*; and Cowley's ode in the *History of the Royal Society*. Cf. II. v, Arg. n., above, concerning William Gilbert and the identity of Astragon.

Typhis: Helmsman of the Argos, and inventor of the ship's tiller according to Pliny VII. lvi (tr. Holland, i. 190).

Thule: Supposed, in classical antiquity, to be the northern-most part of the world.

45 *Paros . . . white*: Pliny XXXVI. v (tr. Holland, ii. 564 ff.) says that marble from the island of Paros is noted for its whiteness.

Sparta . . . Green: Cf. Pliny XXXVI. vii. Green Lacedaemonian marble, or green porphyry is brighter than any other marble.

Araby . . . blushing Onychite: Pliny XXXVI. vii refers to 'onyx marble', which is associated with Arabia, but which came from the part of Egypt on the Arabian side of the Nile.

Misnian Hills . . . Blew: *Misnia* was the Latin name of Meissen, in Saxony. According to Pliny, a bluish marble comes from Lesbos.

48 God's Fav'rite-King: David, the Psalmist.

53 ff. Cf. *Aeneid* i. 446 ff., where Virgil describes the mural art in Dido's temple, representing the War of Troy.

53 Pencils: Not lead pencils, but brushes (cf. Pencil in *OED*); similarly in stanza 73 below.

60 universal Herd: Marvell echoes line 1 in 'Upon Appleton House, to my Lord Fairfax', 455-6.

63 ff. Compare Milton's description of Adam and Eve in *Paradise Lost* iv. 287-324. Harbage (*Sir William Davenant*, 1935, p. 195) says, 'It is amusing to

compare the lusciousness of the picture of Eve in the Garden composed by Milton the Puritan, with the excessive modesty of a similar picture composed by Davenant the Cavalier.'

66–70 The mural of the Flood and Ark is especially appropriate in view of II. v. 21–68, where Astragon's academy metaphorically becomes a Noah's Ark preserving true philosophy.

69 Such . . . Death: Cf. 'The Christians Reply' (*Shorter Poems*, ed. Gibbs; '73, p. 335) stanza 9, where a similar sentiment is expressed in a slightly different metaphor.

73 Where life *Came out*, etc.: Cf. Dryden's 'To Sir Godfrey Kneller', where the artistic theory is strikingly similar to Davenant's. For example, lines 7–10:

> Such are thy pictures, Kneller: such thy skill,
> That Nature seems obedient to thy will;
> Comes out, and meets thy pencil in the draught;
> Lives there, and wants but words to speak her thought.

78 when . . . *May*: Cf. Davenant's *Platonic Lovers* (*Dramatic Works*, ed. Maidment and Logan, ii. 61), and Shakespeare's *Macbeth* I. vii. 24–5, which suggests itself as a possible source of Davenant's figure. Davenant deletes the figure from his own version of *Macbeth*.

84–7 See the *Preface*, lines 959 ff., where these stanzas are quoted but numbered 89–92. Apparently five stanzas were deleted between 1650, when the *Preface* was first printed, and 1651, when the poem was first printed. The missing five stanzas may have appeared between stanzas 72 and 73, for in the first edition of the poem ('*51a*) a *MS* correction changes the catchword on page 194 from *This* to *By*, and stanza 73 ('By pencills . . .') is the first stanza on page 195.

87 Cf. the *Preface*, lines 600 ff., where wit is conceived of as 'the soul's powder'.

II. vii, Arg. *The Duke's . . . cur'd*: These first two lines of the Arg. should be concerned with stanzas 1–3, since line 3 of the Arg. is concerned with Birtha, who appears in stanza 4. Stanzas 1–3 are not about 'The Duke's wish'd health' at all; they are an apology for the long digression in canto vi. 'The Duke's wish'd health' and his wounds are discussed in stanza 83 of canto vi. Stanzas 1–3 of canto vii might possibly be some of the stanzas missing from canto vi (cf. II. vi. 84–7 n.). On the other hand, the Duke's wounds and his health are taken up again in II. vii. 20 ff., and this should be the passage to which the first two lines of the Arg. refer.

2 Then long Opinion to Religion grown: Cf. I. iii. 32 n.

3 *Pyrol*: Wintergreen, an old remedy for wounds (*OED*).

4–19 Birtha's 'knowing innocence' reminds one of Dryden's Eve in *The State of Innocence*, and, as with Davenant's own Eve (II. vi. 63–4), her purity is almost negated by the poet's over-emphasis. Cf. also Davenant's handling of Miranda in his adaptation of *The Tempest*.

8 spring . . . Flowres: Cf. II. v. 29–30 n.

19 *Vervin*: Pliny xxv. ix (tr. Holland, ii. 228) speaks of 'vervain' (or hierba botane, or verbenaca) as good for cleansing and purifying homes, for encouraging merriment, and for treating fresh wounds.

Willow: See John Gerarde, *The Herball or Generall Historie of Plantes* (enlarged Thomas Johnson), 1636, p. 1392: 'The greene boughes [of willow] with the leaues may very well be brought into chambers and set about the beds of those that be sicke of feuers, for they do mightily coole the heate of the aire, which thing is a wonderful refreshing to the sicke Patients.' (I am indebted to Mr. A. M. Gibbs for this reference.)

32 Mindes... bodies wrought: This remark would seem to be in the tradition of the anti-Platonic-love poem. Cf. Donne's 'Love's Alchymie' and 'The Extasie'; and see Cartwright (ed. G. B. Evans), pp. 494–5 and 724 n.

45 *Palm*, and the *Mamora*: Pliny xiii. xvii describes the propagation of the palm. The 'male bristling with leaves erected impregnates . . . [the surrounding females] by his exhalation and by the mere sight of him, and also by his pollen' (Loeb tr.).

Mr. Gibbs supplies me the following quotation from Gerard's *Herbal*, 1636, pp. 1608–9: 'These two trees [the male and female Mamoera], . . . are of the same kinde, and differ only in sex; for the one of them, to wit the male, is barren, and only carries floures, without any fruit; but the female onely fruit, and that without floure: yet they say they are so loving, and of such a nature, that if they be set far asunder, and the female have not a male neere her, shee becomes barren, and beares no fruit: of which nature they also say the Palme is.'

47 Thus to her self . . . *Birtha* talks: Compare Dido's reveries in the opening lines of *Aeneid* iv.

51 purer Organs: Cf. the description of Rhodalind in i. i. 17.

70 as a Pris'ner, etc.: Cf. i. iv. 42 and note.

89 seed: See i. ii. 1 and note.

ii. viii. 24–46. Cf. the *Preface*, lines 405 ff. and note.

38–9 Cf. the *Preface*, lines 1449–53.

40 The theme here is akin to that of *Leviathan* ii, 'Of Commonwealth'.

44 seel'd: *Seal* means to close the eyes of a bird. Some seel doves' eyes to avoid vertigo and thus make them soar higher (*OED*).

53 Bid all our Worthys to unarm, etc.: From Gondibert's glib renouncing of responsibility arise all the conflicts to follow.

iii. i. The publisher's gloss, 'Written by the Author During his Imprisonment', is probably not altogether accurate. Davenant was captured shortly before 28 June 1650 (Masson, iv. 193) on his way to Virginia. But in the *Preface* (lines 1577–84) he indicates that the Third Book of *Gondibert* is nearly ready for the press, and he dates the *Preface* 2 January 1650. Undoubtedly he worked on *Gondibert* in prison between his capture in June and his death sentence in October (see p. 414 below), but probably more by way of revising the Third Book than composing it.

2 Throng . . . love: Cf. II. iv. 46 and note.

10 *Hybla* Hony, or *Arabian* Dew: Hybla is traditionally one of the places where the best honey is found, according to Pliny XI. xiii (tr. Holland, i. 316). The concept of sweet dew in Arabia may possibly stem from the manna described in Exodus 16:31 as tasting 'like wafers made with honey'.

44 According to Harbage (*Sir William Davenant*, p. 183) the reader is here 'darkly threatened with a tragedy', but only for the purposes of suspense.

46 This is the earliest hint of the plot against Orna, which is developed in the *Seventh Canto*. See stanzas 54 ff. below and note. The plot of this sequence has precedents in Shakespeare's *Much Ado*, Bandello's 22nd story in the *Novelle*, and *Orlando Furioso* iv–vi.

49 conjunction: 'An apparent proximity of two planets or other heavenly bodies; the position of these when they are in the same, or nearly the same, direction as viewed from earth' (*OED*). Cf. *John Milton: Complete Poems and Major Prose*, ed. Merritt Y. Hughes, *Paradise Regained* iv. 382–93 n. and 385 n. Hughes explains that conjunction 'was an unfavorable "aspect" in astrology'. Astrology had been attacked by, e.g., Pico della Mirandola, Calvin, and Bishop Carleton (ibid.), and Davenant, as a proponent of the 'new philosophy', would, of course, be using the term poetically here, rather than philosophically.

53–7 In Kynaston's *Leoline and Sydanis* I. lxxxii ff., Sydanis must open a chest which contains a page's suit and disguise herself in male clothing. Like Davenant's Gartha she is at first utterly dismayed.

56 that old Snake . . . like Man: The 'Serpent' of Eden was pictured with human features in, e.g., the Sistine Chapel.

III. ii. 1 plights: Engagement, plighting (*OED*).

6 *Arcadia*: In Sannazzaro's *Arcadia* one lived 'without envy of another's greatness in modest contentment of his lot' (Laurie Magnus, *Dictionary of European Literature*, 1926). Sannazzaro stands in the background of the *roman à clef*, with which *Gondibert* has some affinity.

70 Cf. Browne's *Pseudodoxia Epidemica* VII. xviii. 5 concerning Milo, who was strong enough to lift a bull, owing to his having lifted it every day from the time when it was a calf.

100–8 Cf. the virtues enumerated in the 'Poem on His Sacred Majestie's Most Happy Return . . .' (*Shorter Poems*, ed. Gibbs; '73, p. 256).

III. iii. 10 *loving . . . an art*: See II. vii. 32 and note. Dying is, in monastery cells, an art.

16 *Podian Saphyr*: Cf. Anselmus de Boodt, *Gemmarum et Lapidum Historia*, 1609, II. xliii. The sapphire was supposed to betray adultery by losing its light.

43–4 See I. iii. 76–7 n. and II. ii. 76–80 n. concerning the curse as a convention.

43 cease: Seize (*OED*).

51 like God . . . judg . . . good: Compare Genesis 1—the refrain 'And God saw that it was good.'

57 This high Hill Pow'r: Compare Shakespeare's image of Fortune on a high hill in *Timon* I. i. 63.

III. iv. 24 Your *Diamond*, etc.: Pliny XXXVI. iv (tr. Holland, ii. 610) enthusiastically praises the diamond's ability to break hammers and anvils and to survive heat. He does not mention 'Oisel's juice', however. Bernardus Caesius (*De Mineralibus*, 1636, p. 589) cites many authorities who aver that a diamond will yield to goat's blood.

26 I am not what I seem: Compare *Othello* I. i. 65.

33 The swelling . . . stream: The Nile's floods fertilize the land along its banks. Cf. Browne's *Pseudodoxia Epidemica* VI. viii.

34 light does tame . . . Beasts: For example, the lion, according to Pliny VIII. xvi, is frightened most 'by the sight of fire'.

43 vertuous Men: Cf. Donne's 'Valediction Forbidding Mourning':

As virtuous men pass mildly away, etc.

and see Tilly §L 245 'A good Life has a good death.'

45 ff. See de Boodt, *Gemmarum et Lapidum Historia*, II, Chapter 53. The emerald is said to break at the defloration of a virgin. Similar powers were attributed to the sapphire (cf. III. iii. 16 n.). In Kynasten's *Leoline and Sydanis* III. ccxxix ff., Leoline gives Sydanis a ring with a carbuncle that can store light.

46–7 Thomas Nicols (*Arcula Gemmea*, 1653, I. xii) says that the Scythian emerald 'is the most noble . . . because of its excellent hardnes . . .'. The Bactrian is the second-best. The emerald from Attic silver mines is fifth on his list, and what he calls 'chalco-smaragdus', which is found in Cyprus in brass, is the twelfth and last in value.

50–51 Cf. III. iii. 16 n.

96 respect . . . grown: See I. iii. 32 n.

97 *And terrible . . . true*. Davenant's metrics are usually much more regular than this.

III. v. 2 kindle . . . Eies: Cf. Davenant's 'The Lark Now Leaves His Wat'ry Nest' (*Shorter Poems*, ed. Gibbs; '73, p. 320) .

5 a deep design on Heav'n: Cf. II. vi. 85–6.

13 Made . . . Grief: Cf. L. C. Martin, ed., *The Poems, English, Latin, and Greek of Richard Crashaw* (Oxford, 1957), pp. 432–4. Martin's notes on 'The Weeper' and 'The Tear' discuss the tradition of Mary Magdalene's tears.

20 *Syrian* Mayd: Rebecca of Aram, who married Isaac (Genesis 24: 11 ff.).

22 Sudds of Amber: No doubt an expensive form of rosin-soap, q.v. in *OED*.

31 Common-wealth . . . fram'd: A rather outspoken allusion to the Commonwealth Parliament.

35–6 Cf. II. vi. 85.

41 weaker Eyes: Cf. *Preface*, l. 845 n.

50 Ironically, Birtha's 'design on Heaven' is having the desired effect, and by the agency of the one who has been rebuking her for it.

52 The jealous . . . afraid: i.e. jealous (zealous) people are afraid that they ought to be even more afraid, when they are frightened to death already.

55–8 Compare Birtha's arch innocence in II. vii. 4–19.

64 *Eaglets*: See the *Preface*, line 845.

66 *Manna*: Cf. Marvell's *Ros* and 'On a Drop of Dew'. Cf. Exodus 16: 21.

75 Assemblies . . . wilde: A jibe directed at Parliament, perhaps.

III. vi. Davenant suddenly shifts to a lighter tone for Ulfin's advice to his son, and for the seduction of Goltho.

2 Hill . . . time: See III. iii. 57 and note.

10 check: To aim reproof or censure at (*OED*).

14 *Indians*, etc.: Cf. Montaigne's 'apology' for cannibalism in the essay 'On Cannibals'.

18 *Talkers*: Cf. II. v. 44.

22 Be kinde to Beauty: Cf. II. iv. 18 and note.

27 *Clephes*: Cf. II. i. 10 n. The present reference is presumably to the Porta di S. Zeno (if to any real place at all), because the other two western gates of Verona are 16th-century structures. If Clephes on an elephant was once a statue there, however, it is not now.

31 a black Beauty: For possible connection between Dalga and the 'black handsome wench' from whom Davenant is supposed to have taken syphilis in 1630 or 1631, cf. Nethercot's *Sir William D'avenant*, pp. 91–2.

42 *Circania's . . . Cinamon*: The circanea is a bird of circular flight (Harper's *Latin Dictionary*). Perhaps this is another name for the bird which Pliny x. xxxiii (tr. Holland, i. 288–9) describes as an Arabian bird called Cinnamologus, which builds its nest of cinnamon twigs. The natives, he says, use the nests for cinnamon.

56 All hair: Compare the enchanted horse which Faustus makes out of straw in Marlowe's *Faustus* IV. v^b. It turns back into straw in water. Possibly Davenant intended 'all fair', but there is no authority for an emendation.

61 Ulfinor is of a satirical bent, like his father, Ulfin.
Mandrakes grones: Cf. Browne's *Pseudodoxia Epidemica* II. vi. 1, where Browne discusses the beliefs that mandrakes groan when pulled up and that it is death if you go about pulling up mandrakes in the wrong way.

63 *Oxes Eie*: Nautical: a 'bull's eye', i.e. a little dark cloud that portends a storm.

69 a closse Swallow: 'Conrad Gesner (*Historiae Animalium Lib. III. qui est de Auium natura*, 1585, pp. 549–50) mentions that the swallow remains in her nest all winter as though dead, and revives in the spring . . .' (Rhodes Dunlap, ed., *The Poems of Thomas Carew*, Oxford, 1949, in a note on 'The Spring', lines 6–7).

70 Davenant here descends to the mock-heroic.

THE POSTSCRIPT

1 the middle of the Third BOOK: Harbage (*Sir William Davenant*, 1935, p.192) points out that 'At the end of each canto there is usually a graceful peroration.' There is none at the end of III. vi, so the canto itself may have been left unfinished. At any rate, Davenant was using the term *middle* loosely if he called the *Seventh Canto* the 'last' when he composed it later.

2 an equal half of the *POEM*: Although only two, or perhaps two and a fraction, of the proposed five books remained unfinished at this point, the Fourth Book 'ever having occasion to be the longest' (*Preface*, line 514) would perhaps make up the difference between one-half and two-fifths of the poem. That *Gondibert* half-finished is half as long as the *Aeneid* may say something about Davenant's plan and model.

12 strip Nature naked: i.e. as Baconian philosophy does in a scientific vein. Cf. the *Preface*, lines 388–9 and note, and 678–9 and note. See also lines 57–58 below.

12–13 clothe . . . Vertue: This remark suggests that *Gondibert* was to have been a tragicomedy. Cf. Harbage's *Sir William Davenant*, p. 183.

48 ff. Cf. the *Preface*, lines 388–9 and note, and 919 n.

52 last wise Cardinall: No doubt a compliment to Richelieu, as founder of the French Academy.

THE SEVENTH AND LAST CANTO

Arg. Orna *is betrayed*: This, of course, is the sequel of the plot begun in III. i. 46 ff., q.v., with notes. Cf. pp. xv–xvi above.

1 Unlucky Fire: Cotton's complimentary verses start with 'O happy Fire'.

2 Dead . . . herse: See the *Preface*, lines 388–9 and note. Davenant now seems to lament that he has been unsuccessful in his attempt to reform England.

3 *Tullia's* Urn: Cf. II. ii. 87 n.

4 Coins: Cf. II. ii. 66 n. See also Cotton's stanza 7, alluding to commemorative medals.

10–19 This piece on sleep and sleeping Verona balances I. vi. 78–80 and II. i. 3–21. For another prophetic curse, see II. ii. 76–80.

31 Lutes . . . Willows hung: Davenant seems to borrow from the ballad 'Green Willow', or from an Arabic legend about David's playing the harp under a willow after marrying Bathsheba.

46 There . . . Lanthorns: See Cotton, stanzas 3–4, p. 287 above.

46 There . . . lay: Davenant is metrically conscientious, and lines without enough syllables are rare. But see stanza 65, line 1; and stanza 73, line 1.

106 turn the Prospective: Look through the wrong end of the spy-glass.

COTTON'S COMPLIMENTARY POEM

(*Appendix iii*)

1 O . . . Breath: Cf. the *Preface*, lines 144, where Davenant says that heroic poets perhaps 'will in worthy memory outlast . . . all but such as must therefore live equally with them, because they have recorded their names'. For a suggestion that Davenant had immortalized Charles Cotton the elder, cf. Alvin Dust, *The Seventh and Last Canto of Gondibert* and Two Dedicatory Poems', *JEGP* LX (1961), 282–5.

3 Black . . . Night: Cf. *The Seventh and Last Canto*, stanza 46.

4 dark Lanthorn: See verbal echoes of this in *The Seventh and Last Canto*, stanzas 3 and 46.

7 Paper Monument: See II. v. 36 and note, on the 'monument of Vanish'd Minds', which is a library. See also III. iii. 11, where Davenant calls *Gondibert* the 'Mon'ment of my Minde'.

PRINTED IN GREAT BRITAIN
AT THE UNIVERSITY PRESS, OXFORD
BY VIVIAN RIDLER
PRINTER TO THE UNIVERSITY